BURNING

DESIRES

SEX IN AMERICA

A REPORT FROM THE FIELD

Steve Chapple and David Talbot

DOUBLEDAY

New York   London   Toronto   Sydney   Auckland

Published by Doubleday, a division of
Bantam Doubleday Dell Publishing Group, Inc.
666 Fifth Avenue, New York, New York 10103

Doubleday and the portrayal of an anchor
with a dolphin are trademarks of Doubleday,
a division of Bantam Doubleday Dell Publishing Group, Inc.

Grateful acknowledgment is made for use of the following:

Lyrics from "Surfin' U.S.A." by C. Berry/B. Wilson. Copyright © 1963 by Arc Music Corp. Reprinted by permission. All rights reserved.

Two lines from "Her Mouth, His Seed, Her Soul" from *How to Save Your Own Life* by Erica Jong. Copyright © 1977 by Erica Mann Jong. Reprinted by permission of Henry Holt and Company, Inc.

Lyrics from "Go See the Doctor" by Mohanndas Dewese. Copyright © 1987 Willesden Music Inc./Kool Moe Dee Music (Administered by Willesden Music Inc.). Lyrics reprinted by permission. All rights reserved.

Lyrics from "Fight for Your Right (To Party)." Copyright © 1987 Def Jam Music, Inc./Brooklyn Dust Music (ASCAP). Lyrics reprinted by permission.

Lyrics from "Shock the Monkey" by Peter Gabriel. Copyright © 1982 Cliofine Ltd. Administered in U.S.A. & Canada by Hidden Pun Music, Inc. (BMI). International Copyright Secured. All rights reserved. Used by permission.

Lyrics from "Two Little Hitlers" by Elvis Costello. Copyright © 1978 Plangent Visions Music Inc.

Lines from "Daddy" from *Ariel* by Sylvia Plath. Copyright © 1961 by Sylvia Plath. Reprinted by permission of Harper & Row Publishers, Inc.

Excerpt from *Beauty's Punishment* by A. N. Roquelaure. Copyright © 1984 by A. N. Roquelaure. Reprinted by permission of E. P. Dutton, a division of NAL Penguin Inc.

Lines from "since feeling is first" are reprinted from *IS 5* poems by e.e. cummings. Edited by George James Firmage, by permission of Liveright Publishing Corporation. Copyright © 1985 by e.e. cummings Trust; Copyright © 1926 by Horace Liveright; Copyright © 1954 by e.e. cummings; Copyright © 1985 by George James Firmage.

Lines from "Love in Blood Time" from *The Gold Cell* by Sharon Olds. Copyright © 1987 by Sharon Olds. Reprinted by permission of Alfred A. Knopf, Inc.

Portions of this work appeared, in slightly different form, in *Playboy* and in the *San Francisco Examiner's Image* magazine.

Library of Congress Cataloging-in-Publication Data
Chapple, Steve.
Burning desires.

Includes index.
1. Sex customs—United States.   2. Sexual ethics—United States.
3. United States—Moral conditions.
I. Talbot, David.   II. Title.
HQ18.U5C47   1989   306.70973   88-31087
ISBN 0-385-24412-6

BOOK DESIGN BY CAROL MALCOLM

To Ines, Wild Love

To Camille, with all my heart

And to Margaret Talbot, who knew the secret to fun and lasting love, and probably still does

Acknowledgments

WE

would like to thank the following people, whose kindnesses ranged from reading and commenting on early drafts of the manuscript to putting us up in their homes to putting up with us: Gilbert L. Bagot, Jr.; Ruby Bell; Dolores Blalock; Adam Block; Susan Brenneman; Dorothy Chapple; Karen Chapple; Thomas Francis; Mark Garofalo; David Helvarg; Mark Hertsgaard; Ruth Henrich; Sibylla Herbrich; Susan W. Horton; James Rado Jovanovich; Jonathan King; Howard Kohn; Paul Marks; Kent McCarthy; Susan Nadler; and Camille Peri.

We are also grateful for the research assistance provided by Dana Sachs and Ellen Morris, as well as the transcribing services of Tess Joseph and Gaen Murphree.

Finally, we owe a special debt of gratitude to our editor, Paul Bresnick, and our agent, Ellen Levine, for their unfailing enthusiasm and good judgment.

Contents

I N T R O D U C T I O N

T was a hurricane sea, a decade of powerful and dangerous crosscurrents. As the 1980s began, America was still caught up in the most exuberant sexual carnival of modern times. But while the decade was still young, the country was suddenly swept by a wave of sexual terror. The resulting cultural collision, between lust and contagion, hellfire and saturnalia, produced a strange and wondrous era. It was a time of safe-sex porn queens and misbehaving preachers, of jack-off clubs and federal bureaus of teenage chastity, of shameless politicians and recovering "sex addicts," of Contra playboys and infected swingers, of men who howled like beasts to become men again and women who loved them too much, of phone-sex sirens and condom deliverymen, of Beastie Boys and Good Mothers. It was a time of night sweats and fatal attractions, of desires you could burn for.

By the mid-1980s the media, once so eager to sell the sexual revolution, was just as fervently announcing its demise. "The Big Chill" was how *Time* magazine dubbed the new era. America had been "scared sexless," NBC News was quick to agree. But the obituary notices were premature. The sexual revolution was transformed by the 1980s, not terminated. True, the revolution lost its frenetic quality when confronted by the decade's new viral threats and the strong cultural backlash launched by conservatives, radical feminists, and burned-out sexual liberationists. But the underlying currents of the sexual revolution continued to flow through American society.

Teenage sexual activity remained at high levels throughout the decade— even among conservative religious youths. Women continued to dismantle the sexual double standard, drawing closer to male rates of premarital and extra-marital sex. And while the AIDS epidemic took a brutal toll among homosex-ual men, the nation's gay culture was not destroyed. The plague set off periodic panic attacks and spasms of homophobic violence, but the highly publicized disease also had the ironic effect of making the gay male a more familiar and less threatening member of the American family. By 1988, even such an emblem of social intolerance as the caustically conservative talk show host Morton Downey, Jr., could throw his arms around his gay, AIDS-stricken brother on national television.

Still, if sexual play and experimentation were not killed off in the 1980s, they did become deeply entangled with morbid associations. The AIDS virus did not penetrate deeply into the heterosexual population, outside those forsaken city blocks where needles provide the great escape. But the psycho-logical impact of the disease was profound. The puncture wound was deep enough to infect the nation's dream life.

The AIDS terror was as much a cultural creation as a public health crisis, a punishment inflicted by the nation on itself to atone for its years of sexual celebration. America has long been torn between its randy and repressive impulses, a split that goes back to the days of the Puritans. As historians John D'Emilio and Estelle B. Freedman have persuasively argued, those God-fearing settlers of New England were a more passionate lot than is commonly be-lieved, their souls a battlefield between lust and salvation. But this mortal combat reached its most feverish pitch in the decade of the 1980s.

American culture in these years was like a vast aversion therapy experi-ment, *The Village Voice* sex columnist Richard Goldstein observed one day over lunch, and we all were the skittish lab animals. We were stimulated, then shocked, stimulated, shocked.

On the one hand, we were bombarded with arousing images wherever we turned: explicit sex play in daytime soap operas and prime-time TV shows like "L.A. Law," "Miami Vice," and "Moonlighting"; raunchy T-shirts and bumperstickers (SCUBA DIVERS DO IT DEEPER, COOKS LIKE IT RAW); a frank new eroticism in movies like *The Big Easy, She's Gotta Have It, 9½ Weeks, Dirty Dancing,* and *The Unbearable Lightness of Being;* even racy new language in the ever-coquettish Harlequin romance novels ("His knees separated her thighs under her cotton skirt. His hand moved to the fullness of her breast"). The sexual boldness of this period was perhaps best symbolized by the ad campaign Calvin Klein launched for his line of men's toiletries, Obsession. Madison Avenue had never produced magazine ads like this before: naked copper-toned sun worshipers lounging with eyes closed on a bone-white obelisk that thrust toward the sky, the men with oiled hair and the hard, rippling bodies of Spartan athletes, the women with round, firm, buttery-looking butts and the full, melon breasts of the Mediterranean. In another ad, nude honey-colored blondes of Scandinavian purity rolled together on a soft beach towel, a cubist jumble of bosoms and limbs and creamy cheeks. These were ads with a brazenly tumescent mission. Gazing on them made you want to grab the nearest bottle of Calvin's Fluid Body Talc and tumble around with this beautifully contoured flesh until you were drained of all desire.

But at the same time the culture teased and stimulated, it was also jolting us with hair-raising messages about sex: rap songs about venereal disease ("As I turned around to receive my injection/I said, 'Next time, I'll use some protection.' "), safe-sex billboards with skull-and-crossbones warnings, real-life morality tales about politicians and preachers brought low by the weakness of their flesh. It was the 1987 hit movie *Fatal Attraction* that seemed to leave the deepest imprint: sex outside marriage will blow apart your life like a devil wind.

Arousal and punishment, arousal and punishment. We were hot-blooded monkeys in a cruel lab experiment. "Shock the monkey," Peter Gabriel sang, and it could have been the decade's theme. "Shock the monkey tonight."

It is little wonder that in this climate men and women seemed to have a particularly troublesome time pairing off with one another or that teenagers seemed more bedeviled by sexual anxieties than the previous generation. As we shall see, some men sought solace from the increasingly difficult mating game in all-male retreats, while many women sought advice from self-help books that only seemed to make them feel worse about men.

THE NEW EROTICISM: SEX WITHOUT SEX declared a cover story in *Self* magazine, a publication with a true name for the eighties. The voyeuristic Andy

Warhol seemed to capture the spirit of the times when he remarked, "Fantasy love is much better than reality love. Never doing it is very exciting."

Not all of America, however, was withdrawing into sexual isolationism. One of the decade's biggest untold stories was the reinvention of sex. Across the country, backyard tinkerers in the tool shops of Eros played with ways of combining sexual liberation and sexual hygiene, male drive and female sense and sensibility: Rubber Ducky condoms packaged for fun-loving teenagers and custom-made panties with latex crotches; dirty-talk services and masturbation parties for men and women; Laura Ashley–style porn films with feminist undertones; and a new drive to keep the home fires burning in the age of two-income, time-stressed families. The sexual experimentation ranged from the sublime to the ridiculous, but it was all powered by the grand human drive for life and pleasure, and it seemed to us a welcome affront to the medicinal odor and sober mood of the times.

"No book can be fully understood unless the writer discloses the motivation that led him to embark on his onerous task," I. F. Stone has written. So let us be candid. *Burning Desires* is a celebration of smart and dirty sex in dangerous times. We undertook this bawdy chronicle in order to better understand those forces that were imperiling sex in the 1980s and dividing men and women and to shed light on those forces that were keeping the country's sexual pulse strong and true. The times moaned out loud for an unblushing defense of sex.

As the title indicates, *Burning Desires* is a report from the country's erogenous zones, a book based on hundreds of interviews with Americans from coast to coast, including everyday men and women, high federal officials, and those whose names are found in lights. By telling the stories of these memorable people, this mix of citizenry and celebrity, we hope to tell the larger story of sexual behavior and sexual politics in our time.

In the first section of the book, "Repression," we look at the punishment of pleasure, how that sweat monkey got shocked.

Chapter One is a tale of twin obsessions, those who can't stop doing it and those who can't stop thinking about it. At first we meet America's king of swinging and the young Minnesota doctor who brought the unwelcome news to this last bastion of carefree sex. We then examine the new sexual compulsion of the eighties—the "sex addiction" movement and those men and women who tried to clamp a Twelve-Step restraining order on their desire. Chapter Two explores the national crackdown on teenage lust and features rock 'n' roll purity crusader Tipper Gore and her archenemies, the Beastie Boys, as well as the remarkable female chaperons who ran President Reagan's teen chastity bureau—one of whom, we will find out, was apparently no stranger to lust herself. Chapter Three is a morning-after tour of three fabled American party towns—Key West, Florida; Aspen, Colorado; and Chico, California—towns where debauchery finally gave way to the new sobriety, except, of course, under the black buffalo head mounted in the front left corner of the Woody Creek Tavern, where Hunter S. Thompson held forth. Chapter Four is the story of our nation's most randy political leaders—from Thomas Jefferson to Wilbur Mills, the once-powerful congressman whose career was doused in the Tidal Basin, to Gary Hart, he of the good ship *Monkey Business* —and how the rules of the game were changed by the Washington press corps and the new girls on the bus. Our guide through Washington Babylon will be Contra playboy Arturo Cruz, Jr., the Latin romancer of Irangate secretary Fawn Hall, a man who understands much about the American empire yet still cannot fathom this country's passion for inspecting its leaders' bedrooms.

In "Sex Wars," the midsection of the book, we examine how the ancient conflict between men and woman heated up during the 1980s, making heterosexual union even more precarious.

Chapter Five is the tale of Big John, a six-foot-five-inch cop who cries at male-bonding ceremonies while clasping his masculine "power object"—a .380-caliber automatic pistol—to his heart, and his brothers in the new men's movement. The members of this nationwide brotherhood, who bang drums to conjure their absent fathers and howl like beasts to restore their damaged self-esteem, appear more comfortable in all-male company than in engagement with the opposite sex. Chapter Six is a group portrait of five prominent feminists, including Shere Hite and Germaine Greer, that focuses on their deepening disaffection with men and with the act of intercourse itself. It was a decade when fury and disenchantment replaced romance in women's culture, when loving men too much became a psychological disorder.

In "Rebirth," the final section of *Burning Desires,* we explore the brave new world of American sexual ingenuity, how sex was retooled to fit modern specifications.

Chapter Seven is the inside story of the rise of feminized pornography, a unique development in the sexual underworld that was sparked by such erotic pioneers as filmmakers Candida Royalle and Annie Sprinkle, vampire-and-bondage novelist Anne Rice, and Republican porn star Missy Manners. Chapter Eight chronicles the invention and selling of safe sex, and it features on-the-scene accounts of the "World's First Jack-and-Jill-Off Party" and a phone-sex orgy. It also includes a portrait of Surgeon General C. Everett Koop, a conservative moralist who became the Reagan administration's one and only symbol of medical compassion during the plague years. Chapter Nine is a report from the bedrooms of thirty- and forty-something parents, those inventive couples who are searching for ways to keep passion alive between the twin pressures of overtime and feeding time.

Before we proceed with this panoramic tour, allow your two guides to introduce themselves. We are both journalists in our thirties, veterans of the sexual, cultural, and political uprisings of the late 1960s and early 1970s. While we like to believe that we are wiser now, we are not as regenerate or as damning of the past as current fashion dictates. The expansive feeling, the giddy "one big bed" spirit of those days, still strikes us as one of our generation's grander contributions, despite what we now hear from those sourpusses who blame us for everything from AIDS to child abuse, to the decline of the family. Your coauthors, it should also be noted, came of age with feminism and gay liberation, and while the call of these two great American movements for reproductive rights, sexual tolerance, and equal opportunity became our own, our voices remain unabashedly male and heterosexual.

One of your authors, Steve Chapple, was born and raised near the Beartooth Mountains of Montana, a region so cold, he remembers, that the morning after the senior prom of 1967 he turned to kiss his date and discovered that her face was covered with a layer of frost. Though it was June, the cornfield where they had spent the night was frozen. Your other guide, David Talbot, comes from the wilds of Hollywood, where his father, the seasoned actor Lyle Talbot, was among those Mae West once asked to "come up and see me sometime." We point this out because from time to time one or both of us will be forced to intrude in the narrative and we will distinguish ourselves by citing our place of origin. We have kept these intrusions to a minimum because we believe that tour guides should not block the view. But sometimes such first-person intervention enhances the reader's pleasure, and sometimes it is simply unavoidable. Covering safe-sex orgies and sex addiction clinics is after all a very different matter from covering balance-of-trade hearings or merger bids (no matter how sexy corporate stock maneuvers supposedly became in the eighties). Sexual revolution and counterrevolution was one of the monumental stories of the decade and it would have taken greater powers than ours to resist being swept up occasionally in the drama.

This brings us to our final point, a reader's advisory: the following pages contain some explicit, even pulsating, prose. We do not ask your forgiveness. If one side effect of *Burning Desires* is to quicken the pulse of a public gone numb with fear and shame, we remain unrepentant.

D. H. Lawrence once wrote the following, in defense of prose that celebrates sex: "The late British Home Secretary, who prides himself on being a very sincere Puritan, grey, grey in every fibre, said with indignant sorrow in one of his outbursts on improper books: '—and these two young people, who had been perfectly pure up till that time, after reading this book went and had sexual intercourse together!!!' *One up to them!* is all we can answer . . . There's nothing wrong with sexual feelings in themselves, so long as they are straightforward and not sneaking or sly. The right sort of sex stimulus is invaluable to human daily life. Without it the world grows grey."

Should a young or middle-aged or elderly couple of today feel similarly inclined after reading certain sections of *Burning Desires,* we're with Lawrence: *One up to them!*

BURNING DESIRES

·*R* E P R

ESSION

Obsession

was Hawaiian-theme night at the Silver Chain, a long-established Minnesota swingers' club that met regularly at a hotel in downtown St. Paul. From the podium of the hotel's main meeting room, Dr. Keith Henry watched couples in aloha shirts and flower leis arriving for the party. One man was wearing a grass skirt. Husbands kissed other men's wives full on the lips and grabbed handfuls of their flesh. Wives caressed the wrong husbands. Henry had never seen anything like it. "Of course, I tried not to register shock because I'm a professional," he would say later.

Dr. Keith Henry was a thirty-two-year-old physician who worked in the St. Paul public health department's venereal disease clinic, known as Room III. He had finally convinced the leaders of the Silver Chain to allow him to present his AIDS slide show at one of their Saturday night parties.

But only about half the partygoers bothered to hear Dr. Henry's presentation. The rest were filing noisily into the ballroom next door, where more interesting festivities were already under way. To block out the distractions, young Dr. Henry glanced at his notes. Then he gulped and flashed another slide.

"The viral attack rate for the various types of insertive sex is not well known," he declared. On the screen to his left shimmered a computer graphic of a white splotch inside a giant pink cavity. This was a blowup of sperm inside the vagina. "The attack rate for women in vaginal intercourse is generally estimated to be under 1 percent per contact," he continued in his monotone. "But there are a lot of variables. For example, preliminary data suggests that ulcerative diseases of the vaginal area, such as chancroid, syphilis, herpes simplex, and genital warts, can facilitate transmission of the AIDS virus."

Loud, very loud, squeals interrupted him. He looked toward the ballroom next door. "Tell the teacher we're surfin', surfin' U.S.A." The Beach Boys were waxing down their boards on the party tape. Dr. Henry clicked to the next slide, which was an enlarged rectum cake-decorated like the vagina with a sploosh of white sperm. Resolutely, he pushed forward.

"For anal intercourse, the attack rates range from less than 1 percent to 10 percent. This type of intercourse is associated with more trauma and mucosal bleeding, which gives infected semen fairly easy access to the bloodstream."

After the presentation, Henry and two nurses from the clinic brought out their big needles and took blood samples from some of the partygoers behind a screen in the back of the meeting room. "I told them we didn't expect to find anything," Henry recalls. Privately, however, he harbored strong concerns about these men and women.

Dr. Henry had been surprised when the Room III nurses told him that those attractive professionals who periodically showed up at the clinic with cases of gonorrhea or chlamydia were members of a local swing club. *Swinging?* He thought that had died out years ago. Were there really still groups of people who swapped mates like baseball cards? In this cautious age? Studying these people might provide some clues about the spread of AIDS among fast-lane heterosexuals, thought the VD doctor. And he was right.

Forty-four Silver Chain members lined up that warm Saturday night in June 1986 to have their blood drawn. But nobody took Dr. Henry seriously. Not yet. "Hey, Doc, come over here and have a beer," a Rodney Dangerfield type bellowed at Henry. "Don't mind if everyone looks at you like you're a piece of meat."

In this luau atmosphere, the young doctor stood out like a Baptist minister at Mardi Gras. He was dressed in a conservative blue suit and a blue oxford shirt, and he fidgeted more than a lot. "We were teasing him a little bit," smiles a female club member. Keith Henry looks like the sort of person who often gets teased—chinless, slightly paunchy, with glasses that wiggle down his nose and a flat voice that rarely revs out of neutral. It is hard to imagine him splashing in a hot tub with other men's wives.

"Part of me is attracted to the swinging lifestyle, actually," Henry would later confess. "Everybody has a level of sex fantasy, don't they? Even Jimmy Carter, who has always been one of my heroes, lusted in his heart." But the evening at the Silver Chain left him profoundly unsettled. "It reminded me of the way I felt when I saw that gay movie *Cruising,* with Al Pacino. It was about the S&M scene in New York, the heavy-duty leather sort of thing. To be honest, I really felt like walking out, and I had the same sensation watching those couples grope each other at the hotel."

Later that night, as Henry lay next to his wife, he couldn't stop thinking about this world that was so different from his own. It was hours before he could fall asleep. "I was afraid for them."

Ten days later, the results from the AIDS antibody test came back to Room III: one of the giggling beachcombers who had lined up that night, a twenty-five-year-old single woman, was infected. The nurses broke into tears. "She was one of the first women at the clinic to test positive, and the nurses took it hard," says Henry softly. "I was starting them on a roller coaster ride that was wilder and much more ominous than any of their clinic work had prepared them for."

Keith Henry was in for a troubling ride himself, as were the members of the Silver Chain and sexual liberationists throughout the country. Nothing would be the same for them after that night of hula and blood testing. "Sexually active" heterosexuals, in the era's new clinical jargon, would begin to see that it was not just gays and junkies who were at risk, but anybody who engaged in certain high-risk practices. And young Dr. Henry, who struck some as the type who had spent his youth in the medical library, was about to gain a much deeper understanding of human folly and desire.

"Oh my God, I can't believe it," said the Silver Chain club president when Henry called him. "These people . . ." Dr. Henry pauses. "It was clear to me they had all been living in a bubble world for a long time."

Each person who had had blood drawn that night was called in to Room III to receive his or her confidential test results. Henry refused to reveal the name of the woman who tested positive to other club members. But they frantically began to phone one another. "Who do you think it is?" they asked each other. "Did you have sex with her?" It was fear, not desire, that now bound together the Silver Chain. Some husbands and wives even refused to sleep with each other.

Soon a club meeting was called. A few members wanted to keep on swinging. They argued that the circle could be limited to those who had not been infected. But most wanted nothing more to do with the club. After two decades of sexual experimentation, the Silver Chain would soon be broken.

"There was a lot of anger and denial," recalls one former club member. "Some were furious at Dr. Henry: they blamed him for the disbanding of the club. Others pointed out that he had probably saved people's lives."

Henry, meanwhile, widened his study of swingers in the Minneapolis–St. Paul area. "I didn't want to spoil people's fun," he says, "but I had a job to do." He drove across town on a Sunday afternoon to meet with the officials of Sugar and Spice, a club whose membership overlapped with that of the Silver Chain. He talked them into organizing another round of tests.

There was more bad news when these results came back a few days later. Another swing-club member, a thirty-one-year-old married woman, was carry-ing the virus. Like the first woman, she reported that she had engaged in sex with more than twenty-five other club members. Two of these were said to be bisexual males with whom both women had repeated vaginal and anal inter-course. Again, the revelation blew apart the club.

"This woman was very popular, and her fellow club members were very upset," says Henry. "The president changed his opinion about the health risks of swinging. He sent out a letter disbanding the club. I think he was afraid of a lawsuit, and he didn't want the moral responsibility of being seen as a facilitator for transmission."

But other swingers in the Twin Cities fumed over Henry's research. The conscientious young doctor was not just spoiling the party, he was threaten-ing a whole way of life. By the 1980s, swinging in the United States had become a highly organized subculture, with more than two hundred clubs, two big annual conventions, dozens of magazines and newsletters, and scores of party cruises and special events. "In some ways, it mimicked the gay lifestyle in its heyday," observes Henry. "It was a heterosexual version of the same thing, an international social group in which sex was the driving force."

Like gays, swingers are an outlaw sexual population in the bosom of bour-
geois America. They both flout and embrace traditional middle-class values.
Swingers tend to be white, educated, and well-off. Yet they take pride in their
differences from the mainstream. Their fellow citizens sing the praises of
home and hearth, swingers believe, but then sneak out the back door to
adulterous trysts. Swingers, however, make sexual adventure a corollary of
marriage by bringing along the spouse. In a way, swingers are the most
domesticated of all American couples; they keep even their sexual intrigue at
home.

"The general public would like to think of swingers as the scum of the
earth, but the majority of us are your next-door neighbors, family people,
conservative people in some ways," says a woman who belonged, with her
husband, to both the Silver Chain and Sugar and Spice. "Our friends would be
appalled if they knew about us—we're churchgoing pillars of our community.
There was something fun about having a secret life," she adds, a bit wistfully.
"I'm going to miss it. What I liked most was the social aspect, I suppose, the
getting dressed up, the dancing. It was different than the bar scene. It was
more like going to a class reunion."

As he pursued his AIDS study, which he hoped to publish in the Centers
for Disease Control's (CDC) weekly report, Keith Henry began to immerse
himself in this middle-class sexual underground. During lunchtime, he would
visit pornography bookstores in downtown St. Paul. Soon the drawers of his
desk at the St. Paul Ramsey Medical Center, where he worked when not at
Room 111, were stuffed with magazines with titles like *Saints and Sinners* and
Swingers' Almanac.

The world in these periodicals was far more weird and raw than the
fantasies found in the popular men's magazines. Here were black-and-white
snapshots of naked couples from all over the country, real Americans with
real bodies, all advertising themselves. There were lithe young women with
tan marks and French-poodle hairdos, and older women with stretch marks
and heavy breasts. There were men with flour-sack bellies and tattoos, and
men with smooth, taut torsos. Some smiled straight at the lens as if they were
posing for the family Christmas card; some hid their faces behind arms and
pillows like camera-shy gangsters.

They were locked in the most intimate marital embraces. Wives on all
fours received their husbands from behind, loving lips wed themselves to

bone-hard flesh. And they wanted others to share their marriage beds. This white couple was looking for a "big black cocksman" to add to their pleasure. This "hot housewife" wanted to be sandwiched between "clean, gentle, slim" men in their twenties.

Keith Henry could not imagine his wife and himself stripping down in front of a camera and advertising for a couple interested in Greek, French, or B&D. But he wanted to understand these people better. It is the unconventional ones, the young physician had long believed, who "make life interesting for the more boring people like myself."

That's the way Dr. Henry was. At first he would be put off by the peculiarities of different American tribes, then his curiosity would grow, and he would end up feeling fairly comfortable with them. "When I was a med student at Cook County Hospital in Chicago," Henry remembers, "my girlfriend moved into an apartment building that turned out to be totally gay. And the first time I went over there, I was confronted with all these men who were really good-looking and great dancers and witty and knew all the good restaurants and places to go. And here I was, you know, slaving away all day and night at the hospital taking care of poor people. I felt threatened. Then it started sinking in that this wasn't such a bad group of people for her to fall for, as far as having friends. So I got to know the gay community in Chicago somewhat through that connection. And they became just another group of interesting people, like the Auschwitz survivors I got to meet quite a few of in Chicago, or the IV drug culture.

"And that's the way I came to feel about swingers. I'm not going to fall into the trap of passing moral judgment on them. I just wanted to alert them to the fact that they were placing themselves at risk. They were playing with their lives."

Henry was determined to wake up this sexual subculture. They were intelligent people, he felt. Given the correct information, they would surely begin to protect themselves, cut down on their sexual partners, start practicing safe sex. Soon after he received the Sugar and Spice test results, Henry phoned the organizers of the Lifestyles convention in Las Vegas. This was the nation's biggest annual gathering of swingers. He asked to be scheduled as a speaker at the upcoming event.

Incredibly, the CDC was holding up publication of his study, because it contradicted the CDC wisdom of the time that only known risk groups should be tested, not all those who had multiple sex partners. So, in the meantime, Henry would take his case directly to the swinging community. He would shout out the news, he would be their town crier. But like Dr. Stockmann in Ibsen's *An Enemy of the People,* who set out to alert his fellow citizens to the dangerous pollution in the municipal baths, Keith Henry found that not all the townspeople wanted to hear his warning.

"When I got Bob McGinley, the main guy behind the convention, on the phone, he exploded. 'There's no way,' he yelled at me, 'absolutely no way that I'm going to let you come out to Las Vegas and ruin people's fun.' "

The Twin Cities swing clubs might have collapsed under the impact of Henry's findings. But Bob McGinley's operation was another story. McGinley, fifty-one at the time, was the King of Swing—founder of Southern California's Club Wide World, one of the oldest, most successful clubs in the country; president of a national organization of swing-club operators; publisher of a swingers newsletter; owner of a travel agency that specializes in tours for the "sexually adventurous"; and the most vocal spokesperson for "the lifestyle," making defiant appearances on talk shows across America. If this Midwestern clap doctor figured on sowing panic in his empire and threatening everything he had fought for over the years, McGinley thought, he had another think coming.

One Saturday night at the comfortable Orange County house where Club Wide World holds its parties, two men competing for the same woman confronted each other like circling baboons. Swingers like to think they have banished the more primitive instincts, but jealousy bares its dripping fangs now and then at these gatherings. The larger one, a man built "like King Kong," in the words of the party host, had rolled his hand into a big block of a fist and was about to take a swing at the chin of his rival when Bob McGinley jumped between them. "You hit that man and I'll slug you harder than you've ever been slugged." At five-foot-five, McGinley was nowhere near the other man's size. But there was something imposing about his fireplug of a body, his fierce Irish mug. "The man decided not to follow through with his plans," grins McGinley.

There's a lot of fight in Bob McGinley. His father, Dan, took up boxing in the Navy during World War I and later fought a few years as a professional before becoming a housepainter. McGinley himself has the droopy eyelids of someone who has seen the inside of a ring. Sometimes, though, fists are not enough. "I own guns, I'm into firearms," says the King of Swing. "But along with that comes the obligation to use them responsibly."

There's another story McGinley likes to tell about himself. Late one night when he was in bed with his girlfriend, Jan, McGinley got an urgent call from his youngest son, David, who was spending the night in the Club Wide World office. "Dad," he whispered, "I think someone's trying to break in next door."

McGinley hung up the phone and called the police, then grabbed his .380-caliber handgun—the kind commonly used by European police—and dashed for his motorcycle. He got there before the cops, surprised the intruder inside the building, and held his gun on him until the squad cars arrived. "Don't even think of moving," he told the unlucky man.

It's not that he enjoys playing the tough guy. The truth is, he has been more of a lover than a fighter in his life. McGinley has toiled over two decades to create a business operation that is meant to magnify people's pleasure. But you sometimes have to be a scrapper to protect what you have built, he feels. Especially, he says, in a society that looks with scorn and resentment on anything that is sexually novel.

Bob McGinley's first battle was an internal one. He was raised in the suffocating embrace of the Nazarene Church, the same dour religious denomination that shaped young Gary Hart. As a teenager, he struggled to break free from the Nazarenes. Eventually he found his way to the less restrictive Baptist Church. And today he is an ordained minister in something called the Earth Church of the Pacific, a California congregation that caters to social renegades. Like many swingers, McGinley has created himself anew, severing all ties to his past. "There is nothing in my background to suggest what I would become," remarks the sexual entrepreneur. Jay Gatsby with a twist.

McGinley's new life as a sexual maverick was not inspired by any book or philosophy. He is a man of instinct, not letters. Sinatra's hit song "My Way" sums up his outlook on life, he says. He is also fond of quoting a Jack London line he read somewhere: "The proper function of man is to live, not exist."

"That particular statement has a great deal of meaning to me. Far too many people in this world are limiting their lives because of their religious inhibitions or their marriages or group pressure or the government or many other things. I believe that sexual liberation frees one in many ways, but it's very threatening to a lot of people. That married couple down the street that's into swinging is a very real threat, because it's easy to identify with them, and yet their lifestyle opens up all sorts of questions about the way we limit ourselves." The former Nazarene had become a true believer of a very different sort.

It was in this liberated spirit that McGinley decided to abandon his successful career as an aerospace engineer in 1969—in his midthirties, with five children to support—and start Club Wide World with his second wife, Geri, whom he had met at a swinging event. Over the next decade, the club prospered as the countercultural explosions of the 1960s began to ripple through suburbia. At its height, over two thousand men and women belonged to McGinley's club. His house would be jammed with couples on Saturday night.

The evening would start with a lecture on a current sexual or social topic. In McGinley's mind, education was a crucial part of acclimating people to the new erotic terrain. Then he would gather his guests around the fireplace and, wearing a homey-looking bathrobe, tell corny jokes to get the party rolling. ("What do you call an Italian swinger? Why a swap, of course.") The guests would then wander off to the pool or the "playrooms." McGinley believed he was not just running an orgy palace but building an extended family of freethinkers.

As the club entered its second decade, swinging became less of a passion and more of a business for McGinley. He diversified, launching a travel agency and the annual Lifestyles conventions. His marriage to Geri broke up, but they continued working together as business partners. Showing up each Saturday night to host the party began to seem more and more like a chore. "I satisfied my sexual curiosity a long time ago," he says. "That's not to say I've given up sex. But it's like how many steaks can you eat before you say, 'My God, where's a good hamburger?' "

Still, he refused to abandon his voluptuous kingdom. Swinging was his livelihood. McGinley likes to say that he is not "money-oriented. If I were, I'd be a wealthy man." But his thriving operation made him one of the most successful entrepreneurs in the world of swinging, and he valued the freedom this success gave him. "I have gone from a lifesyle of working for other people, working for the government in a sense, with the security clearances and all of that, to being a relatively free individual pretty much in control of my own destiny." He was, at last, his own man, and he owed it all to the business of mate swapping.

McGinley was also aware that people in "the lifestyle" looked to him for leadership. While other club operators took pains to avoid publicity, out of fear of antagonizing neighbors and police, two-fisted Bob McGinley went on camera to trade blows with indignant talk-show hosts and their clucking studio audiences. Just as he was getting the upper hand in these public brawls, however, the hulking specter of AIDS stepped into the ring.

This new sexual terror threatened all the gains of the past two decades. McGinley suddenly saw it all slipping away. It got to the point where only a half dozen couples or so were showing up for his club parties.

He would not give in. Wild fears were being fanned, he believed, by "a priesthood of doctors," killjoy authorities bent on stampeding everyone back to the sexual Stone Age. "I can read the medical literature as well as they can and there's been no evidence that AIDS can be transmitted in a normal heterosexual manner." No doctor was going to tell him how to run his sex life!

After ripping into Keith Henry over the phone, McGinley finally relented and told the physician he could come to Las Vegas. He would not be allowed to address the entire convention, but he could give a talk to a luncheon meeting of club presidents.

Dr. Henry credited the change of heart to his own powers of persuasion. "I could be a great salesman if I ever wanted to make a lot of money," he says. But the King of Swing had his own motives for letting Henry into his conclave. He knew Henry was planning to publish his paper through the CDC and it was bound to have a big impact. So McGinley would try to exert some influence over the young physician. The tough little man with the commanding presence was fully aware of *his* powers of persuasion. "I wanted to know more about this guy," says McGinley. "I wanted to see him firsthand where I could control him."

The lobby of the Hacienda Resort Hotel, which sits at the far end of the neon canyon that is the Las Vegas Strip, swarmed with registrants for the Lifestyles convention and zombie-eyed gamblers who had been up all night. There were silver slot machines, spinning roulette wheels, and blackjack tables as far as the eye could see. Bottle blondes in red-and-black satin saloon-girl outfits scurried about with trays of drinks. Outside, Las Vegas blazed under the August sun. Inside, it was cool and dark, a cave world of pasty-faced people. Keith Henry stood by the artificial waterfall, taking it all in. He had never been to Las Vegas before. The weekend would be a nice break from his routine, he thought. "My schedule and my family responsibilities don't allow for much playtime."

But first there was the luncheon with the swing-club presidents. Henry walked into the banquet room wearing the same blue suit he had worn to the Hawaiian theme party and carrying the same set of slides. He was seated at a big, round table with a dozen male and female swing chieftains. The Swiss steak entree was a disappointment to Henry. "I'm not into that kind of heavy meat." More dismaying was the conversation. "They were all talking about recent parties they had been to. One woman was laughing about another woman she knew who had intercourse with a hundred people in one weekend. 'Boy, she must have an iron cunt,' somebody said. It was all just fun and games to them."

But a cold shudder ran through the room after the dessert plates had been cleared away and the doctor from St. Paul began projecting his morbid statistics and body cavities on the screen. "People were very disturbed," recalls Paul Miller, a Chicago chronicler of the swing scene who was there that day. "It was a very graphic presentation. They kept asking him a lot of questions. It was like none of them ever imagined they might be in danger."

Henry was pleased. Maybe now the AIDS-prevention message would begin to circulate throughout the swinging community. "I sensed the fear in that room." But as the weekend wore on, he felt more and more invisible.

McGinley had refused to let Henry set up a blood-testing booth at the convention, but he agreed to rent the doctor space on one of the literature tables. Henry manned this post faithfully throughout the weekend alongside his stack of cheaply printed safe-sex pamphlets. All around him in the exhibit room was a dazzling bazaar of sexual merchandise: chocolate penises, anal love beads, bottles of musk oil, evil-looking bondage gear, nude video personal ads, and a unique contraption called a Sybian—a leather saddle with a rotating dildo on top. Porn stars with epic cleavages and heroic displays of lacquered hair offered to pose cheek-to-cheek with conventioneers for photos. Few in the passing crowd ventured near Henry; his cheesy black-and-white handout, with words like "infection" and "body fluids" sprinkled all through it, gave them the creeps.

From time to time, McGinley would observe the nondescript, bespectacled physician as he sat at his table. He wanted to take the measure of this man. "I've studied psychology and I'm a pretty good judge of people. I'm a people person," says McGinley. Was there something bottled up in Dr. Henry's sexual psyche that had led him to study swingers? Was his research a way to satisfy some secret craving? No, decided McGinley, this was not the key to under-standing Henry. "As a matter of fact," McGinley says, "he was very profes-sional. I never spotted him ogling. He didn't seem to be overwhelmed by all these good-looking women."

"It just wasn't very arousing to me," says Dr. Henry. "My main reaction watching all these people walking around was to wonder which one of them might be infected with the AIDS virus or some other sexually transmitted disease. What I really felt like doing was jumping up and screaming, 'Wake up!' "

That night, the conventioneers dressed up in their *Story of O* bird masks and topless gowns, their black leather jockstraps and Dracula capes, and crowded the banquet room for the masquerade ball. Keith Henry went in-stead to a comedy show in the hotel. Later, as he turned off his bedside lamp and went to sleep, costumed revelers swept up and down the hallways of the Hacienda, searching for the party rooms. A middle-aged husband and wife had invited younger couples to watch them make love. In another room, dimly lit and hazy with cigarette smoke, an obese woman was being spanked by a dominatrix in black leather as a crowd of naked and half-dressed men and women looked on. "What a beautiful love slave you are," hissed the dominatrix as she smacked her victim's big jelly bottom.

Swinging had given these men and women a way to play out their extrava-gant, if trite, fantasies. By night they were debauched noblemen and ravished maidens. By day they were common folk, the kind you see in RV camps, in their Ban-Lon shirts and K mart shorts, or at the supermarket, in their pastel sweats and Jane Fonda headbands. The swingers movement had brought libertinism, once the sole province of European royalty and Hollywood celeb-rities, to the mortgaged classes. You could satiate your desires on a Club Wide World cruise to the Bahamas and be back in time to take the kids shopping for school clothes. "Swinging," remarked a woman at a convention seminar, "is having your cake and eating it too."

But the "lifestyle" was losing its appeal in the 1980s. "I think it's disgusting," said one of the Hacienda's teenage towel boys, as he surveyed the oiled bodies of the conventioneers in repose around the hotel pool. "Most of them are old and fat, and I'm sure half of them have AIDS. If I was married, I couldn't imagine another guy on top of my wife. I'm faithful to my girlfriends. Once a relationship is over, it's over, and I start seeing someone else."

His was the censorious voice of a younger generation that had come of age on the down side of the sexual revolution. All he could see was wilted flesh pushed toward dangerous extremes in the service of pleasure. There was no doubt about it: swinging was no longer cool. To judge from the crowd at the convention, swingers' ranks were not being replenished by large numbers of young people. Not even McGinley's five grown children showed any interest in their father's way of life. "They all honor me, but I taught them to have minds of their own," he says.

AIDS hysteria, thinks McGinley, is largely to blame for swinging's sagging popularity. "AIDS is not really that significant a threat," he insists. "I'm more afraid of the panic than the disease." This is the message McGinley wanted to deliver to Dr. Henry at the convention before he went back to St. Paul.

Maybe the physician would listen to reason, McGinley hoped. Maybe the final version of his report would not fuel the paranoia. "I thought he was a sincere, knowledgeable person. I liked him personally, I really did," says McGinley in a fatherly way. "I think as he matures, he's going to be an excellent physician."

So McGinley tried to educate the younger man about AIDS and the swing scene. It was a lecture he has delivered many times since then. Swingers are not at risk, he said, because the virus cannot be transmitted through vaginal intercourse "unless there is bruising and that sort of thing." So there is no need to promote the use of condoms. He personally never uses them because "they interrupt sexual play." Swingers rarely get sexually transmitted diseases, he continued, because they are careful. Furthermore, anal intercourse between men "is extremely rare in the swinging community," as is intravenous drug use, so there is little threat of the infection spreading through those practices.

Henry was flabbergasted. What McGinley was telling him flew in the face of the best medical evidence, a sizable body of research literature on swingers' sexual behavior, and his own clinical experience. The CDC had already documented over a thousand heterosexual AIDS cases, and he himself was beginning to treat women who had been infected through vaginal intercourse. Studies also showed that rates of venereal disease among swingers were much higher than club leaders liked to admit and that bisexual behavior between male swingers, including anal intercourse, was widespread.

The man was being willfully ignorant, Henry thought to himself as he listened to McGinley. "That same expression came to mind: he was living in a bubble world. Let's leave aside the fact that there is indeed bisexuality and needle use among swingers. To say categorically there's no risk in vaginal intercourse borders on the fanatic. It may not be as high as sharing needles or anal intercourse, but there is definitely some risk, no matter what people like McGinley say. He doesn't understand the concept of relative risk. I was not saying that swingers should all go out and start buying cemetery plots. I was saying that there's a relative risk that over time is likely to increase. If you engage in sex with multiple partners, if you fail to use condoms, if you jump from party to party, from club to club, you are increasing your chances of being infected. Period."

The doctor and the swing leader came at each other with the best arguments each could muster. They tussled on and off throughout the weekend, trying to wear each other down. Henry was, as usual, patient and even-tempered, but unbudging. McGinley was a growling guard dog, equally determined to protect his way of life. Neither gave in.

In November 1986, three months after Henry's weekend in Las Vegas, his paper on the Minnesota swing clubs was finally published in the CDC's *Morbidity and Mortality Weekly Report*. The first AIDS study of hedonistic heterosexuals, it created an immediate sensation in the press. "It turned into a media circus," says Henry. "We thought we were all prepared. We had talked it all over ahead of time with the CDC, how and when to break it. The story was supposed to be embargoed until midnight November 13. But late that afternoon, just as we were closing up shop at Room III, the TV crews suddenly descended on us. 'CBS Evening News' had decided to break the embargo and run the story that night, and no one else wanted to be scooped."

The swingers story gave the media a perfect opportunity to simultaneously leer and wax indignant, the standard way unconventional sexuality is covered in America. McGinley and other lifestyle leaders had fought for years to create a more normal public impression of the swinging subculture, present-ing it as a fun and wholesome sport. In his Las Vegas convention and erotic travel tours, the sin was carefully packaged for middle-class consumption. Even his "wild, exotic" masquerade ball was run like "American Bandstand," with McGinley formatting the fun like a risqué Dick Clark. But the media hoopla around Henry's report gave the swing scene a sinister cast. In these news accounts, the lifestyle came across like a subterranean world hooked on sex and death.

McGinley was furious. *Now* he thought he knew what made Keith Henry tick, what motivated his damaging report. It was not a smothered sexual desire. It was flaming ambition. Henry was trying to make a name for himself in the burgeoning field of AIDS research, McGinley conjectured. This was a splashy way to do it. "It was primarily a way to get his name in print," asserted McGinley, "to say, 'Hey, look, guys, give me a raise, I'm doing a good job.' And in his desire for recognition, he destroyed two swing clubs."

McGinley's charges stung the doctor. Perhaps the publicity about his report had gotten out of hand; maybe he did revel a bit in all the attention. But that didn't invalidate his report, felt Henry. There was no professional glory in studying a sexual subculture like swingers. "In the heavy science circles," says the doctor, "that stuff doesn't mean much." In the end, there was only the satisfaction of performing one's medical duty, of sending a warning message to a group that had been remarkably oblivious to the threat. But people like McGinley, he felt, were blunting the impact of that message.

After months of calmly listening to the loud arguments of his critics, Keith Henry finally lost patience. "Bob McGinley is an irresponsible man," he says. "He holds himself up as a leader, but he is leading people in a dangerous direction."

The two men had tried to get a fix on one another, to win each other over. But their differences were too great. The man who had dedicated himself to living, not existing, and the man who complained of being a captive of his routine. The man who promoted the full enjoyment of sexual pleasure, and the man burdened with its medical consequences.

"What if Dr. Henry is right, and swingers are in danger," we ask Bob McGinley. "Won't you feel a terrible sense of responsibility if more get in-fected?"

But he turns the question around. "What if *I'm* right?" pleads the King of

Swing. "Wouldn't it be terrible to have given up all this, our lifestyle, just because a particular person has said that it could be dangerous? What if it isn't? What if *I'm* right?"

When "Jack Bonner," as we shall call him, returned to Minneapolis from his year-long trek through the Far East, he decided to call an old girlfriend. He wanted to tell her about his adventures: about backpacking in China, driving an old Harley into the Himalayas, living in the squalid splendor of Calcutta, nearly wasting entirely away with a mysterious ailment in Katmandu. They were the kind of stories the fast-living twenty-five-year-old woman would appreciate. The two had met at a Silver Chain party, back in Bonner's swinging days. He was nearly twenty years her senior, but he had the spirit and curiosity of a college kid.

There was something wrong in her voice though. Bonner could hear it right away. "I definitely need to tell you something," she told him. "We didn't know how to reach you. I took the AIDS test while you were gone . . ." She was the laughing woman at the Hawaiian theme party, the first positive in Keith Henry's study.

None of her other sex partners who had been tested was infected, she assured Bonner. But it would probably be wise for him to go down to Room III just to be certain. Bonner was stunned. "I stalled for a couple weeks, trying to decide whether I really wanted to know," he says. "I had always been very VD-conscious. I never got a sexual disease. Before I left on my trip, I had a complete workup, and I asked my doctor then about taking the HIV test. He said, 'Why give yourself something to worry about?' He kind of talked me out of it."

This time Bonner decided to go through with it. Ten days after having his blood drawn at Room III, he went back to get the results. He knew what they were as soon as he saw the look on the nurse's face.

Weeks later, Bonner was rushed to the University of Minnesota Medical Center with pneumocystis, a lung infection commonly associated with AIDS. He had entered the world of tests and treatment from which none of the afflicted has ever emerged.

Bonner is telling his story in a Days Inn motel room near the university hospital. He has lost a great deal of weight; he barely survived his bout with the infection. His shining blue eyes and his sunken cheeks give him the haunted look of an El Greco saint. There is a feverish intensity to everything he says. He has just come from a checkup at the hospital, where he is part of an experimental AZT treatment program. Bonner says he is determined not to go down without a struggle. But his long conversation with us feels like a last will and testament. He wants to make sure we get it all down right.

"This woman and I don't blame each other," says Bonner, retrieving the first of the afternoon's series of green, medicinal-smelling lozenges from his shirt pocket. His hands tremble as he works off the wax-paper wrapper and pops the lozenge in his mouth. "We don't know for sure who infected whom. You know the other person would never knowingly put you at risk. You can feel as healthy as a horse and still be loaded with virus. In fact, she still feels great.

"A whole lot of AIDS patients freak out. They moan, 'Oh, why me?' They turn to religion, things they never believed in before. But not me. I'm not afraid of the unknown. I look at this bug the way Africans do: it's another way to die. Nobody skips out on death. It's not a particularly glamorous way to go. You don't want to go through it, believe me. But I don't feel gypped. It beats waiting around for your arteries to harden. I've lived my forty-five years full-tilt boogie. I've jammed in a lot. I didn't just dream of doing things—I went out and did them. I have no regrets."

Bonner is not the type to condemn his past. Swinging was a way to revive his marriage, a way to fully indulge his desires. "My wife and I got into swinging in the late 1970s, after fifteen years of marriage. We had gotten married very young—she was eighteen and I was nineteen—and we soon had two kids. I felt like I'd never had enough opportunity to explore sexual possibilities. I didn't want the guilt that's attached to having affairs, and this seemed like the safest way for us to do it.

"There is just no way to avoid getting bored when you've been married that long. You can be creative and all the rest, but it finally gets to be like eating at the same restaurant every night for your entire life.

"You have to let go of jealousy in swinging. When you feel you can share a sexual experience with your wife in the same bed, with her getting pleasure from another man, and not freak out, it's a revelation. We felt stronger in our relationship. Years later, our marriage broke up, but swinging had nothing to do with it. We had both lost interest in that world by then.

"After you have lived out your fantasies, you say, 'I don't need to do that anymore.' Just like I don't need to go back to India anymore either, after all the time I spent there. I know what the people look like, what the food tastes like, what the streets smell like. I don't need to experience it again. I can conjure it all in my head."

But swinging had left him with more than memories. Maybe it was the Silver Chain woman; more likely it was one of the few men with whom he had experimented. In any case, he was now a CDC statistic, one of those chosen randomly by nature as part of its evolutionary plan. That was the detached way he sometimes regarded his misfortune.

None of the first AIDS casualties in the swinging world, like himself, knew of the menace, says Bonner. They were victims of chance, he believes. But the swingers who continue taking risks, he says, have no excuse. They baffle and enrage him. Here he was, a once-hearty man now skeletal and frail, a walking public service announcement. And still many swingers refused to get the message.

"They say Dr. Henry is creating a scare, he's in it for the notoriety, but they're crazy," says Bonner, the eyes in his gaunt face blazing. "He has no ax to grind; he's just doing his job. I've spent years in the business world, and after a while you really come to appreciate people who don't bullshit you. That's Keith Henry. Swingers have their heads in the sand. Is Bob McGinley going to have to get sick himself before he wakes up?"

The first duty of living things is to survive, Bonner observes. He turns McGinley's cherished Jack London quote on its head: if you don't exist, you can't live. For those sick with AIDS, mere existence becomes an achievement. Once drenched in sensuality, Bonner's life has become barren of sex. "I can't see putting anyone else at risk," he says. "I can't do that to another human being. Not even with a condom. They may be 99.9 percent safe, but what if one did break? I just couldn't live with myself.

"That's the worst part of having this disease," says Bonner, his bony hand fluttering toward his pocket for another lozenge, "the feeling that you're no longer desirable."

It was not the same after the release of Keith Henry's report. Swingers throughout the country were forced to consider the tension between their sexual freedom and survival. Many saw a glacier ahead and chose to abandon their pleasure cruise. By 1987, swing-club leaders were estimating that attendance at their parties was down by 50 percent. Bowls of condoms were set out like party snacks at some swing houses. Some club members formed splinter groups of certified HIV-negatives.

But in some ways, the bubble world remained remarkably unchanged. A 1987 Ph.D. study of 181 swingers in the San Francisco area by Deborah Caust of the Institute for the Advanced Study of Human Sexuality concluded that "while most respondents expressed concern [about] AIDS . . . they do not appear to have fully committed themselves to behavioral changes as specified by the 'safe-sex guidelines.' " A Chicago-based group called ABATE (A Barrier Against the Epidemic) tried to enlist club leaders and swing-magazine publishers in a campaign to promote AIDS education and testing among swingers, but the effort met with little success. "The fear seems to have peaked," said ABATE organizer Paul Miller in 1988. "Swing leaders seem to think of me as an alarmist."

In 1987, the year after Keith Henry's mission to Las Vegas, the Lifestyles convention finally held its first open session on AIDS. But the seminar, which featured Bob McGinley and two physicians, seemed primarily designed as a tranquilizer. "There's nothing that's completely safe," declared one of the medical panelists, sounding like the company doctor at an asbestos factory. "If you want to live in a risk-free world, don't ever get in your car, damn well don't smoke cigarettes, don't walk down stairs, don't ever get off your chair."

This was not enough to allay the fears of everyone in the audience, particularly the female swingers. "I'm scared," said a middle-aged woman. "This thing has just ruined the fun for me. You can't go into that dark orgy room anymore without thinking about it."

But Bob McGinley and several other men in the room rushed to contain the female anxiety they felt rising around them. "I feel that's a totally unnecessary fear," McGinley told her. "This disease is not that ambitious; it's hard to contract. But if you must keep the fear, if it's that important to you, then stay out of that dark room." It was vintage McGinley.

Back in St. Paul, young Keith Henry was feeling much older than he did the day he first began wondering about swingers and AIDS. His days are now filled with the immunodeficient: gay men and former swingers, women and children. "I just came back from my eighth funeral," he says late one afternoon, rubbing his eyes wearily, his feet propped up on the desk in his cramped and cluttered office. "I'm starting to get a creeping sense of desperation. There's no way to count your victories with something like this. You know when someone gets infected or dies. But you don't know when you save someone's life through education. Did my report save any swingers' lives? There's no marker for that."

Henry had gone on to publish dozens of research papers on AIDS in the years after his swinging report, studies on AIDS testing and AZT and the varying rates of infectivity in semen. His medical knowledge had grown enormously. But he still found the human element of this disease, the laws of sexual desire, utterly confounding. Doctors like Henry were struggling to medicalize sex. "We're trying to develop a generation of worried well, to change society's sexual behavior," he says. But success continued to elude them.

How could you explain an otherwise intelligent man who keeps risking death in the pursuit of pleasure? Even more troubling, how could you explain an otherwise decent woman who keeps taking lovers to bed even though she knows she is infected? "I've heard that neither one of the two women who tested positive in the swingers study is practicing safe sex. Even though the married woman's husband knows she is infected. It just drives you crazy," he says shaking his head.

"Sexuality is so complex," he continues. "Being intelligent has very little to do with it. Working in a VD clinic, I've heard it all, every excuse imaginable. You know, I should have studied Shakespeare in college instead of subjects— like calculus and physics—that have nothing to do with my time now. Then maybe I could understand the human heart better so I could attack the source of this problem. Human nature," says Dr. Henry, and it sounds like a sigh of resignation, "that's where the problem lies."

Giovanni Giacomo Casanova, the celebrated eighteenth-century lover and adventurer, could not escape the scourge of Venus. His erotic exploits in the castles and taverns of Europe were interrupted by no fewer than eleven bouts with venereal disease. Syphilis and gonorrhea were not properly distinguished at the time, and Italians referred to both as the "French disease." Nor were they properly treated. One infection, bestowed upon him by the mistress of a German baron, left him more dead than alive. Over the years, Casanova's "pistol," as he fondly called his penis, grew scarred from the oozing blisters that periodically blossomed on him. Flames would course through him when he pissed.

Other mortals would have been moved to lift their eyes to heaven and lament, as does David in Psalms 38:5,7: "My wounds stink and are corrupt because of my foolishness . . . For my loins are filled with a loathsome disease; and there is no soundness in my flesh." But not history's greatest lover. As soon as his grievous symptoms had subsided, he would be off in search of his next conquest. These wounds of the flesh, wrote Casanova in his *Memoirs,* are "less honorable perhaps than those which are won" on the battlefield, but "being obtained through pleasure, [they] ought not to leave any regret behind."

He referred to himself, with typical flair, as a "slave of Eros." But in today's diagnostic culture, Casanova would be termed a "sex addict" and undergo public analysis on the talk-show circuit. He had his way with nuns, with other men's wives, with other men. He impregnated his own grown daughter. He couldn't stop himself. As he grew older, his seductions became more frantic and often pathetic. When his charms failed, the aging roué used money. The rational mind of today, filled with safe-sex guidelines, feminist sanctions, and Dr. Ruth verities, recoils from such debauchery. Casanova brings out the clinician in us.

And yet we still get hot. It's hard not to respond to such pure voluptuousness. "The chief business of my life has always been to indulge my senses; I never knew anything of greater importance," wrote Casanova. "I felt myself born for the fair sex, I have ever loved it dearly, and I have been loved by it as often and as much as I could."

He worshiped his lovers; he savored their very scent. "I have always been fond of highly seasoned, rich dishes" and strong cheeses, confided Casanova. "As for women, I have always found the odour of my beloved ones exceedingly pleasant." Four fifths of his sexual pleasure, he declared, came from delighting his bedmates.

Seduction was an endlessly intriguing parlor game to him, involving an elaborate series of moves and countermoves. He did not believe in using force or alcohol to win his objectives, but he was a master at subterfuge. "As to the deceit perpetrated upon women, let it pass," he implored his readers, "for, when love is in the way, men and women as a general rule dupe each other."

Casanova was the product of a more carefree century, before love became weighted with the seriousness of the Romantic movement. "Never did [women] play the virtuous less," wrote a French novelist of Casanova's Paris. "People take a fancy to each other—and embrace. When they get bored, they part with as little ceremony. On meeting again, they re-embrace with similar vivacity, leave each other again and never quarrel."

It's a description that calls to mind Saturday nights at Club Wide World. Casanova is the patron saint of all sexual liberationists. Even as an old man afflicted with gout and an inflamed prostate gland, he refused to repent for the dissolute life he had led. "Happy are those who know how to obtain pleasures without injury to anyone; insane are those who fancy that the Almighty can enjoy the sufferings, the pains, the fasts and abstinences which they offer to Him as a sacrifice . . . All [God] has given unto us has been intended for our happiness."

There is something mad, something repulsive about this Venetian scoundrel's single-minded pursuit of pleasure. But there is also something pure and wonderful about his obsession. Those who live life to excess, realized Casanova, are flirting with death. Yet, at the same time, they are conquering it, by driving away premonitions of the grave with their carnality. "There can be nothing dearer to a thinking being than life," he wrote as he approached death. "Yet the voluptuous men, those who try to enjoy it in the best manner, are the men who practice with the greatest perfection the difficult art of shortening life, of driving it fast. They do not mean to make it shorter, for they would like to perpetuate it in the midst of pleasure, but they wish enjoyment to render its course insensible."

Casanova's death-defying spirit—oblivious to microbes and morals—hovers over today's swing clubs and those other corners of the sexual demimonde still resistant to the new sobriety. It is surprising how many such stubbornly illicit corners still exist in the current climate.

In Detroit we came across the Original Church of Theiatry, a religious order that preaches spiritual bliss through stronger erections and limitless amounts of tantric intercourse. The church founder, a fifty-year-old former nurse named Sister Reverend Mozella Sunshine, tells her followers that men should engage in sex for "as long as they want and with as many women as they want or as many women as need them. A man is supposed to sow his seed all over the place—that makes for a very healthy human race."

Reverend Sunshine does not believe in using condoms, because "with rubbers there can be no exchange of electricity between the male and female. And the exchange of electricity is the experience of God." She dismisses AIDS as a "phony disease." When one disrobes with a lover, she says, "you can tell whether they're clean and healthy. You can see them and smell them and taste them and feel them."

This Detroit priestess holds "meditations" in motel conference rooms and private homes that draw together black and white, young and old. There are dancing, singing, and moments of contemplative silence. Sometimes Reverend Sunshine, a bespectacled black woman with a graying Afro, appears at these services like a Zulu queen, bare-breasted and draped in beads. Sometimes she is completely naked because "God created me in this manner." When the spirit moves them, her followers also take off their clothes and exchange sexual electricity.

One day Reverend Sunshine elaborates upon her religious doctrine in a telephone conversation with us. Like Casanova, she believes "that the sexual is holy, the body is divine, because God created it. Only God can create a body . . . Excuse me," she says suddenly, "pump it up sweetheart. Pump, pump! That's right, beautiful. OK, you keep pumpin' until the towel falls on the floor, and then you get another erection and you do it again." Men come to Reverend Sunshine to help them learn how to control their ejaculations and put steel in their erections. She is supervising one such trainee as we chat with her.

"We call this exercise pumpin' iron, you know, pumpin' the towel," she explains. "He's using the muscles in his penis to lift the towel up and down. Then you graduate to wet towels, then to a lady's purse, then to one of those plastic shopping bags with groceries inside." Reverend Sunshine has yet to see a man who can forklift a grocery bag. "But that is the goal." She is a woman of boundless faith.

America is a vast and reverent country with a multitude of congregations. But few interpret the Scriptures like the Original Church of Theiatry. The God in most of these houses of worship looks with a baleful eye upon lust.

Desire is not a blessing from above in these churches but rather the devil's hot breath in one's ear.

In the 1980s, even the secular-minded began beseeching the Almighty to help them control their bodily urges. Men and women who lusted too much began forming groups for "sex addicts" modeled on Alcoholics Anonymous chapters. These groups are not affiliated with any religion, but as in AA, members invoke a "higher power" to help them break the chains of their cravings. And their meetings, often held in church vestries, have the character of confession, with the "addicts" publicly unburdening themselves of their most intimate secrets.

Many of the leaders of this sexual self-control movement are former liberationists. And there is something equally passionate about the way they throw themselves into their new calling. If Casanova was once their inspiration, it is now his obsessive opposite, St. Augustine, a man who spent most of his life trying to escape his own flesh. One confederation of sex addiction groups is named the Augustine Fellowship in honor of the revered North African bishop who came to prominence in the declining years of the Roman Empire. He is the movement's ideal patron saint, for while Casanova, looking back over his life at the age of seventy-three, announced, "I regret nothing," St. Augustine was wracked with remorse.

In his *Confessions,* the tormented account of his search for spiritual tranquillity, Augustine paints a black picture of his past. He speaks of his student days in Carthage as a "hissing cauldron of lust." He makes himself out to have been a wanton sensualist who shamelessly rooted about in the city's pleasure troughs. But in reality, young Augustine seems to have been quite normal in his desires. He loved the theater, good food, and the bright company of his friends. He fell in love with a lower-class woman, who lived with him for fifteen years and bore him a son. Though they were not married, it was a deep, monogamous relationship.

But Augustine was plagued by his natural appetites, which he termed "the unclean whispers of [the] body." His humanness was a source of terrible anguish to him. This is how he describes falling in love: "My God, my God of mercy, . . . you mixed much bitterness in that cup of pleasure! My love was returned and finally shackled me in the bonds of its consummation. In the midst of my joy I was caught up in the coils of trouble, for I was lashed with the cruel, fiery rods of jealousy and suspicion, fear, anger, and quarrels."

Yes, love can be hell. But while most of us continue inflicting its dark joys upon ourselves throughout our lives, Augustine eventually fled into celibacy. After sadly abandoning his mistress for a socially advantageous marriage that was arranged by his mother, to whom he was deeply devoted, Augustine, at age thirty-two, renounced the physical world for the spiritual. He would struggle for the rest of his life to achieve a state of perfect grace, untroubled by his nagging body, which he saw as "the tomb" of the soul. He believed that he could only achieve inner peace by rejecting the world of the senses and devoting himself entirely to God.

But earthly desire held the holy man in its grip. After swearing off sex, he continued to be plagued by his love of food and drink. Though "drunkenness is far from me . . . there have been times when overeating has stolen upon your servant," Augustine confessed. And he was mortified by the persistence of his erotic dreams. "During sleep where is my reason, which, when I am awake, resists such suggestions and remains firm and undismayed?" he wailed. ". . . Is it sealed off when I close my eyes?" Fifteen hundred years before Freud, Augustine had discovered the haunting power of the subconscious.

With God's help, Augustine pledged in his *Confessions,* he would conquer even these unwitting, nocturnal desires. "The power of your hand, O God Almighty, is indeed great enough to cure all the diseases of my soul," he wrote. "By your grace it will no longer commit in sleep these shameful, unclean acts inspired by sensual images, which lead to the pollution of the body: it will not so much as consent to them."

Augustine explained the permanence of human evil in psychological terms. The pleasure derived from past sensual acts is "inflicted" on the memory, he believed, compelling us to repeatedly commit our sins. But by invoking the power of God, he declared, those who are truly determined can break the compulsive force of habit and find lasting joy and peace.

As with Casanova, there is something breathtaking about his ambition. These two great figures represent the poles of sexual obsession. While the master of seduction sought to conquer mortality by sating his senses, Augustine tried to do so by subjugating his flesh and becoming pure spirit. Not only would he refrain from sex, he would banish Eros from his sleep. In this way he hoped to win release from the tomb of his body.

More than fifteen centuries after Augustine, God's creatures are still being driven crazy by love and desire. People fall prey to lust and ruin their good marriages. They prowl the streets at midnight in search of quick satisfaction. They lose themselves completely to the wrong lovers. They are "lashed with the cruel, fiery rods of jealousy and suspicion, fear, anger, and quarrels."

And in their anguish, some gather in small, secret groups, confessing their sins, like Augustine, and crying out for deliverance from the coils of passion.

"Nina," as she wants to be called, is celebrating nine months of sexual "sobriety" with about a dozen other recovering addicts at the home of her "sponsor," whom we will call "Gary." * "No sex with myself or anyone else, that's the contract I have with myself," she explains. "I slipped a few times on the masturbation, but I still think of myself as basically sober."

Nina is sitting with her women friends at the living room table, which is spread with wooden bowls of guacamole and tortilla chips, platters of ham and cheese, and steaming casserole dishes. The men are huddled in conversation at the opposite end of the room. There is no dancing, no flirting. The lid is on tight here tonight. A woman with a brunet ponytail glances at us, then turns instantly away. She has the timid, darting eyes of a forest mink.

"Masturbating is definitely bottom-line behavior for me," continues Nina, by which she means it's a proscribed pleasure. Addiction-speak is the primary language spoken at this party. "There's a real fine line between masturbation that is acting out or numbing out and masturbation that is nurturing. It's not always easy to tell the difference."

Nina's plain features are unembellished with makeup. Her cheeks glisten with sweat. It's a hot, moist night in Minneapolis, the capital of the sex addiction movement. Everyone is dressed in shorts and T-shirts or light cotton shifts. Nina is braless, but it does not seem appropriate to notice this, considering the occasion. We quickly look away.

Nina says she must always be on guard against temptation. "Romance is still very much alive in my life. The other night I went dancing and got tranced out. You have to be careful." Another night, an attractive friend invited her to go swimming by the light of the moon in one of the city's warm little lakes. Nina went home to put on her bathing suit; her friend was

* Some names and biographical details in these tales of "sex addiction" have been changed at the request of those interviewed.

waiting outside in the car. But she couldn't go through with it. "I decided it would be safer to go over to my sponsor's house." Gary, her sponsor, has helped keep her on the wagon on more than one occasion.

At thirty-two Nina has the tough, weary air of someone who has long been battling her demons. A few days after the party, she tells us her story over bottles of mineral water at a glass-and-chrome bar on Hennepin Avenue. Her father was an alcoholic. Her oldest brother molested her. Another brother raped her twice. "He and I are extremely codependent," she says.

"After I grew up, I spent a lot of time seducing men—men with powerful intellects, men who were athletes. The kind of men I felt would never like me for me. When I had sex with them, they were under my spell. It was emotionally satisfying, but not physically. I never had orgasms with anyone but Bruce."

Bruce is devoted to Nina. They have been involved for fourteen years. For a time, they were married. But throughout most of their years together, Nina was relentlessly pursuing other men. "Sometimes I would be having four affairs at the same time," she says. "I would go out dancing with friends and end up in bed with them. It looked good on the surface, but I was in a lot of pain. Bruce has been monogamous the whole time, and he never knew about me. I didn't know how to live with Bruce and balance that with all the fun of going out with other men. I felt terrible guilt because of the secrecy. I knew Bruce would never accept me having other lovers. After waking up with some guy, I'd have to sedate myself by smoking pot."

It was during treatment for her marijuana dependency that Nina realized she was also addicted to sex. "As soon as the drugs were gone, that's when the urge for romance and sex really skyrocketed. I started gaming with my drug counselor. He and I were sexual once."

In 1987 she decided to quit her job as a newspaper layout artist in Florida, sell her belongings, and check into the sexual dependency unit of the Golden Valley Health Center in suburban Minneapolis, the country's first inpatient program for sex addicts. "During my four weeks there, I went deep down into my childhood and did a lot of anger work. I had very little sexual drive there. Men angered me; they disgusted me. Then I began to see that the men in the program were hurt little boys, like I was a hurt little girl. We began to see each other as people instead of sex objects." Nina still looks angry.

We think back to Nina's sobriety party. There was indeed something

boyish and girlish about the people there that night. It was like a preadoles-
cent birthday party, before the hormones start working their black magic,
with the boys on one side of the room and the girls on the other. These men
and women in their thirties and forties seemed to have made their way back
to an earlier state of innocence.

"Oh, I can't go near the lakes," one man told us that night when the
conversation touched inevitably upon the sticky heat and the best local swimming spots. Behind his horn-rims his eyes were as wide and frightened as a
child's. We assumed he did not know how to swim. But he meant something
else. "You know—all the girls in their swimsuits. It's too dangerous. I'd start
acting out again."

After completing the program at Golden Valley, she was broke, Nina says,
resuming her story over a second glass of fizzy water at the chrome bar. But
she decided to stay in Minneapolis awhile, in the therapeutic company of the
area's many other recovering sex addicts, before returning to her life in
Florida. She found a cheap room in a downtown dormitory run by a women's
charity. She began attending as many as five Sex Addicts Anonymous meetings a week. It became a way of life.

Faithful Bruce is waiting patiently for her back home. Nina talks to him on
the phone once a week. She says she is looking forward to rejoining him when
her "recovery is more solid." Her sojourn in the north, says Nina, has brought
her greater insight. "I've learned that sleeping with other men was a way to
avoid intimacy with Bruce. Intimacy is hard work." She sounds resolute but
not very enthusiastic.

The busy world of sex addiction therapy—with its sobriety parties, its
secret meetings, its intimate revelations, its late-night pleas for help—can be
hard to leave. It can, in fact, be almost as enthralling as a frenetic sex life.

Sexual desire became pathology in the 1980s. Suddenly groups appeared all
over the country for people who felt miserable about their physical and
emotional cravings. Their urges were incompatible with their family life, with
social convention, with the dangerous new viral reality. And yet they could
not seem to control their lust through willpower alone, so they flocked to a
growing number of self-control fellowships for moral support. In Minneapolis
and St. Paul, it was Sex Addicts Anonymous; in Boston and Northern Califor-

nia, Sex and Love Addicts Anonymous. There was an organization for gay men called Sex Compulsives Anonymous. Each group had its own founder and inspirational tract, known as the Big Book. And each adopted the Twelve-Step recovery method of Alcoholics Anonymous, in which members are first asked to acknowledge that they are powerless over their addiction and that their lives have become unmanageable.

Some groups set stricter criteria for recovery than others. Every member of Sexaholics Anonymous, a Los Angeles–based organization with some three hundred chapters in the United States, Canada, and Germany, is asked to forswear all sex except that with his or her spouse. "Other groups feel this is too hard a requirement," the group founder, a man known as Roy K., tells us. "They redraw the boundaries to include masturbation and homosexual relationships. But in the long run, that's nonproductive. About half our members are single, so they're totally abstinent. But we don't feel abnormal or deprived.

"Freedom from sex can be completely normal. I was totally abstinent in my marriage for fifteen months, and it was the best period of my life and my marriage. Ridding our marriage of sex revealed the dependency pathology I had on my wife. But I was finally able to take lust out of my relationship with my wife, thank God. Once I had let go of all expectations of sex, I felt no need for sex.

"Our goal is to stop lusting, to stop the internal pathology that fuels the addiction. It's so hard to stop lusting, for gay men to stop staring at men's crotches and hairy chests, for heterosexual men to stop drinking in the bodies of women with their eyes. They have created their own idols that they can't live without.

"I myself have been free from the tyranny of lust since January 1976, but I'm tempted every day. I take no credit for my recovery. In our gutter illness, our depraved, perverted sickness, we've discovered a loving God who apparently can do for us what we can't do for ourselves. Once you open that door, it's a marvelous odyssey into love, life, and family."

None of the other fellowships are as Augustinian in their ambitions as Roy K.'s group. But their shared ideal is a monogamous relationship free of such stimuli as pornography, flirtations, and frequent masturbation. Their members are men and women who feel deep shame about falling short of this goal. Sex addicts meetings draw together a colorful and diverse cast of horny priests,

Peeping Toms, gay cruisers, lovelorn women, party girls, ladies' men, erotica collectors, fetishists, and onanists.

They are in terrible distress and they feel compelled to confess it all: *I looked down the front of a woman's dress when we were making sandwiches for the hungry at the church mission . . . I tried to pick up another patient in line at the VD clinic . . . I got hard looking at the other men's naked bodies in the gym shower . . . I slept with my boyfriend's best friend when he was out of town . . . I cupped the breast of a teenage girl after everybody passed out at a drunken party . . .* All is forgiven, no one is without sin at these gatherings. Sexual sobriety is seen as a lifelong struggle.

It has the feeling of an underground movement. They meet in church basements and attics like the early Christians. They are sworn to secrecy; none of their stories is ever to be repeated outside the group. They do not advertise. Press coverage is generally discouraged. The meetings are not run by professionals. No money is charged. This is do-it-yourself people's therapy.

But as the movement gathered momentum in the 1980s, a professional cadre of addictionologists began hanging out their shingles. They wrote books. They appeared on talk shows. They opened sex addiction treatment centers at six different hospitals. They pushed for official sanction by trying to get "hyperactive sexual desire disorder" listed in the *Diagnostic and Statistical Manual* of the American Psychiatric Association. Such listings are crucial for those trying to create a new therapeutic market, for they make it easier to get grants and medical insurance coverage. "We're fighting the same battle the alcoholism treatment people fought years ago," says Patrick Carnes, the nation's leading sex addictionologist. "It took almost two decades after AA's Big Book was published for the medical establishment to accept alcoholism as a disease."

Six percent of the American population, Carnes tells talk-show audiences and interviewers, is suffering from sex addiction. He does not say how he knows this, but he is a serious, intense man and he looks as if he has studied the matter thoroughly. After writing a book on the subject, Carnes was approached by a California-based medical corporation called CompCare and asked to set up the country's first treatment center at Golden Valley. "We see people who legitimately need to be hospitalized," he says. "We see people who are malnourished, they're exhausted, they haven't slept in days. I mean we're talking about people who are into seventy-two-hour back-to-back sex binges. They're suicidal; they really need a lot of structure and support."

Sex addictionologists like Carnes are in the habit of painting eye-popping pictures like this. They look across America and see an army of salivating junkies hooked on scoring. But not everyone buys their perspective. The addictionologists' main professional detractors are the sexologists, those descendants of research pioneers like Havelock Ellis, Alfred Kinsey, and Masters and Johnson whose work has tended to reduce the shame surrounding sex and to create greater tolerance for sexual nonconformity. The sexologists fight bitterly with the addictionologists, trading blows in their respective journals and at university conferences.

The concept of sex addiction, charge the sexologists, can be used to pathologize all those whose sexual behavior does not conform to conventional morality. Addictionologists assume that there is such a thing as "normal" sexual behavior, their critics complain, when in fact one man's excess is another man's minimum daily requirement. Sexologists do, of course, acknowledge that some people are afflicted by perverse desires—or paraphilia, in their new, nonjudgmental terminology. But so many different freakish habits are lumped together under the circus tent of "sex addiction," they say, that the category is virtually meaningless.

"I had a patient who would wake up at two in the morning, break his contract with himself, and go downtown to buy injection needles, preferably the big ones used by veterinarians," says Johns Hopkins University sexologist John Money. "And he would come home and pierce them all the way through his testicles because he got a thrill from it and it made him come. There was no question in his mind that it was totally erotic. Some people would term him a sex addict, but he wasn't addicted to sex. He was addicted to needles."

Money sees the rise of the sex addiction movement as part of the "sexual counterreformation" sparked by the heresies of the 1960s. "At heart, America is still a nation of puritanical missionaries," he says. After periods of license and indulgence, the country feels compelled to atone for its sins. The history of America, Money wryly observes, is a continuous cycle of pleasure and penance.

None of this point-counterpoint seemed to have much effect on believers like Nina. While the great debate between sexologists and addictionologists raged on, men and women continued to gather in church attics and basements and read aloud from the Big Book. They knew how they felt, and they felt like hell. They had whored and partied away their youth, but now that all had to end. Or they would lose their families, their sanity, or even their lives. They had to clean up their acts; they had to get with the new program. They were too secular to be born again. Psychotherapy was too long and expensive a process. They wanted results and they wanted them fast. The Anonymous groups seemed like their best hope for recovery.

They would "work the Twelve Steps" of the Big Book. "We admitted we were powerless over our compulsive sexual behavior . . . we came to believe that a Power greater than ourselves could restore us to sanity . . . we made a searching and fearless moral inventory of ourselves . . . we admitted to God, to ourselves and to another human being the exact nature of our wrongs . . . we humbly asked God to remove our shortcomings . . ." They would break free from the tyranny of their desire, as Augustine had before them.

Self-control was the passion of the times. There were groups for cocaine users, overeaters, gamblers, big spenders, for every human temptation. As it entered middle age, the generation that had once believed "if it feels good, do it" was now in full retreat from indulgence. Along with aerobics and low-cholesterol diets, the Twelve-Step fervor was one more dogged attempt to gain mastery over the inevitable process of decay. The body, once the source of so much carefree pleasure, was now an implacable foe.

Looking back, it was a miracle his marriage ever survived, says Gary, Nina's sponsor and, like her, a former oarsman on the slave galley of lust. By 1967, the year he graduated from college and got married, he was already "deep in addictive behavior—masturbation, affairs, some voyeurism. I hoped with all my heart that marriage would solve my problem." It didn't.

What happened instead was the 1960s. Gary got taken prisoner by the sexual revolution. He had affairs with women he met at antiwar meetings and food co-op meetings. He had affairs with neighbors and friends. He bought *Playboy* every month, neatly stacking back issues on the bookshelf in his bedroom. Hugh Hefner's square hepcat brand of Midwestern hedonism merged, in Gary's mind, with the 1960s' spirit of free love. He was not running around and cheating on his wife, he told himself. He was liberating his libido; he was building a community of lovers and friends.

Gary's looks, with his curly red beard and wire-rim glasses, are a product of that era. So are his politics. But he now thinks that the unfettered sexuality of the sixties was poison to his system. "It helped spread the addiction," he says. "It encouraged the worst in people. You know, when big shipments of heroin showed up in Harlem, lo and behold, there were more junkies."

Middle age has not soured Gary. He has a friendly, open manner. He is kind to strangers. He is the type who would stop to help stranded motorists. But there is something uncharitable about the way he views his own sexual past. Does he see anything positive about the sexual revolution, we ask him. "Yes," he says grudgingly, "there was some emotional giving and taking under the influence of the sexual drug. But there was no growth that could not have been accomplished some other way. A sunset and a music tape—that's all I need to relax and trip out nowadays. Sexual experimenting is not a gross evil by itself. But so often, one person's sexual experiment is another's emotional torment."

Gary is laid out in bed, nursing a knee that he wrenched while boating over the weekend. He wears a T-shirt, running shorts, and a flesh-colored Ace bandage wrapped round his damaged joint. At forty-two he has the sinewy fitness of someone half his age. Above his bed is a lush nude painting of a reclining woman viewed from the rear. Our conversation keeps getting interrupted by fellow members of Sex Addicts Anonymous, phoning for information and advice and offering condolences about his knee.

Gary is a linchpin of the Minneapolis–St. Paul sex addict community, just the way he used to be in the food co-op. He goes to four meetings a week, he serves as a sponsor for other recovering addicts, his telephone is always ringing. "My wife and kids see my deep involvement in sex addiction work as another extreme," he confides, adjusting the pillow under his knee. "They appreciate my sobriety, but they see me going to the other side of the spectrum. I'm a compulsive personality. I have a compulsion to go to meetings. But that keeps me from being suicidal."

Yes, he says, that's how strange and unhinged it had all become. It goes back, of course, to childhood, he tells us. "It always does with sex addicts. I dressed in my mother's underwear as a kid. I would try to see either parent naked. I was crazy with curiosity about sex. My mother and I had a couple of physical encounters, sexual kissing and hugging. I molested my handicapped sister once; I put my hand on her breast." It all comes streaming out of him as he lies flat on his back. Listening to Gary is like watching a magician pull a never-ending string of colored handkerchiefs out of his mouth.

Gary was raised in a wealthy, conservative home "where nurturing was in short supply." He masturbated every day to make himself feel loved. As he grew older, he says, neither of his parents wanted to recognize how increasingly tormented he was by his addiction. "My parents thought I was crazy, but they blamed it on my left-wing politics." He had always been a puzzle to them. After years of college and postgraduate work, Gary ended up working in a railroad switchyard.

That was where he nearly did himself in. His loneliness and need would close in on him there, among the weeds and rusty remains of old boxcars. "Sometimes I would slip into a train engine if I had the time, on a bitter-cold night, and take out my penis. It might be freezing, it might be ten below, but I had to masturbate. It was a terrible emptiness and pain inside me. If I'd taken a needle out and shot up, it would have been no different." It got to where he often thought of throwing himself under the next hulking boxcar that came kachunking down the tracks.

"On the outside I was holding it together," says Gary. "I did my job, I provided for my family," which by the end of the 1960s included two sons and daughter. But inside him was a cavernous sorrow, a darkness that swallowed all light. Sex felt like the only way out. It was a struck match, the flash of a blue-gold flame. When he had affairs, the heavy gloom seemed to lift. He no longer felt like a lost child. "I got very emotionally wrapped up with my lovers."

But there were, of course, consequences at home. "My wife and I never contracted for an open marriage," says Gary. "She knew about my affairs, and she was deeply distressed. Eventually, *she* started having affairs. She acted out in a desperate way to catch my attention. She was testing her own attractiveness, flaunting her freedom. But it didn't solve her problems; it was just pure pain.

"It didn't hurt at first. Then she started giving me details. She had sex with a macho cop in the backseat of his squad car, with a strung-out junkie. It wasn't sexual jealousy. That's not what bothered me. I was concerned about her health and safety. One case of VD did come home that way, the crabs, not a big one, fortunately. But the whole period was unhealthy. She wasn't sleeping or eating well, she was supertense, she was just as strung out in her way as a junkie."

In retrospect, says Gary, there were other unhealthy aspects to his family life as well. During his recovery, he came to see how he created an incestuous environment at home. "I would insist on my right to walk around naked in my own home," says Gary. "It was very patriarchal. One son was very modest; we would tease him about it. My daughter and I had a game. It happened once or twice a year between when she was eight and sixteen. I would take showers, and she would come into the bathroom and tease my penis. 'That's the ugliest thing I've ever seen,' she would say. If my self-respect had been intact, I would not have allowed that. My wife would get in on the act. She'd say, 'Yeah, let's get a kitchen knife and cut off that cocktail weenie.' My daughter would sometimes reach over and touch it. I wasn't crawling into bed with her; she initiated it. But still . . . the people at Golden Valley were very troubled by this when I brought it up later in therapy. It could have been reportable.

"On other occasions, the kids would pile into bed with me and my wife; there would be roughhousing and my daughter would sometimes be in contact with my penis through the sheets. I didn't have an erotic bond with my daughter, so I didn't realize it was incest at the time. But now I do."

How clear is the light of sobriety! What seemed perfectly natural and harmless in the sixties and seventies, Gary now realizes, actually bordered on the criminal.

He hit the bottom of what once seemed like a bottomless well of addiction in 1984. He had taken "a life-or-death vow" in front of his wife and her women friends never again to commit adultery. They had confronted him in the living room of his home; it was a humiliating experience. But soon afterward, Gary became hopelessly ensnared in the stickiest tar baby of an affair in his life. "I met her at my wife's high school reunion," he recalls, and the memory is not pleasing to him. "She was also a sex addict, a married woman with four sons. She was a very wealthy woman. She would normally never have had anything to do with a blue-collar guy like me, except for her addiction. I was more obsessed than ever before. I took the greatest risks."

They went to restaurants where they could have been spotted by friends of the family. He invented elaborate stories to excuse his frequent absences from home. He was spinning out of control and he just didn't care. The woman was rich and aloof, like his mother, and she wanted him in the worst way. The intrigue stretched on for two years before he was finally caught.

The ensuing convulsions propelled Gary and his wife, for the first time, into the office of a couples therapist. "Through therapy," says Gary, "my wife was able to lay down a final ultimatum: 'One more affair and that's it. No negotiating, no tears, it's all over.' And she had the three kids solidly behind her." The thought of losing his family was unbearable to Gary. He saw the big boxcar rumbling toward him; he saw his body crushed under the steel wheels like an old stray dog.

Gary and his wife clung to their marriage by their fingertips. After twenty years together, their hold on one another seemed more tenuous than ever. They avoided each other's touch. He felt like a guest in his own house.

One night, his wife brought a book to bed with her, reading it and under-lining it into the early morning. The book was *Out of the Shadows: Understanding Sexual Addiction* by Patrick Carnes, and it read like her life. Gary had been going to AA meetings because he had begun drinking heavily and smoking marijuana during his last affair "to kill the pain." "You're not an alcoholic," his wife suddenly told him, putting down the book. "You're a sexaholic."

"That was the turning point," he says. "I was feeling like an old man; I was feeling beaten down and helpless. I finally decided to join Sex Addicts Anonymous in December 1984. The first meeting I went to, I knew I was home at last. I was nearly forty years old and I was finally with people who accepted the worst I had done, because they had similar lives. I was no longer hiding the shame. My recovery started that day, December 4, the date [Black Panther leader] Fred Hampton was assassinated by the Chicago police."

Gary still has the reference points of a sixties activist. But his analysis of what ails America has changed. "The extremely stressful nature of American life sets people up for all kinds of quick fixes," he observes. "Sex is one of them. We live in an addictive culture. I will have a lover's quarrel with this country until it makes treatment for sexual addiction affordable and readily available. This is one area where I will get back on my soapbox."

Now he's on fire with the clarity of his new vision. "Unhooking myself from my sex addiction literally saved my life. My wife and I are finally having a genuine marriage. I'm able to see that joy for me is in monogamy. The thing that prevents someone from being monogamous is spiritual defeat. That's what stops us from bonding with real people and with life itself."

Each story of conquered addiction is filled with its own twists. But at heart they are all tales of rebirth. "I once was lost, but now I'm found/Was blind, but now I see." Overcoming addition is the secular version of finding salvation. There is an ecstatic quality to Twelve-Step meetings.

The mecca of the addiction control movement is the great metropolis of the northern plains, Minneapolis–St. Paul, which, not surprisingly, also contains one of the highest concentrations of churchgoing folk in the nation. Each week, there are some thirty sex addiction meetings alone in the metropolitan area. Greater Minneapolis is dotted with more alcohol and drug dependency treatment centers than lakes. It is the only city with an addiction recovery newspaper, appropriately called *The Phoenix*. Embedded in the city's Scandinavian heritage is a penchant for order and hygiene, as well as an inclination toward pagan excess, particularly during those long nights of arctic cold and solitude.

Many of the recovering sex addicts who make the pilgrimage to Minneapolis, such as Nina, are drawn by Golden Valley Health Center. It is their Lourdes, the place where they shed tears of anguish and pray for miracles. Each year, hundreds of desperate men and women check themselves into Golden Valley's sexual dependency unit for the five-week treatment program. Hundreds more, such as Gary, seek help as outpatients. Inpatient treatment at Golden Valley costs over $12,000. Some sex addicts without medical insurance have been known to empty their savings and sell their belongings to pay for their hospitalization.

The sexual dependency unit is located in a brick building on the sanitarium's rolling, well-kept grounds. Nearby are buildings housing Golden Valley's mental health and eating disorders units. Golden Valley staff members "fight" to get assigned to the sex addicts unit, we are told by one counselor without a hint of a smile, because "the patients there are so motivated."

Those who are admitted to the program promise to refrain entirely from sex, including masturbation, for three months. The patients are kept as busy as monks from the crack of dawn to bedtime with a schedule crammed full of encounter sessions, lectures, and recreation. Still, in a building full of surging hormones, sex is bound to cut loose now and then. When it does, it immediately becomes everyone's business. There is more collective vigilance here than in a Chinese village. "Whenever there were little flirtations between patients, the people would be confronted by the rest of us," says a former Golden Valley patient. "Once a guy propositioned a woman. They both immediately recognized the problem and took it to group to ask for help. People are not allowed to wear shorts on the unit, to be seductive in dress or behavior."

Everything must be shared with the group. The compulsion to reveal approaches the level of true kinkiness. "If someone masturbates on the unit, he or she will usually tell you," says Tammy Horstmann, a young, pretty counselor who worked at Golden Valley for more than a year.

Naturally, not all those suffering from sex addiction are prepared to commit themselves to such a rigorous program. Patient demand has not been as high as Golden Valley's operators thought it would be, according to Eli Coleman, the associate director of the University of Minnesota Medical School's human sexuality program. "When CompCare [co-owners of Golden Valley] started up the facility [in 1984], they were basing their patient projections on Pat Carnes's estimate of how many sex addicts there were in the country," says Coleman. "They thought they were sitting on a gold mine. But that growth has not taken place as anticipated." Coleman attributes the facility's slack business to continuing skepticism in the therapeutic community toward the field of sex addiction and the proliferation of cheaper, outpatient centers around the country as well as the do-it-yourself Twelve-Step groups.

Because of bottom line pressures, perhaps, Golden Valley seems overeager to admit patients. "I had questions about some of the people in the program being there," says Horstmann. The decision to admit someone is based on a twenty-question interview that is generally conducted over the phone. Coleman calls this a "weak" method of evaluating prospective patients.

Your coauthor from Hollywood decided to submit himself to the telephone questionnaire to see where he ended up on Golden Valley's spectrum of sex addiction.

The female counselor's voice on the other end of the line is sweet and sympathetic. Some of the questions, she warns me, may seem too penetrating. She does not want to push me over any edge I may be teetering on and send me skidding into a saturnalian binge. Bravely, resolutely, I tell her to fire away. *Do you feel compelled to have sex again and again within a short period of time?* Well, yes, I answer, a bit embarrassed. I mean, that's what weekends away with a lover are all about, right? She does not answer. She's reserving judgment until the end. *Do you feel your sexual appetite is controlling you?* I have to admit that my sex drive is sometimes a voracious beast. *Do you use sex to escape from worries or troubles or to relax?* Sure, and to express undying love and unveil a woman's mysteries and feel less alone in life and take the edge off my lust and . . .

Have you broken promises to yourself or others about your sexual behavior? Now, she is really getting close to home. I am unhappy to say that I have violated vows of monogamy, that I have sometimes deceived lovers in my search for a life that combines comfort and ecstasy. I think of Casanova's plea —"Let it pass, for when love is in the way, men and women as a general rule dupe each other." But I lack his worldly cynicism. I'm always plagued by guilt.

Has your sexual behavior made you feel scared or different? No, but the interview is beginning to. It's a relief to answer a firm no to a series of questions designed to identify the truly hard-core: *Have you ever exposed yourself . . . have you ever taken indecent liberties . . . have you ever raped anyone?*

"So, does it sound to you like I'm a sex addict," I ask at the conclusion of the thirty-minute interview. "Yes, I could say that. Yeah, I could," answers the counselor. "I mean, when I asked you about frequency and you said sometimes two or three times a day, I would say that is compulsive action." I have visions of Golden Valley orderlies at my door, packing big hypodermics.

Of course, adds the counselor, she will have to consult with the staff psychiatrist before she can offer me a definitive diagnosis. "What kind of insurance do you have?" This, it becomes clear, may be the most important question of all. Since sexual addiction is still not recognized by the American Psychiatric Association as a mental health problem, patients must be diagnosed by Golden Valley as suffering from some related disorder, such as severe depression or chemical dependency, to get their insurance companies to pick up the tab for their treatment. Apparently I was not suicidal, but if something could be worked out with my insurance company, she says, I could be admitted to the treatment center. "I don't see it as medically necessary at this point for you to be on the unit, but I think it could be very beneficial. I think you could learn a lot, let me tell you. You'd fit right in."

Sexologist John Money is, not surprisingly, "cynical" about Golden Valley. Sanitariums like this are in it for the money, says Money. He, too, is unsmiling; the world of sex addiction, or rather paraphilia, is no place for humor. "I'll tell you something else I've heard firsthand about that clinic," he says darkly. "I mean, I've heard it from the actual patients, and that is, if you have a really severe sex addiction—like anything that has to do with mental imagery of sexual murders or severe sadism or masochism—you are turned away from the clinic. So it's pretty sneaky to just take in the so-called easy cases." So wary of sex criminals and other troublesome cases is Golden Valley that, according to one ex-patient, the clinic once expelled a man from the program for sunbathing *au naturel* at a nude beach.

University of Minnesota sexologist Coleman comes to Golden Valley's defense. Despite the weakness of their diagnostic procedures, he says, "these people are not charlatans, and most of the patients are there for good reasons. It really is a pathological population. Those people go there as a last resort when they're really in trouble."

"Sam" is one of those who checked into Golden Valley as a last resort. He says it flat out: "The program saved my life. I had been planning my own suicide." He is a big, bearded, middle-aged man with a southern drawl as thick and rich as pecan butter. He looks like a man whose appetites have always been prodigious. Raised a Baptist, Sam later came out as a homosexual and pursued a career in the theater. But he was never at peace with himself. He felt driven to peep shows and porn theaters, to dark and heated embraces with strangers. He grew terrified of AIDS. He would lock himself away for days with stacks of flesh magazines and masturbate like a man possessed. Finally he, too, came across Pat Carnes's book. "It hit the nail on the head." He sold most of his belongings, packed what remained in two suitcases, and flew north to seek deliverance.

It was Carnes who drew him to Golden Valley. The architect of the country's first inpatient program for sexual addiction is, Sam feels, "a brilliant intellect, a brilliant healer. If anyone deserves a monopoly on this growing field, it's him." Working with Carnes at the sanitarium was "the chance of a lifetime," says Sam. Carnes can inspire cultlike devotion among recovering sex addicts. "He has these incredible penetrating eyes," says Sam with reverence. "And he uses them to great effect."

Right now the penetrating eyes of Patrick Carnes are burning directly into ours. He is telling us about the revolutionary significance of addictionology. Professional healers and scholars from different fields, he says, are joining forces to explore "the obsessional life" that underlies sexual addiction, alcoholism, overeating, and other tyrannies of the spirit. Their great insight, he says, was to recognize that these terrible cravings are all linked and can all be broken by using the Twelve Steps of AA. "The Twelve Steps is one of the major intellectual happenings of our time. Because we live in an addicted culture."

His voice has become a grave whisper. He wants to make sure we appreciate the import of all this. There is nothing striking about Carnes's appearance. He is a forty-three-year-old man with a receding chin and thinning blond hair. But those relentless little eyes! They lock in on you like a Stinger missile. If he feels your eyes taking evasive measures, Carnes will reach out and jab you in the arm to reclaim your unblinking attention.

Carnes is expounding his ideas over salmon with dill sauce at a Holiday Inn near downtown Minneapolis. We each have one glass of a California sauvignon blanc. He will pass up dessert. He is a man in control of his appetites.

Unlike Sam and other former Golden Valley patients, we had not been impressed by Carnes's *Out of the Shadows*. The book, crammed with case studies of sexual torment, lacks the subtle insights and literary quality of a work by Krafft-Ebing or Havelock Ellis. Patients are trotted out to illustrate Carnes's simplistic theories about compulsive behavior and then promptly dismissed. Moreover, Carnes seems to be rigidly conventional in his sexual outlook, quick to classify those who take pleasure in frequent masturbation, multiple relationships, pornography, or the services of prostitutes as deviant. His book has the unimaginative feel of courtroom psychiatry.

But in person, Carnes is given to a livelier play of mind. As he finishes his glass of wine, he toys with a theory about the root of sexual addiction that sounds the same as Casanova's. Compulsive sex, he says, is an attempt to deny death. Men and women in our culture, he observes, try to obliterate the unbearable consciousness of their mortality by immersing themselves in sensuality. "In fact," says Carnes, "we try to avoid all sorrow and discomfort. We have a pill for everything; you never need to be uncomfortable. But without discomfort, you don't have spirituality or poetry or art. You'll recall that in the ancient myth, Orestes carried the curse of his family. He had killed his mother, Clytemnestra, to avenge the murder of his father. She had done some obscene things to her husband. So Orestes is pursued by the three Furies. But when he meets the challenges set up for him by the gods, the Furies are suddenly turned into three sources of wisdom. That's true for all of us. Out of our sorrow comes creativity and wisdom. But addiction blots out that pain."

Carnes adds, "I feel that we should put commercials on TV that say, 'Have you had some pain today?' " And he looks dead serious. Carnes *always* looks dead serious. "We are *that* out of touch with pain. And, as a result, we are becoming more and more uncreative."

We want to know about Carnes's own sorrows. What Furies chased him through his life and how did he turn them into wisdom? Is he himself a former sex addict? But he won't answer these questions. He's afraid of the media "making mincemeat" out of him. His work with others might be based on the healing powers of confession, but Carnes himself has a healthy reluctance to reveal too much about himself. Among the few biographical details he divulges are that he was raised Catholic, is divorced, has four children, and began his work on sex addiction in the 1970s after counseling sex offenders.

Uncomfortable with our line of questioning, Carnes brings the interview to a close. But he wants to leave us with a final plea. "I'm happy to debate the research or whatever, but the thing that drives me nuts is when people try to pretend that something isn't going on, that families aren't being torn apart, that people aren't suffering. That's when I go nuts."

"Yes, you really seem to be aflame with this," we say politely, looking into those burning little eyes.

"What do you mean 'aflame,' " he says intently.

"Well, uh, passionate about your work."

He thinks about this for a moment. "Yes, no doubt."

Just then, the waiter appears. "Do you want some more wine?" Carnes drives him away with a withering look.

"If I have a cause," he continues, "it's to explain that there really are some hurting people out there who have not had a voice. And I have given them a voice and I've taken a lot of hits for that. I've had conversations with people, who say, with tears streaming down their faces, 'You know, this thing saved my life. I didn't know life could be this good. I didn't know sex could be this good.' So when you hear the critics attack the sex addiction field, call us sex-negative, or say we're trying to put sex under the rug, that's not what these people with tears streaming down their cheeks are saying."

It is so heavy with grief, this world of Pat Carnes and Golden Valley and the Twelve Magic Steps. Lust, here, is a shrieking Fury. It blows to splinters the most solidly constructed homes, it drives away the ones you love, it sickens your body and spirit. There is no doubt about this: sex addicts have suffered its full torments.

But instead of turning this Fury into deeper wisdom, the sex addiction movement aims to extinguish it. All but a renegade minority agree that the times demand a retreat from libertinism. As the ailing Jack Bonner observed, survival must take precedence over pleasure. But the Twelve-Step culture takes what is a grim medical necessity and turns it into cultish dogma. The goal is to reprogram a generation of sensualists.

Sex addicts' stories always seem more intriguing than the banal interpretations they impose on them. Their tales are filled with the great mystery of human passions. Yet the language of addictionology is utterly lifeless. At a Sex and Love Addicts meeting in a Lutheran church near the Stanford University campus, we heard a young man describe his painful effort to date a woman he had met in Twelve-Step circles: "I had been in a state of sexual anorexia for a long time, but I thought she might be the right one because she had a program and a sponsor and she seemed healthy. My addiction was really heating up. But she turned me down. She told me it wasn't personal, but her program just wouldn't allow it." There is an eerie, narcotized quality to the way people in this world describe their lives.

In the past, they were driven from one sexual intrigue to another. Like Augustine, their obsession continues, but in confessional form. They speak endlessly of their exploits and fantasies, in their strange, sedating language. In this way, they hope to drain sex of its power.

Yet, as Casanova recognized, confession can have a very different use as well. "By recollecting the pleasures I have had formerly, I renew them, I enjoy them a second time," he wrote. Meetings of sex addicts are sometimes orgies of remembrance. In recalling the exquisite details of their shame, these men and women not only "enjoy them a second time" but also titillate others with them.

In the AIDS-haunted 1980s, these intimate public confessions constituted one of the only forms of safe group sex. The aim of these group discussions was to snuff out forbidden desires. But they often succeeded in keeping them alive.

"The load of habit," exclaimed wise St. Augustine, bishop of Hippo, "is a force to be reckoned with!"

Grounding Teenagers

ARY

Elizabeth ("Tipper") Gore could not believe her ears. He was moaning and groaning, loud alley-cat wails that shook the family stereo and made the little blond hairs on the back of her neck stick up. But the worst part was the lyrics. Something about an oversexed girl named Darling Nikki who is pleasuring herself in a hotel lobby with the aid of a magazine, and well, she takes him to her castle, which is equipped with many "devices," and when the lights go out, she proceeds to "grind." He could not go into further detail, he sang. But heavens, the way he was screeching, there was no need to.

So this was Prince, the hot young star whose pretty, doe-eyed face seemed to be on the cover of every magazine at the supermarket checkout racks lately. And to think, *she* had been the one to bring home his new album, *Purple Rain*. Her oldest daughter, eleven-year-old Karenna, liked "Let's Go Crazy," the cut they were playing on the radio. And Tipper, who thought of herself as a "with-it" young mom, decided to buy Karenna the album as an early Christmas present.

It was one of those cozy winter days at the Gore residence, a two-story brick Tudor house on a tree-lined street in Arlington, Virginia—the same house in which Tipper herself had grown up. A fresh snow carpeted the front lawn, cedar logs crackled in the living room fireplace, the four kids were scrawling pictures of reindeer and elves to give relatives as homemade Christmas gifts. When Karenna put *Purple Rain* on the turntable, it did not strike Tipper as the most appropriate holiday music, but three-year-old Albert liked to hop around to "Let's Go Crazy" and she had to admit that Prince was a talented musician with a distinctive sound. But then she noticed that Karenna and her girlfriend from next door were huddling by the stereo, furtively replaying a song from the album.

That's when Tipper Gore cocked her ear and caught the lyrics to "Darling Nikki." "At first I was stunned—then I got mad!" she later recalled. "Millions of Americans were buying *Purple Rain* with no idea what to expect. Thousands of parents were giving the album to their children—many even younger than my daughter."

This is what started it all—the Parents' Music Resource Center (PMRC), the Senate hearings, the talk-show appearances, the clashes with Frank Zappa and sneering punk stars, the whole business of the "Washington Wives" versus the billion-dollar music industry. Soon after stashing *Purple Rain* on a shelf high in her bedroom closet, safely out of the reach of her kids, Tipper Gore declared war on "porn rock," a crusade, as she saw it, to preserve the fragile innocence of American youth.

Tipper, wife of Albert Gore, Jr., the handsome young senator from Tennessee who made a strong run for the 1988 Democratic presidential nomination, was joined in her crusade by several other wives of prominent Washington figures. But it was Tipper whose name became synonymous with the rock decency campaign as she barnstormed across the country, rallying parents against the "cultural stripminers" who were leaving permanent scars on the minds of American adolescents.

Her primary targets were heavy metal headbangers like Mötley Crüe, Whitesnake, Ozzy Osbourne, and Iron Maiden—bands whose trademarks are songs studded with unsubtle phallic metaphors and Nuremberg-like concerts that go beyond self-parody. Millions of testosterone-crazed teenage boys find release in the crashing chords of these hairspray-and-leather bands. But Tipper feared that this cock-rock was channeling all that hormonal energy in sexist and violent directions. She also fretted about the impact of cheesecake performers like Madonna on thirteen- and fourteen-year-old "wanna-bees" and, of course, the seductive appeal of that diminutive dark Prince from Minneapolis, who sang unashamedly of the ecstasies of giving head and the indecencies of soiled sheets. "Even the most open-minded parent can still manage a blush—at least, I hope!" wrote Tipper in her 1987 book *Raising PG Kids in an X-Rated Society.*

The rock decency crusade got off to a splashy start in the fall of 1985 when Tipper and other members of the PMRC convinced their husbands to hold Senate hearings on bump-and-grind music. The committee, which included Al Gore, heard the Washington Wives and an array of expert witnesses blame porn rock for teen promiscuity, pregnancies, drug addiction, suicides, devil worship, bad manners—and even the bloody rampages of Son of Sam and the Nightstalker. "Young teens who already think too much with their hormones and too little with their heads," warned a child psychologist, "are succumbing to heavy metal bombardment." The senators heard from their own wives' lips of rock 'n' roll's wilder shores. Of wild-maned stars who strutted about with black leather codpieces, singing songs about men who fucked like beasts and tigresses who ate men alive.

An unlikely collection of musicians (Frank Zappa, John Denver, Dee Snider of Twisted Sister) defended rockers' artistic freedom. ("Masturbation is not illegal," observed Zappa. "If it is not illegal to do it, why should it be illegal to sing about it?") But the record industry, eager to win congressional support for an antipiracy bill that would compensate companies for the revenue lost through home taping of albums, got the message. After the hearings concluded, twenty-two major record companies agreed to put warning labels on albums with sexually explicit lyrics—the Washington Wives' main demand.

In the following months, only a few albums were actually stickered. But the hearings succeeded in creating a censorious climate for rock musicians. In 1986, televangelist Jimmy Swaggart, still brimming with self-righteous anger before his public disgrace, denounced rock as "degenerative filth which denigrates all the values we hold sacred" and held a meeting with officials of the Wal-Mart discount store chain. Soon after, all eight hundred Wal-Marts stopped stocking rock and teen magazines and yanked albums deemed offensive from their shelves.

That same year, Jello Biafra, founder and lead singer of the mordantly witty San Francisco punk band the Dead Kennedys, was arrested and charged with distributing harmful material to a minor for including a sexually explicit poster in the band's latest album. Ironically, the record was one of the few to carry a warning sticker, but the PMRC found the wording too tongue-in-cheek. ("The inside fold-out . . . is a work of art by H. R. Giger that some people may find shocking, repulsive, or offensive. Life can sometimes be that way.")

In 1987, local politicians and police chiefs across the country zeroed in on another favorite target of the PMRC, sassy-tongued rap groups like the Beastie Boys, Run-DMC, LL Cool J, and 2 Live Crew, trying to shut down their shows and, on at least one occasion, arresting a performer (LL Cool J) for slow-grinding on a couch while singing his sweet-hearted ballad "I Need Love."

Later, during the 1988 presidential race, in pursuit of Hollywood support, the Gores would tell entertainment executives that the porn rock hearings had been a mistake, that they had no intention of sparking a censorship campaign. But as the music moguls bluntly informed them, their regrets came a little late, for the hearings had marked the official beginning of the crackdown. Adult America was once again declaring war on rock and its forbidden world of teen lust, a war fought off and on ever since sweaty black men from the South began howling about "Long Tall Sally" and "Maybelline," and Elvis started shaking his money-maker. But this time the leader of the moral crusade was not some caterwauling backwoods preacher but a young liberal politician's wife with bouncy blond good looks, a big crush on Bruce Springsteen, and a fearsome determination to keep the jarringly frank way some pop stars sang about sex from robbing her kids, and other kids, of their childhood.

Tipper Gore was one of a colorful cast of morality crusaders who made their entrance on the national stage in the 1980s, Big Chaperons bent on upholding an idyllic vision of American youth. They varied widely in their philosophical underpinnings, from the Ralph Nader–style reformism of Gore to the religious conservatism of the women who ran President Reagan's teenage chastity program. The strategies they pursued were equally disparate, from the corporate pressure campaigns of the PMRC to the sexual reeducation efforts of the federal chastity officials. But their fundamental analysis was the same: teenage America was in the throes of a crisis, as evidenced by the exploding rates of pregnancy, abortion, sexual disease, and suicide. This crisis was precipitated by an onslaught of modern forces—pop music, rock videos, teen films, liberal sex education, birth control programs—all of which destabilized the family by undermining parental authority and pushing teenagers into libertinism.

Tipper and the other chaperons were bent on stemming the tide of cultural change so that boys and girls would correspond more closely to what *they* had been in their youth. It was a quixotic crusade, but it touched a deep chord among grown-ups in the age of Just Say No.

Opponents like Zappa compared Tipper and her comrades to wrathful ayatollahs, trying to clamp a moral lid on the nation. But he got her wrong. After all, she didn't burn *Purple Rain* in a down-home Tennessee bonfire: she just banished it to her bedroom closet. And didn't she and Al both admit during the presidential campaign that, yes, they had smoked a little dope when they were younger (although, of course, in retrospect they wish they had never done it)? Tipper was no religious zealot; she was the epitome of liberal young motherhood, a Big Chill Mom who was as devoted to the project of parenting as she had been to marching against the Vietnam War and for civil rights at Boston University in the late 1960s. She prided herself on her tolerance. But like many young parents, she had begun to have second thoughts about the 1960s and feared that today's teens were trying to match or go beyond the excesses of her generation.

She had read her Gesell and Piaget, she knew about developmental stages, that there was a proper time in a child's life for everything. And thirteen or fourteen or fifteen was just too early in her book for a kid to hear about some singer's tasty "sugar walls" or another's rock-hard cock that's "gonna nail your ass to the floor." They're just growing up too young, she thought.

"If you don't try to shield them from sadomasochism and all this explicit kind of stuff until they're ready to handle it, then you're robbing them of their innocence, their one time in life to be somewhat carefree," she sighs one day during the 1988 presidential race, while riding the dusty back roads of Iowa in a campaign worker's old Plymouth. Her hazel eyes are filled with the sadness of it all. "It's not that I want a clean, sterile world. But why commercialize sex and violence and shove it down kids' throats at a younger and younger age in the form of songs and videos?"

Tipper was not the only authority figure railing against rock in the 1980s. There were the Peters Brothers, a pair of publicity-mad preachers from Minnesota who kept torching piles of album covers (because the records themselves gave off toxic fumes), challenging Prince to public debates, and playing the role of the outraged rubes on the Phil Donahue and Ted Koppel shows. And there was Allan Bloom, a crabby middle-aged professor from the University of Chicago with a grudge against rebellious youth that dated back to the 1960s. Bloom's best-selling book *The Closing of the American Mind* was an unrelieved diatribe against all things young, including rock 'n' roll, which he charged turned life "into a nonstop, commercially prepackaged masturbational fantasy." Killjoys like Bloom, sputtering with rage about the indolent pleasures of adolescence (particularly, for some peculiar reason, the naughty joys of onanism), are forever sprouting on the American landscape. His book was only the latest in a long line of screeds to tap into the country's deep well of resentment against the "pubescent child whose body throbs with orgasmic rhythms," in Bloom's panting words.

But these were the censorious voices of the past. Tipper represented the future of rock-bashing. She was the Good Mother, the very symbol of concerned young parents everywhere. Rock musicians, who often have a better line on teenagers' deepest desires than do Mom and Dad, mocked this Pollyannish view of adolescents.

"Today's parents want to wrap their families in a cocoon against the outside world," scoffed twenty-nine-year-old Jello Biafra as he awaited his obscenity trial. "Part of this has to do with the amount of escapist drugs these people used in the late sixties and early seventies, which allowed them to trip out into this fantasia world. Now that they've become yuppie parents, they're trying to build a material, real-life fantasia world with all their money. And one of the ways they do that is to come up with these precious artifacts known as their children. They treat their children as artifacts and pets rather than as people.

"Parents who sit on their asses and let the police and the courts and the censors do their ethical work for them are the laziest, most chicken-hearted people of all," continued Biafra. "They're not doing the work themselves, they're not sitting down with their kids and saying, 'OK, you brought home a record I don't like. Let's discuss it.' Most parents are scared to death of communicating with their kids. They'd rather pay fifty grand to send them to military school or a private mental hospital than to sit down and talk with them. It shouldn't take that much courage to talk with your own children or, on the other hand, to have a loving conversation with your parents."

Liberal pundits, however, rallied around Tipper and her cause. Columnists

Ellen Goodman, Mike Royko, and William Raspberry heartily applauded her efforts, and she even received a warm response at a New York civil liberties conference held during the Statue of Liberty festivities in 1986. "The civil libertarians present liked her approach of relying on community pressures rather than legal constraints, of asking not that any record be banned but only that parents be given an opportunity to discover before a purchase was made what their children were buying," reported the New York *Times*.

Of course, in a climate where the mere presence of a warning sticker is enough to ban records from many stores, the line between parental awareness and censorship seems exceedingly thin. But this did not trouble her supporters. She struck a chord in their nostalgic hearts when she exclaimed, "There's a big difference from Elvis Presley singing 'Little Sister' to Prince singing 'Sister,' which is a glorification of incest, . . . or the Rolling Stones singing 'Let's Spend the Night Together' " and some heavy metal outfit yowling about bondage. "Give me innuendo again!" she fairly shouted, and it rang out like a parental bugle charge.

Now Tipper Gore's version of the sixties is not the way everybody remembers it. There was, of course, raunchy Janis Joplin and the electrically erotic Jimi Hendrix, who had a habit of jacking off his guitar onstage until it exploded in flames, and sultry, demonic Jim Morrison, who sang of Oedipal lust and once showed a Florida audience what was underneath his black leather pants. But this is not the way Tipper prefers to remember it. She and Al were married in 1970 to the sweet strains of "All You Need Is Love." It's the big-hearted innocence of the period she likes to hang on to.

As a teenager, she herself played drums in a rock band that performed Beatles songs at high school dances and Democratic Party rallies. One immediately assumes that Paul would be her favorite Beatle, but interestingly, it turns out to be John. As a child of the sixties, Tipper knows how much this reveals about her. "He was the coolest," she says a little coyly. "I liked his intellect, and I thought he was sexy."

Her childhood in suburban Washington was not free of sorrow. When she was four, her father, who ran a heating and plumbing supplies business, divorced her mother, and she was raised mainly by her maternal grandmother. Divorce was not common in those years, and she was sometimes taunted by her classmates for "having no father." "Drumming really got me through adolescence—it really did," she says.

Tipper, whose grandmother impressed upon her the importance of preserving her virginity "because the man of your dreams would never marry a loose woman," was a self-described "good girl." When she was sixteen, she discovered her first and only real love when she met Al Gore, the son of the liberal patrician senator from Tennessee, Albert Gore, Sr., at a high school prom party. He was about to graduate from classy St. Albans prep school in Washington and go to Harvard; he was well-mannered and good-looking; he came from the right family. Her grandmother heartily approved. Good girl meets good boy; good girl gets good boy.

It was not strictly a white-gloves-and-corsage courtship. The young couple would work up a sweat now and then dancing to the records of James Brown, the master of hump-till-dawn soul music, a possessed performer whose act was much more sizzling than anything onstage today.

Tipper, the nation's leading watchdog of rock, finds nothing ironic about this. "I think you still had to use your imagination a little with him; he was within bounds. Look," she says, warming to the subject, "there's nothing wrong with rock being very primal. It can unleash energy and even sexual feeling. It's a sexual, sensual form of music, but I don't think that's bad. In fact, I actually like that." Tipper, in the midst of a presidential race characterized by an unparalleled amount of prudery, is shot a warning look by her alert press aide. But she plunges on: "Well, I do. I have nothing against the primeval appeal of music—I understand it, I feel it myself, I think it's fine."

It came out at unexpected times, the primal Tipper, the down-and-dirty Tipper. But she knew how to stay "within bounds." After graduating from Boston University, she married Al, a man who also "played by the rules." Even though he opposed the Vietnam War, he did his duty by volunteering for the army and serving his six months in Southeast Asia as a military journalist. After that, Al's career read like the resume of someone destined for the political summit: staff reporter for the Nashville *Tennessean*, Vanderbilt Law School, four terms in the House of Representatives, election to the U.S. Senate, reclaiming the seat once occupied by his father, and finally, the run for the White House—all before he had turned forty. Prince Albert of the Tennessee Valley, "Doonesbury" dubbed him.

Meanwhile, Tipper, who considered for a time becoming a child psychiatrist and worked part-time as a newspaper photographer, gave up these pursuits to devote herself to their four children and Al's promising political career. When she and Al got married, Tipper remembers thinking, "Here is a man who is going to make my life very interesting." And she was right. Becoming a Washington wife allowed her to get involved in a number of high-profile volunteer activities, from the Capitol Children's Museum to a national photo exhibit that dramatized the plight of the homeless. But it was not until the rock decency campaign was launched that Tipper found her true calling. It recharged her life. Not that her days with Al and the kids were dreary: she loved being a mother, and as she blurted out one day on the Iowa campaign trail with touching candor, she still found Al "incredibly sexy."

But by throwing herself into the rock world, she became a teenager again. It gave her a way to play hooky from the joyless, adult world of politics. Between campaign appearances, while the car was being tanked up, Tipper would hit the magazine racks in the one-stop markets to pore over the latest heavy metal fanzines. There she would be, crouched on the floor of the market riffling the pages of *Rip* magazine like some pimply skateboarder. "Oh my God, look at this," she would exclaim when she came across the lurid photo of a particularly nasty-looking band or found herself being attacked in print by Anthrax or Megadeth in typically crude fashion. These rock 'n' roll bad boys seemed obsessed with this good girl, and she, well, was kind of obsessed with them too. Most of them were so gross that you would never actually want to speak with them in real life, but it was kind of fun to hear them talk dirty to you in these teen mags, to have some sort of secret dialogue with them.

Sometimes her crusade threw Tipper into the company of these grown-up delinquents, and she found herself warming up to the more intriguing ones. Frank Zappa, who even her husband gushed over during the porn rock hearings ("You're a true original!"), invited Tipper out for drinks after the TV lights were turned off. They repaired to a Capitol Hill bar called the Monocle, where Tipper stuck to Perrier and Zappa browbeat her in his nasty and charming way. She was tickled to be the target of his barbs, she found it amusing when he called her a "cultural terrorist," she told him she still had a Mothers of Invention album from her college days, the one with "Suzie Creamcheese" on it.

She even hit it off with Jello Biafra when they met backstage at "The Oprah Winfrey Show." On camera later, they tore at each other's throats. But Tipper, the good girl who had become the Good Mother, found her heart going out to this young, pale, handsome punk star who was so full of spleen about modern life. She felt the pain, she says, beneath his fury. "He was the most cynical person I have ever met. Really. So hopeless and so bitter . . . and so intelligent. And I felt, What has happened to you to make you like this?" It may be the most-likely-to-succeed types such as Al Gore that good girls end up marrying, but it's the sullen ones in tight jeans who get under their skin. The ones who are just crying out, you know, to be saved.

Even more surprising, Biafra, American punk's master of invective, song-writer of acidic social commentaries like "Holiday in Cambodia" and "Kill the Poor," mocker of all moon-June sentiment in music and life, found that *Tipper* was getting to *him*. Biafra's indictment on obscenity charges had bro-ken up his band, wrecked his small record label, and turned him into a full-time champion of the First Amendment. He was the Lenny Bruce of the late 1980s, a cool, brash artist forced to put all his time into a trial that was to become a major test of rock musicians' artistic license. Biafra blamed his woes on the hanging fever sparked by the "bouffant-encrusted thought police in Washington." Nonetheless, he found Tipper "disarmingly pleasant and charm-ing. Much more magnetic and attractive in person than she comes across in photos or on the screen. If you're going to have an organization of prudes who are going to decide what the rest of us can hear and see, then you might as well have a sex symbol as your spokesperson. She's very attractive."

Tipper, the Washington housewife with the sensible cotton dresses and the all-American looks, a sex symbol? It was a surprising observation from some-one used to the Morticia look-alikes who crowd the club scene. But the point is, Tipper got to him and he found himself opening up to her a little, telling her about his ex-wife, a woman he had deeply loved, and how she had bled his savings, stripped the house, and run off with a man he had once pulled back from the brink of suicide while the Dead Kennedys were on a road tour. Biafra, already cynical about his fellow human beings and the uses they made of love, had grown even bleaker.

"We live in a selfish, coldhearted society right now," believes Biafra. "We've reached the point where not just the act of love, but the act of trusting is so dangerous that many people just don't anymore. Because a gesture of trust in the eyes of those people whose life philosophy is 'Winning isn't everything, it's the only thing,' a gesture of trust to people like that is a sign to them that now is the time to take advantage of you."

Like others who come out of the punk art scene, Biafra feels that pop culture's obsession with sex and love has become a form of social control, pushing the rat's pleasure button so it doesn't bother to find a way out of the maze. Sex may have had a liberatory power in the beat and hippie cultures, these jaundiced younger artists contend, but it has long since been rendered lifeless and mechanical by the engines of corporate entertainment.

Grim thoughts like these prompted the Dead Kennedys to illustrate their *Frankenchrist* album with *Penis Landscape,* a painting by a Swiss artist named H. R. Giger, whose attitude toward sex is also unrelievedly grim. Biafra saw the painting, which depicted rows of scabrous hard-ons penetrating equally putrescent vaginas, as a metaphor for "the vicious cycle of exploitation, how we fuck each other to get ahead." There was nothing titillating about the hideous poster, as the jury at Biafra's 1987 trial in Los Angeles agreed when it failed to give young Assistant District Attorney Michael Guarino the conviction he had eagerly sought. As rock critic Greil Marcus, an expert witness for the defense, testified, Biafra and the Dead Kennedys are a band that is "very suspicious of pleasure."

The fact is, rock 'n' roll in general was markedly less tumescent during the 1980s than it was in the preceding three decades. The new school of angry young artists that emerged at the end of the 1970s—whose most articulate voice was Elvis Costello—saw the mating game in its starkest terms ("Two little Hitlers will fight it out until/One little Hitler does the other one's will"). Superstar Michael Jackson tried hard to be "bad" in the 1980s but just came across sexless and weird. As the decade wore down, Bruce Springsteen gave up the open road and girls who strapped their arms around his engine for the quieter pleasures of home (though this turned out to be a temporary idyll). And even vampy Madonna toned down her act, which by her 1987 world tour seemed no more scandalous than a Bob Hope USO show. Disco, the thumping sound of gay sexual freedom in the 1970s, made a comeback, but the message was drastically different. "It's a Sin," a 1987 dance-floor hit by England's Pet Shop Boys that was full of self-loathing and recriminations about past pleasures, caught perfectly the spirit of the times. Only the irrepressible Prince still seemed to like fucking.

This is what made Tipper's crusade so ironic. For the most part, rock in the late 1980s was a limp thing. Dominated by aging stars with flagging libidos and newcomers who were extremely wary of sex or strangely disinterested in it, rock came to reflect the antisex sentiments of the culture at large—and the antisex sentiments of Tipper herself, a woman who had learned to bottle up the James Brown in her.

Into this dead rock 'n' roll party burst the Beastie Boys, three white rappers from New York whose album *Licensed to Ill* soared to the top of the charts in 1987, becoming the biggest-selling debut LP in the history of CBS Records. By mixing rap, the schoolyard rhyming of the black inner city, with doses of punk and heavy metal and creating a class-clown stage act that recalled the Three Stooges, Jerry Lewis, and John Belushi, the Beastie Boys won the hearts of a generation of teenagers who were fed up with hearing Just Say No.

Like black rappers, they sang of whores, glue-sniffers, crack dealers, and stickup artists. But this street stuff didn't come across as the real thing in the mouths of these middle-class Jewish boys. What struck a chord with their predominantly white audience, what jolted them like the long-awaited school bell at the end of the day, were the songs about popping cans of Bud, ditching class, and mouthing off to your parents. This, in the Age of Sobriety, was the sound of freedom. The Beasties' anthemic "(You've Gotta) Fight for Your Right (to Party)" was the most radical statement of teenage liberation these stuffy days had produced. Delivered at the end of their concerts, it never failed to get the kids on their feet, punching their fists into the air. ("Your Mom busted in and said, 'What's that noise?'/'Aw, Mom, you're just jealous, it's the Beastie Boys!' ")

The three men in their early twenties, with their ripped jeans, T-shirts, and crooked baseball caps, were the essence of "Boy," of "snips and snails and puppy dogs' tails." They chugalugged cans of brew onstage, pumped up a giant hydraulic cock, invited girls in the audience to bare their breasts ("Yo! Cleveland—let's see some tits!") and dance in their go-go cages, and contractually required concert promoters to provide them with bowls of colored condoms backstage. They were enough to drive parents crazy, especially the Good Mother. It was in the Beastie Boys that Tipper Gore found her truest enemy, for beastly boys will forever be locked in mortal combat with Good Moms.

They really got her worked up. She was at her most scolding when she started talking about them: "They would go over to the girl in the cage and take her blouse off, and she was nude from the waist up and they put their mouth on her breast . . . sucking breasts—I mean, it's an erotic act. In front of kids at any age. Is that OK? It's not just fun and games and blowing off steam—it's bringing a strip show to kids of any age without prior notification to the public. I happen to think some people might say it also denigrates women, it turns them into nothing but sex objects." Tipper was raising a valid point: Is it OK at any age? But we doubted that a brawl between the Beastie Boys and the PMRC was the best way to resolve the question.

Then there was the matter of the Beasties' dirty mouths. "They say everyone uses foul gutter language in society," continued Tipper. "Well, I don't talk like this. We're living under the tyranny of the explicit, where some people cram it down your throats and act like it's normal. Well, it's not necessarily normal: there are some parts of the country where people don't appreciate that kind of language and are trying to raise their kids not to do that."

Apparently, however, not in Manhattan: "The PMRC can suck our dicks," announced Adam Yauch (better known as "MCA," the Beastie with the unshaven mug and the toughest pose), foul words spat out in his nastiest New Yawkese. Other rock celebrities criticized and ridiculed Tipper, but none with the fourteen-year-old brashness of the Beasties. It was this in-your-face attitude that again and again got the boys in trouble as they toured the country.

As word about this "Sodom and Gomorrah on wheels," in the overheated language of Gannett News Service, local authorities began to clamp down on the traveling show. In Seattle, operators of the civic auditorium canceled a scheduled Beastie Boys concert after receiving "intelligence" from the police about "potential [teenage] rumbles." In Cincinnati, the police chief announced that *his* intelligence indicated "that this act is garbage" and vowed that his vice squad would be out in full force to monitor the show, a warning that panicked parents and kept thousands of kids home. "It *is* garbage, but it's not violent garbage," retorted the Beasties' Adam ("Ad Rock") Horovitz. In Columbus, Georgia, the police chief vowed to arrest the band if they ever showed their snot-nosed faces in his fair town again and the city council passed a "Beastie Boys ordinance" against lewd rock acts, a law later used against fellow Def Jam artist LL Cool J. In Jacksonville, Florida, city officials slapped an ADULT SUBJECT MATTER warning on concert tickets, until a federal judge finally ordered it removed forty-eight hours before the concert.

It was as if adult authorities throughout the nation had decided the Beastie Boys were a contagion that must be stopped before infecting their young. Their act was raucously sexual, it was smart-assed and New York, and perhaps most alarming of all, it brought together white girls and black boys in a highly charged environment—particularly when the band was billed with premier rap group Run-DMC on their 1987 Together Forever tour. It was obvious these shrewd New Yorkers knew how to shake up the heartland.

The hysteria raged even higher when the band took their show to England in the spring of 1987, prompting one Tory member of Parliament to call for a ban on their concerts. ("Our children will be corrupted by this sort of thing.") The Fleet Street press launched a frenzied attack on the "crudest pop band in the world." (WE HATE THE BEASTIE BOYS screamed one typical headline.) With Maggie Thatcher, the ultimate iron-corseted nanny, in the process of being swept back into office for a third cheerless term, sad, old Britain seemed in no mood to put up with the boyish antics of the Beasties.

There was no doubt about it: for those who wanted to explore the teenage id, the turbulent underbelly of American adolescence in the subdued 1980s, on the road with the Beastie Boys was the place to be. We hooked up with them, appropriately, in swampy, decadent New Orleans, where the band always felt right at home. "The whole economy here is built on alcohol and transvestites and nudity and sex and partying," observed Mike Diamond (a.k.a. "Mike D."), the sweetest, most polite Beastie. "There's everything here, even black magic, that's why I love this city so much. The stuff you see on Bourbon Street is a lot worse than you'll ever see at one of our shows. I mean, how can our show corrupt kids who grew up in this environment?"

But that's precisely what some city officials were warning would happen if the concert at the University of New Orleans Assembly Center went ahead as scheduled. The nationwide campaign to ground the Beastie Boys and the libidinous forces they unleashed had caught up with them even in this city of flesh peddling and mumbo jumbo. In the hours before the performance, the band's lawyer huddled nervously with concert promoters and police officials to work out an agreement that would allow the show to go on. The Beasties' act had long since been tamed. Gone was the monumental phallus, gone were the topless dancers. But New Orleans city fathers wanted further concessions: they were especially anxious to be assured that there would be no simulated masturbation onstage. (There it was again—that age-old parental phobia.) The band agreed and the show went on.

Backstage before the show, the Beasties are still full of spunk. "What these parents are trying to do is make sure their kids never hear anything about what's going on in the world," growls tough guy Adam Yauch. "Tipper Gore's kids are going to grow up not knowing about sex and they're going to catch AIDS. Kids are just naturally fucking rebellious—they're going to do whatever they're told not to."

Yauch, his scrawny frame slumped in a dressing room couch and his eyes already bleery with beer, gets especially revved up when we mention his favorite book, *Hammer of the Gods,* the tawdry account of Led Zeppelin's rise to fame and fortune. These were rock's glory days, feels Yauch, the days when superstardom brought something close to absolute power, and Zeppelin, the progenitors of heavy metal, took full advantage of this power. The British band reveled in the decadence of the road, and the lurid tales of their American tours achieved mythic proportions: fishing from a seaside hotel balcony in Seattle for shark and fucking a drunken groupie with the nose of the fanged beast (in reality, it was a red snapper), trying to rip the clothes off a female *Life* magazine reporter, practicing black-magic rituals from the pages of Aleister Crowley, and besotting themselves with drugs and drink.

"That book's my favorite shit," announces Yauch. "I remember reading it before we were famous, when we were so sick of everyone like the Thompson Twins and Duran Duran and George Michael and all those faggots ruling the whole fucking rock 'n' roll scene like a bunch of pussies. And I remember a quote from Led Zeppelin's manager, where he said something like, 'Led Zeppelin lived at a time when rock stars were treated like gods, and they could do anything they want, and it'll never be like that again.' And I just looked at that book and said, 'You've got another think coming, because we're going to fucking do it.' And then our album started taking off."

Sure enough, as the group stormed across America, wild stories of wretched excess began to circulate about the Beasties. There was the time they puttied up the glass shower in a San Francisco hotel room to create a giant swimming tank in which to cavort with groupies, but when someone opened the door, the room flooded and the floor caved in. And so on. The problem with these stories was that they sounded too contrived, dredged from the imagination of someone who had overdosed on *Porky* movies. And it

turned out that most of them *were* invented. There was something a little
wimpish about the real-life Beastie Boys, trying too hard to follow in the
footsteps of their merciless rock gods and instead coming across as the sexually frustrated nerds in their songs.

There is no crush of beautiful young women backstage after the New
Orleans show, the bowl of ribbed and colored condoms remains untouched,
even the presence of Adam Horovitz's new girlfriend, teen cinema queen
Molly Ringwald, provokes little excitement. Serious girlfriends seem like in-
truders in this world of arrested adolescence. When Horovitz, son of screen-
writer-playwright Israel Horovitz *(Author! Author!; The Indian Wants the Bronx)*
first took up with Ringwald, fellow Beastie Yauch blasted him in the press as a
traitor: "Ad Rock hangs out with Molly a little while, next thing you know
he's watching *Pretty in Pink* on TV all the time like there's no tomorrow. The
fucking dude: we went to New York for two days and he went to L.A. to
party with her. He's chinking out on the whole band. He's a pussy, right! Tell
her to come to New York!"

Despite's Yauch's hostility, it appeared to be a perfect match, the pairing of
two teen icons. The full-lipped young actress with the auburn mop top had
come to symbolize female adolescence in the 1980s through her portrayals of
smart, sexy, hypersensitive girls in movies such as *Sixteen Candles* and *The
Breakfast Club*. Horovitz, who looks like a young Eddie Fisher, was the ultimate high school wise guy, the kind who would finally wear down Molly's
resistance in the movies. But Molly seems ill at ease backstage in New Orleans
tonight, a little embarrassed by her uncouth boyfriend.

When Horovitz, in a moment of restless boredom, snatches a slice of
American cheese off a banquet table laden with chicken, cold cuts, and
bottles of beer and splats it against the wall of the sterile little dressing room,
Molly rolls her eyes and sighs, "Oh Gawd." And when he begins to tell a Sam
Kinison gay-bashing joke, the media-savvy actress quickly tries to cut him off
("I really don't think you want to tell this joke . . ."), and when that fails,
she demands that our tape recorder be turned off before allowing him to
plunge ahead. *(Question: Why are gay people so skinny? Answer: You wouldn't feel
like eating either if you had a dick in your mouth all day.)*

Homosexuality makes the Beastie Boys nervous. They were going to call
their album *Don't Be a Faggot*—by which they meant "Don't be a coward,
stand up for what you believe in," according to Mike D.—but CBS vetoed the

idea. Along with the gay-bashing humor, there is a lot of grab-ass, a lot of sexual taunting backstage with the Beasties. It is the eroticized homophobia of a boys' locker room. Maybe it was because they spent so much time together, snapping towels at each other's butts in a sense, that they felt a need to keep frantically asserting their heterosexuality.

But it was not just fear of homosexuality: there was a fear of sexuality itself at the heart of the Beastie Boys act. While the music of earlier rock 'n' roll bad boys, like the Rolling Stones and Led Zeppelin, was drenched with sex, the Beasties' music was filled with ridicule, as if that were the only way to deal with something so overpowering and threatening as physical desire. You could easily imagine a night of fucking and howling with Mick Jagger or Keith Richards—in Yauch's worshipful words, "Those guys had balls"—but it was tougher with the Beastie Boys. Like the archetypal adolescent male, they were obsessed with girls, the mysterious *other,* but you did not get the feeling they ultimately knew what to do with the opposite sex. Their fantasies about Tipper were more about spite than lust. "I'd like to shave her head and cover her with whipped cream," crowed Yauch, "handcuff her to a pole and take off all her clothes and humiliate her."

In the end, the Beasties proved to be one more product of the times, a band whose underlying message was that sex is gross and stupid. Their teen-age fans, however, heard something else. To them, the band's swagger seemed like true rebellion, a spitwad at the head of an increasingly punitive adult America. And the boys' empty sexual boasting felt like pure license, all the permission their fans needed to start partying. It took only a few minutes on the floor of a Beastie Boy–Run-DMC concert, packed with fired-up black and white kids in laceless high-topped Adidas, skintight black jeans, T-shirts, and heavy gold chains, to realize why parents were so jittery. This was a party without parental supervision, the kind that could wreck the furniture and waste the carpets. And it was a *mixed* party (a rarity in today's rock), a sweaty, seething, dangerous compound of different races and sexes.

During the concert in New Orleans that summer night, a small army of vice cops keep a lid on it all. But afterward, in the steamy French Quarter, it comes spilling over. Packs of excited girls, their dresses plastered to their skin by the awesome humidity, roam the hallways of the ornate, antebellum Royal Orleans Hotel, where the Beasties are holed up, scrawling words of devotion in lipstick on the hotel walls. The heavy air outside shakes with the loud thuds of "Fight for Your Right to Party," booming out of cruising cars. Frat boys with glistening bare chests bellow at the moon, tanked on ice-cold Hurricanes, the sickeningly sweet but potent house specialty at Pat O'Brien's. On Rue Dauphine, a mulatto girl packed tightly into a pair of red pedal pushers like a hot andouille sausage has jammed a pretty white boy into a doorway and is working her hips against his with shameless abandon.

That Beastie Boys shows should unleash the pent-up energies of male adolescents was no surprise. The real news from the front was the extent to which girls were joining in, and even leading, the celebration. In suburban Detroit the following week, at the Pine Knob Music Theater, the scene is more menacing, more juiced with testosterone. Helmeted police on horseback and dune buggies patrol the grounds, but chaos reigns on the dusty, teeming hill overlooking the stage. Thunderbolts of sound from Olympian speakers shake the earth. Boys misbehave, girls are groped by strangers. One black teenager with a porkpie hat and a mouthful of blood spits insults at the crowd. It is a hellish vision out of Hieronymus Bosch, out of *The Road Warrior*. The girls love it. "The guys here are really rude, outrageous, and free with their hands," says eighteen-year-old Gina. "This music causes aggression. It's loud and exciting and these people get crazy. But I love it, I love it to dance to."

Seventeen-year-old Megan, a tall, sturdily built girl with jet-black hair, lipstick, and nail polish, wearing a revealing black tank top, black jeans, and black boots, takes big swigs from a king-size bottle of Cherry Faygo spiked with vodka and testifies about the aphrodisiacal powers of rap music. "I mean, we partied before the Beastie Boys were ever invented. It's just more fun to do it while you're listening to their music." Of course, nowadays, she quickly adds, you've got to slap a rubber on guys. And what if they refuse to wear one? "They can go to hell. I say, 'Later, dude—no glove, no love.' " Doesn't she think the Beastie Boys' act puts down women? "Actually, I think they're really worshiping them. Even though they have them in a cage, they're up there onstage, and they have all these songs about looking for girls. I mean, it's what they live for—beer and women. It seems like they can't live without us."

Backstage, after the show, nineteen-year-old Shawn, a short blonde with green eye shadow and an abbreviated black skirt, says she felt excited to be one of the girls plucked from the audience to dance in the notorious cage.

Didn't she feel kind of humiliated? She and her girlfriends answer in unison, "No way." In their eyes is utter disdain. *Look, lighten up. It's all a big joke and we're in on it.*

It was cock energy that powered these shows, but these girls were not in the least intimidated. In fact, it seemed to amuse and excite them, they grabbed hold of it for their own pleasure. The teenage girls down in these rock 'n' roll trenches seemed like a hardy new breed, perfectly capable of taking care of themselves without being brought under the protective custody of the PMRC and other guardians of adolescent welfare.

This impression is reinforced by an incident that takes place on the 1988 Gore presidential trail. Tipper is gamely working the sparse crowd at a county fair in Indianola, Iowa, shaking hands in pungent cow sheds baked by the sun. The Washington housewife is a little stiff, talking with the grizzled guys in their John Deere caps, but her face lights up when she chats with Debbie, a seventeen-year-old farm girl with a ponytail and freckles, wearing a T-shirt and cutoffs. Tipper is genuinely impressed: this high school senior has raised five hefty steers by herself on her father's farm, and here she is in competition with tobacco-chewing men twice and three times her age. Well, this kind of gumption just makes you feel darn good about the next generation of women, thinks Tipper. They clearly *all* aren't strung out on MTV and Calvin Klein sexual imagery.

As Tipper moves on to the next outstretched hand, we have a chat of our own with Debbie. No, she never heard of Tipper Gore before, but she thinks the idea of a parents group trying to regulate rock 'n' roll is "a little ridiculous. I mean, I listen to heavy metal and I'm OK. I like Mötley Crüe, Whitesnake, AC/DC. They say that some of these bands' lyrics are Satanic and all that, but I don't really listen to the lyrics. I just like the sound, it's exciting." And is she bothered by the explicit sex in this music? Does it put ideas in kids' heads? A sheepish grin, a quick sideways glance to see if the man in the next stall, spritzing water at his bull's asshole to keep away the flies, is listening. No, she reports, the pleasures of the flesh were not introduced to the Indianola High student body by the hair-gel boys from L.A. and London. The farm kids, it turns out, discovered these pleasures on their own.

When we repeat this conversation later to Tipper in the campaign car, she looks like she has just squished a cow pie with her high-heel. "Oh no!" she shakes her head in disbelief. "That all-American girl!"

Teenagers, even all-American ones, are simply faster than the nation's chaperons care to know. After rising sharply in the 1970s, sexual activity among U.S. teenagers began to decline slightly in the early 1980s. But adolescents throughout the nation are still being deflowered in unprecedented numbers. We know this because the mating habits of American teens have been scrutinized more rigorously than the amorous exploits of Rwanda apes. Pollsters, psychologists, family planners, government researchers, teen magazines, and educators are constantly launching expeditions into teenage erogenous zones, trying to penetrate the veil that adolescents desperately, and often futilely, draw around their privacy. If, as the late French philosopher Michel Foucault observed, the attention that contemporary Western society lavishes on sex, the compulsion to tell all, is yet one more way of controlling this primal force, then American teenagers—probed, surveyed, and discussed to the point of distraction—are, with the possible exception of gays in the age of AIDS, the most regulated sexual beings in the country.

These are some of the things we know about teenagers and sex, as a result of the exhaustive snooping of curious adults: More than half have engaged in sexual intercourse by the age of 17 (a 1986 Harris report). The majority of these boys and girls feel intercourse improved their relationships (a 1985 *Rolling Stone* magazine survey). The average age for a girl to have intercourse for the first time is 16.2 years, and 15.7 years for a boy (the Center for Population Options, 1987). In some inner-city areas, the average age of sexual intercourse can be as low as 12 (a 1985 Johns Hopkins study).

Sometimes, even experienced teenagers are astounded by their generation's sexual precociousness. "Kids are fast nowadays," we were told by Maria, an eighteen-year-old Hispanic mother with big brown eyes and a serious demeanor who is enrolled in a program for teenage parents in San Francisco's Mission District. "I heard a ten-year-old the other day saying 'Hey, did you get over on that girl?' I said, 'What? That little kid?' You hear boys saying things all the time like 'Yeah, we pulled a train [today's slang for a "gang bang"] on that girl the other night.' I think it's usually just talk, but once in awhile you'll really see a girl do stuff like that."

Our talks with teenagers around the country—at high schools, teen counseling centers, music clubs, and rock concerts—made all the polling data jump to life. While girls often still feel the pressure to act more demurely, there is no doubt that their sexual appetite equals that of boys. "Most kids just can't wait to have sex, and it's not just the guys," said Naomi, a seventeen-year-old who edits the newspaper at her suburban Cleveland high school. "Girls sit around and talk about sex all the time." "I feel perfectly comfortable exploring and doing anything and everything in bed," stated fifteen-year-old Debbie, a young woman who projects the self-confidence of Dr. Ruth and who indeed counsels fellow high school students in suburban Los Angeles about sex. "You know, I just think, Hey, no foreign objects."

So sexually forthright is the new Teenage Girl that some boys feel positively hunted. "I've been pushed to have sex too hard by women several times," complained Jason, a sixteen-year-old baby-faced blond who works as a volunteer in the same counseling program. "And it's really hard for men a lot of times. Because saying no is not a real macho thing to do."

But if teenage girls and boys are more sexually experienced today, they are also surprisingly uninformed and anxiety-ridden. American teenagers get pregnant and give birth and have abortions at much higher rates than do kids anywhere else in the Western world. The Alan Guttmacher Institute estimates that less than half of American teenagers use contraception the first time they have intercourse and 15 percent *never* use it. Teenagers are also disturbingly ignorant about AIDS and other sexually transmitted diseases, even those adolescents who live in cities hardest hit by the epidemic. A 1986 report published in *American Journal of Public Health* found that 40 percent of the students surveyed at ten high schools in San Francisco did not know that using condoms was an effective way of preventing transmission of the AIDS virus.

The notion that girls can't get pregnant if they do it standing up or if they douche with Coke still holds sway in some teen circles. So does the conviction that only sluts would plan for a date by going to a birth control clinic. Despite their randy ways, kids are still tyrannized by physical self-loathing, and the subject of masturbation often produces more anxiety than conversation about intercourse. "Kids are so negative about their bodies," observed Amy Loomis, who runs a program for teenage parents in San Francisco that has become a national model. "When I counsel them about masturbation, they get so uptight. Well, if you can't touch your own body, you're not going to be able to put on a condom or insert a diaphragm. There's a real rigidity about sex out there."

Overwhelmed by the possibilities and risks in today's sexual arena, some kids seek firmer ground. In Minneapolis, teenagers who like their parties to stay within bounds go to the Beach Club, a night spot that conjures up a more wholesome past of milk shakes and sock hops and Annette Funicello movies. Clean-cut kids in Benetton casuals, and some with lacquered hair and crucifix ear studs, flock to the club to hear metal bands that replace Satan with God and syrupy "contemporary Christian music" combos. Dancing is strictly forbidden by the club proprietor, an energetic former youth minister named J. L. Glass, because "I don't want some guy rubbing up against a girl on the dance floor until I have to come in and referee it. I don't care how saved the guy is, when you start dancing you're appealing to the flesh. He's got hormones that don't stop at saved."

These sentiments were echoed by born-again teenagers at a massive youth rally in the New Orleans Superdome sponsored by a national conference of Evangelicals in the summer of 1987. It was the very weekend that the Beasties slouched toward New Orleans, and teenagers throughout that unholy city were raising hell. But under the Superdome that night, the devout young believers were burning off their adolescent energy in other ways. Legions of boys and girls in skimpy running togs went storming around and around the stadium's perimeter, carrying huge flapping banners and flags, whipped on by the chanting faithful in the bleachers, earsplitting gospel music, and a colossal electronic sign that beamed messages of eternal love. After this grand display of youthful vigor, the sweaty teenagers fell into each other's arms, laughing and squeezing one another.

Pulling himself away from a breathless blond girl with inflamed cheeks, Tony, a handsome nineteen-year-old University of Kansas freshman with a sculpted torso and long brown hair held in check by a white and purple headband, paused to talk with us about the temptations of youth. Many were the women who had lusted for Tony in their hearts, he revealed, for God had blessed him with good looks and a self-confident manner. He had succumbed once, but he prayed that he would not do it again until he was married. Girls, with their intense yet delicate emotions, had to be constantly resisted; some you could not even kiss without "giving them the wrong idea." Yes, there was much reveling in the flesh on his campus, because "secular kids go along with whatever is happening, and that's what's happening now." But he also saw more and more students, eager for something to believe in, turning to Jesus.

The fear of sex hangs heavily over youth rallies like this, in particular a terrible uneasiness about the sexual freedom of young women. A disquieting sense that when the female of the species starts becoming a sexual predator, then our moral universe has lost its alignment and anything can happen. Though more obvious in fundamentalist youth culture, these deep-seated feelings of sexual guilt and anxiety are not limited to Bible-quoting teens. By the mid-1980s, studies by university researchers and psychologists began to identify a creeping "erotophobia" among young people.

This country's absurdly high rates of teenage pregnancy, venereal disease, and sexual neuroses amount to a savage indictment of sex education in America. Sex instruction of one sort or another has become a regular feature of U.S. school curricula, and public support for it is widespread. But because of the determined, well-organized opposition of a conservative minority, the vast majority of sex education courses are timid and sketchy, more distinguished by what is missing than by what it taught. The principal classroom taboos are sexual pleasure and technique, masturbation, homosexuality, and abortion. Many courses are still taught by embarrassed gym coaches and driver education instructors with all the depth and feeling one might find in a football playbook or motor vehicle code manual. Other schools tag sex instruction "family life education," a less politically volatile term, and cram it between such unrelated topics as drug abuse and death and dying.

These morbid associations were reinforced when the subject of AIDS was introduced in sex education classes. Liberal, pro-family-planning educators saw the epidemic as an opportunity to begin talking more freely about condoms and nonrisky types of sexual play. But, as taught in most schools, AIDS instruction has only become one more instrument of sexual terror wielded against impressionable kids. The emphasis is not on the joys of safe sex but on the poisonous specter of dread bodily fluids. Columnist Ellen Goodman was among those observers noting the bitter irony of "a generation of parents who struggled out of one sexually repressive era [only to] find themselves anxiously ushering in another. Add one more sad entry onto the list of AIDS side effects: We may once again teach our young to be afraid of sex."

Some sex instructors do manage to dispense detailed, useful information in a way that affirms both the glory of physical pleasure and a teenager's right to control his or her own body. So rare are these creatures in today's censorious climate that they assume heroic stature. Hene Kelly, a "family life" teacher at San Francisco's Woodrow Wilson High, is one such legend, a woman whose teaching style is so bold and exuberant that she has achieved notoriety even within her relatively tolerant school district. She touches, she squeezes, she works her classroom like Phil Donahue on ecstasy. She is not afraid to make her kids feel sexy. "Ooh, you're so cute. I love your new haircut. I may let you meet my daughter."

While many sex ed classrooms are draped with more warning signs than a nuclear test site (AIDS alerts, chlamydia alerts, pregnancy alerts) and blunt exhortations to remain chaste, Kelly's classroom features a poster titled GOOD REASONS TO SAY YES TO SEX ("To show love, to make a baby, for pleasure, to release sexual tension"). Kelly does fret, of course, about her young charges ("I worry about them every time the weekend comes around"), but she delivers her admonitions in a decidedly unprissy way: "Hey, don't get any STDs [sexually transmitted diseases] and don't get pregnant!" she booms in her bullhorn voice as the kids file out after the bell.

Kelly is a short forty-six-year-old woman with pretty brown eyes and a fondness for shapeless housedresses that are often adorned with teachers-union pins or buttons with urgent messages. The daughter of a Jewish rabbi, she graduated from the University of Chicago and began her career as an English teacher but later switched to sex ed. ("I never want to teach reading again. You put a dirty picture in front of a teenager and they'll find a way to read the caption.") Kelly and her husband, also a public school teacher, have two children.

Her kids at Woodrow Wilson, a worn-out but clean school near Candlestick Park with a predominantly black, Hispanic, and Asian student body, receive an education that is rich in practical details ("I tell them saliva is the best lubricant. They go absolutely nut-fuck: 'Oh Gawd! Spit?' ")and humane values ("I tell the boys, 'This girl is a person, not a vagina. What if she were your sister or daughter?' "). But she is best known for her cucumber lessons. "I bring in the biggest cucumbers I can find to show how rubbers can stretch to fit any size, because some boys always say, 'Mine's too big.' One little Chinese girl's eyes got big as saucers when I held up a really impressive cuke. I said, 'Don't worry, Saundra, they're not all this big.' I show how sexually active you can be with a rubber by blowing it up, swinging it around my head, doing all sorts of things to show how durable it is."

Midway through her condom demonstration one day, the Woodrow Wilson principal walked unexpectedly into Kelly's classroom. Unfazed, Kelly promptly drafted him to serve as a model. "I made him stand there holding the cucumber at groin level while I rolled on the rubber. But as I was putting it on, he got nervous and jerked it away and the tip of it snapped off. One of the kids piped up, 'You've always wanted to do that to someone in administration, Mrs. Kelly!' I said, 'Alright, next let's demonstrate how to insert a foam applicator,' but he made a quick exit."

Despite the tenor of the times, Kelly refuses to expurgate her lessons. "If they fire me for being so outspoken, I don't care," she declares. "I'd give out birth control devices in class if I could. I don't disagree entirely with the abstinence message, but kids have the right to say yes too. Most of us are going to at some point in our lives, so it's my job to prepare them for that moment."

But sex education in America, on the whole, is aimed at shutting down teen hormones. Date rape, incurable infections, dangerously defective contraceptive methods, emotional trauma—these are the goblins that dance in the minds of teenagers once they have been marched through the vale of tears known as "family life." The principal target of this antisex reeducation campaign is female adolescents, whose "girls just want to have fun" spirit of independence is increasingly threatening to the guardians of family and state. This explains why New York's sensational "preppy murder trial" in 1988 became a morality play in the pages of the tabloids and women's magazines, a cautionary tale about teenage girls who pursue sex with too much gusto. As interpreted by the more primal elements of the media, eighteen-year-old Jennifer Levin was not simply a victim of square-jawed former altar boy Robert Chambers but a victim of her own ferocious appetites. WILD SEX KILLED JENNY in the pithy analysis of the New York *Post*.

While the feminist movement has, for the most part, established a woman's right to control her body, the nubile forms of teenage girls remain largely under the dominion of adult authorities. By 1988, nearly half of the fifty states had passed laws placing a teenager's right to abortion in the hands of her parents or the court. Conservative pressure has also succeeded in curbing teenagers' access to contraceptives, by preventing many school-based clinics from dispensing birth control devices.

Studies have demonstrated that these clinics can delay teenagers' sexual initiation, increase their use of contraceptives, and cut pregnancy rates. But conservative opponents such as Phyllis Schlafly of the American Eagle Forum and Judie Brown of the American Life League have charged that the clinics "encourage children to behave like animals" and are part of a plot by the "promosexual lobby" to make kids sex-crazy (as if that required a lobbying effort). When a high school in Portland, Oregon, opened up a clinic in 1986, local witch-hunters marched on the school and condemned the clinic coordinator as a "devil worshiper" and "whoremonger." The following year, Florida Governor Bob Martinez began defunding school clinics in his state, saying that sex counseling was the responsibility of parents.

While chasing the Trojan-pushers off campus, the enforcers of teen morality broadened their attack to include sex educators and textbooks deemed ideologically impure. Schlafly helped ban a textbook from the Seattle public school system that expressed tolerance for premarital sex and homosexuality. According to an American Life League pamphlet, books such as this were spreading "psychological venereal disease" and stripping students of the "shame, disgust, and morality that are the natural inborn mental dams that control base sexual urges." Instilling shame and disgust about sex, particularly in teenage girls—this was the goal of those conservative elders who had charged themselves with the proper rearing of today's overly stimulated youth. And, for a time, it would even become the official policy of the U.S. government.

The crusade against adolescent sexuality in the United States has a long, colorful history. It was an obsession with the "secret vice" of masturbation that drove two quintessentially American characters, Sylvester Graham, of graham cracker fame, and John Harvey Kellogg, father of the celebrated cornflake, to invent their wholesome staples in the belief that a bland diet helped put a damper on youthful sex drive. (So pure were Graham's dietary strictures that today's adulterated cracker would not pass his muster.)

Kellogg, a licensed physician, carried this curious campaign even further, presiding over a fashionable sanitarium in Battle Creek, Michigan, and writing a series of highly popular health books in the late 1800s that raged against the practice of "self-pollution." His suggested treatment for chronic masturbators is chilling to read, given the prestige and influence he enjoyed in his day. "In females," he wrote in *Plain Facts for Old and Young,* "the author has found the application of pure carbolic acid to the clitoris an excellent means of allaying the abnormal excitement and preventing recurrence of the practice." His remedies for young male offenders were equally severe: he recommended circumcising younger boys "without administering an anaesthetic, as the brief pain attending the operation will have a salutary effect upon the mind, especially if it be connected with the idea of punishment," and, for older boys, sticking one or more silver sutures through the foreskin of the penis. "It is now impossible for an erection to occur, and the slight irritation thus produced acts as a most powerful means of overcoming the disposition to resort to the practice."

The surest way to determine whether a child was engaging in self-abuse, Kellogg further counseled, was to burst into his or her bedroom and throw off the bedcovers. A throbbing erection was, of course, damning evidence in the case of boys, but female suspects required closer inspection. In guilty girls, "the clitoris will be found congested, with the other genital organs, which will also be moist from increased secretion."

These de Sade–like ravings did not prevent Kellogg and his wife from being entrusted with the care of forty-two foster and adopted children during their long marriage. "Kellogg's self-image was that of a kindly benefactor, and not that of an avenging terrorist out to destroy youthful sexuality," observed Johns Hopkins sexologist John Money in *The Destroying Angel,* a mordant study of the antisex impulse in American life. But it is creepy to contemplate the possessed doctor, who took to garbing himself all in white and keeping frequent company with a white Australian cockatoo in his later years, prowling the halls of his twenty-room Battle Creek mansion in the still hours of the night, uncovering his young charges and searching eagerly for signs of moistness and tumescence.

Kellogg and his wife never had offspring of their own, since he had a deep aversion to sexual intercourse. The one indulgence this internationally renowned health expert seems to have allowed himself (other than his passionate struggle with young lust) was a daily enema, which was administered each morning by a sanitarium orderly after Kellogg had consumed his cornflakes.

The antimasturbation propagandizing of Kellogg and other nineteenth-century American purity crusaders continued to haunt the nation's youth well into the next century. According to Money, "Moral squeamishness about masturbation did not officially disappear from American medicine," until 1972, when the American Medical Association's Committee on Human Sexuality finally declared that "masturbation is a normal part of adolescent sexual development and requires no medical management," a sentiment echoed by the moralistic *Boy Scout Manual* around the same time. But even today, some religious groups continue to exhume the musty teachings of Kellogg. "If you are tempted to masturbate," counsels a contemporary Mormon tract against onanism that reads remarkably similar to those penned by the flaky Kellogg, "think of having to bathe in a tub of worms, and eat several of them as you do the act."

The crusade against youthful desire took a different shape during World War I, as moral reformers inside and outside of the federal government cracked down on the sexual high jinks around military camps. "Girls apparently of good families drive up in their cars and invite the soldiers who happen to be along the roadside near the camp to come to supper to a roadhouse or the nearest city," clucked a disapproving physician at the time. "The results are the usual ones."

In what would become the pattern throughout the century, the nation's moral wrath was directed mainly against young women, who were supposed to be setting a high standard for sexual conduct but who apparently were being driven crazy by men in khaki. Moral crusaders fretted that "the girl problem," as it became popularly known, would lead to the spread of venereal disease among the troops and "drain the virility" of the doughboys. Between 1918 and 1920, agents of the federal Commission on Training Camp Activities rounded up thousands of fun-loving teenage girls and camp followers, along with women suspected of prostitution, and incarcerated them in detention facilities, many of which were secured by barbed wire and guards.

After World War I, as the nation's youth threw itself into a frantic celebration of life and women's rate of nonmarital intercourse began to converge with that of men, moral centurions again went marching against female impropriety, as symbolized by the flapper. Charging that the new music and faddish dances of the 1920s brought out the devil in youngsters, police began posting strict regulations in dance halls and the U.S. Surgeon General distributed a dire warning to the managers of these "amusement places." Even Henry Ford felt prompted to denounce the popular music of the day as "monkey talk, jungle squeals, grunts and squeaks and gasps suggestive of cave love [and] camouflaged by a few feverish notes."

As historian Allan M. Brandt has observed, Ford's scornful attitude toward popular culture was ironic in light of the fact that "it was . . . the automobile that many identified as the principal cultural culprit. The automobile provided the dangerous combination of mobility and privacy that invited new sexual mores."

In the 1970s a new generation of moral crusaders, reacting against another notorious decade of rampant partying and sexual emancipation, again attempted to clamp down on youthful exuberance. Their dream of restoring American teenagers to a mythical state of virtue and innocence was given a strong boost in 1980 by the election of Ronald Reagan. During the Reagan years, teenage purity would, for the first time in American peacetime history, become government business.

In 1981, Republican senators Jeremiah Denton of Alabama and Orrin Hatch of Utah pushed through the Adolescent Family Life Act (popularly called "the Chastity Bill"). Thus began a strange federal experiment in sexual-behavior modification, a program run out of a sterile-looking wing of the Department of Health and Human Services (HHS) by a series of female officials with the roguish zeal of Lieutenant Colonel Oliver North. These czars of chastity relied on government-funded brochures and school curricula rather than silver sutures and vials of carbolic acid to accomplish their ends, but the underlying conviction was the same as that which animated the bizarre doctor of Battle Creek: sex is too dangerous a force to be left in the hands of children; adults must throw back the bedcovers.

The teenage chastity program dispensed millions of federal dollars to developers of "cold shower" sex ed courses with titles like Saying No and Meaning It and encouraged pregnant teenagers to consider adoption, rather than abortion. Conservatives saw these efforts as a moral alternative to the federal government's family planning program, which funds some forty-five hundred birth control clinics around the country. These clinics, frequented by poor women and teenagers, are viewed as dens of iniquity by purity crusaders, who suspect them of promoting promiscuity and abortion. President Reagan and his conservative allies in Congress knew they lacked the votes to kill the family planning program, so they did the next best thing by setting up the rival chastity program within the same bureaucratic wing of HHS, the Office of Population Affairs, and putting them both under the direction of women who made no effort to disguise the fact that they strongly favored the abstinence approach.

The Reagan administration's war on teen "promiscuity" was launched with a flurry of pious rhetoric. "The most effective oral contraceptive yet devised is the word 'no,' " intoned Senators Hatch and Denton. The women who ran the chastity program were convinced that American teenagers, confounded by the sexual complexities of modern life, would welcome this stern and simple guidance. But as the Reagan administration's first term drew to a close, having spent over $30 million on teaching kids to say no, the program's most ardent backers had to concede that teens were still saying yes in truly distressing numbers.

In addition, the Office of Population Affairs' own research was beginning to turn up some unwelcome information about its educational strategy. Many of the projects funded by the agency stressed parent-child communication, in keeping with the conservative belief that sex education belonged in the home instead of the classroom. But agency studies revealed that parent-child discussions had no discernible impact on girls' sexual activity, and even more unsettling, father-son chats seemed to *encourage* the sowing of wild oats.

Federal chaperons began to appreciate just how intractable were the forces of sexual change. Not even the family, which conservatives liked to romanticize as the bedrock of American decency, was proving to be a reliable ally in the campaign to regulate adolescent sexuality. Sexual license and liberalism seemed to have taken root everywhere one looked, including—to the extreme mortification of Washington conservatives—the drab, fluorescent-lit offices of President Reagan's chastity agency.

Fortunately for the abstinence program, the complete story of the Marjory Mecklenburg affair never made it into the press. But it made for sizzling conversation within the HHS bureaucratic maze long after Mecklenburg had been banished from the department. After her downfall, conservative morality crusaders would sniff that, well, they had never completely trusted Marjory, she wasn't really and truly one of them. Before coming to Washington, hadn't she broken from the right-to-life movement back in Minnesota to start her own antiabortion group, one that supported contraception? But all this was hindsight. During her first couple years as deputy assistant secretary for population affairs, the nation's chief guardian of embattled teen virginity, Marjory Mecklenburg had been a heroine to the Moral Right. She had won their hearts when she authored the notorious "parental notification" proposal, better known as the squeal rule.

The Mecklenburg proposal would have required federally funded clinics to immediately report teenagers seeking contraceptives to their parents. Its manifold critics, including thirty-nine states, the American Medical Association, the American Bar Association, the Salvation Army, and scores of newspapers, charged that the squeal rule would scare teenagers away from clinics and result in more pregnancies. (Indeed, many teenagers stopped going to Planned Parenthood clinics during the widely publicized debate that raged around the proposal, in the apparent belief that it had already gone into effect.) The squeal rule was eventually struck down by the courts, but not before the ambitious Mecklenburg had won a name for herself in the Reagan administration as a true believer. She might have supported teenagers' birth control rights before coming to Washington, but now she was gung ho for youthful abstinence.

The former Minnesota housewife suddenly seemed on the political fast track. There was even talk of her running for the U.S. Senate from her home state. But there were signs that Marjory Mecklenburg was not all she appeared to be. In July 1983, muckraking *Mother Jones* magazine revealed that the Reagan administration's top propagandist for youthful celibacy had been pregnant before she married her husband, gynecologist Fred Mecklenburg. Copies of the magazine circulated quickly throughout the Office of Population Affairs, but since the mainstream media did not pick up the story, there were no political repercussions, and Mecklenburg dismissed the whole business, at least in public, with a laugh. By then, however, members of her own staff were beginning to have funny suspicions about Mecklenburg, for it seemed increasingly clear to them that their moralistic boss was leading a secret life.

As Mecklenburg came under withering political fire during the long battle over the squeal rule, she seemed to draw closer and closer to her top aide, a paunchy, balding career civil servant named Ernie Peterson. Peterson was not beloved by his fellow employees at the Office of Population Affairs, who variously called him a "liar," a "conniver," a "skunk," and worse. They would tell the story of how Peterson suddenly became a devout, pronatalist family man on the eve of Reagan's election in 1980, in hopes of endearing himself to the new administration, prominently displaying a Bible and a papier-mâché stork on his desk. Peterson quickly made himself indispensable to the new chief executive of chastity, counseling her about the Byzantine world of bureaucratic Washington.

In the beginning, Mecklenburg was viewed by her staff as a gracious and open boss, one who would make a point of dropping by office birthday parties and jogging with her employees. But as time passed, she withdrew more and more into a world occupied only by her and Peterson. The two became inseparable: they would huddle together in her office, they lunched together, they even occasionally accompanied each other down the hallway when one had to go to the bathroom. At meetings, they flirted and giggled like love-struck teenagers and shared whispered secrets, according to others in atten-dance. When she felt besieged by office pressures, Mecklenburg would some-times retreat to Peterson's office, lying down on the couch in his darkened room, with the attentive bureaucrat sitting by her side. It got to the point where her top staff members could not have an audience with Mecklenburg without Peterson hovering at her elbow and dispensing advice.

Then there were "the sightings": Mecklenburg and Peterson seen cuddling in a car in the HHS parking lot and various other locations around Washing-ton. It all seemed wildly improbable. "I mean, Marjory was an attractive woman, she dressed beautifully, she was an articulate and gracious person, a doctor's wife, she was connected to some high-powered political people," says one former OPA employee. "The thought of her taking up with this kind of slobby polyester bureaucrat was unbelievable." But more and more staffers were beginning to believe just that: the Office of Population Affairs was in the throes of a torrid affair.

Of course, no one except the principal parties knew for certain whether Mecklenburg and Peterson were romantically involved.* But that is the way it seemed within the chastity bureau—and in Washington, appearances are everything. "Whether or not they were having sex was a moot point," says

* Mecklenburg declined to be interviewed for this book. Peterson did not return repeated phone calls.

the former Mecklenburg aide. "They were constantly together, closer than a married couple, and they were becoming more and more isolated."

It was their out-of-town jaunts that finally brought down the odd couple. Between May 1983 and November 1984, they logged thousands of air miles together, flying on seventeen separate occasions to far-flung conferences around the country and holing themselves up in hotel rooms at taxpayers' expense. Conference attendees reported that Mecklenburg and Peterson were in the habit of breezing in and out of these gatherings, sometimes staying for as little as fifteen minutes.

The kicker was their trip to Denver in November 1984. Mecklenburg and Peterson wanted to see her son, Karl, the hard-hitting linebacker for the Denver Broncos, play during that winning season, so they scored a couple complimentary tickets for the November 18 game in Mile High Stadium and charged two more plane tickets to the federal government. A week and a half after booking their flight to Denver, it was suddenly announced in the Federal Register that there would be a training workshop for prospective OPA grant-ees in Denver on November 19—conveniently one day after the Broncos game. As usual, the two scurried away from the workshop soon after conclud-ing their opening presentations.

Word about the jet-setting twosome eventually got back to Capitol Hill. Senator Denton, the stern father of the chastity program, was not amused. He had not been sent to Washington by the good people of Alabama, after spending years in a Hanoi hellhole as a POW, to see his best efforts to morally revive the nation mocked by a couple of indiscreet paper-pushers, by God. "Someone in Denton's office asked me whether it was true that Mecklenburg and Peterson were having an affair," recalls a former OPA staffer. "The rumors were really flying. That meant that Denton was going to sell her down the river. When you get mired in a sex scandal in Washington, you suddenly have no friends—especially among conservatives. They're so concerned with people not having sex that it becomes a fetish with them."

When an HHS investigator came to interrogate Mecklenburg and Peterson about their wanderlust, they vehemently denied any wrongdoing. It was all legitimate government business, insisted Mecklenburg, adding that she always took Ernie along for the ride because the portly bureaucrat provided her with expertise as well as protection from the dangers of the road.

The investigation into the alleged misuse of office travel funds found no evidence of criminal wrongdoing. But the higher-ups in the department no longer had faith in Mecklenburg's judgment. Columnist Jack Anderson was known to be working on a story about the Denver trip. If reporters started looking at the office romance angle, it might be even more embarrassing.

Here was President Reagan's leading crusader against young lust—a woman whose mission was to curb access to contraceptives, reinforce parental authority, and promote youthful self-discipline—and all the while her office buzzed with gossip about her own shameless indulgences: a married woman rumored to be chasing around the country with her married aide. HHS Secretary Margaret Heckler was not sympathetic. She was going through her own personal difficulties at the time, with her estranged husband accusing her in court papers of cruelly withholding her sexual favors for more than twenty years of their marriage and driving him to adultery. Secretary Heckler made it clear: she wanted Mecklenburg out.

C. McClain Haddow, Heckler's chief of staff (who himself would be forced out of office under a cloud, a common fate among those who staffed the Reagan administration), broke the news to Mecklenburg. "There were a lot of questions being asked about her conduct regarding her travel and the Denver trip and then the appearance problem that occurred with one of her staff people," says Haddow diplomatically. "I told Marjory that she would have to assess whether she was in a position to continue effectively in office." To put it more bluntly, the chastity czar could spare herself and the administration a lot of grief and embarrassment if she went quietly. Mecklenburg resigned on February 26, 1985—just hours before the Jack Anderson column appeared— citing a desire to spend more time with her family and taking a parting shot at those anti-Reagan bureaucrats who had conspired to bring her down. Peterson, too, took the tumble, dispatched by his unforgiving superiors to bureaucratic Siberia, a dreary administrative outpost in Maryland involved with refugee health problems, far from the Washington vortex where he had thrived.

After the Mecklenburg affair, Washington conservatives were determined that sex never again rear its leering head in the ministry of chastity. Mecklenburg was succeeded by an ideologically unimpeachable Catholic right-to-life activist named Jo Ann Gasper, who kept seeking martyrdom by trying to defund Planned Parenthood clinics. When Gasper's repeated defiance of Congress and the law eventually succeeded in getting her fired, Senator Jesse

Helms engineered the appointment of one Nabers Cabaniss to the chastity post.

In Nabers Cabaniss, the Moral Right had at last found the ideal woman to run this unique branch of the federal bureaucracy. For the attractive Nabers Cabaniss, with the soft Alabama drawl, fetching smile, dancing brown eyes, and light spray of freckles, was a twenty-nine-year-old virgin. Righteous conservatives were always carrying on about staying pure until marriage, but few seemed to actually practice what they preached. Among these curiosities was the unaccountably chaste Nabers Cabaniss.

Nabers Cabaniss was part of the new wave of zealous young conservatives who had come to Washington with the Reagan administration. Like the New Deal alumni who staffed Democratic administrations for decades after FDR, they saw themselves as having gained the political know-how and connections to run the federal government and perpetuate the true-blue Reagan brand of conservatism for years to come. Cabaniss's circle of Washington friends was drawn from these young true believers. In what little time remained them after their longs days of slashing away at the regulations and social programs that were the legacy of liberalism, these young Reaganites got together for beers or games of tennis or Bible readings.

Cabaniss frequently went out with men from this circle, but these dates never ended in bed. This apparently did not strike her young suitors as abnormal, because many of the men and women in her circle were also virgins. The comely chastity official would spend the final moments of her day wrapped not in the arms of someone like that nice young lawyer who worked in Ed Meese's Justice Department but in the embrace of the Bible or one of her favorite novels, like *Madame Bovary,* a book she found "terribly relevant."

Cabaniss preferred classical literature and music to the superficial, sex-drenched stuff being churned out by the pop culture machine. She esteemed works of art that had a moral dimension, that explored the consequences of human actions. Contemporary culture was awash with sensation, Cabaniss and her conservative friends believed; it was steeped in the selfish ethic of "If it feels good, do it." But sex outside of marriage could have calamitous results, as Emma Bovary came to appreciate.

Nabers Cabaniss had learned this during her student days at Princeton in the late 1970s, "when it was more like anything goes." She had seen coeds jumping into bed with young men, and other students who were struggling with their sexual identity—were they gay or were they straight? And it all made her shudder, for what she saw was not the elation of sexual discovery but terrible suffering and turmoil. "I always resisted the sexual revolution," she tells us one hot summer day, sitting behind her desk at the Office of Population Affairs, dressed in a white fishnet blouse, blue skirt, and blue pumps. "Maybe, by the time I got to college, I could see more clearly the emotional consequences of all that experimenting. I'm personally convinced that it's women in particular who have been harmed by the sexual revolution. I've seen too many women who have been hurt in relationships where the woman and man had very different intentions. I frankly would rather avoid that kind of pain."

Yes, it is true that her generation is witnessing the end of the double standard for men and women, but the new single standard is a lower one. "I would rather see women calling men to a higher standard than joining them on their lower level," she informs us. "I do think that women frequently have a civilizing influence on men."

Cabaniss, the daughter of a retired army colonel, maintained a military sense of discipline throughout her college years, even in the midst of bacchanalian revelry. "Nabers never touched drugs," her college roommate, Liza Schlafly Forshaw, daughter of Phyllis Schlafly, would later tell a New York Times reporter. "She never engaged in premarital sex. She seldom drank, and when she did, it was very abstemiously. She never experienced the kind of alienation from her parents that so many college students do."

This kind of behavior might have seemed odd at Princeton in those years, but when Cabaniss arrived in Washington with a horde of other Reagan youths, she felt she was not alone. Suddenly she was surrounded by many other ardent young conservatives who were willing to put their cause before their pleasure and who respected the old-fashioned virtue of self-restraint. While liberals were out wallowing in the sensual, they would be changing history.

Cabaniss simply found nothing juiceless or dull in a life without sex. "You can date without having sex," she says. "There's sports, there's travel, there's, well, lots of outdoorsy kinds of things. You can have more fun, in fact, because your parameters are clearly set; therefore, you don't have to be constantly asking yourself where your boundaries lie. Everybody, obviously, has sexual desires. But, no, I don't desire something that I believe will ultimately cause more harm than good. So I am quite willing to forgo temporary pleasure to avoid what I believe would be long-term pain."

Of course, some people in her office were skeptical, thought that she must be a sex demon underneath it all. But those who worked closely with her knew that she lived her life according to her convictions. She simply had no unseemly cravings or habits, at least none anyone could discern: she did not smoke, overeat, or drink too much. She was prepared to forgo sex and marriage forever if the right man did not come along.

There was something ethereal about her temperance. The selfless Jesuit priest played so mournfully by Jeremy Irons in *The Mission* was one of her favorite movie characters. In her denial of the physical, in her utter rejection of the excesses of youth, Nabers Cabaniss was the perfect embodiment of the New Sobriety that reigned in the public arena in the 1980s. Even her name sounded appropriate, like something out of *The Pilgrim's Progress*. "I think desires need to be channeled in a constructive way," she resolutely believes. "Many things in life involve exercising self-restraint, and I think we're better off for it."

The family planning types just shook their heads in wonder at this "oddity" whose programs had such a major impact on the sex lives of teenagers and poor women. "Her lifestyle is such that she has no way to empathize with the women her program administers to," asserted Scott Swirling of the National Family Planning and Reproductive Health Association. "She is in no way typical of the average thirty-year-old, who is concerned about pregnancy and birth control and sexually transmitted diseases. She is off in her own netherworld—if she can find me another chaste thirty-year-old professional woman in Washington, I'll be astounded."

Cabaniss admits that she at first felt very embarrassed to be working on "the sex issue." It was "no place for a young unmarried girl." She wished with all her heart that the Reagan Revolution had seen fit to put her to work instead on welfare reform or health policy, anything else. But once she embraced her duties, she came to feel there was nothing peculiar about putting a virgin in charge of federally funded birth control clinics. "I don't think you need to be a murderer to counsel murderers," she tells us.

There it is again, that morbid equation. To the new breed of conservative ideologues, sex outside the sanctions of church and state is a chamber of horrors. Nonmarital sex may not be exactly tantamount to murder in their minds, but it certainly brings wretched suffering and sometimes even death. The men and women who came of age before her generation had simply gone too far in their pursuit of pleasure, Cabaniss and her fellow young Reagan revolutionists believed. Feminism had pounded a deep crack in the family; homosexuality was not just an "abomination against God," in her estimation, but as the AIDS epidemic raged uncontrollably, clearly "a destructive option," a lifestyle that "leads to pain"; and heterosexual promiscuity was also revealing itself to be a poisoned apple.

"There is a culture out there that has not abandoned the traditional norms," remarks Cabaniss in the waning hours of that sultry Washington afternoon. Her voice has a solemn weight that belies her tender years. "I think there is a growing change among women, and perhaps men too, a growing conservatism in people's lifestyles. And truly, AIDS has had something to do with that. But I think it goes deeper than that. I think there's a general awareness that the sexual revolution has not been a bed of roses."

These pious conservatives in their twenties and early thirties felt that it was up to them to clean up the debris of the 1960s, to attempt nothing less than a rollback of the sexual revolution, which they saw more as a sexual reign of terror. They were the new idealists in this age of sobriety, trying to create a utopian society that was the exact opposite of that envisioned by the free lovers of the past, but no less radical. It was a daunting project, but for one remarkable moment in American history, they enjoyed the full sanction of the federal government. And being young and hopeful, they knew this mission would not end with Ronald Reagan's presidency, that at some point they would be given another chance to remold the sexual behavior of America.

As Ronald Reagan rode off into the sunset, family planning activists predicted that his administration's bold experiment in sexual reeducation would leave no lasting imprint. But this was wishful thinking on their part. The chastity czars at the Office of Population Affairs and the conservative movement that backed them up did succeed in shifting the debate about adolescent sexuality in America. As a result of the teen purity crusade, the abstinence message was thoroughly incorporated into family planning educational campaigns, albeit with a less moralistic tone. In 1983, Planned Parenthood president Faye Wattleton proudly announced that the organization's fastest-selling pamphlet was *It's OK to Say No*. By 1987, even Douglas Kirby of the Center for Population Options, a frequent critic of Reagan administration initiatives, was declaring that "it would be good national policy to stop all sexual activity until after high school graduation." Kirby had not entirely abandoned his liberal convictions, however. "I wouldn't rule out kissing and necking for teens."

Saying no to unwanted sex, of course, is a perfectly proper act of self-assertion. Discriminating teens and adults exercise this option on a regular basis. But by the end of the 1980s, the dominant message being delivered to American teenagers was that they had not merely the right to say no but the obligation. Thousands of school districts throughout the country are now using programs developed by Evangelicals, conservative Catholics, and sex phobics with funding from the Office of Population Affairs—programs that teach premarital sex is inevitably degrading and dangerous. This barrage of propaganda has not succeeded in stopping teenagers' sex drive, but it has made adolescent sex a riskier and more anxiety-ridden affair than it is in those parts of the developed world with a less punitive attitude toward youthful pleasure.

In classrooms in suburban Chicago, St. Louis, Los Angeles, and small towns throughout the South and Midwest, boys and girls are chanting slogans like Control Your Urgin', Be a Virgin; Pet Your Dog, Not Your Date; and Don't Be Dips, Stop at the Lips; and memorizing Sex Tips for a Safe Date, such as "Don't let any part of anyone else's body get anywhere between you and your clothes. Avoid arousal." It's all part of OPA's most celebrated reeducation program, called Sex Respect, which was created by a young, relentlessly perky, former Illinois high school teacher named Coleen Mast, a woman who is against contraception (even for married adults), R-rated movies ("They are designed to turn you on"), and the notion that everyone is entitled to a sex life (It's a privilege only those who are cut out for marriage should enjoy). In her school workbooks, cartoon students with zombie stares recite lines like "Hey, I learned how to have fun on a date without having to prove myself!" Mast, like the other antisex educators of the era, prides herself on being tuned in to American youth. But no teenager talks this way. No *human being* talks this way.

An air of wacky unreality surrounds much of today's sex education. The task of molding adolescent sexual behavior has fallen into the hands of a curious collection of sober citizens—men and women whose unbending ideas about the pleasures of the flesh put them way out of touch with most teenagers. No kid in a country as big and ripe as America should have to fight for the right to party. But that, alas, was the fate of those coming of age in the days of Tipper Gore and Nabers Cabaniss and Sex Respect, in the days of Big Chaperon.

The Morning After

EVEN

at the peak of its sexual revolution, America could not be compared to ancient Greece, when whole temples were erected to fair-bottomed women and entire cities went wanton for nights on end, the men dressed as satyrs, the women "raving on from peaks higher than the clouds," as Pausanias tells us, holding orgies to Dionysus, while legions of beautiful boys engaged in kissing contests, boy on boy, the way Iowa farmers might compete in pig calling during harvest, with the winners bestowing garlands on their proud mothers.

And we never exactly became Roman Italy in the time of the Caesars, when the cult of the Bacchanalia swept north toward Rome, the men "prophesizing like madmen, their bodies distorted by frenzy," the women initiating their own sons in lust. On weekends Americans don't use the sight of criminals being torn apart by lions to get all hotted up.

No, we lack the stomach for true Olympian depravity, being such egalitarians, and with all that baggage left over from Plymouth Rock too.

Still, not so long ago these United States witnessed the hottest sexual celebration of modern times. And nowhere did the flames jitterbug more out of control than in certain party towns. It was fun, fun, fun, till Daddy took the T-Bird away.

What happened in these special places when the party lights went out across America? It would be possible to chart the course of the sexual revolution by chronicling the changing mores in these wild towns. Thus, during our cross-country tour, we chose to lay over in Key West, Florida; Aspen, Colorado; and Chico, California. The first two towns are legendary. The last has been voted the top party campus in the country by a jury of peers.

What makes a great party town? Not size, although New York, New Orleans, and Las Vegas come to mind. Key West is a much better place to spend a Saturday night than the nearby city of Miami; Aspen always makes Denver seem dull; Chico just simply jumps better than UCLA or Wisconsin or Yale. Natural beauty seems to help. A casual constabulary doesn't hurt. Neither does a rootless population with better-than-average looks and less-than-average self-restraint. A great party town seems to attract people who have fewer limits, the kind of folks who are willing to stare too long into the sun, as Bruce Springsteen once sang, because that's where the fun is. This was the basic party mix that made these towns get up and dance. But by the late 1980s it had all changed.

The reasons were different in each case. In Key West, an outlaw town that went too far, sobriety came in the form of a walking AIDS nightmare. In Aspen sexual excess gave way to 1980s greed, the cult of fitness, and an only-in-Colorado narcissism. In Chico the party wound down when authorities turned mean and clever.

Suddenly, everywhere, even in these dance hall towns of America's good-time frontier, it was the morning after. While it lasted, though, it had been one wild and woolly night.

Key West

Jim Mayer had a way with women. There always seemed to be someone new, even after he got married. Coeds down for a week in the Key West sun, singers in local bands, party girls who liked to drink in his noisy, cavernous bar with the legendary name Sloppy Joe's. The bar where Hemingway used to chase away the "black lonelies" with Scotch and sodas and his special "Papa dobles" (white rum, lime juice, a half grapefruit, and six drops of maraschino).

Some claimed that Mayer's success with women was due less to his seductive charms than to his ample supplies of cocaine. "You know how the joke goes," snickers a local charterboat captain. "How can you tell when a Key West woman is in love? '*Sniff.* I didn't know you had a sailboat.'" But there was more than a trace of male jealousy in comments like this.

Mayer had mischievous green eyes and a thick, dark mustache. He wore a silver earring in one pierced lobe. Those who fell for him said he looked like a Caribbean pirate. He was full of the reckless drive that quickens the blood in some women. He had fought with the Green Berets in Vietnam and had come home alive. He had run drugs, it was said around town, and had made a small fortune. Maybe he felt he would always come out unscathed. "He was just full of life, very charismatic," says one of his former girlfriends. "Anything he wanted to do, he could do, and I mean anything."

Becoming part owner of Sloppy Joe's made Jim Mayer particularly proud. He saw himself as a Hemingway man: soldier, adventurer, the type of man who pits his strength against the world. Like Papa, he took up boxing, and he had a ring built inside the bar.

He was in his late thirties, but when a young boxer full of muscle challenged him, he immediately accepted. "That's who he is, he never backs out of something," says the ex-girlfriend. "They went three rounds and they called it a tie. But I saw it, and he definitely won. He's an amazing man."

But the tide suddenly shifted on Jim Mayer.

"Nightmare" was the nickname his friends had given him, because of his proclivity for pushing the Key West party principle to alarming extremes. But nothing he had done before approached the nightmarish nature of this.

Word about Mayer buzzed quickly all over the island during that week in March 1988. Locals refer to this instant transmission of town gossip as "the coconut telegraph." As usual, Buddy Owen, owner of B.O.'s Fish Wagon on the corner of Duval and Fleming (SEAFOOD AND EAT IT), was among the very first to pick up the message. B.O., a Key West native, drew a wide assortment of customers, from cops to coke addicts, with his hearty "bubba" humor and his unrivaled conch fritters. And they all had stories to tell him.

"Hey, B.O., did you hear about Nightmare?" says a bony, stray dog of a man with a patchy growth of whiskers and a jumpy-eyed look. "He was harpoonin' and—" B.O. cuts him off. Young guys with habits depress him. Besides, he has already heard the story. "Jim Mayer had no regard for anybody," says B.O., flipping a couple more fritters in the deep fryer, after the skittish dude has made his exit. B.O. has a tightly packed, oil-drum body and a handsome, bearded face that looks a decade younger than his forty-eight years. He is wearing red shorts and a T-shirt with South Florida humor: IT DOES SNOW IN KEY WEST.

"People tried to get him to cool it, but he didn't listen," continues B.O. "Not long ago, he had an outbreak of shingles. It looked like someone had taken a claw hammer to his forehead. But he kept right on going. I said to myself, 'If anyone gets AIDS, he does.' "

That was the word. The man one friend called "the most promiscuous person in Key West" had been infected with the dread virus—after playing around with needles, according to the most commonly told version of the story. Mayer had known for a long time, it was said, but he had continued his hyperactive sex life without warning anyone. Now his wife was seriously ill. And dozens of young women who had slept with Mayer, as well as their male partners, were rushing to the local test center.

Key West is not the kind of town where people talk about the "wages of sin." But there were those who began to talk about the island's "bad karma."

Key West has always loved its outlaws. This is fortunate, since the town seems to collect them the way a trawler's net scoops up shrimp. It is known as "the Last Resort," "the End of the Road," a steamy, scoundrelly coral island at the frayed edge of the continental United States, closer to Havana than to Miami by sixty-four miles. "This is the last stop, boy," says bar owner Vic Latham, a former business partner and bubba of Jim Mayer's. "You don't make your stand here: you either leave the country or die." Latham made his final stand in Key West after hotfooting it out of New Orleans in 1970 "one step ahead of the law."

A good quarter of the island is under the flag of the U.S. military. Sears, Winn Dixie, and other stucco-walled citadels of American culture have also established outposts here. But the heart of the island is unlike anywhere else in the country. Fancy antebellum houses with gingerbread trimming and cool, dark verandas sit side by side with bleached-to-the-bone shacks. There are

Cuban bodegas on the corner, and stalls where old black men sell sponges and seashells. The streets are shaded from the tropical sun by plants with unnaturally bright hues of red, pink, purple, and fuchsia. Colors from a Rousseau jungle. Jacaranda, bougainvillea, poinciana, frangipani—even the names of the local flora make you feel you have departed America.

At the end of each day, there is a special ritual along the quay that juts out from Mallory Square. People by the hundreds gather as the sun slowly extinguishes itself in the blue-green waters of the Caribbean "in a blaze of refulgent glory," as John James Audubon described the Florida Keys sunset long ago. And it is a strange, curve-of-the-earth sun, fat and glowing and red as blood. When the last little flash is swallowed by the sea, the crowd applauds as if at the opera.

Over the years, the island has been a haven to pirates, rumrunners, drug smugglers, and assorted misfits. The *contrabandistas* achieved folk-hero status in the 1970s, when marijuana money propped up the crumbling local economy. The Key West police department tended to look the other way. City officials with a piece of the action were periodically nabbed by federal drug agents. In 1982 the mayor announced that Key West was seceding from the Union, to protest a traffic-snarling drug blockade thrown up by the U.S. Border Patrol on Highway 1. "They're treating us like a foreign country so we might as well become one," thundered the mayor as he was installed as the first Prime Minister of the newly proclaimed Conch Republic.

Conchs (with a hard *ch*), as Key West natives call themselves, after the pink-lipped, cone-shelled mollusks that abound in local waters, have a crusty sense of humor. Shortly after hoisting their new flag, the townspeople announced their surrender, in hopes that the vanquished republic would become eligible for American aid.

Vices and eccentricities that would draw the lash back on the mainland are shrugged off on this tropical isle. "You can do anything you like here," David Wolkowsky, local aristocrat and patron of the arts, likes to say, "as long as you don't frighten the horses." Novelist Thomas Sanchez, who stopped off on "this tawdry, vicious piece of real estate" on his way to St. Martin's in 1981 and decided to stay, calls Key West "Dodge City on the Gulf Stream."

But outlaw towns still have their codes. "Even though Key West is known for dope and sex, we have our commandments," says Vic Latham. "And commandment number one is, you look after your bubba, your brother. It's a town where loyalty always rides above legality. You don't bullshit the bullshitters here, 'cause we're gonna hear about it the next day."

In the 1980s, however, the bubba code began to lose its binding force. As the marijuana trade gave way to cocaine and crack, smuggling took on a violent, jittery edge. Deals were no longer made between fishermen and college kids over a handshake and beer. The Colombians moved in, then the Panamanians. Scuba divers exploring the wonders of the reef would find bound and gagged bodies dropped like anchors among the coral and turtle grass.

Sex in Key West, once characterized by its raunchy innocence, also got meaner. The story of the "Blister Sisters" always got laughs when it was told on the docks at Garrison Bight and in the bars along Duval Street. Two college coeds from the north, sisters, came to Key West one summer to work at a resort hotel. They were young and beautiful. They were virgins. And they were both courted by the same man, a local charterboat captain in his twenties whose handsome face was already bloated with drink. He slept with one sister when he knew he shouldn't, during one of his herpes outbreaks. Then he slept with the other before his lesions had healed. He was their first lover and they would never forget him. The Blister Sisters. That's what he called them when he told the story.

People laughed. No one knew the two women. They were out-of-towners, like the thousands of others who overran the island during peak season, in their pink flamingo T-shirts and aqua-rimmed shades. But no one laughed when they heard about Nightmare.

Jim Mayer always liked to be the main attraction. His wedding to Valerie Maloney in 1983 had been a typically flamboyant affair. It was held in the backyard of his friend Sunshine Smith, singer Jimmy Buffett's manager. "He wore a white tuxedo and an Arab headdress," recalls Smith, a thirty-six-year-old woman who had been part of the youth wave that washed up on Key West's shores at the end of the sixties. "He was lowered into my backyard by a crane. He was not about to be outdone by anybody, even his bride."

Five years later, all of Key West was talking about Mayer. "There was panic everywhere," says Noreen Sofranac of the Monroe County AIDS Education Project, which runs the local test center. "Maybe this is what it took for the straight party crowd on the island to realize that AIDS is not just a gay problem." Local health officials had a list of more than thirty women who had slept with Mayer, according to the coconut telegraph. All were now fearfully awaiting their test results.

As the telegraph kept clicking, Mayer denied everything. He was suffering from cancer, he told friends, not AIDS. But as the panic turned to rage, he and his wife, Valerie, wisely decided to board their sailboat, *The Papa*, with their four-year-old son, Jesse James, and ride out the storm in Bimini. "He may turn out to be a one-man epidemic," fumed one former friend. "He's no different than Jack the Ripper, except he did it to women with his dick instead of a knife. No one cared if Jim got it from a needle or a shot up the ass. But the fact that he kept fucking around a long time after he knew he had it— Well, I'd say that definitely broke the bubba code."

Key West still had blood in its eye when Mayer and his family returned the following month. His wife did not have long to live, it was said, and she wanted to die at home. The coconut telegraph kept updating the story. There was talk of violent revenge. Some said Mayer had stationed armed guards outside his house. An old friend claimed Mayer was threatening to shoot him for talking too much. People said there was no telling what a man like that might do.

In late April, Valerie Mayer died of AIDS-related pneumonia. Her physician had concluded that Jim Mayer was "the primary patient" and had counseled him "about what it means to test positive and be at risk." But Mayer continued to deny he was infected, claiming he was the victim of a "vendetta." Maybe he really believed it, friends speculated. Maybe he just could not accept how bad it was all turning out.

"I think Valerie died as much of a broken heart as anything else," says Sunshine Smith. "I went to see her a couple weeks before she died. She said to me, 'I feel like I got badly cheated by life.'

"She was a sweet girl, a homemaker. She made her own clothes, her own curtains, she took care of the baby. I don't think she was ever able to make the bridge to Jim's fast-lane world. He wasn't what she hoped he would be. I took out a bottle of wine and drank a toast with her. I'm not into mourning. I said, 'Have a good trip and save a seat for me.' "

By the time Valerie was buried, the story had broken in the Miami newspapers. Never had Jim Mayer been the center of so much attention. The story got bigger in following days when a twenty-five-year-old singer in a Key West band sued Mayer for access to his medical records, claiming that she had been his lover for the past year and was pregnant with his child. The singer's own tests indicated that she had not been infected with the AIDS virus. Reportedly, none of Mayer's ex-lovers who flocked to the AIDS Education Project that spring tested HIV-positive. But because of the long incubation period for the virus, the singer asserted that she had an "urgent need" to know Mayer's HIV-status to determine whether her life and that of her unborn child were in jeopardy.

In a landmark decision, a Monroe County judge agreed with the young woman, ruling that her medical rights took precedence in the case. But to protect Mayer's privacy, the judge limited access to his files to the singer and her physician. After viewing Mayer's records and consulting with her physician, the singer decided to have the baby "because it may be the only child I can ever have if I later turn positive," she tells us, sounding on the edge of tears. "At twenty-five years old, I didn't really want to have children, and I certainly didn't want to have children with somebody I didn't really know or thought was somebody else. But that seems to be my choice right now."

She performed with a girl group that sang oldies like "He's a Rebel," "Leader of the Pack," and "Then He Kissed Me." Unabashed songs of devotion from a less cynical era. Songs about bad boys with good hearts, the kind of boys parents never approved of. "We're girls with attitude" is how one of the women explained their act. "Our dads don't want us to go out with these guys. But we see the one good thing in them."

She and the other group members wore slinky black dresses, B-52 hairdos, and yard-long eyelashes. Her stage name was "Baby Tracy." "Sexy, soulful, and innocent," read their press kit. "Baby Tracy believes true love really exists."

She believed it truly existed between herself and Jim Mayer. He was her only lover, even though she could not have all of him. "The only side I saw of him was wonderful, faithful, charming, caring—totally the opposite of what I found out later.

"He can talk to you and figure out right away how to appeal to you. I mean, it could be raining outside, and he could convince you the sun was shining. I'm not exaggerating one bit. It's a craft. He's a magician. I'm not a stupid woman.

"At this point, of course, I don't believe a word he utters. I kept making excuses for him, because I couldn't believe that any human being could do that to anyone else, especially someone he loves. But I'm not going to be fool enough to stick around."

Baby Tracy was losing her innocence. And yet . . . "Who knows, maybe he'll rehabilitate himself and become a wonderful person and we'll get married. He wants me to marry him. I'm a very faithful and loyal type of person. If I love somebody, I love them. But I don't know— I think that's a gleam of hope that will probably never happen."

It was in that cold-blooded springtime that Key West outlawry lost the last of its glow. How could you romanticize hard living after Jim Mayer? In the end, it seemed, he was not a "one-man epidemic." His wife was the sole casualty that season. But the trembling and disgust the tale inspired stuck with people.

The end had been coming for some time. Most of the 1970s party generation—the smugglers, writers, musicians, bartenders, fishermen, gays, and sailors who had made Allen Ginsberg's "heavenly connection to the starry dynamo" in the Key West night—were now dead or in detox or behind bars or leading lives of sober responsibility. Mayer had been one of the few to keep howling late into the eighties. You did not have to be a runny-nosed beach girl in search of her next line to want to be around that kind of charged-up masculinity. He knew more about life than most other men of the era. He knew there was more to it than staying fit and assembling the right portfolio. But he took it too far.

"There's too little laughter around nowadays, too few people devoted to wild fun," says the wise saloonkeeper Vic Latham. "It really is an art form, being truly devoted to fun without fucking over someone else." The man who knows how to do that, says Latham, that's a man of heroic dimensions.

Latham is a man of heroic physical dimensions. He stands six-feet-five and weighs 270 pounds. When he laughs, which is often, the great tremors shake his impressive belly and the eyes above his gray-flecked beard crinkle with sly glee. It seems that most of his fifty-two years has been spent trying to master the grand male art form of raising the roof without bringing down the barn. "There's a fine line between fast living and antisocial behavior," he says, finishing off one more gin and tonic at his bar, the Full Moon Saloon.

The bar is favored by Conchs and local writers. The jukebox is loaded with Creedence Clearwater. The place is cool and dark, with a low-slung ceiling, like a boat cabin. On the far wall, frozen in one final, glorious leap, is a 369-pound blue marlin caught by Latham's friend novelist Philip Caputo, in Havana Harbor. "Two of his wives wouldn't let him hang it at home, so it wound up here," grins Latham. "Caputo broke Hemingway's record with that fish."

In the 1970s, Latham was one of the local literary crowd's favorite stimulants. He could be counted on by writers like Tom McGuane and Jim Harrison to help propel things to vertiginous heights. "In the good old days," he recalls over another gin and tonic, "I was drinking a quart of whiskey a day, not to mention freebasing and such. I would go visit an AC/DC couple I knew and we'd do drugs for days around their pool. I'd fuck her while he played around with his boyfriend.

"We'd have these theme parties at my house. I'd stir up a big barrel of sangria and declare it a Mexican fiesta day. In the middle of the party, I'd go out to take a leak on my front lawn and there would be McGuane and Elizabeth Ashley fucking in my bushes. There was nothing sick or decadent about any of it. It was just freewheeling as anything. If you got into a serious relationship, you'd protect it. Jim Harrison stayed with his wife through it all."

Those days, shrugs Latham, are gone. "Only Katmandu can last forever." Not long ago, he married his fifth wife, a woman exactly half his age. "Every time I wanted a child," he belly laughs, "I married one." But this one was different. "I probably respect her more than any woman I've ever known and more than 95 percent of the men. She's got a good head on her shoulders. She's a writer. She dropped out of grad school in Washington to come down here to cover her brother's business. Now she's working on her first novel.

"I'm fifty-two—I can't drink sixteen hours a day anymore," he says, taking a healthy slug from yet another gin and tonic. This major alcohol transfusion has yet to make a discernible impact on the big man. But his drinking companion, whom he insists match his intake, is growing unmistakably befogged. "We have a six-month-old son now, so I've stopped a lot of that shit. The days of 'They all look lovely at closing time' are pretty much gone. People realize how much they have to lose. It's not just your marriage, but maybe your life and somebody else's life that's on the line." Nightmare still haunts the bars of Key West.

Despite his advancing years, fatherhood, and the temper of the times, big Vic Latham has not entirely given up his indulgences. "McGuane is no longer allowed to see me when he comes to town," he says with a great, rolling laugh. "I guess I'm a bad influence." He treasures this bit of wickedness like an old war medal.

Nowadays, Thomas Francis McGuane lives on a ranch near McLeod, Montana, with his wife Laurie, the sister of his good friend Jimmy Buffett, and their eight-year-old daughter, Annie. But he often returns to Key West, where he lived from 1968 to 1980, to go bonefishing, a lifelong passion. No writer is more closely associated with the Key West of the sped-up seventies than McGuane. His Key West novels *92 in the Shade* and *Panama* are filled with the chaotic spirit of the times. They are the stories of haunted young men digging in for one final stand "on the scrambled edge" of American culture, as McGuane once described Key West. McGuane writes about the drugs, the sexual recklessness, and the general atmosphere of decay with cool reserve and humor. But below is a well of moral distress.

McGuane's own life in those years seemed as frenzied as the lives of his characters, jacked up with large doses of sexual and chemical stimulants. He was one of America's most highly lauded new writers. He was a tall, handsome, dark-eyed man, with thick black hair down to his waist. He was young in the age of youth. It all seemed his for the taking. "Writers have to bear the tomfoolery of giving so much to the world; you begin to think that you might as well fuck everyone along with writing books for them," says McGuane today, with a wry laugh. "Sort of the Allen Ginsberg failing."

In the mid-1970s, McGuane found himself in the grip of two highly publicized love affairs, with actresses Elizabeth Ashley and Margot Kidder. Meanwhile, his wife Becky, by whom he had a son, became romantically involved with actor Warren Oates. McGuane complicated his life further by casting all three performers in the film version of *92 in the Shade,* which he shot in Key West in 1975.

At the time, McGuane and his lovers had a lofty explanation for this minuet. As Ashley later recalled it, "We decided that [we] were going to be pioneers on the frontier of a Brave New World, guinea pigs in a Grand Experiment in breaking the rules and expanding the boundaries. We would follow our sexual instincts wherever they led us, tell each other the truth, and see where the lines actually were."

But the flint-eyed Warren Oates did not see things quite the same way. "Bullshit," he told Ashley after she laid out the Grand Experiment to him. All he wanted was to run off with Becky. Ashley could have McGuane.

In the end, after the utopian architecture had collapsed and the dust had finally settled, Becky was married to the star of *92 in the Shade,* Peter Fonda. And McGuane was married to Margot Kidder, who bore him a daughter. The Grand Experiment was turned into pulp romance in the pages of *People* magazine and Elizabeth Ashley's kiss-and-tell autobiography *Actress.* Readers of Ashley's unabashed memoir would learn that she and McGuane had a taste for magic mushrooms and public sex, once having their way with each other at a Milford, Connecticut, matinee of *The Sting.* "We were both consumed in a frenzy of terminal horniness," reported the actress.

McGuane's marriage to Margot Kidder lasted only nine months. Two years later, he married Laurie Buffett. He first set eyes on her while laid out on the floor of the Chart Room, Key West's literary watering hole in the seventies. Their union has proved resilient. The dedication to McGuane's 1979 novel, *Nobody's Angel,* reads, "For my beloved Laurie, still there when the storm passed."

Today, McGuane tells us, he looks back on all this elaborate sexual plotting "with a sort of bemused, semivacant smile. I mean, it now seems so utterly futile that I can't believe I ever thought it would work!" He lets out the kind of good, pure laugh that only the deep cushions of time make possible. "It just seems there's something that approaches biological fact, something that people can't seem to overcome, alas! The jealousy, the dashing back and forth between two lovers, the losing weight, and feeling basically unhappy all of the time. Of course, there's that kind of gust of oxygen as you charge from liaison to liaison. But the whole thing is intrinsically comic. Ludicrous and comic, with a kind of bathetic underpinning."

But wasn't there something else, we ask, something touching about this generational effort to love more than one person? "Yes," agrees McGuane, "it all derived from this kind of oceanic warmth that people have at a certain stage of their lives. But as you go on in life, you begin to suspect that the real state of affairs is solitude. And even nesting and pairing off is simply the final illusion. In fact, I see in my oldest children, who are around twenty, a recognition of something that my generation is still having a hard time facing. Namely, that it's very logical for everybody to have his own quarters and his own marbles and all this other stuff is highly illusory."

McGuane is sounding gloomy to himself, and his life has held too much pleasure for him to come across like that, so he offers a midcourse correction. "I don't have any great remorse about those times, although my life was hugely disrupted by those years. I do have a lot of really happy memories. In one sense, it was easier to work in that kind of environment, when there was a breaking wave. I feel sorry for the younger writers today, because there's not much happening anymore. And I think that must be kind of hard, to get out of bed in the morning and do your job when you don't get the feeling that you're carrying the mail for your generation.

"My father, who was a businessman from Michigan, used to come down to Key West in those years and say, 'What the hell is everyone doing here anyway? Why aren't they up north working?' He thought the whole world was falling apart, to see all these young people driving down here to be part of this sweaty pile. There may be some validity to his remarks. But, on the other hand, it's like the saying goes: How do you know what's enough until you find out what's too much?"

Nowadays, concludes McGuane, if he is excessive about anything in life, besides fishing, it is fathering. "I think to have a daughter at age forty is to be really positioned for total concentration. In fact, I'm sometimes criticized for being too into fatherhood at this point. I'm totally absorbed by my eight-year-old, Annie; without exaggeration, she's really the main thing in my life. She's sort of my great pal. She's even a fisherwoman."

That ecstatic declaration—How do you know what's enough?—is no longer the motto of Key West, though to the weekend visitor that might appear to be the case. The bars are still raucous. The drugs are still abundant. (McGuane reports that his twelve-year-old niece recently went to a Key West junior high school party where crack was the refreshment of choice.) And the briny tide-pool scent of sex still hangs heavily over the island.

The souvenir shops that blight Duval Street display T-shirts noted for their in-your-face raunch. (A typical one pictures a bikini-clad beauty washed up on shore, with the unsubtle inscription IF IT SMELLS LIKE A FISH, EAT IT!) Young gay men, stripped to their baggy white shorts in the blazing sun, cruise by one another exchanging barracuda looks. A local singles club devises a unique icebreaker for their parties: each man is handed a bolt at the door, each woman a nut. They must find the right fit before the evening is over. Another night, the men are made to run races with plantains stuck firmly between their thighs.

And yet Key West seems a town at war with its desires. The island uses its slatternly image as a come-on to the tourists. GO ALL THE WAY urge the billboards along the route to Florida's southernmost key. And the locals do appear to have a one-track mind. "It's the heat; I just get so goddamn horny after a day on the beach," a city hall secretary blurts out while we're waiting to see the mayor one afternoon. Strangers are forever saying things like this to you in Key West. But you soon begin to suspect that it is all just talk. Key West today swings its hips and has a dirty mouth and wants it oh so bad, but the truth is it's terrified of going all the way. The reason is obvious: Key West is afraid of what it might catch.

A gay businessman mourns the end of a fifteen-year affair with a young married telephone lineman. "I met him on the beach when he was a teenager. There are a lot of secret romances between gays and Conchs in this town. He's too afraid of having sex with me now. I can't tell you how that makes me feel." The housekeeper of a Key West blue blood, known for her savory key lime pies, declares, "I had to give up my outside man. I hated to see him go, but I'm married and he ain't. He was bringing other ladies home. People are worried now; it just ain't as fun anymore."

AIDS is not the only goblin that makes people keep their distance in Key West. Like so many on the mainland, young men and women here seem to recoil from indoor fireworks, the tumult of love. "Every now and then I'll spend the night with an ex-boyfriend, then I'll drift back to celibacy," says thirty-one-year-old Debra Benedict. "It's easy, it's safe, no muss, no fuss. Sometimes sex is just entirely too much trouble. I would love to have a stable, long-term relationship that is past the infatuation stage. The passionate stage of a relationship just takes up too much energy."

Ironically, Debra used to run the dating service in town, Meet a Friend. "I feel much less crazy and complicated when I'm dealing with other people's romantic problems," she says. But the service lasted a mere six months; she could only make three successful matches. She is not the only person in Key West wary of complications.

Debra talks faster than a speedboat. She has a habit of unclipping her long, black, shiny ponytail and pulling it back from her head in tighter and tighter nooses before clipping it again. She has an immediately pleasing face, long, pretty legs and a torso kept slim on Caribbean fish and health food. She likes to speed walk around the island; it's hard to keep up with her.

One night she accompanies one of your authors to dinner. We're double-timing it down Simonton Street to Louie's Backyard, a restaurant that works wonders with snapper and mangoes and boasts a fine view of the Atlantic. Debra is dressed like a young Audrey Hepburn—sleek black dress, long satin gloves, and a hat with wings that keeps threatening to take off as she marches briskly into the sea breeze. Debra has a taste for retro fashion; her wardrobe is plucked from the thrift stores and garage sales that she and her gay friends frequent. "I've always had gay friends," she says. "They appreciate my efforts much more than straight men; they appreciate my style. They love me every way but sexually."

Debra once lived with a man, but he moved out after six months, she says over a candlelit fish dinner on the balcony at Louie's. Below we can hear the slopping of the sea. "It was a personal-space thing, the disarray, the invasion of someone else's goods. Seeing someone else's things in my space is a distraction and irritation. Whenever a friend leaves a book or clothes at my house, I can't wait to return it."

Debra drinks Perrier at dinner. "I won't associate with the drugged or intoxicated," she says. But she is more fun than she sounds. Later we go dancing at Back Street, a gay disco full of pumping sound and light. In her tight, black sheath, she cuts a seductive figure on the dance floor. Her hips move like a palm bending in the wind.

On the way home, we walk by the Alligator, a pornographic video arcade on Duval with a disreputable back room. The Alligator has achieved landmark status of sorts by being the only furtive sex establishment remaining in Key West. I'm curious; Debra is curious. She gamely escorts me into the mine-black, gummy-floored back room. Shadow men peer at us as we grope our way down the hall into a video booth. In the aquarium light of the video screen, we can see holes poked in the side walls large enough for pink sea serpents.

You can switch video channels to satisfy a range of desires. Debra seems particularly interested in a loop featuring big, sculpted Jeff Stryker, whom her gay friends have told her is the hottest man in porn. We watch, bunched together in the booth, as the nude Stryker works himself into a lather in a shower. The tips of Debra's winged hat tickle my ears. There is no way not to laugh, stuffed snugly inside our sex dream machine, with the milk-colored splotches on the screen. But the whole experience is more than a little sexy too.

Afterward, I walk Debra to her car and she says good-night. I have just experienced, it would seem, today's archetypal Key West date. Off by a tropical beat or two, highly suggestive . . . yet restrained.

Nowhere on the island is desire more reined in than in the gay bars and guesthouses of Key West.

The island has long been a gay playground. Tennessee Williams first arrived in the 1940s, drawn by the sun, sailors, and social tolerance. "The Conchs accepted the gays in those days," an old fisherman tells us. "Hell, half of them had gay sons. When you spend a lot of time out on those fishing boats with other men, you begin to get ideas. Key West had the highest rate of sodomy in the States."

But as more gays began moving to the island and buying real estate, tensions developed. There were violent incidents. Tennessee Williams himself was jumped by several young toughs in 1979 and knocked to the ground, while ambling drunkenly down Duval Street one night with a friend. The assault received national publicity, though Williams later downplayed the whole thing. "It didn't even accelerate my heartbeat," remarked the playwright.

By the mid-1970s, Key West had become Fire Island South, the wildest tropical port on the gay sexual tour. The island was famed for its discos and debauchery. But gay Key West today is like a Disneyland version of the past. It looks the same, but the spirit is missing.

Families in Bermuda shorts no longer stumble over men coupling openly on Higgs Beach. The gay bathhouse was turned into a fat farm after its owner died of AIDS. The local parish of the gay Metropolitan Community Church quadrupled in size between 1986 and 1988. And La-Te-Da, one of the first—and most orgiastic—gay guesthouses, now has TV sets in its rooms. "I resisted for years," says Larry Formica, the proprietor. "But people have stopped partying. We get mostly couples now."

Key West's gay leadership welcomes these signs of growing temperance. "Having fun doesn't have to end in an orgasm," Richard Heyman, the town's first openly homosexual mayor, tell us.

This new respectability came at a high price. Like Greenwich Village and San Francisco's Castro district, gay Key West was electroshocked out of its immoderate behavior. Key West has one of the highest AIDS case rates in the world, though the city is reluctant to acknowledge this, for fear of stampeding the tourists. By early 1988, the official AIDS toll on the small island had topped one hundred. Local AIDS counselors and physicians estimated the true figure was perhaps five times as high.

Despite the chipper pronouncements of city officials, gay Key West does not seem to have smoothly adapted to the plague years. It is a community of containerized emotions; its contents are under high pressure. "Many of my clients ran away to Key West to escape all the AIDS suffering," says Tom Rooney, a forty-nine-year-old gay therapist at the Mental Health Care Center of the Lower Keys. "I call it 'the geographical cure syndrome.' But they bring their problems with them. They're in paradise, but they're still miserable, wondering why they're still drinking too much and flitting from body to body."

There is a pervasive fear and melancholia, periodically alleviated, for some men, by bursts of feverish pleasure in the back room of the Alligator, in the coral bed of the old submarine canal, or in the mangroves near the Beach Club. "They'll do something stupid one night and then come to me the next day and cry, 'Oh my God, what have I done?' " says Rooney. "I want to slap them and yell, 'Get your life together!' " Rooney himself seems a deeply dispirited man. His young lover, he tells us, is suffering from ARC (AIDS-related complex). They are both celibate.

There is sex and death here, but it does not seem appropriate to bang the drum slowly for Key West, for there is sex and life too. We see it one white-hot afternoon on Fleming Street, when two towheaded college-age boys go sailing past the rustling palms on a rickety rented bicycle. One boy is perched atop the handlebars, a purple bougainvillea flower stuck saucily behind one ear and his head thrown back in abandonment. The other boy, stripped to the waist and slick with sweat, pumps away, oblivious to passersby. It is a vision of casual male eroticism that seems typically Key West.

And we see it much more intensely late one night at the Copa while waiting for Gloria Gaynor to come onstage and belt out "I Will Survive." The Copa is a vast, two-story disco complex on Duval, complete with stage, balcony, elbow-room dance floor, game room, piano lounge, patio, and—at last count—five bars. It used to be a blue-movie theater, boasting the longest run of *Deep Throat* in the nation. The air is still thick with lust.

On this Friday night, the dance floor is hip to hip with men and a few women. For the most part, the crowd is white, thirty-something, and dressed in the lazy, beachcomber style of southern Florida: baggy cotton pants, holiday shirts with pink flamingo or coconut tree prints. But one dancer immediately stands out. He is younger, he is black, and he radiates the dazzle of marquee lights. Except for his eyeliner-thin mustache, he is a girl: lithe body, narrow waist, small bubble of a butt. His hair is cut asymmetrically, shaved close to the head on one side, long, shiny, conked curls on the other. He is dressed like a disco Valentino: white silk turtleneck that stops short of his belly button, black caballero trousers, black calfskin boots. And he dances like a sweaty angel. It feels like a blessing just to watch.

His body is fluid against the harsh synthesizer beat. He spins as if he is caught in a whirlpool, one hand waving free. He makes all the others on the dance floor look as though they are simply going through the motions. Dozens of eyes are on him, and he knows it. One minute, he is dancing with a young blond man, and the next, with a dark-haired woman. They cannot stop touching him, because they realize that his inspired performance leaves them out, and they want some of what he has. The blond man grabs him around his bare waist and twirls him around, to feel his body against his own, to possess him. But the dancer just laughs.

He belongs to everyone this night. It is an exhibition of flagrant promiscuity. Gay Key West may have battened down most of its dangerous desires, but tonight at the Copa they are flapping ecstatically about. The dance floor, in the AIDS years, has become a living museum display, one of the last reminders of the orgiastic past.

Later, he comes over and strikes up a conversation with the more Hollywood of your authors. He flirts, he plays with my hair, he touches my chest and arms, his hands are hummingbirds constantly in flight. We sip margaritas and he tells me his story.

His name is Keith Jones, he is twenty-two, and he is something of a local celebrity. He grew up in Key West; his mother is a ward clerk in a hospital and his father works at the naval base. In high school, Keith won "lots of trophies" as a running back on the football team. But he had more fun sneaking out nights to go dancing at the Monster, a legendary gay night spot no longer in operation. When he was eighteen, he told his mother what he had known since he was at least fourteen. His older brothers gave him a hard time about it until his mother told them, "If your father and I can accept Keith, then you can. If you can't, you can move out."

While dancing one night at the Copa, he was discovered by a theater producer, who gave him a chorus role in a cabaret show in Munich. But Germany was cold and gray and now he was back in Florida, looking for another dance show. In the meantime, he was blowing away the competition at Backstreet and the Copa.

Men are always falling for Keith. "A man from Boston wanted to marry me," he says. But Keith has a boyfriend. "He's a hairdresser in Miami. He's Cuban, and he's very possessive. I have to explain to him that I'm a star in Key West. He calls me every day and tells me he's in love with me."

AIDS does not seem to be the circling hawk in Keith's life that it is for the older generation of gay men. He says he does not give it that much thought. He never slept around, he says, so he doesn't miss those days. He took the AIDS test and it proved negative. Nor have any of his friends succumbed to the virus. When he does have sex with someone new, "I'm always very careful. I insist on rubbers and I don't let anyone shoot inside me."

On the dance floor, though, Keith is wanton. Each night, he allows himself to be ravished by several partners and even more voyeurs. I see more symbolism in all this than Keith does. "Is dancing a replacement for sex?" I ask. He lets out a loud laugh. "Honey," he shakes his head, *"nothing* can replace that."

Our last morning on the island, we get to thinking again about the bubba code, that unwritten code of roguish chivalry that once guided male behavior in Key West. You can break the law, get drunk every night, and bed as many women as you can—or so went the code—as long as you do it with a certain charm and humor. "The problem with a town of unbridled opportunity like this," Tom McGuane had told us, "is that a dangerous individual like Jim Mayer can run amok without the usual checks and balances."

But the rascally innocence of Key West's past is preserved in at least one place on the island—at Captain Tony's Saloon on Greene Street, the original Sloppy Joe's, where Hemingway first laid eyes on Martha Gellhorn, the woman who would become his third wife. The bar is owned by the legendary Tony Tarracino, a salty old dog who is the living embodiment of the Key West masculine ethic. In the course of his seventy-one years, Captain Tony has worked as a professional gambler, operated a fishing boat, run guns to Castro's rebel army (then ferried Cuban refugees to Miami after Fidel took power), married three times, and sired thirteen children by five different women. "I'm always looking for my next kid's mom," he likes to say.

On our way out of town, we decide to drop in on Captain Tony to talk about love and sex and women. We have been told that he is a wise man on these subjects. He is sitting at the bar, working his way through today's first pack of cigarettes. Overhead floats a plastic shark with a shapely mannequin locked in its jaws and other nautical junk. The bar stools have the names of famous customers painted on them: TENNESSEE WILLIAMS, WALTER CRONKITE, ERIC CLAPTON. The joint is loaded with old Key West charm. So is Captain Tony.

He has a gravelly voice and a face that has been cured for decades in smoke and Scotch and Caribbean sunshine. He has the strong, gnarled body of an old fisherman. He's a character out of Bukowski, with a more amiable disposition. It's no problem getting him to talk. He once sold his life story to Hollywood, but the movie was never released.

"I took over this bar in 1962," says Captain Tony, letting out a soft swirl of smoke. "In those days, it mixed together Cubans, shrimpers, sailors, and gays. I was the first to bring drag shows to Key West. Tennessee and Truman Capote would be here, dancing together like two grandmothers. Truman would take care of guys in the alley and lose his false teeth. I would get afraid for him—he'd follow big marines right into the bathroom.

"We had U.S. senators in here, Tallulah Bankhead, Elizabeth Taylor. The genteel love to squish their toes in shit. They say I fucked Anna Magnani once, but I don't remember. I was a heavy drinker in those days."

Captain Tony is getting warmed up now. "You've got to be a fuckup to find the woman of your dreams," he says. "You've got to always be stumbling around searching. You never know when you'll find her.

"I've had ten great romances in my life. All my favorite women have been stormy. I had a mad romance once with a Puerto Rican; we used to claw away at each other. She finally got me in the thigh with an icepick. But later that night, she gave me the best blow job of my life.

"You only fall truly in love once in your life. Mine was Stacy, a beautiful fag hag. She ran the bar with me. The gays loved her. She was special, very gentle, intelligent. We were together for seven years. But I didn't know what I had; I was a fucking fisherman. A friend told me, 'She's so beautiful, Tony, one day you'll have to give her up.' One day I came home from fishing and she was gone. I had always told her she should leave when she wanted to. But she ran off with my air conditioner and $500. I shot twenty-two holes in her picture. The taste of her, the smell of her, I can still remember it all." The old sensualist has told these stories so many times, he sounds like an actor reading his lines.

As we leave, Captain Tony hands us an autographed poster featuring his grizzled mug, cigarette dangling predictably from his lip, and his guiding philosophy. "All you need in this life," reads the insciption on the poster, "is a tremendous sex drive and a good ego— Brains don't mean a shit." Countless tourists have left his saloon clutching this souvenir. Captain Tony, we can't help but reflect, has become an amusement in his old age, one more stop on the Conch Train tourist ride.

This, it seems, is the current fate of outlaw sexuality in Key West. It has become picaresque and harmless. Like Captain Tony's plastic shark.

Aspen

"Springtime in the Rockies," says the pilot of the Denver–Aspen commuter plane. "Ding ding ding," he mimics the sound of a ship's bell into the intercom. "That's my secret signal to tell even the flight attendant to put on her seat belt." The single stewardess sits down, and quickly. Fastens her belt. "We'll be going through some clouds upon our descent into Aspen, and if you passengers in the front begin to hear sounds like rocks hitting the plane, don't worry, because it's just the deicer at work flinging ice from the propellers against the body of the aircraft. Just part of the deal." Within seconds, ice is rapping the windows. "Sounds like we're being attacked by machine guns, doesn't it?" asks the pilot in a maddening, reassuring, innocent Colorado twang. John Denver at the controls. By now the plane is shaking like a wet dog. Drinks are being spilled across the carpet. Tourists look afraid. Locals do not. "Banana Days," says the pilot over the intercom happily, the hump season between winter and spring.

"New money doesn't know how to party," says Steve Crockett, angry. "Fifteen years ago in Aspen you partied because it was a full moon or because you'd just climbed a fourteen-thousand-foot peak or because a friend got killed in a bike accident or just because it's great to be alive in the Rockies. These new people, the L.A.–New York crowd, they party to relieve their dull, mediocre lives. They're followers making the scene. In the old days, we were the scene. You'd go into the Pub in the basement of the Wheeler Opera House, and in the first booth would be two rocket scientists thinking out loud, and in the next booth would be two guys writing a song, a good song. In the next, somebody'd be getting a blow job. In the next, they'd be duking it out. And outside all of a sudden you might hear someone riding their motorcycle down the steps! It was hilarious, wacko. People shot out the streetlights. You didn't go to parties. The whole town *was* a party."

Steve Crockett is not new money. His mother's family were Boston blue bloods, he says, from Chestnut Hill. His father's family is Virginia military: "West Point, my father and grandfather both, and before that, the Confederacy." Steve Crockett's great-great-great-grandfather was Davy Crockett, the frontiersman. ("Put as many 'great-greats' in front of his name as it takes!") As he talks, Crockett is standing next to the sheriff of Aspen. "Steve still wears a coonskin cap," explains the sheriff, Bill Braudis.

"On my dick!" says Crockett.

"Yep, on his dick," agrees the sheriff. "That's the kind of guy he is."

"Mass follows class," continues Crockett, who is thirty-nine. "That's the first law of social mobility. Old money revitalized Aspen thirty years ago, and then our generation put the town on the map. Next came the first wave of movie stars like Jack Nicholson and Jill St. John, who were escaping L.A.

They'd dress like locals and blend in. They wanted to emulate us because we were real. All the new celebrities like Don Johnson care about is seeing and being seen. They're pretentious, ostentatious people who wear fur coats and drive the hottest toys and die for the right reservations at the right place at the right time. It's all hat and no cattle now. These people would rather shop at Boogies than get laid!"

Boogies . . .

Aspen, Colorado, the coolest stomping ground for department store billionaires, outlaw millionaires, rock stars of taste, adventuresome classical musicians, cutting-edge skiers, freehand rock climbers and criminally risk-taking upside-down mountain road competition skateboarders, is now a paradise divided against itself, old money versus new, funk versus glitz, community preservation versus resort-town greed. Some even say that in Aspen today, money has become more of a turn-on than sex itself.

And the symbol of these divisions, strangely enough, has come to be the wildly successful restaurant and fashion emporium that occupies the high-priced corner of Cooper and Hunter streets like a jewel. Like a chancre, Crockett might say.

Eat Heavy, Dress Cool is the motto of Boogies. The building is new and brick, opening to a glass-and-brass atrium that caps the design like the top of a percolator. The layout is clever. To get to the diner upstairs, you must walk through the clothes the way you have to walk through the casino to reach the restaurants in Las Vegas.

Upstairs, a burger and fries, with malted, costs about $7.50. Downstairs, a rhinestone-and-jean vest from Tony Alamo of Nashville might go for $750 and a bomber jacket from North Beach Leathers, $650.

"Bomber jackets for $650!" fumes Crockett. "Hey, my father had a bomber jacket. I like bomber jackets. But my father was a real bomber. He flew B-25 bombers in World War II. What's real, what's fake in Aspen anymore? It's all mimicry. These guys are the marketers of contemporary trends."

Boogies is the clothing store equivalent of the Hard Rock Cafe, the trendy but mass chain of rock 'n' roll restaurants. Elvis Presley's 1955 Corvette convertible is on sale ($90,000–$100,000) next to a vintage Harley Davidson motorcycle. A restored neon-blue greyhound from a bus station leaps across a wall. Glossy blowups of Brando, Elvis, Little Richard, the Lone Ranger, and Marilyn hang upstairs. A poster advertises the movie *Diner,* in which Mickey

Rourke played "Boogie." The clerks wear name tags of their favorite TV and movie characters: CUPCAKE, BAMBI, LAVERNE, ANGEL, RATSO RIZZO. Late 1950s to mid-1960s rock blasts from speakers everywhere: Stones, Martha and the Vandellas, Marvin Gaye, Buddy Holly, Richie Valens, the Beatles.

There's a compelling sexiness to Boogies. The music is breezy and bright, dozens of women and men with racing bodies are trying on sweaters all around, dozens more stare at the dashboard car sculptures, folks are dancing in stocking feet, the food is sloppy and fun. But the curmudgeon Steve Crockett is right. It's sexiness in the service of sales. The rebel sex gods of two generations, Marlon, Marilyn, and Mick, have been trotted out of their mausoleums to move hot leather off the racks.

"The music is happy music, shopping music," says Sandy Cohen, the thirty-four-year-old designer and part owner of Boogies. Cohen's own heroes, he tells us, are the conceptualizers of Banana Republic and Fiorucci's.

Cohen is well aware of Steve Crockett. "He's a trust-fund kid. I don't know how much he gets a month or from where, but he doesn't have to sleep in the real world." He pauses. "Controversy has been good for business."

Cohen, in town now for two years, is from southern Florida. He's handsome, with a long stick of a nose, shrewd and introspective at the same time. Black hair falls to his shoulders. One ear is pierced with a stud. His own outfit, black sweatshirt over loose black pants, he describes as antifashion.

"It's no sin to make money, and it's no sin to want to spend it," he says. "Crockett talks how expensive everything has become in Aspen. So someone bought a house for $30,000 thirty years ago and sells it today for $1.1 million. What's wrong with that? So Chris Hemmet sells his home at the base of Aspen Mountain for $16 million. What's wrong with that? He started out as a bellboy. He's entitled. So Steve Crockett wants Boogies to leave town. He's never even been inside the store."

"I have a classic car myself," replies Davy Crockett's descendant. "It's a 1951 Hudson. The first time I shop at Boogies, I'm going to drive that car through the front door."

Above the door at Boogies, on the inside, is a neon sculpture in smoky red: JUST SAY NO. "I think that's funny," Cohen says, "but I also happen to believe it. I'm the straightest human being you'll ever meet. I've never smoked pot. I only drink wine on the holidays." Cohen is married. He has an eleven-year-old daughter. "I am fidelity personified. People just aren't as promiscuous today.

Girls don't go downtown as quickly. There's a muffler on things. People want to know each other first."

Sandy Cohen does not like to party. Sandy Cohen may be the future of Aspen. The Sandy Cohens have the Steve Crocketts worried.

"The making of money may or may not be as big a turn-on as sex these days," the mayor of Aspen corrects us, "but the *display* of money has certainly become the new sport around here."

The mayor of Aspen is sitting in his wife's bookstore, the Explore, which is also a coffeehouse. The mayor, Bill Stirling, is an intense talker with piercing light blue eyes and a mane of gray hair above a carefully trimmed beard. Dressed in a gray shirt and brown corduroys, he is drinking cappuccino, but he could have chosen Ethiopian Harrar, or Jamaican Blue Mountain, which goes for $5 a small pot, $25 for large. There is a selection of imported teas, Italian cremes, and what the menu calls a "water bar." All waters are $2.50 a glass, and come from springs in Iceland, Belgium, Honolulu, and elsewhere. The bookstore is elegant and soft-spoken, like its owner, the mayor's wife, who is Katharine Thalberg, daughter of Irving Thalberg, the movie mogul on whom F. Scott Fitzgerald modeled the hero of *The Last Tycoon*. The bookstore is carved out of an old Victorian. "It's hard for anything new to have character," the mayor says at one point.

In the early 1970s, when the future mayor moved to Aspen after setting up storefront counseling centers for Vietnam veterans in Harlem, he was a carpenter in the summer and a bartender in the winter. "There was a wonderful egalitarianism in Aspen then," says Stirling, whose father was an Episcopalian minister in West Palm Beach. Stirling is now in his late forties, as are about a third of the town's residents, the mayor believes. "Nicholson, Angelica, Hunter Thompson could sit in the Pub listening to the jukebox and nobody would bother them." Stirling first met Jack Nicholson when he served him beers on the deck of Little Nell's, the grill that was for two decades the public party center of Aspen. Nicholson would order in a parody of his own style: "Two beers, two weenies . . ." "I couldn't believe the fun of Aspen then," remembers Mayor Bill, as friends and detractors alike address him. "People would haul big yellow kayaks right up the slope." Then at five-thirty they would ride them downhill to Nell's with a whoop and a holler, and start partying.

The beauty of the mountains, the charm of the old silver-boom architecture, the world-class skiing, and the downscale magic of Ph.D. dishwashers hoisting Coors next to trust-fund millionaires had turned Aspen into a mix-and-match watering hole by the early 1970s. Hunter Thompson had already run for sheriff on what might be termed a modified Great Society platform of "guns and drugs" and lost, but fellow reformers were swept into office. John Denver moved in and wrote "Rocky Mountain High."

With the stars came camp followers. Condo frenzy began. Condo cancer, as Steve Crockett would phrase it.

"John Denver was single-handedly responsible for ruining this place," Crockett fumes. "The guy's a bohunk from Nebraska with fewer brains than a fence post. He literally shit in his own nest by singing that Aspen was the greatest place in the world and inviting every bozo in Kingdom Come to enjoy it with him." Others less flamboyant would later estimate that when Don Johnson moved to nearby Woody Creek from Los Angeles, the number of beautiful women cruising through Aspen increased a good 15 percent.

At the same time, the mayor tells us, "Cocaine was becoming ubiquitous. There was this feeling that you could make major withdrawals at night as long as you made heavy deposits the next day. It other words, it was OK to get very hammered if you got up early and went to work or skied all day."

The mayor believes this "schizophrenic duality" was a 1970s perversion of the old Aspen concern for unification of mind and body. In the 1950s, Aspen had turned its back on the golf-course-and-pointy-bra ethic of postwar America to attempt a mix of the intellect and the supremely physical. In the summer, the Big Questions would be answered at the Aspen Institute for Humanistic Studies, a think tank in the Great Books tradition founded by Walter Paepcke, chairman of the Container Corporation of America and a trustee of the University of Chicago. The winter would offer some of the fastest racing in the world.

By 1980, however, "Lives were being ruined by cocaine and alcohol," believes the mayor, while new houses were beginning to sell for as much as a million dollars and remodeled Victorian homes for almost as much. The cost of living was driving ski bums and summer philosophers to bedroom communities "down valley." The neighborhood was being trashed in reverse. Aspen was losing its best partiers the way Colorado wilderness preserves lose their wildest animals when fancy backpackers flood the woods.

"It used to be that the actress out from L.A. on a break in the shoot would go home with the lift-operator or the dishwasher—provided he was the hottest skier. Now they want to look at your portfolio," a snow plow driver tells us. "I'm a doctor," explains a partier in the back of the Paradise night-club, "but among the stars and trust-fund babies I'm just another worker bee. The leading aphrodisiac among women in Aspen is now money and power." "If you want to get laid today and you're not rich," adds waiter Ron Hodge, "you better have one hard body."

The realization that the town was seriously out of balance finally sunk in after the murder of a mysterious sportsman named Steve Grabow.

Grabow, thirty-eight, was one of the hottest skiers on the Ridge, as well as a major importer and distributor of cocaine—about $35 million worth a year, according to federal authorities. He was the perfect representation of Mayor Bill's schizophrenia, a man on the cutting edge of sport who dealt big dope. On a cool December day in 1985, Grabow finished a game of tennis at the Aspen Club and climbed into his jeep. An explosion ripped through his buttocks and left a pool of blood and intestines across the asphalt of the parking lot. Even for a town that had long lived well on contradiction, a cocaine kingpin terminated outside the sports club was too much. Aspen was about to change from a sex-and-drugs high to a health-and-fitness high.

"It's a sophisticated group that knows its limits," smiles Danny Wardwell with that small, calm, quizzical smile he has now. "The third time I wanted to go off and do coke by myself I thought maybe a pattern had set in. This woman was ready to go home with me—great skier, blond, beautiful, every-thing I liked—and yet I just wanted to do the drug.

"I decided not to go to the Betty Ford Clinic because I didn't want to be surrounded by celebrities. I was worried treatment might become just another phase of partying. I went to a smaller place and made myself like a fly on the wall, observing. Then the doctors warned me not to go back to Aspen, but I thought, This is where my friends are. People love me. They wouldn't think of offering me even a glass of wine now. I guess I got addicted to ritual."

Danny Wardwell is a man of near-movie-star looks. His face is strong, the eyes black, his graying hair full. He has the body of an old skier, with thick legs and muscles that lie in bulges along his arms and shoulders like sleeping animals. For most of the seventies and eighties, Danny Wardwell was what in Aspen they call a player. He owned or managed a number of restaurants, and many of the wildest parties in town started in a Wardwell joint (sometimes in the meat freezer), continuing after hours until a dozen giggling, sniffling people would wind up in his apartment or skiing down the mountain at dawn. There was a sense of exploring life all the way and beyond at a Wardwell party, people say. The bigger bashes even acquired a special name: Danny Wardwell's Fun Hog Parties. "I guess I was the Pied Piper," he pauses. When Wardwell pauses, his eyes seem to drop back over the years. "Funny times . . ." he says quietly in an upstairs suite at the Hotel Jerome. "I remember trying this as an opening line once: 'Have you ever done a six-way?' "

His companion doesn't laugh. She raises an eyebrow. She doesn't want him to name names. In Aspen, people will share anything about themselves, but the code is to protect celebrity friends. Wardwell catches her look and turns general.

"I guess you could say for me it was a different party every night for twenty years. Being confined to Aspen, I understand people who have trouble coming out of the joint. It's utopia here."

Her companion laughs with him now. "When I go to L.A.," she says, "I suddenly remember there really are people who are fat, unhealthy, and ugly."

Everybody laughs at that.

Next day at lunch Wardwell eases into an antique upholstered chair in the Jerome's Tea Room. "That woman really hurt me last night," he smiles. "You know, I like her much more now than I did fifteen years ago. Women in their thirties are always hammering on you to have children. You can't talk to them. But when they're past that stage, you don't have to go through a ritual to have a little affair." He lifts the menu, weighs it, lets it drop back to the white tablecloth, "You get some pretty loose older gals. Jesus!"

Danny Wardwell was with Spider Sabich the day Claudine Longet shot him. There are many local legends in Aspen—Nicholson, John Denver, the writer Leon Uris, the late arts patron Walter Paepcke, gonzo boy Hunter Thompson, six-foot-six-inch Sheriff Braudis, Don Henley, Jill St. John, and

Buddy Hackett—but Spider Sabich was the man all the girls wanted to fuck and all the boys wanted to be.

"Spider was the only really good pro in America," a ski instructor will tell us, "and you could pronounce his name. His living here brought all the best skiers in from Europe. Plus he was a nice guy, the nicest. I even liked him, and he went to bed with my ex-wife."

Longet was a strong presence too. Beautiful in a town of beautiful women, she was French and arrogant, an actress divorced from singer Andy Williams.

"Spider and I used to shoot rats with that gun," says Wardwell in a voice so quiet as to be wistful. "We'd take it down to the dump. It must have cost, I don't know, thirteen dollars. It had a bad safety. Claudine didn't mean to kill him, although I think she had hatred for him at that moment. The gun just went off and hit Spider in the gut. If Claudine had really wanted to kill him, she would have shot him in the head." There is a long pause this time.

"I hated Claudine for what she did," Wardwell finally says, his voice soft as snow. "Spider was like a brother to me. I cried at the funeral, and I don't cry. Wardwells don't cry. Three hundred years of WASP Wardwells and we don't cry. They asked me to testify, but I thought I was too prejudiced, too close. I didn't want to be the one to put her behind bars for thirty years, because it really was an accident, even if Claudine had anger in her heart. Claudine had a Latin temper."

Shot once with a .22-caliber bullet, Sabich bled to death. After Longet's trial in 1977, she received thirty days in the Pitkin County Jail, which she spent painting a mural. Later she married one of her lawyers.

"It's taken me a long time to deal with Spider's death. I don't know if I ever will. My anger gave way to forgiveness. Claudine loved him and didn't mean to kill him, our guy, Aspen's guy." He pauses. "I used to handle it by having another beer or—" Wardwell puts his finger alongside his nose and snorts.

"The plane didn't arrive, that's what went wrong." He shrugs. Perhaps it could all have been different. Sabich and Wardwell were planning to fly to Las Vegas for a ski show and a few days of end-of-season partying. Sabich and Longet were breaking up. The day of the trip Longet and Wardwell talked on the phone, says Wardwell. Longet wanted to know if Wardwell's girlfriend of the time was going with them. "Tell me, Danny," Wardwell mimics Longet's French accent. So Wardwell told her his girlfriend was indeed going, and as he spoke he suddenly understood that until that minute Longet had not realized that she, Longet, would not be going, that Spider had cut her out of the trip. Spider, says Wardwell now, had not discussed it with him. Then the group found themselves unexpectedly stranded. The plane couldn't land in Aspen because of bad weather. Sabich met with Longet one last time, and she shot him.

But Wardwell wants to talk about the future now. "Everything's different," he says. He's sober, he's off cocaine, he's reformed, except for older women, and you can only go so far. "This town will either become the next Gstaad or it'll end up like Waikiki," he says.

Wardwell prefers elegance, "planned elegance."

Next day, outside the Aspen Grove Cafe, we run into another serious ex-partier, the old comedian Buddy Hackett. The story is told that Hackett likes to go up to beautiful women in discos and restaurants, roll his wonderful goitered eyes, and say, "Excuse me, goils, I'm a newcomer to Aspen. Can youze show me the way to your condo?"

At sixty-four Hackett has more twinkle in his one good eye than most younger comics have bad jokes. He agrees the story is true. "But I can't drink as much now. One drink in the morning, one in the evening," he says. "These days, a good party to me is jogging five blocks without puking."

Not everybody in Colorado perceives excess to be a problem, however. The New Aspen Sobriety comes to a screeching halt, we find, under the black buffalo head mounted in the front right corner of the Woody Creek Tavern, seven miles north of town.

There Hunter S. Thompson is enjoying a dinner of chicken and spaghetti with a tall water glass full of bourbon and two little jiggers of what appears to be cream and Kahlúa, set on either side of his plate like muddy eggcups. Thompson, the author of that true-crime classic, *Fear and Loathing: On the Campaign Trail '72* as well as *The Great Shark Hunt* and *Generation of Swine*, lives up the canyon. The tavern functions as his clubhouse. He does not walk in and take a seat. He makes an entrance. The bartender shouts out, most people stop eating and look up, the drunks at the pool table call his name.

Thompson nods and throws up an arm to acknowledge the fans. He is like a barbarian king stepping out of the forest into the circle of a campfire. These are his people: bums, boozers, and Bronco fans; truckdrivers, outlaw millionaires, and rock stars with second homes.

Thompson does not so much move as angle his body across the room. He walks like a large upright ant. Not staggering but not in a normal manner either. His head, which is enormous and strange-looking, the flesh stretched tight across high cheekbones, the eyes sunken, the hair cut rough, as if with garden shears or a straight razor, where he isn't completely bald—this basketball of a head bobs around on its own as if it were unconnected to his neck and shoulders. Hunter Thompson looks exactly like a six-foot-four-inch newborn baby whose mother has been drinking for weeks.

Seated and talking, Thompson says he doesn't follow the changes in Aspen anymore. He rarely visits the town, he claims. They don't allow smoking there, he says. And he lifts the menu from a pack of Dunhills, the way a gambler might take his napkin off a derringer, and plugs the butt of a fresh cigarette into his Franklin Delano Roosevelt holder. The ashtray is filling with butts. "Woody Creek is an oasis," he says, jabbing a hand toward the smoky pool table and the sign behind the bartender that reads NO SNIVELERS.

"We don't allow the swine up here," mumbles Thompson in his trademark growl. By "swine," he means health addicts and real estate developers from nearby Aspen, mostly.

The bard of Woody Creek is willing to talk about AIDS in southern Florida, branding rituals among college fraternities, sex and money in Aspen —but only for a minute. What really gets him hot and sweaty is the upcoming permit hearing on the Woody Creek gravel pit.

Gravel! Greed! Pollution! "The relationship between Elam [owners of the gravel pit] and Pitkin County is the same as between the U.S. and the military industrial complex!" the lawyer representing Thompson's side of the argument had railed a week before. "I don't go around trying to tear up your yard," Thompson had shouted at the lords of the gravel pit during the last hearing, "I don't even know where it is. If I did, I would."

Hunter Thompson has plunged into the Great Gravel Pit Debate with the joy of a hungry grizzly coming upon a clearing of feasting nudists.

Since Thompson, unlike Danny Wardwell, Buddy Hackett, the mayor, and most of the rest of Aspen, has not let health concerns sidetrack him, he has plenty of energy to devote to the important things in life, like real estate development. Development is big money in Aspen, and as we are discovering, making money—and stopping money from being made—is the new erotic entertainment. Far from being boring, the endless hearings over new hotel construction, wilderness access, and gravel pit policy take on the character of catfights in a whorehouse. It is a battle royal between rebels and establishment, but this being Aspen, the antidevelopment rebels are usually just as rich as the greed-heads, so called. The real party action in town, we are about to learn, now takes place at Pitkin County Commission hearings, no longer in the meat locker of a Wardwell nightclub.

The nefarious gravel pit sits in a hole on the flat above the tavern, about two miles down creek from Thompson's house. For a gravel pit, it is very pretty, very Aspen, sunk low and lined with high-tech machinery, but to Thompson it is *The Pit of Hell*. Woody Creek residents want county officials to monitor pollution at the pit, reroute the access road, and limit the duration of the company's operating permit.

Some pretty heavy timber testified at the first pit hearing. Outlaw millionaire Don Johnson of "Miami Vice" showed up, and rock star Don Henley, formerly of the Eagles, flew in from Malibu, where he was recording his next album. The two Dons, as they are called in Aspen, are Thompson's neighbors. Good neighbors, too, since they don't seem to complain when live fire erupts long after midnight outside the Thompson residence.

The fluorescent lights were bright in the ancient brick courthouse in the center of Aspen where the hearing was held. Henley and Johnson kept their sunglasses on, even though it was nighttime. This caused Pitkin County Commissioner Tom Blake to don his own sunglasses. In Aspen, being a county commissioner is a lot bigger deal than being a movie star or a rock idol, and Blake, who usually drinks a couple cans of cold Coors at meetings, did not want to be upstaged.

"I'm sorry I won't be able to stay around to watch democracy in progress here," said Johnson, who is currently the most famous and least likely upholder of the New Aspen Sobriety, since after a lifetime in the lobby of the Hotel California, he publicly swore off cocaine and liquor. Johnson needed to leave the hearing early for a film shoot. But he and Henley had been bitten with the populist bug. "Some of these stars try for twenty years to be accepted," another county commissioner would tell us. "The Great Gravel Pit

Hearings made these guys instant locals." From L.A., Johnson and Henley soon sent Commissioner Blake a present—a "fabulous, bitchin' assortment of the latest shades from France, Italy, Japan, etc."

"Dear Tom," the Dons wrote Blake, "It's so lonely and difficult being us. We're just so darn misunderstood. Sometimes, rich, famous sensitive guys like us simply have no choice but to retreat behind our dark glasses so we can be left alone to contemplate life's deep, dark secrets. When we've got our sunglasses on, we feel safe, but, more importantly, we look cool—and you know, Tom, looking cool is probably the most important thing in life. In America, if you look cool, you don't have to know anything, or say anything, or be anything, or stand for anything. All you have to do is look cool and people love you! Ask Reagan! . . . These things are going to change your life, Tom. You're finally gonna get it all!—the bucks, the babes, the power, the respect that you deserve!"

At the April 12 hearing, the general manager of the gravel pit, a calm giant named Hal Clark, shows up in aviator's sunglasses and a "Miami Vice" cap. The pit boss has a sense of humor. Don Henley, his adversary and the man who is paying much of the legal costs for the opposition, looks much more earnest in a white dress shirt and washed jean jacket, his hair pulled behind his head in a short tail.

The thinking man's redneck, County Commissioner Fred Crowley, yet another reformed party animal *in extremis,* is there. Crowley is one of the people Thompson called "swine" at the Woody Creek Tavern, but Thompson himself is not present. "I was worried Hunter might show up with his golf clubs," Crowley tells us later in his gravelly bark. This is an allusion to a recent incident at the Aspen Municipal Golf Course when Thompson pulled a shotgun from his golf bag and fired a salvo at the wayward ball of a foursome that had gotten too close, or else at his own hopelessly hooked ball, or perhaps simply to discourage one of his partners whom he suspected of cheating. Motivation is often unclear in Aspen. One of Thompson's partners, "60 Minutes" correspondent Ed Bradley, says that he happened to be looking the other way at the time and was unable to see a thing.

"Hey," Commissioner Crowley tells us during the break, "I like Henley and Johnson personally. I even like that Looney Tune Thompson. But rich people in Aspen think they shit little golden pellets. Nobody wants a hotel or a gravel pit next to their home."

At a predetermined moment, the Woody Creekers call for a show of support. Which means that two thirds of the audience whips out sunglasses and puts them on. In opposition, Commissioner Crowley installs pink Groucho Marx glasses at the end of his own red nose. The hearing lasts from seven to midnight, and most of Aspen stays up to watch the show on closed-circuit television.

"This is the way Aspen used to be in 1974," Don Henley tells us afterward. "People getting together and deciding things." In the seventies, Henley had cowritten "Life in the Fast Lane." Now he, too, seems to be turning into the concerned country gentleman.

"Call it a new sobriety if you want, but what's happened is that people have set down roots in the last ten years. We're older," he says, "and we don't like what a certain type of money is doing to this town. I especially don't like the kind of money Donald Trump and Mohammad Hadid [an American-Palestinian investor] represent." Rival moguls Trump and Hadid have been trying to construct a $100 million Ritz-Carleton hotel at the base of Aspen Mountain. "Trump and Hadid are assholes, and you can quote me on that," says Henley.

Joining the new baby boom yourself? we ask. "Not me," says Henley, always the straight man. "I'm into population control."

In Aspen, unlike Key West, the fear of AIDS has not contributed much to the antiparty mix. The aging of the seventies generation, the switch from drugs to health, and the preoccupation with money—making it, displaying it, protesting its rudeness—are all more important.

"AIDS may be a valid paranoia in New York and San Francisco," John Glisman, an emergency-room physician, tells us, "but it was only a brief hysteria here. AIDS is the kind of virus you've got to bend over backward to get. The gays lowered their hygiene to the level of a Third World country."

Glisman, or Dr. Bud, as everyone calls him, says that a couple of years ago healthy heterosexuals flooded the hospital to be tested, but these skiers, rock climbers, and kayakers in peak condition soon realized they were clearly HIV-negative. Today heterosexuals are relieved but no longer as promiscuous. "I still sportfish. I no longer sportfuck," as a patrician gentleman tells us. AIDS became a joke told on less fortunate urban areas.

At the third annual Aspen Gong Show, for instance, first prize went to Ed

Cross and the Aspen Condoms, a repeat engagement advertised as "The Second Coming," and second place went to a guitarist named Muff, billed as being from San Francisco, who sang of the gay life in a tune called "Muff, the Tragic Faggot," a reworking of "Puff, the Magic Dragon." The Aspen Gong Show has often served as a repository for the darker side of the town's unconscious. It's easier to laugh at other people's problems. The simple fact is that Aspen believes AIDS to be a *them*, not an *us*, disease. At least one local gay man has died of AIDS, and his lover committed suicide; but both deaths were hushed up. In Aspen there is an unkind horror of anything unclean.

This horror is narcissistic, but it is Aspen's narcissism, ironically, that has saved the town from the fate of Key West. Whereas Key West refused to call a halt to its sexual carnival, Aspen recoiled at the spectacle of drug dealer Grabow's murder and abruptly changed from a sex-and-coke high to a health-and-sport high. Aspen is like a beautiful young skier. Indulgent, superficial perhaps, certainly overly concerned with looks, tan, and technique. But perfectly willing to abandon any vice that interferes with winning. The nightmare of a Jim Mayer would be hard to imagine in this most perfect of mountain resorts.

The downside to Aspen's narcissism is that perfection attracts notice. Aspen may be killing the goose that laid the golden egg. The more pristine the mayor and the county commissioners keep the town, the more unique the place becomes. The more developers of the tacky Waikiki and Donald Trump variety are forced to conform to the Victorian elegance of the Aspen ideal, the more the truly rich want to buy here. "It's becoming the Palm Beach syndrome," says Sheriff Braudis. "The town is starting to revolve around a few seasonal millionaires, and the guests at their parties are all the same people in tuxedos staring at each other."

"New money," Steve Crockett repeats, "doesn't know how to party."

As Banana Days broke up and turned into summer, Sandy Cohen and about twenty-five other guys packed up on their Harleys ("no rice burners allowed") and buzzed over Independence Pass to Leadville for ice creams.

"Just like the Hollywood people," Cohen explains, "the young actors and the young studio execs who want to hang out with the young actors. It's fun. It's just like the fifties, being on Harleys."

"If Hollywood goes moped," says Steve Crockett, "then next year the

Boogies crowd will turn in their Harleys and ride pink mopeds. You gotta pray for a recession or holocaust or an AIDS plague. It's the only way out."

Aspen. Land of the rich and reformed.

Chico

It is raining buckets through the soft foliage that covers Chico, California, in the spring. A police car drives slowly by the little party. Its spotlight grazes the off-campus bungalow. John Manning, at this moment a fairly inebriated student resident of the new Chico—that is, Chico after the wondrous bonfire-in-the-street hellzapoppin' riot of 1987—jumps to attention. His friend, a former officer of the Tekes, the Chico State fraternity proud to claim Neil Armstrong and Ronald Reagan as national alumni, shakes his head. "Better turn it down," he says to Manning. "Heat of the Night" by Bryan Adams is playing on the small stereo, but hardly blasting.

A drunken kid in the living room unwinds his long arms from a chubby girl in a blue minidress. Like everyone else, he is holding a plastic glass full of vodka and grape juice. He sets the drink down on a packing crate coffee table. "Did he really flash on us?" the kid asks.

"Yes, turn it down," says Manning, disgusted.

"Damn," says the kid, but he turns the music to a whisper.

"It's so hot in Chico," *Playboy*'s campus party critic wrote before that big Pioneer Days riot of 1987, "it'll make your skin bubble." That year *Playboy* declared Chico State, which is 180 miles northeast of San Francisco, to be the Number One Party School in the nation. Now, a year later, Manning rails, "Living here is like being in that movie *Escape from New York,* you know? Our parties are monitored! Our every move is marked! We're prisoners!" Manning throws up his hands in hurt exaggeration. Manning's a big guy, thick and gangly at the same time, a bit like Chico's famous Sir Joseph Hooker oak— biggest oak in the world, they say. But he has a serious point.

We visited Chico, California, twice, first in the spring of 1987 and then a year later. In 1988 the easygoing party capital of collegiate America was undergoing a hideous clampdown. As well as facing certain new sexual realities . . .

Nineteen-year-old Mark Loper sits in the command center of Big Mike Condoms delivery service, which happens to be Mark Loper's bedroom. Loper is Big Mike's sales manager. A red mountain bike hangs on hooks over his waterbed. A Commodore computer is nestled into the bookshelf. "Girls come in," smiles Mark, "they say, 'You're a pervert, right?' because I have six hundred condoms beside my bed."

The condom delivery service in the comic strip "Doonesbury" is modeled after an enterprise like Big Mike's, which was one of the first in the country. It's a full-service concept. Students call into Mark's bedroom hotline, and order up Nuda Plus or Conture Form-Fitting or Stimula Vibra-Ribbed. Colors are no longer available. The price is three for $3, which includes delivery. If customers want, they can have Extra Strength with nonoxynol-9, the spermicide that offers additional protection against the AIDS virus. "Females," says Mark, who is a business major from Placerville, "often purchase our optional condom wallet, which keeps the condoms secluded. That way, they don't have to fumble through their purses." Females, as Mark calls them, account for some 40–50 percent of purchases. Mark plots all sales and customer demographics on his computer. Big Mike's makes as much money from its T-shirts as from actual condom sales. It's become cool in some circles to sport a T-shirt that says PROTECTED BY BIG MIKE on the back. "Especially by females whose boyfriends are named Mike," explains Mark.

At precisely 12:06 A.M. a call comes in.

"Big Mike's . . . You're interested in a regular fit? . . . Uh-huh . . . First name? . . . Uh-huh . . . Address? . . . Rio Linda off the Esplanade . . . All right, I shall be there in fifteen minutes."

Condom run!

Mark throws a coat over his SPUDS MCKENZIE, THE ORIGINAL PARTY ANIMAL T-shirt, the one that has Spuds surfing in sunglasses, and we pile into Mark's new Toyota GTS sportscar. This vehicle, as Mark refers to cars, goes 155 m.p.h. when he wants it to. John Lee Hooker is playing on the tape deck. Mark hits a switch and the headlights pop up from the shiny hood. *Vroom!* Condom run! It makes no sense at all, to us, to scream through the rain-slicked streets of Chico in a $20,000 sports car to deliver condoms worth $3. But then profit does not seem to be the entire motive behind Big Mike's. "We want to make condoms a household item," says Mark, "rather than something to be feared."

Mark sweeps his hand across the interior as he makes a crisp left turn through a yellow light. "Look at this rain. I think it's romantic."

Soon enough, we pull into the parking lot of a modern apartment house complex. Mark raps politely on a green door. A suave blond kid wearing only a white Chico State sweatshirt and skivvies appears. It is dark behind him.

The kid arches his eyebrows. "Big Mike's?"

Mark hands him the little fake-suede condom wallet full of Stimula Vibra-Ribbeds. "Could you sign our disclaimer?"

"First name OK?" asks the kid, which we thought was pretty savvy.

"Sure," says Mark.

The disclaimer slip states that condoms during intercourse are not 100 percent safe in the prevention of sexually transmitted diseases and pregnancy and that Big Mike's is merely a distributor. Mark also hands the customer a one-page safe-sex fact sheet.

The kid does not read the disclaimer. He signs with a flourish, tips Mark a dollar, and disappears into the dark apartment, as many as three rounds of protected and untold pleasure awaiting him.

"Girls are the ones who think about AIDS around here," a blond sorority woman is telling us, "because they have a hidden agenda. They're really more worried about getting pregnant than they are about catching some STD. AIDS is a great excuse to ask a guy to put on a condom."

Her friend, our hostess, nods. The day after the condom run with Big Mike's we are attending a preparty sorority party, which means an off campus warm-up to one of the big events of the year, the annual all-Chico sorority-fraternity dance. Like John Manning's party, this one is small. All over town, police and campus authorities are cracking down.

The little cottage is painted mud-brown, and there is an aquamarine 1968 Mustang in the driveway. On one wall of the living room hangs a poster for *Friday the 13th,* and on the other wall, one for the "Art of the Vatican" exhibit. The guests are cute as buttons, everyone wearing pastel shorts and T's, the girls, especially, all a little butterfattish. Since Chico is such an innocent place at heart, it seems to attract innocent bodies. Our hostess has blue eyes and black hair and a pin on her shorts that says WHERE'S THE PARTY? A tall goof, easily six feet six, picks up a heavy stand lamp and holds it behind his head. "Am I in your light?" he asks the hostess. Before she can answer, he whips out a black Luger with his other hand and shoots her across the chest. From her purse the hostess grabs a little pink pistol of her own and fires back. A royal waterfight ensues. The guests are armed. Under a steady stream of water and giggles, we ask questions about AIDS and the changing sexual behavior among riotous and innocent youth.

AIDS is a scary thought, these students tell us, but Chico is seen to be an insular community. There are no needle drugs. Gays live in far-off San Francisco or Los Angeles. *Don't you know any gay people on campus?* No, everybody insists. And they keep drenching each other with water pistols, until the guns run dry. Then the kids stop to tank up on Welch's Grape Juice and cheap jug vodka, which seems to be the cocktail of choice about town.

We decide to check the new sexual attitudes in a more scientific way, with a survey. Fortunately, Professor Gayle Kimball, director of ethnic and women's studies at Chico State, has already conducted one.

Kimball is a gender scholar who wrote *50–50 Marriage* and *50–50 Parenting*. She is a tall woman with a flip of dark pepper hair and a fast laugh. Everything and anything holds meaning for Kimball, whether it is her seven-year-old son's habit of hunting salamanders and birds ("Hunting seems almost instinctual in small boys") or the memory of the dark "necking room" at her own sorority on the UC-Berkeley campus in the mid-1960s. "I would have been mortified to go in that room, but it held a certain fascination for me."

The little class survey makes for interesting reading.

A majority of the fifteen women responded that what turned them on the most visually was a guy's eyes, and that neck and ear kissing turned them on the most physically. For the sixteen men, it was the figure as well as the eyes, and oral sex in addition to neck kissing. No men and only two women were virgins. Everyone looked forward to monogamy in marriage. One girl had tried a homosexual experience, but none of the boys, with three boys answering "Fuck, no!" "Absolutely not!" and "No way, never, gross!" Three boys said they had been sexually abused by homosexuals. Three girls had also been abused, presumably by heterosexuals. Breast size mattered to only four of the boys, and penis size mattered to only two of the girls ("The bigger the better," and "Size is a great deal"). Thirteen of the boys felt "positive" when girls initiated matters ("Love it!" or "Love it, want it, wish for it"), while only seven of the women felt comfortable doing so. The guys always climaxed, and the gals usually did, except for three. In short, Kimball's class was a red-blooded bunch, neither prim nor promiscuous, although perhaps a bit more fascinated with sex than other undergraduates, or why did they bother to take the course?

Now to the meat of the matter. Only four of the women responded that AIDS had changed their sexual behavior, while seven of the men did. But the women in Kimball's class who did worry expressed their feelings strongly: "Abstinence is fine for me till I meet someone I love and *trust*. AIDS is a killer. Why should I take a chance with a one-night stand?" "I feel really strongly about making the guy wear a condom, not because I'm afraid of getting pregnant—that's mutual—but because of diseases! It's scary." "Yes, I'm less sexual and, if sexual, more protected." Many of the women who made no changes in response to AIDS were in relationships, they said, but the others offered no explanation. The men were equally laconic, but of those who made changes, the change was to wear a condom and "get around less."

By and large, then, students in Chico seemed only mildly cautious—aware of new risks, sometimes worried—but hardly as obsessed with health as Aspenites had been or as demoralized as the betrayed Conchs of Key West. "Students are concerned," explains Kimball, "but they think, 'It won't happen to me.' Then they go to a party and get drunk and meet some luscious person and forget everything."

But on our first visit to Chico, students were even less concerned. Back then, Big Mike's was only a gleam in Mark Loper's eye; a sorority woman would not have thought to use AIDS as a polite excuse to induce her date to slip on a condom in order to protect against pregnancy; and men did not shrug and find it prudent to "get around less."

No, in the good old days, in the middle 1980s, things were a bit wilder on the Chico party front. Balls out, actually.

Soon after Police Chief John Bullerjahn arrived in Chico from Palo Alto, California, he went on an introductory patrol. It was a balmy spring evening, he told us on our first visit to town, in 1987. The dry heat of the valley had cooled. The new chief admired the serenity of Bidwell Park, one of the largest slices of urban greenery in the country. At the edge of the city, which nestles against the Sacramento River just west of the Sierras, the almond orchards were blooming and the delicate bushy trees seemed to be strung with white popcorn. The musk of dogwood and magnolia filled the air. The chief cruised through the old downtown area, with its red brick buildings. Downtown was as quiet as Bidwell Park, but then, just past the university, the patrol car entered Fraternity Row. To the new chief, something seemed wrong, very wrong. There was a strange sound that Bullerjahn would later describe tersely as "the hum."

At first the chief thought the hum might be a bad electrical generator or even millions of swarming bees. He commanded the sergeant to stop the car. They rolled down the windows. The hum increased.

"Sergeant," asked the chief, "what's that hum?"

The sergeant smiled. He started the car again and they drove on a few blocks. Here was the source of the problem: a medium-sized white house in the middle of the block. The hum wasn't bees. It was people. Hundreds and hundreds of them sitting on the roof, hanging out of the windows, milling across the lawn, doing what Chicoans do best—partying. The chief started counting guests. He quit at twelve hundred.

Bullerjahn would learn that the gathering, a "hummer," was nothing more than the fraternity kickoff to Chico's main event, called Pioneer Days, a week of beery debauchery held each spring—until 1988.

For several years, Pioneer Days had been getting out of hand. Many of Chico State's fourteen thousand students were skipping classes. The fraternities had collapsed the two weekends of the celebration into nine days of hard partying. Motorcycle clubs in the Sierra were marking the event on their calendars. Something had to be done.

University president Robin Wilson, the science fiction writer and former master spy for the CIA (of which more later), declared, "Every time a group of students does something to reinforce the image of this school being a party school, they are lowering the value of their degrees." Chief Bullerjahn sent patrols into the frat houses with sound meters. The Greeks capitulated.

Not so the off-campus residents of the "Zoo." The Zoo is a several-block-square apartment complex officially named Sierra West Apartments. It is clean and modern enough, but the Zoo had become to partying what the Okefenokee Swamp is to alligators.

Certain residents were bitter that Robin Wilson was trying to civilize Pioneer Days. They pasted up flyers around town advertising a bring-your-own-keg party for the upcoming Saturday. The affair was to begin at eleven in the morning. By afternoon, three thousand revelers had shown up. Perhaps another thousand more would join them by sunset.

Who is to say what makes a good party? Certainly three or four thousand people and an unlimited amount of beer do not hurt. A hot spring day helps too. A pool for skinny-dipping also. The thrill of a phalanx of armed police hovering in the street, conferring with the owners of the apartment complex. Hundreds of stereos blaring Run-DMC, Talking Heads, and Bob Seger. Then as the night wears on, a few bonfires in the trash dumpsters, fueled from time to time by a fresh sofa or bookcase.

"At night the flames *were* a little dramatic, OK," Chief Bullerjahn explained. "But people have got to let off a little steam. That's almost healthy. It wasn't a moral event, but we don't see ourselves as moral guardians. Within the boundaries of the law, people have a right to party. Look, it was a ten-to-twelve-hour event with that many thousands of people, and nobody was raped, robbed, or beaten. To my way of thinking, that does not connote a seriously negative event."

Still, there was the little matter of the branding. . . .

PARTY WAS PAINFUL FOR BRANDED PARTICIPANT the Chico *Enterprise-Record* headlined it. "A Chico man who passed out at a mammoth weekend party awoke to find he'd been branded on his right arm by so-far unidentified attackers."

The picture that accompanied this report showed a twenty-one-year-old car mechanic naked to the waist. A crown of elfin curls circled his head. A white gauze bandage was pulled back from his right shoulder and underneath was a three-inch red welt in the shape of the letter C. The mechanic looked bewildered. This must have been what *Playboy*'s party critic meant when he said the town was so hot it would make your skin bubble.

But what did this disgusting pink C stand for?

Our first guess was that the C stood for Chico, but Chico lovers usually get a bumper sticker with a heart on it and leave it at that.

Since truth, the amusing darker truth of undergraduate life, was our business now, we made it a point to ask. The best answer came from a sophomore with black wet-moussed hair. She was not shy. "I know those guys. The C stands for Coors, Copenhagen, and a derogatory word for girl."

Aptly put.

We drove to the scene of the crime. Fortunately, we were driving a lung-red 1952 Buick Super, the car with the whale-mouth grille. At the last minute, we had thought to ask the commuter airline that flies to Chico International if they took dogs. No, said the clerk. The plane was too small, especially for ninety-pound malamutes. So we were smoothing around College Town, U.S.A., in a classic car with a backseat big enough to mate sheep in, accompanied by a very large and, to most people's way of thinking, vicious-looking husky. Arctic Ed does not brake for dobermans—or Spuds McKenzie either. All of this is to say that for this chapter we happened to be traveling with icebreakers, which counts in searching out party maniacs.

We pulled the Buick up to the end side of the Zoo, where half a dozen guys were drinking beer and tossing around a football, including big-as-an-oak John Manning, who with Gayle Kimball would become our Chico Virgil. These guys were big and they were fearless. Ted Mahoney, a six-foot-three-inch madman with narrow-set blue eyes and a shock of blond hair, reached down without introduction, grabbed Arctic Ed by the upper jaw and tossed about a pint of beer down Ed's throat. We were shocked. Ed was shocked. Everybody else laughed. Tomorrow Mahoney—who sleeps under a Budweiser quilt, his head on a Budweiser pillow, with his most prized possession, a framed picture of his dead German shepherd, on his nightstand and a framed picture of the second most important thing in his life, his girlfriend, on his dresser—would be in a foul mood, since he would be thrown out of the Graduate when a friend accidentally breaks a shot glass full of tequila, and still later he would be forced to disarm a neighbor in the Zoo who was thinking of slicing him up with a kitchen knife simply because Mahoney had offered the neighbor's angry blond girlfriend a place to sleep on his couch. Such is college life.

Manning and Mahoney offered a tour of what the Zoo was like during the Pioneer Days kickoff party. They pointed out the pool where kids were skinny-dipping, the location of the burning sofas, and so forth.

"You really want to know what happened that night?" Manning finally asked. "Come on."

We put Ted in the backseat with Ed and cruised over to a dilapidated pseudo-Tudor structure a few blocks away. Above the front door of this Nor Cal Animal House was spray-painted COORS! It was not sober handwriting.

Inside was mayhem. It was an hour after sunset, but everybody seemed to be getting up. The decor made Manning's disheveled bungalow look like the Metropolitan Museum of Art.

These guys called themselves the Booze Pirates. Sure they were at the Zoo that night. Sure, they were into branding. The Booze Pirates had done a branding in Hawaii one time, and at Notre Dame, and at a college in Colorado. "Once," yelled our friend Manning, "you guys even tried to brand me! Remember?" Manning, who was wearing one of those CHICO #1 PARTY SCHOOL IN THE U.S.A. T-shirts we kept seeing around town, had wriggled out of the chair before the Booze Pirates could get a good grip on him.

A short, muscular guy named Kevin Steil had been taking a nap. He had to bartend at the Graduate that night. He yawned and pointed to his shoulder before he threw on a yellow Hawaiian shirt.

There it was, another three-inch C. This one was brown and smooth, a chiaroscuro swirl of artistic scar tissue.

Did the branding hurt?

"Nah," said Steil. "Maybe a little afterward. Once I brushed the scab against a door. That hurt."

Aren't you worried they're permament?

"No, they fade in about six years," he said. "Then you have to burn the brand back on."

The original C, like the later brands, was fashioned from a coat hanger. The prototype C still exists, burned into the wall behind the spice shelf in the kitchen, beneath a plastic Art Deco Coors lamp.

"We didn't even know that guy," said Steil. "He showed up at the party at the Zoo, and somebody said we were going to be doing some branding, and this guy was drunk. He really wanted to go first, and so we sat him down in the chair and"—Steil put his two fists together and made a shove gesture, like a cowboy branding a heifer—"so we did it, and then he came on to the girls too much. He was so drunk, we put him outside. He wanted it." Steil had hard eyes.

"You guys ever consider joining the army?" we asked.

"We got our own army," said one Booze Pirate.

These guys seemed to be wolf-packers, more comfortable in the company of other men. Were there any female Pirates? Well, one, somebody would explain. The girl really wanted a C on her breast, but the guys didn't feel they could do that. The woman insisted. So the Pirates burned a small and ladylike C on her forearm.

This was like talking to vampires on their day off.

Breakfast with the Booze Pirates made us late for dinner with Gayle Kimball. Naturally, Gayle was fascinated to hear of the branding. "Jesus," she said, "that's aberrant behavior." To Kimball, the Pirates were at once similar to, and different from, other college men in transition from adolescence to adulthood. "Most young men want to be part of a group," she said, "push limits, take risks, see how virile they are. Football players, for instance, go out on the field and get banged up and crunched in part to prove they're not pansy-assed. There's a theory along these lines that says males need to break away from their mothers, and part of the process is proving they're not like women.

"But the branders are pushing beyond social limits. They're accepting a lot of pain—so much it almost makes you think they're feeling guilty about something, that the branding is a form of self-punishment. In the old days, trappers and woodsmen could push out their aggressive anger on the frontier, and for thousands of years before that humans were hunter-gatherers. It's unrealistic not to acknowledge that we may be carrying some of that inheritance. The branders could be seen as creating their own little hunter-warrior society, only these days there's no real outlet for their aggression and they've turned in on themselves."

To Kimball, the branding constitutes an initiation ritual, a painful act that proves a boy has the courage to become a man. In this view, the Booze Pirate branding ritual is really not very different from the tattooing of a boy's face in tribal society or the cutting of his foreskin. "About the only male initiation ritual left in America is getting your driver's license," said Kimball.

The crazy pain of these rituals has a purpose too. "At first it must be awful," said Kimball, "then afterward it turns to euphoria. Ultimately it becomes transformative. Women don't need these rituals so much because they have the birth process. Think how similar that is. First there is great pain, then intense euphoria, and afterward you are by definition an adult. Men don't have that, and some men need ritual more than others, especially if they are the sort of guys who may be ambiguous about their virility or who have less advanced social and intellectual skills, and the Booze Pirates qualify, compared to other Chico students, who are a pretty slick bunch of young people."

After the Booze Pirates, Kimball agreed to help show us a more civilized side of campus life. We were beginning to agree with her that American society offers a very unclear path to adulthood.

We started out at a "101" party sponsored by the Red Barn, an elite group of fun-lovers. Admission was by membership only, and there was a firm list at the door. It was like crashing a New York club, except that the Red Barners had a good reason for being restrictive. This party required an equal number of boys and girls.

Even from a block away we could hear the whistle, every sixty seconds like a foghorn. As we got closer, you could hear the giggles too. Another minute's pause . . . some sort of shuffling . . . another seal trainer's whistle . . . more giggling.

In the backyard of a one-story house, the Red Barners had set up about fifty folding chairs in a big circle. All the guys were sitting on the chairs. The girls were sitting on the guys' laps. Inside the circle were some kegs, Miller and Miller Lite, and a platform where Steve Bass, the whistle-blower, stood. Bass, known to everyone as "Iguana," was a charmer. Iguana would blow his crazy whistle and everybody would hold out a glass. Pourers ran around the circle and filled the glasses. Iguana would blow again. The girls would jump up, or try to, giggling and wobbly, and smooch onto the next lap clockwise.

The idea was to swallow 101 glasses of beer, getting to know fellow club members in the process. Break the ice without falling off chair or lap.

By the time we arrived with Professor Kimball, the Red Barners had already finished sixty-six rounds. At round sixty-nine (get it?) Iguana tooted his ridiculous chrome whistle, shouting, "Time for a switch! Everybody up! Men on women!" There was a lot of whooping at this. The place looked like a seal refuge at the height of rut. Kimball leaped up with the best of them. Perhaps she appreciated the nonsexist turn of events. Perhaps she was glad to be part of an adolescent initiation ritual that was nonviolent. Although, who knows? Discipline was breaking down. . . . All good, clean fun, of course, especially for Professor Kimball, who was, unlike everybody else, a teetotaler. "Getting smashed is not my idea of a good time," she said.

Iguana laid into his whistle like a drunken coastguardsman. Later he told us that the Red Barners never made it past ninety rounds.

When *Playboy* picked Chico as the Number One Party School in the nation, President Wilson had said appropriately, "I'm appalled, horrified, disgusted." He seemed to mellow a little after the magazine decided to photograph the women of Chico State. "I'm not overjoyed, but what can I do? 'Let us pray that we have a sound mind and a sound body,' " he quoted Juvenal. "We are delighted at Chico State to display for all comers our sound minds."

When one of your authors met with Wilson in 1987, he had thrown up his hands. "Needless to say, I'm not thrilled by the situation. College presidents don't usually like their universities to be known as party schools."

A former spy with the CIA, Robin Wilson was an unusual character for a college president. Wilson had been in clandestine operations in Berlin. "I was a case officer. The German word for that is *Spionmeister,* or 'master spy.' A case officer would have a string of agents, to whom he would give assignments under clandestine circumstances—give them money and so on."

Wilson was a big-bellied jolly fellow who laughed a lot. "Maybe," he said on that first visit, throwing up his hands once again, "we should just put a big papier-mâché olive in our thirty-foot satellite dish. It already looks like a martini glass anyway."

A few weeks later, closer to the beginning of Pioneer Days, Wilson appeared to have second thoughts. "I don't think any town wants to put up with what Palm Springs and Fort Lauderdale put up with," he said in a statement. "If we see a great influx of outsiders, I will take the thing [Pioneer Days] out in the backyard and shoot it in the head."

Unfortunately, it proved to be a bad year to keep a good riot down. *Playboy*'s designation in its January issue had ensured media attention, and then MTV, the rock 'n' roll channel, began to broadcast that adventurous viewers might want to "check out Pioneer Days and see if the Number One Party School in the nation lives up to its reputation."

It did. Thousands came north, some in chartered buses with CHICO OR BUST!!! on the sides. In the traditional off-campus kickoff, some two thousand students and outsiders did a lot of beer drinking, a certain amount of bottle breaking, and bit of sofa burning. One hundred and twenty-five police were called in from outlying towns; seventy-five celebrants were arrested and thirty injured.

Wilson blamed outside agitators and MTV. "I feel totally suckered by MTV. It was a scurrilous abuse of journalism . . . a cynical piece of work . . . trying to entice people to come here and then filming the ensuing carnage."

"We weren't even there," protested MTV vice president Doug Herzog, although the channel had asked Wilson's permission to film Pioneer Days for a "School's Out Weekend" special.

The Booze Pirates and others assumed it was all a big setup. They believed that Chico State may have had enough with Pioneer Days and was looking for an excuse to call the whole thing off for a few seasons.

After the university took the festival into the backyard and shot it like a rabid dog, as threatened, the city council decided to create its own party: Rancho Chico Days. Except that Rancho Chico Days was to be a sober affair. No drinking. No bottles. They even banned paper cups along the parade route.

The day after the parade is the Coors Omnium Bicycle Race. We meet on a street corner with Booze Pirates Bill Merrell and Kevin Steil while packs of racers on ten-speeds shoot by us and the crowd cheers. We expect that by now most of the guys may have graduated from branding rituals to knocking over liquor stores. We are wrong.

Most of the guys are studying hard now in order to graduate. The older Pirates already have jobs. The Booze Pirates have also given up competitive drinking. For several years at Riley's, their tavern hangout, the Pirates had finished first in the keg-drinking contests, where teams of ten guys would see who could drink a sixteen-gallon keg first. But as they have aged, they have declined to take part in the contests. As for the branding, this still goes on, but most new recruits elect to take the hot C on their right leg, a more discreet location. Most interesting, five members of the club are to be married by the end of the summer, and two have already taken the fall. No more wolf-packing. You'll have to have Booze Pirate reunions, we joke. Turns out they already have. The boys rented a houseboat on Lake Shasta, packing away a dozen kegs or so, and partied for a week.

Like John Manning and his friends—and the sorority women too—the Booze Pirates believe Chico is losing its community feel. For as long as anyone could remember, Chico State had been a strange pocket of paradise, like Sugar Mountain in the old Neil Young song, a place where nobody could grow old. True, things had gotten a bit crazy by the middle of the 1980s, what with three hundred twenty-one-year-olds jumping on bikes every Friday night and pedaling from bar to bar, tanking up on draft beer and laughing, until they fell asleep in each other's arms under the big trees like a ball of puppies. For more than a decade the kids had partied at the drop of a hat and for any reason. Nobody was ever hurt—or at most rarely. It was all so different from the rich suburbs where most of these children were from. There, in Marin or Orinda or West Los Angeles, as students explained to us again and again, nobody said hello on the streets; in fact, there were no streets, only cars, and it was all phoniness and California isolation. These students had chosen Chico State over anonymous San Diego or UCLA to get away from that.

So the times had changed. The mix was complicated, but the vectors all pointed in the same direction: too much drinking had led to riots, and riots had embarrassed the university and the town. Rules were put in order. A clampdown was imposed. Sobriety was not as fashionable yet as vodka and grape juice. Chico was not yet Aspen. But the direction was toward moderation. As for sex—well, sex in Chico had remained loose long after the rest of the country had chilled out, but now the students of Chico State, too, had suddenly become wise beyond their years. What makes youth what it is, that blissful ability not to think, was disappearing as quickly as coeds who didn't know the meaning of "STD."

We prefer to remember the town from the year before. Late one night, we had wandered into Hey, Juan!—the closest thing to a bohemian hangout in Chico, a small and loud bar where few entered sober and none left that way. As we arrived, a group of seven students were climbing on each other's backs to form a pyramid. Everybody clapped when the last kid clambered on top and raised a glass. We made our way to the back. There a group of English professors and a hale fellow named Steve Krakel, who had once driven from Chico to Managua in five days for sport, were downing pitchers of Sierra Nevada ale, the local brew. The conversation oscillated from *Playboy*'s attempt to promote "The Girls of Chico" to the two feral razorbacks penned in a cage in the back of a truck outside the bar, to the course of true love. Gary Thompson, Chico's local poet, squeezed his wife. It was his fortieth birthday.

He was shy and he was loose, but he raised a glass and freely quoted e. e. cummings:

> since feeling is first
> and kisses are a better fate
> than wisdom
> for life's not a paragraph
> and death i think is no parenthesis.

Chico, California. Party Town, U.S.A.

Washington Babylon

CHAPTER 4

NE

night in Georgetown, the fashionable brown-brick center of white Washington, while lovesick cicadas with red eyes buzz and bat against the windows and the air conditioner, as they have not done in the District for exactly seventeen years, Arturo Cruz, Jr., talks of how he once worked his way through the better whorehouses in Granada, Nicaragua, with a man old enough to be his father. This man at first enjoyed Arturo's company, and they had laughed out loud together and drunk rum, and the older man turned Arturo on to some tricks of the night, since Arturo was still very young.

But then Arturo began an affair with the man's daughter. This girl was beautiful and she was a virgin, but like the cicadas, she was awakening.

Her father could not handle what was happening. At first, he welcomed Arturo to his door and watched as he took his daughter to dinner. Much later that same night, if it was a weekend, he might find himself beside his prospective son-in-law in some elegant old plaster house where women made love for money. Both men grew confused, remembers Arturo. The older man, in fact, eventually became so agitated that he nearly suffered a heart attack.

Arturo draws a parallel between the father-son-daughter triangle in Nicaragua long ago and his more recent affair with Fawn Hall, the iron-lipped secretary to Lieutenant Colonel Oliver North, the patriotic enigma of the Reagan administration's Iran-Contra scandal. Arturo believes that the older men at the White House were jealous of his relationship with Fawn Hall. Only this time the jealousy did not carry an Oedipal aspect but rather a political one. What rankled these old goats was that Fawn, the secret long-haired beauty of their powerhouse basement, could fall for a foreigner.

"Oliver and the others were always trying to help the Nicaraguans," says Arturo, "yet they condescended to the real ones. It was Communism they cared about, not us."

Cruz, thirty-three, is the son of Arturo Cruz, Sr., the development banker who was once a member of the Sandinista directorate, as well as Nicaraguan ambassador to the United States. The elder Cruz resigned when he concluded that the new regime was becoming totalitarian and moved to the United States, where he became one of three top Contra leaders, only to step down again in 1987 when he decided that the Contras, too, were undemocratic. His son Arturo had been a Sandinista working in the revolutionary foreign ministry but had followed his father to Washington. There he soon became the leading ideologist of the Contras and principal aide to Eden Pastora, the legendary Commandante Zero who had been the Sandinistas' most famous battlefield commander before he, too, changed his mind and turned up as field marshal on the CIA's southern front. The Cruzes were complicated and sophisticated exiles.

For us, Arturo Jr. became the perfect guide to the Washington of the late 1980s. Wry and ever curious, he is both in love with the imperial capital and repelled by it. He can party most of the night near a Teddy Kennedy and still be shocked when some woman twenty or thirty years younger goes home with him. "Who is she sleeping with—the man or the senator?"

And like any ambitious young man from the colonies, he also brings with him a sense of perspective often lacking in the metropole. "There is more than a feeling of decline in Washington," he says. "There is total anarchy. What is the national purpose? What do you Americans want? What are you willing to defend? The old elite is tired, that political class that came over on the *Mayflower*. These people lack vitality, the blood. Such a powerful country, such incredible resources, yet your ruling class is so innocent. You require the cynical nature of us foreigners, the new Vietnamese, Cuban, and Nicaraguan immigrants. We have very big egos," he laughs. "We are convinced we can succeed anywhere. The problem is, by the time my generation of foreigners is ready to take over in this country, it will be too late to save the empire."

Always "the empire." In the summer, the younger Cruz is reading *The Decline of the West* by the bald German Oswald Spengler. By fall, Arturo has decided Spengler was "an idiot," and is paging through Jaroslav Pelikan's *Excellent Empire: The Fall of Rome and the Triumph of the Church,* as well as Paul Kennedy's *Rise and Fall of the Great Powers.* Come spring he has graduated to the hard stuff, Edward Gibbon's eighteenth-century classic *The Decline and Fall of the Roman Empire.* In the last years of the Reagan era, foreign-born and native intellectuals alike are running scared: was the American Century winding down after barely four decades? First came Cuba, then Vietnam, then OPEC, the overthrow of the Shah, the hostage-takings, the inroads of Japanese and German commerce, and, of course, the little revolution in Nicaragua.

Perhaps, Arturo sometimes mused, America's current sexual constriction is an outgrowth of an empire in decline. If a powerful country perceives itself as threatened from without, does the resulting anxiety produce a moral panic? For instance, at the beginning of the nineteenth century, the British—not yet in decline but nevertheless racked with syphilis and worried by the possibility of a French invasion following Napoleon's rise to power—had clamped down in the extreme on sexual frivolity. Similarly, the retrenchment that seemed to be occurring in the United States in the 1980s might be more than a reaction to AIDS and family disintegration, more than a swing toward couch-potatodom as wastrels of Arturo's baby-boom generation finally decided to have children. The zipper tightening might in fact be a reaction to foreign competition. Yes, the sexuality of an era could be linked to its politics, Arturo was willing to believe, although exactly how was always hard to say.

Besides possessing a sense of history, Arturo made a good observer, too, because he had an eye for the details. Seated at a luncheon beside Secretary of State George Shultz, he blocks out conversation and notices the secretary's watch: a Patek Philippe. Arturo is a student of watches. "A Pentagon guy would have a Rolex, the way the most powerful generals in Latin America do, including Castro. Castro has two gold Rolexes. Not that the Rolex is not a perfectly good watch. But it is a watch for generals." Like the decade, Arturo does not have morals. He has eyes.

Yet when it comes to love, Arturo is sincere. This is part of his charm. That hot night in the summer of 1987, as Oliver North was about to complete his testimony on Capitol Hill, Arturo tells us how he first met Fawn.

Cruz was talking to a State Department official. The man smiled at one point. "Arturo," he said, "you've got to see Colonel North."

"Why?" asked Arturo.

"Because he has the most beautiful secretary."

Cruz liked this idea, and a few days later he had occasion to visit North's offices across from the White House. He looked Fawn Hall over—her tousled hair, clean good looks, and imperfect teeth—and for some reason he told himself she wasn't beautiful enough.

A week later he again had business with North. This time, after staring at her for a few seconds, he decided that he would fall in love with this Fawn Hall.

The office was a small one. North, according to Cruz, drew him aside.

"Why are you looking at my secretary?" the colonel wanted to know.

"She's going to be my woman," said Arturo.

"What?" said North.

Cruz just stared at the colonel. For Arturo, the matter was decided.

Cruz is an intense, sharp man, very handsome, although the attraction is not so much in his looks. He is not Omar Sharif, even though his lips curl and his eyes are a dark riverbank green, and the bones of his face are strong. The attraction may be his ever-boyish charm. Boyish charm is a hard thing to define, of course, and it can cut both ways, especially as a young man ages. One time in Washington before he met Fawn Hall, Arturo fell in sight-love with the dark-haired daughter of a general. This woman was beautiful, like nearly all of Arturo's women, but she regarded him with, he remembers, an utter calm. He would ask her out. He would try to kiss her. The general's daughter always pulled away. She was several years younger than Arturo, but one evening she looked him square in those jade green eyes and told him that the reason she could never love him was that to her he would always be a boy.

Arturo laughs when he tells this story. Laughs and shrugs. He shifts from leg to leg, offers good red wine, which he doesn't drink himself, having given up most liquor a few years back, then slides into the desk chair before his Apple computer. The little Apple is flanked on the one side by his Ph.D. thesis, a part of which will be published in *The New Republic* a few months later under the cover title "The Absurdity of Nicaragua," and on the other side by a framed picture of then revolutionary Pastora and Edelberto Torres, the grand old man of the Central American left. Because of his history, Colonel North once asked U.S. counterintelligence agents to find out if Arturo was pumping Fawn for secrets to give to the Sandinistas. The officers determined Cruz was not a double agent, only love-stricken. Next to the picture of the old Communist is a photo of Mexican revolutionaries from the early part of this century. Arturo remarks that peasant armies, be they Contras or Zapata's peons, often fight savagely. Peasants don't fight, they murder, he shrugs, and it is a chilling shrug this time. Arturo does not lose sleep over accounts of Contra atrocities.

Cruz stands up. He sits down. Though he jogs several miles each day from his little apartment in Georgetown to Arlington National Cemetery and back, he never seems to slow down.

Even with the rented air conditioner on full blast, the room, with its hot, bright lights and books everywhere, is too warm. Arturo apologizes. He asks formal permission to change his clothes. He emerges from the bedroom in blue cotton shorts, running shoes, a polo shirt. He makes a joke about the cicadas clogging the air conditioner. Talks of how his father made the transition from Sandinista director to Contra leader to wealthy neutral, exiled in Miami with those ever-beached Cubans. He smiles at the mention of the Cubans. The CIA believed right-wing Nicaraguans to be pretty much the same thing as right-wing Cubans. They all had Mexican last names, right? He shrugs.

A Cruz shrug is a definitive gesture.

It is always tentative. When Arturo shrugs, he is asking a question that is up to the listener to answer. Arturo Cruz, Jr., is not the simple Central American peasant that occupies the imagination of American liberals. Arturo was educated at American University and Johns Hopkins. He greatly admired Oliver North, but with a shrug and a laugh, he agrees with North's own awkward assessment of himself that he, gap-toothed North, could never be a member of America's tribal elite the way certain newer, richer, and better-educated immigrants hoped to.

A week later we are seated on a bench along the Potomac. It is a sunny afternoon, too bright for the cicadas, who seem to prefer the night. Arturo cannot get Fawn Hall out of his mind. They broke up five times, he says. Each time, he admits, it was his fault.

He talks of their first date. Fawn asked him if he wanted to go to a certain movie. She asked him, he says, because he was too shy to ask her. Although Cruz can remember very well the pastel colors on the buildings in the small coffee towns of Nicaragua that he visited with his grandmother when he was a boy, he cannot recall the name of the movie. He does remember that Fawn drove her red Pontiac Fiero. Arturo usually refused to drive the Fiero because he considered it to be a hopelessly lame American imitation of a Ferrari. And he cringed at its personalized license plate: FAWN-3.

"How could I," shrugs Arturo staring at the boats on the river, "marry a woman whose name was Fawn? Really, Fawn was her given name. Yet I loved her. I loved that woman."

What Arturo loved about Fawn Hall is that she ordered his life. She helped him find his apartment. She was as loyal as a Latin woman. She still kept pictures of him in her bedroom, even now, as she testified before Congress. She had chosen him to be her man. Once, according to a source close to the National Security Council, when Arturo ran a brief mission to Europe for Oliver ("Ol-ee-ver," Arturo pronounces it), he promised Hall that he would be back in three days. Then North and the higher-ups decided the mission required more time. Arturo refused to stay any longer. But North would not take no for an answer. Finally, Hall stormed into North's sanctum and told him that if he did not allow Arturo to return as promised, she might never speak to Oliver again. Arturo loves this story. It tells him that Fawn Hall was more loyal to him, the Nicaraguan, than to North, the American colonel-boss, and it tells him as well that she was tough. Cruz believes that American women are tougher than other women—harder to deal with, but tougher. His nickname for Fawn Hall is "the Tough One."

At the movie, Fawn excused herself to go to the bathroom.

"What are you going to do, Fawn," shrugged Arturo, "pee or pooh?"

Fawn Hall was shocked. Nobody had ever spoken to her this way. To millions of Americans glued to the Contragate hearings on television, Hall was the bitch-princess of bureaucratic sangfroid, all legs and loyalty. But she was, after all, just a secretary who had grown up in the tract-house wasteland of suburban Washington, D.C. Fawn was impressed by rank, by stretch limousines, by Secret Service guards, by lines in front of certain clubs like Pisces in

Georgetown—by all the imperial affectations that made Arturo Cruz, Jr., shrug and laugh.

So Fawn stared at Arturo in the movie theater and Arturo smiled tentatively; and then, suddenly, they both cracked up. There was magic here. Fawn could not stop laughing. It was a strange line for him to use on a first date, this "pooh or pee," Arturo shrugs on the bench beside the Potomac, but it worked. He had her. And she had him. Like most of the world's great seducers, Arturo employed a mix of calculated boldness with genuine innocence, boyish charm with adult vulnerability.

As he talks, Arturo's eyes wander to a boat crossing in front of us. It is a family of, we will discover later, Venezuelan tourists.

"Look at those Latin girls!" sighs Arturo. "Look at the way they move! They're born that way! It is they who teach the boys!"

The girls, three of them, are about fifteen or sixteen years old. They are wearing short shorts in the July heat, and it is true that they move with a certain adult . . . swing.

"Oh God," says Arturo a few minutes later, "my dear Fawn, I could never live with her unless I cheated." A year later he will tell us, "I would have been willing to marry Fawn, although because of the difference in our cultures, it would not have worked." But this day he talks about Fawn Hall's upper lip. Arturo draws his index finger across his own upper lip. Fawn already has little wrinkles there, he says. "I loved that woman," he says. All the while Arturo is watching the progress of the Venezuelan pleasure craft.

A couple hours later we will be walking through Georgetown and Arturo will insist that he does not want to gain a reputation as a womanizer. He is adamant! And soon after he says this, a new BMW pulls up to the stoplight beside us. Arturo looks at the woman driving. She is dressed down, in old blue jeans and a white tank top, because, figures Arturo, why should she dress up? She's driving a new Beamer. He examines her. "Look at her! American women!" Arturo shrugs. He raises his hands. He smiles. What can you do? he is asking. Everywhere, all the time. And later he will admit that he simply cannot do without a woman, not since he was seventeen. "I cannot live without love. That is my tragedy." Then he will add with hysterical simplicity, "All's I want to do is get married and settle down and raise a bunch of babies in the country, babies and dogs." And a minute later, "No, no, no. I know that would bore me."

Cruz changes his mind a lot. First the Sandinistas, then the Contras, then some hopeful third path. First Fawn Hall, then a Los Angeles actress, then . . . Sometimes Arturo wishes desperately that he could go back. But he knows that the Sandinistas, just like Fawn, would always wonder if he was about to jump the fence once more. Arturo is one of those emotional chameleons who wants to be loved by everybody and ends up being loved by nobody.

But the exile's eyes are now on that Venezuelan boat. Last night in a restaurant where a Soviet diplomat once defected, Arturo spoke Spanish to the Bolivian bartender, a woman with a saucer cup of black curls. He watched her as she went for our drinks, and some mention of Bolivia or Che or Soviet defectors started him talking about a visit he once made to Cuba, where a fortune-teller told him that he would soon quit one love cycle and begin another. The new cycle would last thirty-five years. Days after he left Cuba, Arturo divorced his wife. (This woman, he says, once threatened to cut off Arturo's testicles with a pair of scissors because of an incident with an airline stewardess, but to elaborate now would divert us.) Arturo believes Fawn Hall may still be the woman of the new thirty-five-year love cycle.

The Venezuelans are docking.

We saunter over. And here is where you must begin to understand the complexity of someone like Arturo Cruz, Jr. The three girls step off the boat onto the dock, giggling. Their father ties the rope to a post. Their mother fastens her eyes onto Cruz. Latin mothers are nobody's fools. But Arturo is tongue-tied. He doesn't know how to begin. He walks past the boat and gazes out across the Potomac.

And so one of your authors, not unadmiring of South American youth either, asks point-blank where the family is from, where can we rent a boat like theirs, isn't it hot on the water today—a series of questions to open relations. So Cruz turns around and immediately chooses the most beautiful of the three daughters. "I'm a Contra," he says.

The girl freezes. Later Arturo admits he had made a mistake. Venezuela is not exactly a war-torn Central American state. Venezuela is in fact the most boring place in Latin America, and few in the American media have ever been there because it is a democracy, the Venezuelans don't run cocaine, everybody votes and has enough to eat, and, quite frankly, they're afraid of Contras.

Cruisin' with the Cruz!

Your authors and Arturo retreat to our bench in the sun. The Venezuelan girls are just practice.

The daughter Arturo had hit on, he says, reminds him of the girl Anastasio Somoza had married. Remember now, that Arturo is talking a mile a minute, as always, time being short in this life. This girl was much richer than Anastasio Somoza, the first Somoza America helped to impose on Nicaragua in the decades before the Sandinistas took power. The girl's father did not want her to marry Somoza, because though charming and intelligent, the first Somoza was considered to be merely a peasant from what in Nicaragua were called "the towns," and so the father sent his daughter away to college in the United States. But Somoza's uncle wanted his nephew to marry whomever he loved, and the uncle, who was also Arturo's great-uncle, was even richer than the girl's father. The uncle gave Somoza the money to go the United States to be with his love. But still the girl's father refused. He brought her back to Nicaragua. So the uncle of Somoza and Arturo called in certain debts which were owed by the father. The man gave in. His daughter married Somoza.

Arturo's stories often tell like fairy tales but the morals are always realpolitik.

Somoza made the right marriage, but just as importantly, so Nicaraguan legend goes, he acquired the right mistress, who was the wife of the American ambassador, called "minister" in those days. She was a European woman much younger than her American husband. Everybody—everybody in Nicaragua—shrugs Arturo, knew that the wife of the American minister was sleeping with Somoza, and nobody cared, really. In fact, getting into the bed of the wife of the minister was seen to be a victory for the locals, not unlike Arturo's seduction of Fawn Hall under the noses of Colonel North and the others.

Everybody in Nicaragua also knew that the third Somoza, as opposed to the first, had a small "organ." This is another instructive story, says Arturo. "That Somoza-3 was smaller than Somoza-1 in body held significance in the imagination of the people since Somoza-3's politics were suffocatingly smaller as well." Arturo shakes his head at such a complicated parallelism. The point is that everybody knew and nobody cared. But how ever to understand a country like America? In America, unlike Nicaragua, nobody knows and everybody seems to care. The affair of this Democratic Senator Hart, for instance. "In Europe or Central America, Hart would have been elected. So he fucked a beautiful woman. So what is wrong with that? I think the American public used his moral behavior as an excuse. In their subconscious, they must not trust him. I am really puzzled by this Hart thing." Arturo throws up his hands with an extra vigor. "But then I don't understand American women to begin with, and if you don't understand the women of a country, how can you fathom the rest of its culture?"

Arturo was closer to an answer than he realized, however. Empire and decline, the Cruzer's twin preoccupations (after love), were a big part of the explanation. Yet it would take an ideological enemy to make the best sense of it all.

"Is there, in your opinion," the German magazine *Der Spiegel* asked Gore Vidal in the summer of the cicadas, "any connection between the rise or fall of an empire and the standards of public interference in the private lives of the rulers?"

"If anything falls," the liberal author of *Lincoln, Myra Breckinridge,* and *Empire* replied, "everything is questioned about those who are in charge of the fall. When everything was rising, no one questioned Julius Caesar's or Augustus's private lives."

"There is a lot of tension building up in our society," Vidal, the acerbic patrician, would expand in an interview with *Playboy.* "We're going broke, we're losing our place in the world, the quality of life goes down and the public educational system is gone. So what shall we talk about? Anything that can distract the folks from taking revenge on the country's owners, who have ripped us off. Let's talk sex."

So let's.

The fun and games hardly began in the Reagan era, of course. It is just that from the 1940s to the 1970s—that fitful stretch of Roman prosperity—nobody, press or public, questioned much the private lives of America's presidents and lesser rulers. Most of the truth-telling began recently.

But let's consider the past.

Thomas Jefferson seems to have sired six children by a beautiful slave named Sally Hemings. By some accounts, he loved her as much as he had his wife, who had died, but he always refused to free Hemings or the children, even in his will. Early-nineteenth-century wags sang a ditty about Jefferson to the tune of "Yankee Doodle Dandy":

When press'd by loads of state affairs,
    I seek to sport and dally,
The sweetest solace of my cares
    Is in the lap of Sally.

She's black you tell me—grant she be—
    Must color always tally?
Black is love's proper hue for me—
    And white's the hue for Sally.

Fifty years later James Buchanan quite possibly became the first gay President. Never married, he roomed for twenty-three years with Senator William Rufus de Vane King of Alabama, who, upon leaving to become ambassador to France, wrote him, "I am selfish enough to hope you will not be able to procure an associate who will cause you to feel no regret at our separation." Buchanan was known in his time as "Betsy Buchanan," but whether he ever consummated his relationship with King may never be proven.

The tragedy of Lincoln's life was that he may have infected his wife, Mary, with syphilis, and this is why she ended her days in the insane asylum.

When it was discovered that Grover Cleveland had fathered an illegitimate child, the opposition hatched the jingle "Ma! Ma! Where's my Pa? Gone to the White House, ha, ha, ha!" But when Cleveland owned up honestly and told how he still supported mother and child, the country sympathized and elected him.

Warren G. Harding, no stranger to scandal of all stripes, was a womanizer of the first order. Though married, he was involved with the wife of a department store owner for fifteen years. The Republican National Committee paid her $20,000 to keep quiet, plus $2,000 a month. Harding also began an affair with a twenty-year-old, Nan Britton, and once made love to her in a White House closet to avoid detection by his wife.

Franklin Roosevelt died with his mistress, Lucy Mercer, beside him, not wife Eleanor.

Dwight Eisenhower yearned for Kay Summersby, his aristocratic jeep driver. ("His kisses absolutely unraveled me." He was "hungry, strong, and demanding.")

John F. Kennedy made love to Marilyn Monroe and smoked marijuana with Mary Pinchot Meyer, the divorced wife of the CIA official in charge of spying on student and labor groups inside the country. Kennedy enjoyed swimming nude in the White House pool with two voluptuous secretaries whom the Secret Service code-named "Fiddle" and "Faddle," and he took up with Judith Campbell Exner, the innocent architect's daughter from Pacific Palisades who had nearly simultaneous affairs with Frank Sinatra and Sam Giancana, boss of the Chicago Mafia. (Kennedy, Exner wrote in *My Story,* preferred the woman on top. "He was having trouble with his back, but there is something about that position, if not arrived at naturally, that makes the woman feel that she is there just to satisfy the man.")

For his part, Lyndon Baines Johnson liked to play a little game with his sleep mask, his mistress of twenty-one years finally told *People* in 1988. WAKE ME ONLY FOR SEX OR GOLF was printed on that mask. This was before he ever played much golf, added Madeleine Brown, who claimed to be the mother of Johnson's illegitimate boy, Steven, now thirty-six.

When Senator Dan Quayle was chosen to be Vice President George Bush's running mate in 1988, an old scandal resurfaced. During a golfing vacation in Florida in 1980, Quayle had shared a cottage with two other Republican congressmen and a lobbyist with platinum-blond hair named Paula Parkinson. Parkinson's lawyer reported that the lobbyist told the FBI that Quayle wanted to sleep with her but that she was too busy in the master bedroom with Tom Evans of Delaware. Later, Parkinson allowed that she had had sex with "less than a dozen" congressmen and that one hypocrite slipped her $500 to have an abortion while at the same time voting against reproductive rights on the House floor. "At least I'm honest," said Parkinson, who is now reported to be a waitress in Texas. "I've never changed my story and I don't carry on and then have my picture taken with the wife and kids. My morals might be low, but at least I have principles."

In 1988, even Richard M. Nixon, thought to be the least likely candidate for sexual scandal in the history of the presidency, was reported by journalist Shelley Ross to have had a long-standing relationship with a Hong Kong hostess named Marianna Liu. (Liu now says the friendship was purely platonic.)

These recent revelations of uncommon men and common lust were prompted by that fascination with the Emperor's nakedness that suddenly follows the fall. In years past, Lincoln and Jefferson were deified, Kennedy protected, and Roosevelt sanitized. There was a reluctance to see the nation's leaders as all too human until we were forced by circumstances to question ourselves in other ways too.

The new interest in private lives was hurried along by the changed media of the eighties. Press and television were "Murdochized" as Australia's most ambitious emigrant hit the States running. An overdue feminization of the Washington press corps had much to do with it all, too, as we shall see soon in detail in *l'affaire de* Hart.

But was there maybe something more than symbolic about the arrival of all those damn bugs? Those bizarre seventeen-year-old locusts who chose the humid summer of 1987 to emerge wet and glistening from the ground and mate high above cherry trees and Washington Monument, pumping away like Texas schoolteachers until sweat and gravity brought them back to the ground once more? Insect love. Everywhere we went in Washington that summer, cicadas flew into the faces of senators and janitors alike.

Perhaps scandal has no bounds. Perhaps God has six legs. It was around the time of this cicada summer that the nation was treated to a public whipping of its television evangelists. The Reverend Jimmy Swaggart, one of America's most popular churchmen and first cousin of none other than rocker Jerry Lee Lewis, would first imply and then straight-out charge that his rival televangelist Jim Bakker of the PTL (People That Love/Praise the Lord) loved church secretaries as much as he loved the Lord Jesus. But after Bakker and his wife, Tammy Faye, she of the double eyelashes, were driven from the temple like the money changers, Swaggart's own turn at the pillory would come when it was revealed unto the public that he cared as much for sex games and New Orleans prostitute Debra Murphree as for his wife of thirty-three years. This was as much a shock to us as to the rest of America's faithful. In a 1986 visit we paid to Swaggart in his offices at the World Ministry Center in Baton Rouge, we noted his affection for his comely wife, his view that rock 'n' roll was the new pornography and that Mother Teresa might well burn in Hell, and other such things, and we wrote, "Jimmy Lee Swaggart understands the hairy swamp monkey of fear and desire that is the American subconscious, because Jimmy Lee feels *the fire.*"

America would learn, too, that the religious-talk-show host Pat Robertson, son of a senator, may very well have talked his way out of front-line duty in the Korean War and that Oral Roberts, no slouch in the telebucks department either, threatened to wither away like a dust devil in the Sinai unless the poor and gullible of the country tithed up $8 million to save him.

With corruption so rampant in temple and forum, it was probably no accident, then, that in the next to last summer of the Reagan era, a natty blond zealot from West Virginia named Carl ("Spitz") Channell admitted to a scam bold enough to make even a television evangelist blush: raising private money for a covert government program, the funding of the Nicaraguan "freedom fighters." Channell promised the dollars would go for grenade launchers and Piper Cub airplanes. But no matter what Elliott Abrams and Pat Buchanan vouched to Texas donors, less than $5 million of the $10 million raised by Channell's National Endowment for the Preservation of Liberty went to Arturo Cruz's Contras. Some of the funds went to Channell's male companion, who lived with him in a Rock Creek condominium, and other associates.

In the same months, the very heterosexual mayor of Washington, Marion Barry, showed up below the window of *Jet* magazine's June "Beauty of the Week," who was twenty-three-years-old at the time.

"Who is it?" asked the sleepy young woman.

"It's your mayor!" shouted Barry, who was wearing a blue velour running suit and a duck-billed cap with, yes, MAYOR emblazoned across the crown. His limousine waited at the curb, and he was for some reason holding a walkie-talkie.

Mayor Barry, like Malvolio in *Twelfth Night,* would provide comic relief, denying again and again during the cicada summer that he had done lines of coke or enjoyed a bit of French sex under the table at one of the Fourteenth Street strip clubs or broadly abused the broad definition of "minority contracting" for minority gain.

But if Barry and his buddies appeared to be robbing the plantation commissary, the white folks across town were looting the nation.

Time published its famous indictment of supply-siders, the hundred Republicans who "faced allegations of questionable activities." ASSAULTED BY SLEAZE, SCANDALS AND HYPOCRISY, AMERICA SEARCHES FOR ITS MORAL BEARINGS. "Whatever happened to ethics?" the magazine trumpeted on its cover.

Corruption was rampant, but what really turned on the boys and girls aboard the media bus was sex. Issues of double billing, no-bid Pentagon contracts, oil giveaways in Wyoming, and Ronald Reagan's financial relation to his wealthy Hollywood supporters were harder to pin down. Investigative reporting, so fashionable a decade earlier with Watergate and the exploding Ford Pinto and other business scandals, was *outré* in an era of unabashed greed. Hard reporting also cost a lot of money, led to libel suits, and just wasn't as sexy as—well, as Oliver North's underwear.

There were as many rumors as cicadas in Washington, and one of the best concerned Fawn Hall's boss, Oliver North. It was said there existed a video of the colonel at a gay orgy arranged by Spitz Channell. North was supposed to be sitting on the floor in the middle of a living room carpet sipping a cold beer and wearing little more than his famous grin. A lot of very savvy and well-paid people believed there really might be such a tape because Colonel North's personal history was a bit darker than the White House let on. In December 1974, North, then a lieutenant, had suffered a mental breakdown. He had been picked up brandishing a .45-caliber pistol and crying of suicide. In the strongest version of the story, North was dressed only in his skivvies and was running through a cornfield near his house raving about "boys" and shouting "I'm no good! I'm no good!" North spent twenty-two days in Bethesda Naval Hospital. A doctor wrote "delayed battle stress" on his file.

Penthouse reporter Eric Nadler traced the rumor of the orgy video to a Contra leader who felt betrayed by North. Nadler met with this former Somoza officer at a Miami Beach hotel. "It is not clear whether North actually participates or merely sits there in his underwear watching what goes on," said the Contra.

ABC's contact for the tape was Phil Mabry, a Contra fund-raiser from Texas who crops up in the Tower Commission's report in a letter from Fawn Hall. She congratulates him for "dedication and ambition" in support of the "freedom fighters." "The video was made by somebody who wanted to keep Oliver North under control," said Mabry.

ABC was not convinced the Ollie Orgy tape existed, but the network invested considerable money and three weeks to find out. "It was all a bit crazy but then so was the sale of arms to the Iranians!" Karen Burnes, ABC's on-air Contragate reporter, now with CBS's "West 57th Street," tells us. In hindsight, the salacious video may have been a plant calculated to divert some of the best Contragate reporters from harder secrets that would not surface until months later, such as North's and Vice President George Bush's connections to Contra leaders who were smuggling cocaine. If its "World News

Tonight" staff could secure the Ollie video first, ABC knew it would score the sleaze coup of the decade. Just two months earlier, a couple of Miami print reporters outside a Capitol Hill town house had brought down the leading Democratic contender—and Senator Hart's tryst was with a woman, and only one of them at that. Think of what a video of Colonel North cheek to loin with Spitz Channell and friends would mean on national television. This was Washington Babylon. This was number one during Sweeps Week. If only the tape was for real!

There were several attempted viewings, the first in a Washington hotel with Bill Lord, then executive producer of "World News Tonight," present. The tape turned out to be blank. Lord was furious. But since Mabry had proved credible on the earlier Spitz Channell revelation, the network decided to give him a second chance. The meeting took place in a motel in South Carolina. Again Mabry claimed to have the tape. It was so fresh, he said, that he had not had a chance to look at it himself. Frank Snepp, the ABC consultant on the story, slowly slid the cassette into the VCR. Snepp, the ex-CIA officer who wrote *Decent Interval* about the fall of Saigon, betrayed no emotion whatsoever. "One takes a measured approach on these matters," he tells us later. The television filled slowly with black-and-white dots. It stayed that way.

Thinking that perhaps the TV was not working properly, Snepp suggested the scandal hunters quickly visit a video store. "It was a setup for comedy, that scene," remembers Snepp. "The manager got very impressed with who we were. When I told him this would not be a video suitable for viewing by children, he cleared the store." But once again, and for the final time, the video was blank. "Pure hash," says Snepp.

"We felt that he had betrayed us," said Karen Burnes. "We were let down and disappointed. Phil was visibly shaken and could only reply that his source had let him down."

But that's show business, and show business is what the big-time media has become.

Despite the new media glare, of course, sex was hardly banned in the imperial capital or driven underground. We would talk to vice cops and psychiatrists this summer, even pay a visit to Nancy Reagan's hairdresser and stop by the panda cage at the Washington Zoo, where Ling Ling was welcoming the visiting Hsing Hsing, with unfortunate results. In our researches, we began on the ground floor, not with the high and mighty but with those who service them. The sex business had been deregulated during the Reagan years, we discovered, just like the airlines. Rather than established houses, there were now hundreds of escort services and free-lancers.

"I have a congressman that I do regularly. I call him 'Miss Dirty,' " says Mya, whose eyes are green and whose skin is smooth and dark. Mya is twenty-two. Her father is a colonel. "The congressman likes to put on women's stockings, then have me humiliate him. He says his family treated him like dirt, that he needs it. He laughs a lot, even when I whip him. I whip. He laughs. The one thing he asks is that I don't leave bruises. He has a pretty weird sense of humor. With him I do what I call safe humiliation." She giggles.

"The only way that politicians are different, as far as I can tell, is that they worry about performance. They always try to please me. I say, 'No, no, I'm here to please you.' They're all men. That's the bottom line."

Mya was a cheerleader who sang in a Gospel youth choir and taught kindergarten at a religious summer camp where Jerry Falwell once autographed her Bible. She still wears two small gold crosses around her neck. "They set off my red nails."

"It's not like I've slept with the entire Congress, but in my opinion, Republicans are better tippers. My friends and I are worried the Democrats will take over after Reagan. Oh God, you know, first AIDS, then the Democrats!"

Like Mya, Bobby charges a hundred dollars a session. Bobby has been hustling since he was twelve. Today he's wearing white overalls, a pink golf shirt, and white Reeboks as he sips a rum and coke on the patio at Mr. P's, a gay watering hole near Dupont Circle. His face and body are a little puffy. "Nobody wants a skinny boy these days"—he laughs—"AIDS." Not real humble, Bobby keeps rubbing the bulge in his pants. "Ten inches hard," he smiles.

Bobby caters to the Pentagon crowd. "I get a kick out of how carefully they hang up their uniforms."

Bobby's eyes dart over the men in Mr. P's as he tells the story of a Washington VIP who lives in Georgetown.

"He'd bought three town houses in a row and knocked down the inside walls. There was a fountain in the lobby. We did a few lines of coke; then he showed me his bedroom. There were whips and chains and handcuffs all over.

He said he wanted me to do the wildest thing I could think of. I thought, No point in beating the shit out of him. He'd probably enjoy that.

"So I handcuffed him to the bed. Greased up his ass nice and slow, and rubbed my ten inches in the groove to get him all hot. Then I jumped up and took his wallet and keys, dropped them downstairs at the front door, and split.

"Seven the next morning, the maid arrives. She'd been told never to come into the VIP's bedroom because of all the whips and chains, right? But she figured there's been a burglary or worse. She runs upstairs and there he is, still all tied up, greased, and naked!

"Later in the morning he calls me. He said he'd never been so humiliated. He sent me an extra hundred dollars in the mail. I liked that job."

At first glance it seemed ironic that homosexuality and other unsanctioned activities were so widespread at the end of the Reagan years. Ronald Reagan and the Republicans came to Washington promising, among other things, to merge private and public morality and restore the American family to the perfection of a Norman Rockwell tableau. But perhaps the problem all along had been that the Reagans just weren't what people thought.

Daughter Patti: Lived out of wedlock with a member of a cocaine-using rock band, the Eagles, until she married her yoga teacher. When she refused to attend the funeral of her own grandmother and wrote *Home Front,* a revealing roman à clef, mother Nancy cut off relations.

Son Ronald Jr.: Ballet dancer who became an editor of *Playboy* magazine. Decided to marry only after the boldest of the palace media intimated he might be bisexual.

Adopted son Michael: Wrote in his autobiography that until he was ten years old, he believed the family's black maid to be his true mother. (BESS, YOU IS MY WYMAN, NOW YOU IS as *Esquire* put it.)

The President: Admitted to a friend that after his bitter divorce from "Falcon Crest" star Jane Wyman, he slept with so many starlets in so many one-night stands that he sometimes forgot where he was and whom he had woken up beside.

The First Lady: Long a believer in astrology, Nancy even postponed the President's first press conference on the Iran-Contra scandal until the alignment of the stars was right, according to former White House chief of staff Donald Regan in his memoir *For the Record.* Regan stated that the First Lady also had her astrologer, later revealed to be Republican socialite Joan Quigley of San Francisco, draw up Mikhail Gorbachev's horoscope so that the President might gain insights into the Soviet leader's behavior before the summit meetings. Though the Reagans derived much support from America's Christian Right, the Christian faithful have long considered astrology to be a science of the devil. The First Lady was also hardly an opponent of abortion, contrary to her "profamily" image. "I don't give a damn about the right-to-lifers," she reportedly told Regan, as she insisted that references to abortion be taken out of one State of the Union speech. And Mrs. Reagan once allowed her interior decorator to sleep with his male companion in a bed at the White House.

The Hollywood background of the Reagans was always spicier than Republicans were allowed to know. Nancy was the goddaughter of the famous lesbian actress Alla Nazimova. Nancy Reagan's father abandoned the family when she was a baby. Years later, she declined to go to his funeral. Described as "ambassador to the world's children," she did not bother to visit her own grandchildren until some years after they were born, and then only because a gossip columnist raised a stink. Her best friend was Betsy Bloomingdale, whose husband Alfred was a leading member of the President's kitchen cabinet. Bloomingdale, founder of Diner's Card and heir to the department store fortune, kept his mistress, Vicki Morgan, on a $10,000-a-month retainer and exhibited an insatiable predilection for sadomasochistic sex. What Bloomingdale, who accompanied Nancy and his wife to the wedding of Prince Charles and was appointed to the Foreign Intelligence Advisory Review Board, liked to do most was whip bound prostitutes until at last he attained his erection, then jump immediately into bed with Vicki Morgan for a very quick climax.

What is most interesting in all of this is not the hypocrisy of the Reagan family but rather that the Reagans were not so different from most other families of our time (excepting perhaps for violent Uncle Alfred). Consider that nowadays half of American marriages will end in divorce, that 28 percent of all children live in single-parent homes, that 15 million women have had abortions since 1973, that close to a majority of married men and married women have had affairs, that a majority of teenagers and college students have tried marijuana or cocaine, and that up to 10 percent of the adult population is believed to be bi- or homosexual.

Americans, at least in our time, seem to want not righteousness but the illusion of righteousness. Jimmy Carter believed that the path of righteousness was difficult and that it took discipline. He lost the presidency. Ronald Reagan was a positive thinker. To him, it was enough to declare righteousness. Reagan was a big hit.

Like the Reagans themselves, most Americans wanted to believe that they, too, were something they were not. Or more accurately, that they were something they had not been for a very long time.

Politics first became prime-time sex farce on a wonderfully wild October night in 1974 when exotic dancer Fanne Foxe, "The Argentine Firecracker," born Annabella Battistella, dark, buxom, and sloe-eyed, jumped arms akimbo and screaming into the Tidal Basin at two in the morning while a hopelessly drunk Wilbur Mills, then Democratic chairman of the House Ways and Means Committee, blinked from inside the silver-and-black Continental. This was the night the rules changed.

Before, senators could stagger to the podium drunk, as Huey Long, Harry Truman, and Joe McCarthy had done. Congressmen could keep apartments off the Hill to entertain young power groupies. Nobody would report any of it.

But this night, when a local television crew caught a freak call on their police-band monitor and raced toward the Jefferson Memorial thinking a congressman was in the process of being kidnaped, the cameras were on. They would not stop rolling through ABSCAM and the disrobing of Rita Jenrette, through the unmasking of Bob Bauman, the gay "gentleman from Maryland," through the downfall of Senator Gary Hart and beyond.

"I always led the kind of exemplary life you could hang on a tree and point to," Mills tells us. He is now a corporate tax specialist in the Washington office of the New York law firm Shea and Gould. Long ago Mills had wanted badly to be President, but few took him seriously. If he could not be an angel on the winning side, Mills would play the devil's game instead.

Today his gaze is sad behind thick glasses. His right eye is almost shut. His right hand shakes from time to time, and he holds it unobtrusively with his left. But his voice and mind seem air-conditioned. At eighty-four Mills is still a frank country boy.

"I was an alcoholic. I had blackouts. I thought I had a malignant tumor. I was taking medicine for a back problem. I always thought I was a better doctor than the real McCoy."

Mills had gone to the Silver Slipper, where Foxe performed, and afterward, three men and "a carload" of women started off. The driver, "a Nixon fellow," neglected to turn on the headlights. By the Jefferson Memorial the car was speeding. The U.S. Park Service police pulled them over. "She [Mills doesn't refer to Foxe by name] jumped in to draw attention away from me. Wrong move."

Mills did not act like a man spooked by bad publicity. Over Thanksgiving, he stumbled blindly onto the runway at a club in Boston's Combat Zone where Foxe, rechristened "The Tidal Basin Bombshell," was strutting her stuff.

Those cameras whirled away. Mills was like a big muddy dog that doesn't know he can't walk into the clean living room. He made a show of invulnerability when his committee chairmanship was stripped from him. "This won't ruin me. Nothing can ruin me." But he did not run for reelection. "I could have won," he shrugs. "If people will elect a man drunk, they'll elect him sober. But I was tired."

Mills had been one of the sharpest characters on the Hill. He was Congress's expert on tax policy. Medicare might not have been possible without Mills, who led Ways and Means for twenty-two years. "We enhanced retirement benefits, helped the aged and the self-employed as they had never been helped before. A lot of people live better today because of what I did," he says, and he's right enough. He looks straight through us as he talks, still assessing the damage. "You won't get headlines for helping little old ladies," he says finally.

Was he framed?

This is a question Mills had thought about. "A hit man over at CIA told me so. No. A high-up Arab told me the Jews did it. No, Jews were my friends. Nixon was mad as hell that I succeeded in getting a tax on textile imports when he had failed, but it would be ridiculous to think he set me up for that. No, I blame myself, and maybe her a little. She wrote her book. It was full of lies. She wasn't pregnant by me. Turned out, I couldn't have gotten her pregnant. I had an incompetent problem." *Didn't he sleep with her?* "Oh, I guess I did."

Fanne Foxe quit stripping. She said she didn't want to cause any more embarrassment for Mills. She married a man who would become a commodities broker, but times turned tough for the couple along the way.

"Toward the end of 1977," she told Rudy Maxa of the Washington *Post*, "I was home alone, and my older daughter was supposed to have gone to a party. But she said to a friend that I didn't look too happy that night and she wanted to come back home early. They found me unconscious on the living room floor. I don't remember how many sleeping pills I swallowed. Maybe thirty. I did it coolly. I wasn't drinking. I just took the pills with a glass of water. I was really tired. Everything was just piling up, piling up. I guess the way [the Mills affair] was taken hurt—most people blamed me for what happened, and it wasn't like that at all. I don't really know what I was expecting from such a situation. I imagine I was expecting to be received better because it was a sad story."

The media had acted like frat boys at a stag party. It was first blood.

Foxe continued with her life. At forty-four she had a baby, and even finished a six-hundred-page novel about the legendary nineteenth-century Argentine wife who was executed for her love affair with a priest.

There is a photo of old Mills sitting on a park bench in a duffer's hat and a black overcoat, his arm around Fanne Foxe. She is wearing a leopard-skin coat, and it would be easy to use the title of her little book to describe them: *The Stripper and the Congressman*. But there is something sweet about the picture, an almost serene quality. With one hand, she clutches his; with the other, she strokes his calf. Neither Mills nor Foxe wears the glazed rabbit look one notices years later in the famous photo of Donna Rice on Gary Hart's lap. Perhaps the congressman and the stripper were in love after all.

Even though their scandal hit in 1974, Fanne and Wilbur played like an old Jayne Mansfield movie, big tits and too much booze. Theirs was a 1950s scandal. Wonderfully salacious, a hoot, poignant, sad in the end, but issues of Character were not raised as they would be in the scandals to come. Mills made a mistake, and he paid for it. Fanne Foxe was unjustly stereotyped, but this was par for the course too.

The first modern sex scandal would fall to the Jenrettes, Rita and John. And it would be a doozy: yuppie greed, two spreads in *Playboy*, a faithless wedding night followed by a stand-up session under a mink coat between two pillars guarding the Capitol, $25,000 "or so" found in an old shoe, betrayal, reconciliation, redemption, and the introduction of the bimbo perplex to American journalism.

In 1976, John Jenrette was a thirty-nine-year-old congressman from South Carolina who was going places. His wife, Rita Garlington Jenrette, twenty-six, was from Austin, Texas. Not stupid, she had graduated cum laude from the University of Texas and had been research director of the state's Republican Party. Not too poor, her family owned a fifteen-thousand-acre Brahma-bull ranch in Jasper County, among other things, and she had grown up in a horseshoe-shaped mansion. She liked to trace her mother's line back to 1066 and the Battle of Hastings, and she was a recognized Daughter of the American Revolution—at least until the second *Playboy* layout.

So she was appalled when she first met John. "He was wearing white shoes and a yellow, orange, and green plaid jacket . . . but he just had something. He's so good-looking, those white pearly teeth. He looks into your eyes. He makes you think that you're the most important person in the world. He is the epitome of the political animal. I'm sure I would like him much more had I not married him. He's the kind of man who should never be married. Ever, ever, ever!"

Rita remembers that immediately after their marriage ceremony, John had flown to South Carolina for what he told her was pressing political business. In fact, she believes, he was saying goodbye to an old girlfriend. When he returned to the capital, though, he invited his new wife to visit him during a late-night session of Congress in order to consummate their marriage. Rita met him at the appropriately named Members Portico, which overlooks the city. She was wearing a mink coat and high heels and little else. They made love standing up between the columns. "The night was really cold." She laughs with a sudden Texas cackle. "It sounds racy but men and women should do things like that. I've always been a free spirit. I was thinking, Well, isn't *this* exciting. This is one way to keep a marriage interesting."

Rita Jenrette was "the little kid with the glasses who studied too much." Then she turned fifteen. She became a cheerleader and official football sweetheart of Austin's St. Edwards High School. She was an enthusiast, a brainy go-getter, Texas-style. At the same time, she was beginning to look like Mae West after aerobics. Even today, her body is a mix: hard cheekbones and small intense eyes set in a heart-shaped face, Icelandic blond hair, a pouting lower lip, large breasts, dancer's legs, and an hourglass waist.

Washington had not seen a political wife like Rita Jenrette since Dolly Madison. The Washington *Post* picked her as one of four blondes to watch out for. "We were hot social property," remembers Rita. As for husband John, the *Post* said the congressman was "the arithmetic of power."

Rita was impulsive and fun-loving, but loyal. She enjoyed getting up at four in the morning and flying to South Carolina to shake hands with the common folk at the factory gate. This was exalting. Ten years later, she volunteers at shelters for the homeless.

When Jimmy Carter's people swept into Washington, over a hundred FBI agents set up a sting operation to catch corrupt legislators. A former con man posed as an Arab sheik named Kambir Abdul Rahman. Rahman operated from a rented Georgetown house wired for sound and video. The cameras caught one senator and six congressmen who offered to support various outlandish schemes, from real estate projects to titanium-mining companies, in return for significant cash bribes. The operation was called ABSCAM, for "Abdul scam." Congressman Jenrette was offered $50,000.

"I've got larceny in my blood," he told the hidden cameras. "I'll take it in a goddamn minute."

"When I heard those tapes in court," says Rita now, "I thought I had married a different person."

At his trial in the fall of 1980, Congressman Jenrette claimed that what he had really said was: "I had alcohol in my blood. I'll do anything to get out of here."

It was a good try, but the jury did not believe him. He would eventually spend thirteen months in prison.

Suddenly Rita was being referred to in the press as "Lovely Rita," after the Beatles song about the meter maid. *Playboy* asked her to write an article about her experiences as a congressman's wife. She flew to Chicago, and there the magazine's editors encouraged her, she remembers, to dress up in a silk blouse and pose for some test shots. Back in Washington, John Jenrette asked her, "Who wants to see a twenty-nine-year-old woman in the nude?"

"All of a sudden there was a fire burning inside of me, like I'll show you! I remember sleeping on the couch that night and thinking, Just stay away from me, John."

During the next several months the couple would fight and break up, then reunite, usually in a moment of mad love. John Jenrette flew to Florida for several days just as Rita returned from Chicago. She was, she says, putting her dirty clothes into the little hamper in John's closet. "There was this brown suede shoe in the middle of the closet floor. We are both very meticulous people. I thought, What's this shoe doing here? I picked it up to put it back on the shelf, and all this money fell out, more money than I'd ever seen at one time. I went, Oh shoot, am I on camera like John was? Maybe, they're setting me up, too!"

The shoe contained two packets of $100 bills and a third packet of $20, $50, and $100 bills. The total was $25,000—"or so."

Jenrette panicked. She called the number her husband had given her in Florida. A Cuban woman answered the phone. Rita demanded to speak to John. The woman was confused. " 'Listen, lady, I know he's there with you. Put him on!' A man came on the line. 'Ma'am,' he said, 'there's nobody here by that name.' 'Listen, buster,' I said, 'quit covering up for your sister! I don't care what John's doing. Put him on!' Then I suddenly realized: John had given me a fictitious number.

"It was two in the morning now. I thought of throwing the money in the Potomac, giving it away," she remembers.

On Sunday, John Jenrette finally called and explained that the money was from a certificate of deposit. He had, he said, brought the cash up from his safe in South Carolina and stuck it in the shoe for safekeeping. Rita believed him. But, she says, without her knowledge her lawyer called the FBI. The FBI compared the serial numbers with the serial numbers on the ABSCAM bribe money believed to have gone to Congressman Jenrette and the serial numbers matched.

Rita Garlington Jenrette looked innocent, if very, very naive.

Then came the April photo spread in *Playboy*. Demure in an ostrich boa, vibrant in motorcycle leathers beside the Capitol, alluring in black stockings on a coyote-skin rug—she was no longer innocent. The slightest shock of pubic hair waved between her Texas thighs like a tuft of prairie grass. She was everything a titillated public had hoped for, the first yuppie sex symbol, rich, fluent in four languages, and butt-naked.

Seven years later, during dinner at the Cafe Destin in Manhattan near her Central Park condominium, Rita Jenrette spots Alexander ("Lexo") Toradze, the Russian pianist. Toasts are mounted. Toradze, in exile, is about to perform at the Kennedy Center in Washington. Jenrette has a leading role in a hit play. It is called *A Girl's Guide to Chaos* by Cynthia Heimel, directed by Wynn Handman at the American Place Theater. Rita plays a single woman named "Rita," and at the table she agrees to repeat her best lines, which are as appropriate as the title of the play and the name of the restaurant: "Never lead a sensible life. The moment you decide you're a grown-up now and must put away foolish things like dancing all night or cruising down strange highways is the moment your life is over. Have adventure. Opt for the unknown. Ride the freedom train all the way to the other side. God protects drunks, infants, and feisty girls—girls who are up for anything!"

Toradze claps.

"I think that's it," laughs Jenrette.

What angers Rita Jenrette about the scandal (or as she usually phrases it, "those times") was that everybody took her for a bimbo or, worse, a gold-digging bimbo. "I didn't marry John Jenrette because he was a congressman. He married me because he needed a blond, intelligent woman from a good family to be by his side so that he could go on to higher and higher office."

Americans, she feels, have a love-hate relationship with The Blonde. It is not easy being blond and intelligent in this country. You may find that women, as well as men, refuse to take you seriously. Men, because that's the way a lot of them are; women, because they can be jealous judges, says Rita, and we are reminded of the closing lines from *Esquire* cartoonist Lynda Barry's *NAKED LADIES! NAKED LADIES! NAKED LADIES!* "By [high school graduation] the girls in *Playboy* were clearly the enemy. They were going to get all the guys and we'd never get any guys, not even the creeps, and even if we ever did get a guy, they could take him away from us just like that. Because every man in the world would always want them way more than they would ever want us because they were beautiful and we were ugly. It put us in a bad mood for the next ten years."

The media want a sexy bimbo at the center of their circuses, insists Rita, whether it's Jim Bakker and Jessica Hahn, Wilbur Mills and Fanne Foxe, Gary Hart and Donna Rice, or John and her.

But, Rita, what about Playboy? *You weren't quoting Kierkegaard on top of that coyote rug.*

"Doing *Playboy* was not the most negative thing anyone's ever done," says Rita. "It's not being Attila the Hun, and it's not being Mother Teresa, either."

This is a good line, but Lexo Toradze gets the last laugh. "KGB and American media," the exile Toradze shrugs, a lot like Arturo Cruz, Jr., "different reasons, same results."

One of the fun things about sex scandals for the rest of us is the pictures. Think of the *Time* magazine shot of Wilbur Mills, the king of common sense in another life, who really did decide how much corporations were taxed or whether Medicare would become a reality, stepping onto that Combat Zone runway. Or of lovely Rita, upended on her coyote skin, neither coy nor degraded, to her way of thinking, only a Texas princess wondering what all the media fuss was about.

But there are no pictures of Robert Bauman the morning he awoke in the Madison Hotel and crawled to the bathroom on his hands and knees, his wallet emptied and his wedding ring stolen, his overnight lover long gone to the pawnshop. That day would be the last day Bob Bauman would take a drink of alcohol. It would be too late.

Congressman Robert Bauman was the archconservative Republican who waged war against the Democrats during the Carter years. A tough and clever parliamentarian, Bauman cracked the whip against the administration's gasoline tax, aid to the new Sandinista regime, and, most ironically, extension of civil rights to America's homosexuals, of which Bob Bauman was one.

"Speaking of incongruity," Bauman wrote years later. "Here was a conservative member of the U.S. Congress attired for that role in a suit with vest, sipping bourbon with two scantily clad young hustlers in a noisy, smoke-filled barroom only blocks from the U.S. Capitol. One in the morning and a million miles from home and reality. . . .

"Not just the Honorable Bauman, member of Congress, but convert to Roman Catholicism, married and the father of four, a leader and spokesman for the American conservative movement. Friend of Ronald Reagan, William F. Buckley, Jr., parliamentary scourge of House Speaker Tip O'Neill and the liberals on Capitol Hill."

On the Wednesday after Labor Day in 1980, Congressman Bauman, "the gentleman from Maryland," as he likes to refer to himself, was visited by two

FBI agents. The agents told him that he had been observed visiting gay bars and soliciting sexual acts from young men, some of them minors. Although the District police under Mayor Barry now looked the other way, his actions were federal felonies.

Bauman was stunned. Not because the agents were wrong in their charges but because he had been caught, and he was in the midst of an important reelection campaign. Bauman was heavily favored to win the Eastern District of Maryland. Afterward, he wanted to take on one of the incumbent senators of that state, Paul Sarbanes. Bauman would always believe that his exposure and conviction for soliciting sex from a teenage nude male dancer were the result of political opportunism. The Carter Democrats wanted to stop him from entering the Senate, he believed.

Perhaps Bauman was correct in his paranoia. A joint District police and FBI probe investigated nine other congressmen and senators who enjoyed sex with their own gender, but only Bauman, an ambitious thorn in the side of the Democrats, was charged.

Perhaps correct, but sour grapes nonetheless. Undercover officers told us that Bauman was as discreet as the Washington Monument on a moonlit night. He frequented the rough-trade bars in a three-piece suit and cruised street hustlers from behind the wheel of his big blue Mercury with congressional license plates.

With Election Day only three weeks away, articles containing leaks from the government's files appeared in the Baltimore and Washington papers. Buzz words like "pederast," "closet homosexual," and "blackmailed legislator" did not give his campaign spin. The jokes were relentless. *How do you separate Bauman from the boys? With a crowbar. Do you know what position Bauman will have in the Reagan administration? Solicitor general.* On billboards, pranksters crossed out the FOR in Bauman's slogan FOR ALL THE PEOPLE and spray-painted BLOWS. Bauman lost a safe seat, by a few thousand votes.

All his life Robert Bauman had desperately wanted to be part of the normal world, the conservative world. Yet, since the moment Bauman's drunken father told him he was adopted, Bauman had felt the outsider: "You know you're not my son, Bobby." His father added, "You better Goddamned straighten up, because if you don't, you can just get the hell out of here."

"I felt tears rolling down my cheeks . . . No wonder no one wanted me.

My own parents, my own mother, father, whoever they were, had not wanted me either."

The future congressman's secret world deepened when he realized at military school that his strongest feeling was "an involuntary reaction to the sight, smell, and feel of other boys . . . a frightening force from deep within my being."

"I came to hate myself," wrote Bauman, "because of the presence within me of this horrible weakness, this uncleanness of spirit over which I seemed to have no control."

In the summer of the cicadas, Bauman is very tanned, wearing white shorts below a yellow cotton pullover, sandals, and the sort of round eyeglasses Harold Lloyd made famous in the silents. Divorced, finished as a politician, he does not appear to be a happy man.

"I'm sorry I'm out of the closet," Bauman tells us. "I'm sorry I'm gay. Well, I don't mean *sorry*. I am the way I am. But if I had the choice, I wouldn't have chosen this way of life. Strike the 'sorry.' I've begun to deal with it."

Bauman now lives in a slightly seedy Capitol Hill house with peeling paint and an unwatered lawn. It is a long way from Glebe House, the farm on Maryland's Eastern Shore where he had lived with his wife and four children. The only sign of former glory is an enormous oil painting of Warren G. Harding, an interesting choice. As we talk, the ex-congressman's tiny fox terrier tears at a hamburger Bauman has prepared for it in the microwave.

Bauman is angry, but Bauman is chastened. Bauman often refers to himself in the third person. Former conservative friends and colleagues like Lyn Nofziger, soon to be convicted himself, no longer deign to return Bauman's phone calls. Bauman is not allowed a seat on President Reagan's new national AIDS commission. Bauman is broke. Bauman has become D. H. Lawrence's "Prussian Officer," the tortured German soldier who disgraced himself with the love that dare not speak its name.

We play armchair psychiatrist. *Were you so tough and ruthless as a politician,* we ask the fallen congressman, *because you were trying to compensate for what in your heart you knew to be true?*

"If you are asking me," he replies, "if I somehow said to myself, I might be a fag, so I must appear to be macho, I would say, no. I just delighted in the game of politics, and I knew the rules, and other people didn't."

Does it strike you as odd that there are so many gay men in—and about—the Reagan administration?

Bauman will not answer. But it is worth quoting from his book:

> There are many men in leading positions of power who are homosexuals and yet appear regularly in the media as the leaders of our nation. Gay and closeted, many of them are married and have families. They serve in Congress, the Reagan administration and White House, the judiciary, military, and Washington power circles. . . . [At] all-male parties sometimes they bring their younger male friends with them (derisively known as "twinkies") and sometimes they are accompanied by lovers of many years. Some are close friends of the President, some serve on the staff of the national political committees of both parties, and some aspire to higher office. Some regularly appear in public as leaders of the conservative movement and some few even resort to the hypocritical tactic of attacking homosexuality and gay people in their public role. Later the same day they retire to bed with another male after spending an hour or two at a gay bar.

One could say that the gentleman from Maryland was trapped as much by himself as by the FBI. He had already stopped his heavy drinking. If he had found a way to tell his constituents honestly that he was gay, he might have stood a chance at reelection. This is what two Massachusetts congressmen, Barney Frank and Gerry Studds, did. Studds was caught in the congressional page scandals in 1982, but he admitted all, with a Washington shrug, and because he had a fine record as a legislator, just like Bauman, he was returned to office. In an interview with the Boston *Globe* in May of 1987 Frank said, "If you ask the question: 'Are you gay?' the answer is: 'Yes. So what?'"

Studds and Frank, however, were liberal Democrats, and Bob Bauman was a point man for the new Republicanism. Homosexuality and right-wing politics did not mix well. At least they were not supposed to.

The truth is that one can be secretly gay and still blow the bugle for God, flag, and family. History is full of such examples. Baron von Krupp was pinning little gold bombs to the shirts of his lovers as the Nazis pinned pink triangles to less fortunate gays destined for the camps. J. Edgar Hoover, who lived for four decades with FBI subagent Clyde Tolson, was often referred to by the Kennedy brothers as "that queer son of a bitch." G. Harrold Carswell,

Nixon's failed appointee to the Supreme Court, was arrested after allegedly soliciting a male undercover officer in a Tallahassee, Florida, rest room; and, of course, there was Cardinal Francis Spellman of the bellicose China Lobby, and Roy Cohn, the famous aide to Senator Joe McCarthy, who later became a fixer lawyer for the Mafia. Cohn is dying of AIDS as we chat with Bauman, and Cohn's Roman orgies make Bauman's fearful forays play like a choirboy's picnic.

But in the eighties, an era of full disclosure, gay conservatives had a problem. Liberals, at least those elected from uncloseted districts such as West Hollywood, San Francisco, Boston, and Manhattan, could be honest. But an important segment of Republican strength in these years came from the profamily, antihomosexual Christian Right. To Republicans, out-front homosexuality was the kiss of death, and there was no easy way out of the closet, as the case of Terry Dolan showed.

Dolan was the New Right's most celebrated fund-raiser. Founder of the National Conservative Political Action Committee, he had helped to raise $10 million for President Reagan's 1980 election and, at the same time, to knock out key liberal senators such as Frank Church and George McGovern. Angry that he would not leave his own tormented closet to lobby the administration for bigger AIDS research budgets, Larry Kramer, author of the novel *Faggots* and the play *The Normal Heart,* had once thrown a drink in Dolan's face. Like Roy Cohn, Dolan never publicly admitted his sexual preference. When he died in 1987, the Washington *Post* listed the cause as AIDS. This provoked Dolan's brother Tony, who happened to be President Reagan's chief speechwriter, to take out a two-page ad in the Washington *Times,* at a cost of about $5,600, to deny it all. "My brother died a holy and heroic death," Tony Dolan later told us. But Bob Bauman had spoken at a memorial service for Terry Dolan.

"I believe that Terry no longer cared if people knew what he was dying of," Bauman tells us, "and he talked to his attorney about turning his house into an AIDS hospice."

But the fact is that Terry Dolan went to his grave without making a public statement about the nature of his illness or sexuality.

"Terry Dolan didn't give a shit about his community," a prominent Washington fund-raiser for gay causes tells us. "The Reagan administration attitude is faggots and drug addicts are better off dead, period. These closeted gay

Republicans who won't stick their necks out to increase AIDS funding are monsters. I don't know how they live with themselves. How can you deny your family, your brothers? I wouldn't give Bob Bauman the sweat off my balls."

In his autobiography, *The Gentleman from Maryland,* Bauman was careful not to surface his Republican colleague Dolan, but Bauman had no problem mentioning the Massachusetts Democrat Barney Frank by name: "The witty liberal Barney Frank appears at Washington's annual Gay Pride Day in a tank top with his usual young companion."

"This was outrageous," Frank tells us rapid-fire from behind his desk in the Rayburn Building. "That guy was not my lover. Bob Bauman needed a little juice to sell his book."

Frank is a rough, tough, jocular guy who was raised at his father's truck stop in New Jersey. He talks with the fast gravelly clip of a tractor-trailer changing gears, looks like nothing so much as a muscular loaf of white bread, and is many things that gay-bashers imagine homosexuals not to be.

"For a gay man or a lesbian to be actively part of an administration that oppresses other gay people is despicable," fumes Frank. "There is a right to privacy, but I don't think there's a right to hypocrisy."

Barney Frank was the first Democratic congressman to declare without having to that he is gay. "I became convinced that my refusal to answer the question of whether or not I am gay, although I think I had a perfect right to refuse, would be interpreted as meaning it was something I was afraid of." A majority of his constituents lauded his honesty.

But Frank believes America has only reached "an intermediate stage" in its willingness to accept gays as elected leaders. "I think an entrenched senator could now come out and survive" the reaction, but it would be "unlikely," says Frank, for a gay or lesbian to be elected to the Senate if he or she were not already an incumbent.

Just why are homosexual leaders so taboo to American voters? A strain of homophobia, of primal sexual repulsion, runs through the body politic, of course, and this is the root of the matter. But conservatives, especially religious conservatives, also believe that homosexuality could spell the end of the family and of American civilization. In defense of their case, conservatives often cite the decline of the Roman Empire. But this view is a modern myth. The Romans, like the Athenians before them, not only tolerated bisexuality at many points during their prosperous reign but were ruled by emperors who generally preferred boys to women, given the choice. Of the first fifteen emperors, only one, Claudius, had tastes in love that were "entirely correct," as Edward Gibbon put it. And yet the Roman Empire lasted five hundred years. Furthermore, it was not creeping sexual decadence that brought down the Romans. The barbarians and imperial overexpansion did the trick. If religious conservatives allowed a more accurate reading of history, then they and their fellow Americans might elect a gay President—even a Bob Bauman —with no ill effect, save shock.

Old snow covers the walkways outside the auditorium like a stained sheet. Inside Wawanak Building at the University of New Hampshire the heat is turned so high that the thousand undergraduates in their pullovers and boots fidget behind the rows of sweating politicians in tweed sportcoats and L. L. Bean rubber loafers. The row directly in front of the stage is a picket fence of predatory boom mikes and minicams.

Onto the stage file the candidates for the New Hampshire Democratic debate: Paul Simon, Al Gore, Bruce Babbitt, Richard Gephardt, Jesse Jackson, Michael Dukakis. Then comes Senator Gary Hart in an old brown jacket and Hush Puppies.

Nine months before, in May, Senator Hart, then the likely candidate for his party's nomination and already leading Republican Vice President George Bush in the polls, had insisted to a New York *Times* reporter that his private life was as pure as Aspen snow. Hart had even dared journalists to follow him. Two reporters and a photographer from the Miami *Herald* did just that. Outside his Washington town house, they caught Hart in a tryst with Miami model Donna Rice. Weeks later Ms. Rice, of the vacant smile and the wondrous thighs, told reporters of a wasted, drunken, naive voyage of puppy lust aboard a yacht called *Monkey Business,* bound for Bimini. Photos were produced. A reporter from the Washington *Post* then confronted Hart with a smoking-gun file of secret meetings with other women. Hart resigned, chastised and steaming but admitting nothing, only to return to the presidential race in December. This was a surprise, and the media was outraged. But Senator Hart vowed to let the people decide.

This cold night in New Hampshire, John Chancellor is the debate's moderator. Chancellor is the fatherly essaysist of the nightly NBC news. His introduction of the other candidates has been dull and correct. No allusions to Paul Simon's bow tie or mallardlike gait, to Albert Gore's rock-bashing wife, to Gephardt's vanishing eyebrows, or to the resemblance between Bruce Babbitt and "Crazy Jim," the character on the old TV show "Taxi," or the way Massachusetts governor Michael Dukakis has all the personality of the little greased man on the wedding cake.

Suddenly, Chancellor's voice drops: "Gary Hart, a candidate who resigned his seat in the Senate to campaign for the presidency, only to resign once again after reports of his involvement with a Miami model became public"—here the moderator widens his famous owlish eyes—"which poses the eternal question, Will you still love me in December as much as you did in May?"

The audience gasps. Without warning or cause, Chancellor has disrupted the level playing field.

It is the existential moment for this year's existential candidate. What would that old Irish womanizer JFK have done in Hart's place? Or that even older Irish Hollywood womanizer, Ronald Reagan?

Reagan had been presented a similar problem in 1980 when a moderator of the Republican debate in New Hampshire had tried to stop him from speaking. "I paid for that microphone," growled Reagan, and the nation decided then and there that Ronald Reagan was not too old to govern.

And only days from now Vice President George Bush would snarl back at CBS anchorman Dan Rather when Rather insisted on asking Bush what he knew of the Iran-Contra scandal and when. Bush's sudden bellicosity helped offset the "wimp factor" which had dogged him for months.

Hart could do the same thing, and do it first. In trying to knife him, Chancellor has bared his own neck because after months of raucous scandal the country is ready to punish the media for giving them exactly what they want. This is Hart's big chance.

He could swing back as he did during a much less important speech a week before at Boston University. "How do we know that you will pay more attention to your oath of office than you did to your wedding vows?" someone had asked.

"First of all, my marriage vows are my business, not yours," returned Hart, to immediate applause. "Second, if to prove that I do make mistakes, people have to hide in my bushes and peep in my windows [Miami *Herald* reporters maintain they did not hide in bushes or peep through Hart's windows], I think they have to go to extraordinary lengths, and third, let's talk about judgment and character. Judgment's knowing what's right; character's having the courage to do it. And I would not . . . sell arms to terrorists . . . lie to Congress . . . shred public documents . . . pass the buck. I'll leave judgment to the American people."

So Hart has a fighting chance if he can just treat John Chancellor like any other ill-mannered heckler who dreams of Donna Rice swimming toward him through moonlit seas. Who is John Chancellor anyway but a pompous network bubble brain who thinks he is a better man than the elected senators, governors, and representatives he is introducing this night, simply because he is paid a fortune each year to deliver high school orations on the nightly news and they are not?

Hart sits on stage as shocked as the audience below, his gnarly Nazarene hands politely folded in his lap.

"Mr. Chancellor," he begins meekly, "I am here tonight to talk about how we are to pay for our Democratic shopping list, to talk of defense and taxes. These things are more important than the questionable taste of your introduction," and then his voice winds down like a sleepy puppy's. Hardly the home-wrecking Beast of Bimini tonight.

The audience of college students and native pols is enthralled: a senator, the former Democratic front-runner, brought down before their eyes like a star quarterback caught whacking off in the shower by the coach. So this was the Senator Hart who had sinned for the tabloids, who had deserted his constituency of Colorado construction workers, computer programmers, and Hollywood New Age money men to *schtup* a ditzy party girl fresh from "Miami Vice." It must have been fun while it lasted. But Chancellor has him in the stocks now.

More than others, "the American people seek out purity and innocence in their leaders," social philosopher Richard Sennett once wrote. We put our sages on pedestals, but we take great enjoyment when they fall. Sennett has a theory of why this is so. The early American Puritans practiced an important ritual of *inspection*. They believed that "man alone, in his sinfulness, is too weak to prove himself worthy in the eyes of God, and so the community must take part, too. Inspection, open discussion of a moral lapse, public penitence—by these means are men saved, and by these means the strings of the community are bound ever tighter." In trumpeting the escapades of Wilbur Mills, distorting the bimboism of lovely Rita, spotlighting Bob Bauman in his conservative closet, and hounding Gary Hart, the press is merely doing "the culture's dirty work," that is, serving as the means that we descendants of the Puritans may once more inspect our leaders.

Still, the media has a life of its own. This was never truer than during the Reagan era when the media had become Murdochized and, with less self-awareness, feminized.

"The Hart affair was the inevitable consequence of the gradual and inexorable deterioration of news standards over the past fifteen years," Mark Hertsgaard, the author of *On Bended Knee: The Press and the Reagan Presidency*, tells us. "All presidential candidates are arrogant and egotistical. They always will be. A lot of powerful male politicians have the opportunity to screw as many women here in Washington as they want, and many take advantage of it. In 1984 you could have caught Jesse Jackson in flagrante delicto any night of the week. It wasn't that Hart dared the media to check out his exemplary social life; that's just the media's own excuse for what they did to him. When Rupert Murdoch bought the New York *Post* in the late seventies, a sensational tabloid style took over many of the working-class papers in this country and then the networks, first CBS. Suddenly something as stupid as the marriage of Prince Charles became legitimate news. What you had at the start of the 1988 presidential campaign was a room piled high with straw and gasoline. In that context, it didn't take much of a flick of the match to say, 'Let's get Gary Hart.' In that context, who cares who flicked the match? The rules got changed on Hart."

This is one view.

A more direct opinion is expressed by Beth Frerking of the Denver *Post* at a small dinner the night of the traditional Democratic debate in New Hampshire. "I'm not exactly pure," Frerking, who is thirty and recently married, tells us, "but if my husband did to me what Gary did to Lee, I'd run him down and shoot him between the eyes. I'm a pretty good shot, too."

To which her friend Kathy Kiely, thirty-two, of the Houston *Post*, replies, "You know what Hart should do is take the sheets he says he didn't sleep on with Donna Rice, cut them into one-inch squares the way the Beatles did, and auction them off to pay his campaign debts."

Hard words. But the Hart affair struck strong chords. The saga of the senator opened a flood channel of anger in many American women, deep pools of resentment toward the men in their lives who had cheated on them, or left them for others, or done them dirty and wrong, or even evinced the barest of Walter Mitty sideway glances at the backsides of waitresses twenty years younger. And for the first time, there were women reporters and columnists who saw the personal as very political indeed.

"A feminist sensibility has seeped into the public consciousness sufficiently to make philandering appear to many at best unattractive, maybe unacceptable and possibly even alarming where the candidate's emotions and psychology are concerned," Suzannah Lessard wrote in *Newsweek* of the Hart affair. "Viewed from this perspective, the real issue in the Hart controversy was not Hart's 'judgment,' as some have argued, but the question of womanizing."

But realistically, how should a politician in a failing marriage like Gary and Lee Hart's handle the devil of sexual need?

"Get a divorce like the rest of us," Elinor Clift, the beleaguered liberal of TV's "McLaughlin Group" says to us, and crisply.

"I am told," Ellen Goodman tells us when we pay a visit to her office at the Boston *Globe,* "that Hart treats women horribly in the morning. At least they say Ted Kennedy makes breakfast."

"Hart lost the betrayed women's vote," Kathy Arnst of Reuters tells us in the pressroom before the New Hampshire debate, "and that's 95 percent of women. The press is mostly men, and they overlook this. We're angry. I can't be objective. I was the Lee Hart of my own life. I was going out with a sports reporter. It was the 'Slap Maxwell' story! I wanted to take Lee aside and say, 'You can do better.' If Hart wasn't happily married, he should have divorced her, but to do this to a woman with two children . . . All men are shits, and Gary Hart is proof of it!"

A river was flowing that was deeper and stronger than Arturo Cruz, Jr., understood. Without realizing it, poor Gary Hart had become America's monster of the id, his wayward penis a lightning rod.

But why do public men get caught, and why only some of them? Bad luck, political enemies, newshounds—these terrors stalk all politicians. A Kennedy, a Johnson, or a Jesse Jackson manages to avoid scandal, or at least deflect it, while the Harts, Baumans, and Millses go down in flames.

We hold a number of meetings with a man who has long been an under-cover officer with an intelligence agency in Washington. He is an intense but nondescript person. Our most memorable meeting takes place in a McDon-ald's. As we talk, a commotion suddenly erupts at the cash register. From the back where we are sitting, it looks as if a robbery is in progress. Our source rushes to the front. Instead of a robbery, a man buying a cheeseburger has fallen to the floor in an epileptic fit. Our source pulls out a two-way radio from his suit pocket (which surprises the McDonald's management), calls for an ambulance, and then returns to the little molded plastic table where we are sitting.

This intelligence operative had been called in to observe as Bauman cruised street hustlers. He knew a great deal about Wilbur Mills, a sex scandal allegedly involving Spiro Agnew and the Mafia, the case of John Jenrette, and the off-duty behavior of George Bush and Jesse Jackson.

"They get off on it," the intelligence officer says simply of those who get caught. As these men begin to understand that they are being followed and observed by police or press, he suggests, the strange delicious pounding thrill of what they are doing is actually enhanced. "They get harder," says the intelligence officer in the rear of McDonald's. Then instead of growing fearful and cutting back, these politicians often take even greater risks.

Wilbur Mills lurched onto the Combat Zone runway in Boston even after he had been videotaped drunken beside the Tidal Basin. John Jenrette jour-neyed to Florida and South Carolina for more money and different women all the time Rita Jenrette was trying to raise bail. "Stop me before I fuck again," a political consultant had once said of Senator Hart, only half tongue-in-cheek. Congresswoman Patricia Schroeder gives us the polite version: "A rational person would not do what Gary did if he wanted to be President."

"The pressure is just so constant and intense," says Rita Jenrette. "I think some politicians just want off the treadmill somehow, and so they begin to send out signals."

But since these are consummately ambitious men who have spent their lives on a fast track of their own making, they cannot easily step down or may be afraid to. They want to quit, but they don't know how. So they begin to behave like the alcoholic who binges more and more wildly until his world comes crashing down around him. They create a situation that finally forces others to take notice and intervene to stop them when they can't stop themselves. Behavior that appears to be crazy and self-destructive from the outside may actually be serving a logical emotional purpose. It is a call for help.

We visit one of Washington's preeminent political psychiatrists, Dr. Constantine Kyropoulos. The doctor is a calm, careful, gay man, fifty years old and a former naval officer, who graduated from Yale's medical school and completed his training at Georgetown. His house near Dupont Circle is hung with nineteenth-century landscapes. The couches are elegant but threadbare, some of them over a hundred years old, the rugs thin and even older. Sitting and talking in this living room full of period antiques is like falling into the time of President Buchanan.

Dr. Kyropoulos comments on the bad luck which seemed to shadow one former congressman from Mississippi, Jon Hinson. Hinson had the misfortune to be arrested for committing an obscene act in a public park, then trapped at a gay movie theater when the building caught fire, and later apprehended while giving head to a twenty-nine-year-old black male librarian in the public bathroom of a House office building. Hinson was like that Al Capp cartoon character who went everywhere with a little raincloud over his head.

"Someone in a responsible position who would exercise such poor judgment about one aspect of behavior is clearly manifesting some desire to be punished, some wish to be caught, some self-destructive, self-punitive need," says the doctor.

How would this need for self-punishment originate?

"The hypothesis held by many, and one that I partially subscribe to," says Dr. Kyropoulos, "is that these individuals, no matter how healthy they may be, have internalized a certain amount of homophobia, growing up in a culture that is basically homophobic, and that this takes the form of what might be called self-hatred, although that's often too strong a word. This self-hatred is sometimes acted out in behavior which is calculated not merely to provide a gratification of the sexual drive but concomitantly to produce a kind of punishment that goes along with having a forbidden or illicit or defective part of oneself. There is pleasure in the pain." And the logic of the formula applies in much the same way to sexually repressed heterosexuals as well.

In other words, if one is guilty but has to have it, it feels better if one is punished at the same time. What we are talking about is "safe humiliation," as Mya, the Washington call girl, phrased it in reference to "Miss Dirty," the congressman she serviced. Except that Miss Dirty, unlike Bauman and others, had his perversion under control. He was not signaling. Presumably he could stop himself if scandal appeared likely, just as Lyndon Johnson did, or Jack Kennedy, who once confided that he had decided to "lay off the poon" as he began his run for the presidency.

To Dr. Kyropoulous the single important quality in a politician is "integrity," which to him means "a kind of honesty of principle, an ability to establish sensible priorities, a recognition that the acclaim of public life comes with certain responsibilities, and I'm not convinced that one's sexual orientation has to be incorporated into that accounting."

But are politicians any different sexually from anyone else? Do they like to mix the pain with the pleasure a bit more than the rest of us? Does a spot of punishment provide release to men who spend their lives controlling others?

"That's like saying that all blacks like anal, or all Hispanics prefer the missionary position, or all lawyers do it doggie-style," a former Washington party girl who is now a California actress tells us. (We had never heard the one about lawyers.) "It's impossible to generalize."

Kyropoulos seems to agree. "You know," he says, annoyed and bemused at the same time, "I've never answered the basic question, Why are some people into some things and other people into others? Why is somebody a tit man and somebody else an ass man and somebody still further a leg man? It must have something to do with their mothers, I suspect. Gee, are we ever going to find out? Is it important? I don't think so."

The good doctor could afford to be arch. His life was stable and he was in, we might say, a depression-free business. Certainly, the weight of empire was not on his back, as it was for more troubled spirits.

Months later we talk with Arturo Jr. on the phone and the interchange is almost exactly as follows:

"I may be the biggest failure in the history of my country!" begins Arturo modestly. "I am in a desperate situation. I don't know what to do with my life. I am already thirty-three!"

"Such a pup," we say.

"Ah, Fawn," says Arturo, ignoring us, "she was the greatest love, not because of her beauty—she wasn't that beautiful—but because of her authenticity, her kindness, that she would put up with someone like me who is arrogant, problematic, confused, and unfaithful by nature. She finally said, 'Enough is enough. Either you get your act together or I leave,' and it so happened that I didn't get my act together. I am getting old!"

"Take heart!"

"What?"

"Take heart."

"Hart? Hart is an idiot!"

"No, no, *h-e-a-r-t,* as in 'take courage.' "

"Oh, oh, I see!" and Arturo breaks into a strong laugh. "I have a new plan," he says only a second later.

"Yeah?"

"Yes. I want to marry a Salvadoran oligarch," he jokes. "I have thought about it. Here I am, a man who likes to read and write who has no sense of practicality when it comes to money, although I still think I would have made a great politician. I'll go to Miami and find a Salvadoran oligarch who wants to have an intelligent husband, and that's it. Then I'll have a mistress in Paris and one in New York. When money is no object, what the hell! We'll have about seven kids in Miami, which should keep the Salvadoran very busy. At night she'll be too tired to make love, so that will leave me free. She'll never find out what I'm up to. I'll only cheat when I travel. That's how life used to be conducted by the old-fashioned playboys. American men are so crazy! They divorce their wives to marry their mistresses. Not me. I'll be happy with my oligarch. What the hell!"

What the hell . . .

SEX

WARS

The Beast Within

"**B**IG John," as we shall call him, steps forward from the circle of sixteen men sitting in the lotus position on the dark carpet and clutches his "power object" to his heart. A power object, as used in "men's movement" ceremonies like this one, is something that symbolizes one's inner strength. Several of the men here, like cofacilitator and psychologist Daniel Ellenberg, chose crystals as their power objects. A lawyer from Berkeley, exhibiting a wry sense of humor, chose a wristwatch. (Time is money. Money is . . .) Another man, an artist, displayed a favorite seashell. Cofacilitator Andrew Michaels brought a small wooden statue of Lao-tsu, the Chinese philosopher. Big John is an Oakland cop. His power symbol is a bit more literal: a .380-caliber automatic pistol.

The clip is out and the hammer is down, but it seems that therapist Ellenberg is a little nervous as he lays a gentle arm around Big John's enormous shoulders. This has to be a therapist's worst nightmare: "Umm, what you said about my mother—I just couldn't, I can't handle that" . . . and then the shooting begins, and this intense men's retreat at Harbin Hot Springs in Northern California turns into a screaming headline with bloody bodies jumbled about every which way.

John stands over six feet five inches tall. His stomach thumps out of his gray Nike T-shirt like a keg of Budweiser. His thinning hair is wild, and his eyes are wilder still, above three days of stubble and a broken nose. Two nights earlier, John had told the group that the woman he loved had left him for another woman. He had not been able to make love in the three years since. Last night, stepping out of another kind of circle, John had tossed a slip of paper into a roaring campfire. On the piece of yellow notebook paper was written the worst judgment John held against himself and the worst judgment he felt women held against him: "I will do anything, anything at all, whatsoever, you name it, for love," he had written, "and you [women] only judge me by the clothes I wear." The little piece of paper had burst into flame like an insect.

Now Big John smiles into a small bedroom mirror perched on a table between facilitators Ellenberg and Michaels. "I am," Big John whispers in a voice so low the rest of us can hardly hear, "a loving and sexual man. And," he intones, as each of us had before him in this ceremony designed to enhance self-esteem, "I love you. I love you," he repeats to his own image.

John turns and faces the rest of us, who are sitting cross-legged before him. Michaels strikes together a small set of brass cymbals behind Big John's head. The men raise both palms and salute him with a burst of male energy. Pistol across his chest, John stares into the eyes of each man, one after the other. The room is so silent you can hear the wind rustling through the manzanita bushes outside. John is crying. He does not blink as the tears roll slowly out of his eyes and down his unshaven face, because he is sad and happy and proud at the same time.

Perhaps it took some two thousand years for women to form the feminist movement. After only a decade or so the men's movement has reached critical mass. It is no longer limited to the Birkenstock-sandals set in Berkeley and Cambridge. The ranks now include cops and dogcatchers, corporate lawyers and computer executives. American men are on the march, God help us all. The elephant has risen, and he's in pain.

Yet these days the guys are not so much interested in learning how to cry as in learning how to lift their trunks and roar! The sensitive man of the seventies is now on a hunt for fiercer, more masculine pleasures.

In the San Francisco Bay Area, Boston, Los Angeles, Seattle, Minneapolis, and other hotbeds of the new masculinity, men can choose from hundreds of events: weekend retreats in the redwoods, workshops, therapy bull sessions, and full-blown ritualistic ceremonies. These gatherings are designed to help men overcome the mortifications of boyhood, break out of "the force field of women," and, ultimately, unleash "the wild man within" (of which, more later). Men young and old are beating drums and remembering about the fathers they never knew. They are laying bare their deepest shame and, more than a little bit, heaping scorn on the dominating women in their lives. Surprisingly, though, sex is not at all a hot topic at these gatherings. The New Man seems infinitely more fascinated with himself than with the ladies.

Naturally, some women—psychotherapist Lillian Rubin, for one—are appalled by these Cro-Magnon goings-on, while other feminists like writer Nancy Friday are saying, "Let 'er rip!" One thing is sure. As with the women's movement, the world will never be the same again. Take "Chas," for instance.

Chas follows Big John at Sunday's self-esteem exercise and his power objects must give facilitators Ellenberg and Michaels as much cause for concern about the direction of the New Man as Big John's dead-black automatic. When the little cymbals chime behind his ears, Chas is clutching to his heart a Polaroid of his pet cat laughing, a copy of the score to Mahler's Symphony No. 2, and an eight-inch wooden dildo spray-painted silver. Afterward, flashing a little insouciant smile that makes him look like a bearded and pudgy Jack Nicholson, Chas tells us the dildo is a self-portrait.

Like an unusual number of men today, Chas seems more comfortable with himself than with women. Earlier in the weekend, the facilitators had asked the men to take crayon and paper and draw a vision of what life might be like with their "ideal mate." It seemed to be kindergarten therapy at first, but the guys threw themselves into the visualization with gusto. Chas's picture was so minimalist that the group could not figure it out at first. Chas, a professor of art at a community college, had drawn a rounded figure on a bed. Three balloons like the circles cartoonists use for dialogue floated above the figure's head. The balloons were empty. The guys assumed the figure was a woman, but Chas quickly explained that it was not. The figure was himself. He was lying on his side on the bed masturbating. "Whacking off," he said.

The rest of us were stunned. Our drawings expressed fears and discord, sure. Nobody knew what the future held and most—except for Bill, who had been married only two weeks earlier and was spending his posthoneymoon in male company—were currently single. But the other drawings had vibrant colors, turquoises, reds, lots of pink. They usually contained a man and a woman, and there was a sense of hopefulness, however goofy.

Chas explained that hope was not part of the picture for him. No palm trees, no cabins in the mountains, no vibrant colors. Love was not an option. Perhaps he had a chemical imbalance, he suggested; perhaps, he had developed from a worthless zygote. (Get a bunch of us guys alone and together, gals, and we quickly start to sound like characters in a Eugene O'Neill play.)

The facilitators were quick to pick up on the root problem. They set up a role-play exercise with Chas. He was asked to choose one of the men to be his mother and another to represent his father. Chas selected an intelligent, intense man with delicate bones and glasses to serve as his mother and an older man from France to act as his father. "Give us a memory from your childhood," directed Michaels.

Now, you have to understand that context is everything in a setting like this. For two days and nights at this eleven-hundred-acre retreat in the California wine country that has become the Esalen of the 1980s, we seventeen men had been sharing personal stories and dancing and deep breathing. Everybody felt pretty comfortable, instantly intense, easily exhibitionistic. Guys seemed able to act out scenes in a few seconds that might have taken years to work through back in the city.

Chas immediately sets the stage: "I'm about eight years old. The old man wanders in drunk. He starts berating my mother. He's going to beat her. I can tell, but for now he insults her. It's a game he likes to play."

"Where are you?" Michaels asks.

"Me? Where am I?" Chas is rocking back and forth, getting into the memory. "I'm behind the stove. I'm cowering behind the stove like a scared little jerk."

Nobody needs prompting. "You're not pretty enough," sneers the Frenchman to the "mother." "You got old. You didn't keep yourself pretty enough—"

Chas tries to say something from behind the "stove."

"Shudup!" shouts the "father" in his French accent.

The Frenchman is good. He's into the part. You can see how drunk he is. He staggers, swaggers, slurs his words. The mother cowers, wilts. But when

Michaels calmly asks Chas if this is what his father was really like, Chas says, "Nah," hunching his shoulders, shrugging as if he were nothing, inconsequential, an eight-year-old little boy hiding behind a gas stove because he was too small and chicken. "No, he never cared what she looked like." That wasn't the problem.

Suddenly, Big John pivots forward on his knees.

"We have another father," says Michaels calmly. We do indeed.

"What the fuck's the matter with this house?" shouts Big John to his wife. The wife, a computer analyst from Silicon Valley, shrinks back in real fear. "You never clean it up!" shouts John. "What am I doing? Why am I working? It's a stinking pigsty you give me!"

Another guy suddenly jumps into the ring, Jessie. Jessie, it turns out, is as gay as Big John is straight, a man who used to hustle guys for money on Polk Street in San Francisco. His mother, and grandmother, too, were bikers, and when his dad or anybody else tried to make him change his ways, he ran for the shotgun he kept behind his toy chest. Big John and Jessie were raised, somebody says later, in the same house. Like Chas, Jessie and John know this action too well. Now we've got two fathers.

"You made him into a fucking wimp!" shouts Jessie at his wife.

"You're drunk," whispers Chas, defending his mother from behind the stove.

"Whadyou say?" shouts Big John, whirling at Chas.

"You're drunk," says Chas, a little louder.

"Is this more like it was?" Michaels says.

"This is definitely more like it," says Chas, biting his lip, beginning to sweat and smile, beginning to really get off on it, because he can't believe what's happening: this is the way it really was! "You have my father down to a T," whispers Chas to the two fathers, who do not smile back.

"Cut your fucking hair," says Daddy Jessie coldly.

"There's this boy down the block, Danny, he's going to turn out right, not like you," says Big John, even more coldly.

Big John turns on the mother all of a sudden. "You've given me a pussy. I'm going to make him a man."

Mother, the computer analyst, sputters, "I'm not— He's not—nngghhh, nngghhh—" is all she can say.

"Can't you speak English?" shouts Big John.

Jessie cocks his arm. He's going to belt her one.

"OK, guys," says Michaels quickly.

The players drop back into the circle.

"Where's your father now?" asks Michaels.

Chas smiles.

"He died!" screams Big John, his face red. "He died in the gutter, didn't he?"

"Yeah, he died just a few months ago," smiles Chas with his ambivalent little Nicholson smile.

"He died in the stinking gutter!" screams big, bleary-eyed John again.

"No," says Chas, calm as the Polaroid of his cat laughing, "he died old and drunk, but not in the gutter—not in the gutter one tiny bit. The bastard died happy."

A pillow appears in front of Chas, pushed there by Michaels. "You're dog meat, old man!" Chas shouts into the pillow, pounding it with his fists. "You're dog meat, and I wouldn't cut you up and feed you to my own dogs!"

We were beginning to like these guys: they didn't wimp around. They got the job done. We didn't much enjoy the exercises where we danced with men or the meatless dinners, but we could see that something was happening here. At first, these guys had seemed too needy. After a day it was clear that they were normal American men who had made a hard decision to change themselves. And being guys, you understand, they were kind of into frontier exaggeration.

But what was most interesting was how the subject always worked its way back to fathers. After all, the theme of this weekend was Love, Sex, and Intimate Relationships. One would think we would mostly talk about wives, girlfriends, sisters, and mothers.

And the group did manage a story or two about virginity, masturbation, sexual guilt, first wives, women who left us for other men or for women, bitches, tramps, good girls, princesses from every possible kingdom in America, and even that rarest of discussion topics in men's circles—as rare as she is in real life—the sexy, caring, intelligent, mature woman with a sense of humor who likes to do the sweaty all night long! But somehow father hunger always nosed its way into the circle like some nearly extinct species of wolf.

The search for the "distant father" has become a major preoccupation of the new men's movement. Perhaps a brief history of the post-World War II American male is in order. Many of today's New Men grew up in homes where the father was hardworking but absent. Unlike idealized TV dads such as Robert Young in "Father Knows Best," who always seemed to be home when Bud and Kitten needed his advice, most fathers toiled long hours in a skyscraper or factory to pay for suburban bliss. When Dad came home, bone-tired, he retreated into some vague male space, leaving Mom to bring up Baby and obsessively scrub the Formica with Spic 'n' Span. Sometimes good old Mom did right well, like Jane Wyatt, and sometimes, she smothered her sons in the love she could not extract from Dad and helped to make home a hell of manipulative game-playing and pointless trank-popping.

In the fifties, Dad was good at bringing home the bacon, but his elevator forgot to stop at emotions. He left that up to Mom, for better or worse, and so the son often began to identify with his mother's problems instead of his father's. He came to view his father's world as remote and coldhearted—and it was indeed a tough place, tougher than anyone may have thought at the time. As gender theorists later revealed, the stress of the gray-flannel world and the shop floor could lead to hypertension, alcoholism, and suicide—if men shut down their emotions. (Some four out of five suicide attempts are by women, but because women often choose pills and razor blades—methods that call attention but rarely do the job—three out of four successful suicides are men.)

When the women's liberation movement was launched, the son—by then a young man—responded sympathetically. He already saw love and sex through the eyes of his mother, since his father had been too busy, drunk, or confused to offer balance. To this young, tenderhearted man, feminism immediately seemed a just cause. By the early 1970s, as the antiwar movement faded, it was also often the scene with the hottest, most interesting women.

And so this new feminist man began to concern himself with day care, abortion rights, the ERA, and stopping violence against women—in short, the feminist agenda. He counseled wife-beaters and picketed against pornography, agreeing with those women who asserted that porn was violence, not some idle pastime of horny onanists. And, of course, he learned to cry and get in touch with his feelings.

Initially, feminists were delighted with this new, sensitive creature. They had created a man in their own feminized self-image. The Pygmalion myth in reverse. But then nagging doubts began to set in. Had they actually created a strange mutation—a soft, weepy hybrid of the sexes who lacked both the cockiness of the old male as well as the dynamism of the new female?

A frustrated feminist writer named Deborah Laake first sounded the alarm in 1983. "Where have all the real men gone?" she asked in a syndicated column. "Wimps and wormboys: what's a woman to do?" Wimps and wormboys! Here the sensitive man had gone out on a limb for his sister-lover. He had supported her, massaged her, learned how to cook *coq au vin,* and what does the ungrateful bitch do? Labels him a wimp, the same homo-epithet that jungle ape John Rambo used on him—superficial, illiterate John Rambo, who penetrated China dolls in Vietnamese forests without hardly a "Howdy-do, ma'am, do you have protection?"

Laake's outburst begins, you might have guessed, when she asks her honey to marry her, with the most circumlocutory rhetoric possible: "I told him, I hoped gently, that I was overwhelmed by the responsibilities falling to me in our union—those of principal breadwinner, head of the entertainment committee, business manager, and mother of souls. Feeling guilty, I told him that it appeared he could not be counted on to contribute much to my care or the welfare of our future family. Having unburdened myself, I leaned back to await Henry's reassurance.

"Instead, he said calmly, 'Yes, I think you're right. I'm just not a suitable choice for you.' "

This is where Laake decides to run her saber through poor Henry. "Wormboys have their charm. They can be sensitive and they often possess the wry humor characteristic of the observer." But, she concludes, they do "not want to carry the ball."

Imagine how John Rambo might react to all this. Deep in the jungle south of Ho Chi Minh City, he makes ready to rescue those MIA's single-handedly. He's got his C-rations and is grinding up insects for protein, tuning into the Voice of America on the shortwave for entertainment. Instead he catches one of those new radio talk shows, "Man to Man," and hears a self-proclaimed Radical Faerie blubbering about ungrateful feminists.

"Suck my cheroot," grunts Rambo as he snaps off the set and calls in an air strike on the station. "These women's libbers created a mule and now they have the nerve to ask where the stallion went."

But strong women weren't the only ones complaining. A growing number of male feminists were also getting in touch with their feelings—very much in touch—and they were mad as hell. "A lot of men feel hung out to dry by the women's movement," says Gordon Clay, a director of the National Council of Changing Men. "A lot of men feel that they, personally, are being held responsible for everything that's macho and wrong in the world today: rape, wife-beating, war. They've been feeling very bad about themselves, and so they're overjoyed to recover their maleness and feel proud about themselvs as men."

And so a new men's movement has risen on its hind legs, displacing (and often incorporating) the sensitive souls of the seventies. Call them "masculinists." At best, they're on a search for the true hearts of men. At their worst . . . well, who knows? We men have been a volatile bunch these last few thousand years. And no one understands this better than Robert Bly, the goose-voiced *paterfamilias* of the new men's movement.

The stage at San Francisco's Palace of Fine Arts is dimly lit and set, like an ancient theater, with plaster columns and enormous masks of the male gods, Hermes, Apollo, and Dionysus. Suddenly the drums hit a frenetic tempo. A thousand men in plush chairs roar like rutting elks, and old Robert Bly, poet, National Book Award-winner, protester of the Vietnam War, organizer of the Great Mother conferences of the seventies, six-feet-two, sixty-two years old, and craggy as the top of a mountain, appears stage center like some Garrison Keillor version of Zeus. He's accompanied by a younger sidekick, storyteller Michael Meade from Seattle.

"If I don't act holy, it's because I'm not," says Bly in his wry, flat Minnesota voice.

"Yes!" several men lift their voices.

"I can't believe how dumb you are to pay $55 to listen to a couple of self-indulgent guys ramble on."

The guys boo him good-naturedly.

Bly loves it. He insults his audience. "You're all patriarchs and inborn rapists."

This time the guys roar with manly delight! Outrageous!

It's like "Donahue" live, only with the door locked. The crowd treats Bly like a randy uncle. They shout things at him: "Robert, when we tell women our desires, they tell us we're wrong."

"So," says Bly, "then you bust them in the mouth because no one has the right to tell another person what their true desires are."

This time the bull-roaring from the audience is not as loud. A dissenting disciple of Bly's named Shepherd Bliss challenges him from the floor. Bliss, who has a Quaker farmer beard that misses his upper lip, is from a military background. Fort Bliss, Texas, is named after an ancestor. Bliss resigned his own commission in the army years ago, after hearing Bly denounce war at a poetry reading. Now he's a leader of the Northern California men's movement.

"Robert," says Bliss, "I feel uncomfortable with the violence in your statement."

"Yes," replies Bly, "I meant, hit those women verbally!"

Later someone actually stands up before the sea of men and relates how his father once caught him masturbating. The father beat him blow after blow across the bedroom until the poor guy fell and cut his penis.

Bloody members! (No wonder there is a retreat from sex going on.) Is this sort of shameless confession cathartic and healing, or is it simply New Age exhibitionism?

"Thank you," says Bly with bright-eyed irony, "for your horrendous story."

It's hard to tell whether Bly is inwardly laughing, but it seems he is. "A lot of my stuff is drawn from my own life," Bly says at one point. "I don't know how true it is, since my life is a combination of the disastrous and the unspeakable."

We had dinner with Robert Bly at a Cambodian restaurant a few nights before his showman-shaman performance at the Palace of Fine Arts. This night he was wearing an elaborate London Fog trench coat with epaulets. The coat was so thick and multilayered that it looked as if it could withstand a rain of muskellunge. His hair was white and full and wild above a quite nice, pink complexion, not alcoholic, the fair skin of a third-generation Norwegian who still lives on a farm. Bly kept ordering fish dishes.

"The male in the past twenty years has become more thoughtful, more gentle," Bly declared back in 1983, "but by this process he has not become more free. He's a nice boy who not only pleases his mother but also the young woman he is living with. I see the phenomenon of what I would call the 'soft male,' all over the country. They're lovely valuable people—I like them and they're not interested in harming the earth or starting wars . . . There's something favorable toward life in their whole general mood and style of living.

"But something's wrong. Many of these men are unhappy. There's not much energy in them. They're life-preserving but not exactly life-giving. And why is it you often see these men with strong women who positively radiate energy?"

Bly picked up this line of thought at the restaurant. "The anger of women in our culture comes partly from the fact that the men are not wild enough," he tells us over fish cake appetizers. "What's the use of being a wild woman if there aren't any wild men around? In her heart of hearts, the feminist woman doesn't want the man to do everything she's told him to. In fact," says Bly with a Minnesotan pause, "she's gotten so sick of it, she's ready to stab the poor bastard."

For Bly, the source of the soft male's weakness is certainly not feminism or even dominating mothers. The real problem, "the wound" that prevents him from being a "fierce" male, in Bly's words, is his estrangement from his father —and this began long ago.

Before the industrial revolution, fathers worked shoulder to shoulder with their sons, in field and shop. A boy knew well who his father was. He knew what it meant to be a man, for better or worse. But when most fathers began to troop off to factory and office, the sons fell into "the force field" of women.

"If our father was remote, as mine was," Bly explained, "our mothers would come to us with their own pain, verbal or otherwise, and we ten-year-old little men sitting in the kitchen were elected to shoulder it. This gives us a lifetime habit of carrying women's pain. If a man picks up women's pain, he's going to drop his own because you can't carry both at the same time. These sensitive men are wonderfully supporting of women in their grief and oppression, but about their own pain they know nothing at all. What we need now are people willing to examine the male wound."

The concept of the wound is very important to Bly and the new men's movement. The most telling wound to the soft male is probably the incest wound. "The mother flirts with the son because the father's not satisfactory. Happened in my family," smiles Bly with a mouth full of peppers and fish. "The young boy receives all his attention from women, his mother. He knows somehow that he's stolen from his father, and this widens the gap between him and his father. These boys crave praise, flattery of any kind. But the boy's sexual organs, naturally, are not useful in this exchange with the mother, only his spiritual nature. So the male gets split in the middle. In later life he can often only love a woman with the lower half of his body, his sexual part, or he can love a woman with his spiritual part, but not both at the same time."

In other words, this is the origin of the whore-Madonna complex so dear to many of us modern lads—wormboys, Rambos, and sensitive studs alike.

"My feeling," continues Bly chewing, smiling, "is that the wounds women receive in our culture are often wounds in self-esteem, very severe, and women have moved in the last thirty years to become conscious of this. But much of the pain men experience is inflicted by their fathers, and can only be healed by men, often men the age of their fathers. And so male feminists, in my opinion, are sort of beside the point."

The point is how to bring back the old ways that made men *men* in a way that modern men can understand and use. No easy trick, since for Bly, the old days could mean 10,000 B.C. Bly believes, borrowing from Jungian psychology and assorted preindustrial cultures, that every human society offers four stages of male initiation: bonding with the mother and breaking away from her; bonding with the father and breaking away from him; finding a male mother, that is, a nurturing wise man like King Arthur (or Robert Bly), who helps the boy-man into adulthood; and marrying what Bly calls, somewhat mystically, an "invisible Tsarina," who is one's true final mate but may also be something far more spiritual, a mating with the universe. (As concerns stage four, it is tempting to quote Gordon Clay on Bly: "Robert is so perceptive two thirds of the time it takes your breath away. The other third he's totally full of it.") About the only stage American men do well, according to Bly, is bonding with the mother.

In the bull-roaring old days, breaking away from Mom was a formal affair and done much better than we do. At about the age of eight or nine, boys were ceremoniously snatched from their mothers by older males. Sometimes they were held underground in caves, as with the Hopi. Sometimes, as with the Kikiyu of Africa, the boys drank the blood of the older men to replace symbolically the milk of their mothers. When the boys returned from this ritualistic period of separation in some other tribes, they smeared their faces with ash, and their mothers cried out and mourned and treated them as dead. Dead as boys, but born anew as men.

"The young boy cannot grow up to be a male without models to demonstrate the tremendous generosity, the spirit, the willingness to sacrifice for the community that the word 'male' implies in the positive sense," says Bly. This is one reason why teenage boys raised by single mothers often seem to fare worst of all, mouthing off, refusing to learn, chafing at the bit, joining criminal gangs. A teenage boy needs a father, and at the same time, he needs a community of good men to take him beyond his father.

In America the public community of older men is mostly negative. In the old days, even a few decades ago, positive old males were immediately visible —like Andy Griffith in Mayberry, you might say. A boy could sit down on the porch outside the sheriff's office and explain with embarrassment that Dad got a little rough with Mom night before last when the mine laid him off. In those days positive older males were sane and nice. They liked kids like you.

But now the big media create the image of the older male, and they seem to glorify crime figures, Wall Street raiders and, until recently, old bulls such as Ronald Reagan. Bly, no Republican, says the desperate hunger Americans have for positive older men explains the surge of young males who voted for Reagan in 1980 and 1984, even though Reagan, in Bly's opinion, is quite infantile, never having dealt with his father's pass-out-on-the-front-porch alcoholism.

During dessert Bly looks up, a little horrified. "I want to make clear to you," he said, "that I'm not trying to cure any of this."

"You're not?"

"Nope, just opening the wound." He laughs and laughs again.

Bly does, however, have something of a remedy for the soft male. It is not as swift and sure as the invasion of Grenada or the air strike against Libya, although it may be equally controversial. Bly's prescription is mythopoetic. "Mythology is the psychology of the ancient world," states Bly, quoting his own personal elder, psychologist James Hillman, "Psychology is the mythology of the modern world."

Bly believes the central myth that civilized man needs to recover, especially the soft-chested male, is the myth of the Wild Man. Some feminists might call this Wild Man "the beast within." The Wild Man myth is based on an obscure fairy tale by the Brothers Grimm called "Iron John." Iron John is an ancient hairy man who is found living at the bottom of a pond. To old Bly, this hairy Wild Man represents the sexual, primitive man that lies at the bottom of the modern male psyche.

In the fairy tale, Iron John is brought back to the castle in a cage. When the young Prince's golden ball, which Bly interprets as the radiant intelligence of the child, rolls into the Wild Man's cage, the gentle monster makes a deal: find the key to my cage and the ball will be returned. Bly points out that the 1970s wormboy looked to his feminine side for the golden ball, but this is not where it was lost. It has been lost in the "deep masculine" of the Wild Man, which is also very different from the shallow "savage masculine" of John Rambo.

The boy is frightened, and runs off, and finally says he has no idea where the key is. "The key," says the Wild Man, "is"—guess where?—"under your mother's pillow." So the boy steals the key, and the two take off for the forest, the Prince riding atop the Wild Man's hairy shoulders, knowing he will never see his parents again.

In some ways, the entire new men's movement can be described as a boy starting out on a long journey into the forest, perched uncertainly on the shoulders of a hairy old man he does not understand yet wants desperately to know.

The incessant, hypnotic drumming begins soon after we step inside the arched wooden chapel of St. John's, an Episcopalian church in the hills of wealthy Montclair, California. "Journey into the Male Wilderness," read the flyer. "Join us for a quest to rediscover what men hold sacred, to explore the seasons of men's lives, to tell our stories together."

Your author from Montana is there, along with about a hundred other men. This is a different crowd from Harbin Hot Springs or the Palace of Fine Arts. Vice presidents of several Fortune 500 companies, accountants, lawyers, two owners of local television stations, quite a few doctors, as well as a couple of downwardly mobile carpenters and a bearded forest ranger. One man who is a minister later tells the group, "I'm about as New Age as *The Wall Street Journal*."

The drumming takes your Montana man over. It is led on congas by Bruce

Silverman, "Drum Master and Psychotherapist." Silverman explains that the beat of a man's heart is samba. Shepherd Bliss, the former soldier who is presiding over today's rites, tells us that "the drum is one of the places where fathers and grandfathers live. They like a slow steady beat."

Bliss asks every man to pick up a drum. We all do—CEOs and forest rangers. The guys shake rattles and tap bongos and whap whatchamacallits. I end up with some weird leather bracelet strung with little leather pouches full of tiny stones. It sounds pretty good. Not too embarrassing. Fun, for nine o'clock on a Saturday morning. Everybody turns into an eight-year-old little man right away. The situation is trancelike. Bliss asks us to think of the drums.

I think of a morning in the Pelhourinho Hotel in the old section of Salvador da Bahia, Brazil, when it was so hot she and I finally had to quit and take a shower, and in the shower we got turned on again, with the water and the soap and the twenty-foot ceilings, and as I smoothed her against the wet wall and she lifted her legs around me, I heard the ba-dooping of the drums through the sound of the falling water. Very good drunks were keeping carnival going on congas that morning in the street far below.

And then with no warning, I think of my father tapping the metal dashboard of our 1957 Chevrolet Impala to the tune of "Happy Jack," by the Who, as we passed through the black forest west of Yellowstone, and the old man jumping out of the same car six months later in the same forest, at twenty-seven below zero, so he could "get some exercise," because it turned out he was dying of pancreatic cancer, and he couldn't tell anybody of the pain, not even himself. And so I led in that Great American motorcar, not understanding the old man was dying, of course, but knowing it was strange that anybody would insist on walking behind a car like a boxer in training when trees were snapping from the cold and the ground had been frozen for months.

And I think of the funny times when the old man drove me out to Yale, college in the East, and we stayed for a night in New York, which he hadn't visited since he was a flyer in World War I (my father having been born fifty-five years before me, in 1893), and the old man asked me what I wanted to do on our night in the big city, so I said, "Let's go to this concert by this group called the Doors," and we did, sitting so close to the stage that Jim Morrison seemed about to split his leather pants. And the old man, seventy-five at the time, aging out anyone else in the audience by a good—a very good—fifty years, stood up with a smile after the last encore, and I asked him what he thought about the music, and he said just about what he said when he used to turn up "Happy Jack" on the car radio: "I like the beat, Steve." Turned out the old man was tone-deaf.

So you see how quickly us sentimental guys, with our wolf deficiency, hunger.

"It's all part of the backlash against feminism," psychologist Lillian Rubin tells us. Rubin is the author of *Intimate Strangers,* the best-selling book on the chasm between the sexes. "The concerns of the men's movement seem to have shifted from the early days when there was a strong interest in figuring out relationships with women. Nowadays, there seems to be a need to make women irrelevant.

"There's something forced and artificial about this sudden obsession with fathers. The real charge in men's lives is around their relationship with women. These men may want to have you believe that women are not all that important in their lives, but if you dig a little beneath the surface, you soon find out that they are very important.

"As for male bonding rituals, there's nothing new about that. That's been going on as long as men have walked the face of this earth. I have no more sympathy for this 'beast within' Wild Man thing than I do for those in the women's movement who are into goddess worship. Both are off the track. Neither archetype—goddesses or male power symbols—have to do with being real human beings. I'd prefer to see us all become more androgynous."

"I personally never got off on the androgynous man," counters Nancy Friday, the famous chronicler of erotic fantasies. "Women want empathetic, sensitive men—but then they don't," she tells us. "Today's successful women can't deal with dominating men in their lives, but that's precisely the type they fantasize about. The contradiction drives them crazy."

("Shades of the whore-Madonna complex . . . in reverse . . . with a lime twist!" mumbles John Rambo, out of quinine, but beginning to catch on.)

"I can see where men would be attracted to these primitive male rituals because they are like the call of the wild, something familiar, primal, in an increasingly unfamiliar sexual world," says Friday. "Men have been asked to break new ground, much of which has been laid out by a contradictory feminism. Women are saying, 'Treat me like an equal,' and at the same time, 'Take care of me.' A great deal is being asked of men. Both sexes are confused.

"It's true that the shadowy father is a very important factor in men's development. When the little boy begins to break away from his mother, that's precisely the crucial point in his life when he needs a father, a male model, to help him figure out what it is to be a man. But the father is generally absent. So little boys get together and decide for themselves. All they have is their cocks to give them a separate identity. They're young and they still operate on the biological level. The fact that their father is away making money holds no significance for them at that age. They can't understand that. They end up rejecting everything associated with Mother as sissy. They have to be everything bad and dirty. The 'boy gang,' to use Jack Kerouac's term, becomes all-important. That's what gives them their identity. And that's what these older guys are trying to find with their tom-toms and male rituals.

"But the charge that this stuff is 'anti-feminist' is one-eyed poppycock. We're all in this confused period together, men and women, good and bad, trying to figure out what the new sexual order will be."

Nancy Friday is right. It is a confused time, a shakedown period between the sexes. Most men, like most women, are doing what they do best— groping, letting themselves be carried along in the strange current that is contemporary America. But sometimes it seems as if many New Men have decided to quit treading water altogether. These guys are heading for the far bank. They are in retreat from sex, from emotional engagement with women. Those up top of Iron John's shoulders are off on a narcissistic journey of self-discovery. "Snips and snails and puppy dogs' tails," Greek Gods and campfires, fathers and grandfathers are what hold their interest now. It may be a necessary and temporary journey. Or it may be that many guys will find they like forest living better than bedroom battles.

If there were one place you would expect to find heat-seeking New Men, still hot and ready to trot, it would be Marin County, home of hot-tub hedonism. With this in mind, we sit in one night at a meeting of the Men of

Marin. The topic this evening: Is Sex Necessary? And the answer seems to be: "Well, not really, it's too much of a hassle." As always, Marin may be on the cutting edge.

More than any other group, the Men of Marin are ordinary guys: a carpenter, a bookkeeper, a computer operator, a pharmacist, a dogcatcher (graveyard shift). It seems to us that Huey Lewis, the just-folks Marin rocker, could have sat comfortably in that circle in the carpeted annex of the county public education building.

The discussion leader, who is the carpenter, thin and articulate, passes around a box of chocolate truffles. The guys begin to talk of this and that, nothing close to the topic of the evening, until the carpenter laughs and says, "Well, maybe truffles are better than sex. What do each of you think?"

We go around the circle.

The bookkeeper, who somewhat boldly describes himself as "a sloppy fucker who used to like to eat out regularly," explains that he has not made love with anybody for six months. "I've checked out of the sexual rat race," he says. "I'd rather get together with friends and talk about computers."

The pharmacist starts to talk about orgasm but becomes more aroused as he explains how in a few days he is planning to climb mountains in Nepal.

The discussion leader says that despite a growing number of sexual opportunities in his life, he often prefers to loll about in bed alone. If his new girlfriend, a truck driver with inconvenient working hours, wants to visit him, great; otherwise, he is content to turn out the lights and be his own best friend.

The dogcatcher shyly wonders how many times a week is "normal."

You coauthors go on a little longer than the Men of Marin, but then they are both first-time visitors.

One of your coauthors tells the group that growing up in Hollywood has hooked him on softly lit love scenes and dramatic complications. He always seems to be torn between two, sometimes three different women. And he wonders aloud if it will all fade out with a happy ending.

And one intense man originally from Montana says that sex sets him apart from his worries, from life itself sometimes. It puts him in a slow playful trance which is as far as he can get from dying and he has seen too many friends, and his brother and his father, die around him.

Much later we think back on Saturday night at Harbin Hot Springs, the time around the campfire when we had thrown those paper imprecations into the flames. As wood burned into ashes, we sang the campfire songs of our generation from "(I Can't Get No) Satisfaction" and "Louie Louie" to "Amazing Grace."

"Amazing Grace/How sweet the sound/That saved a wretch like me."

American men. Still hungering for deliverance.

Perhaps salvation is only a generation away. If the fathers of today become the fathers they never had, their boys may just learn to become both strong and gentle—"fierce," as Elder Bly would put it. Boys would then grow into stout-hearted men who wouldn't let women walk all over them (like our poor friend, the wormboy); at the same time, they would be caring adults who listened to that special woman and loved her all over.

What we need here is a certain synthesis, a happy ending. Remember Iron John in the woods? He's loping down the grassy slope like a naked grizzly. Our frightened Prince holds onto his hairy shoulders for dear life. Somewhere at the bottom of the little valley, we want them to build a house of bark. For seven magic years, Iron John will show the Prince how to chart the stars and cook venison on a spit. Iron John never speaks of women, but his strength is seeping into the Prince until one day, as the Prince is about to shoot a deer with his longbow, Iron John holds up his hand. Over the hill come two Princesses.

One is a giant pine-tar bitch as gross and instinctual as Iron John. Her dugs hang down and her nips are sweet, and she moans as John kisses her. The Prince and Young Princess watch transfixed, but as they do, Iron John and Ms. Pine Tar evaporate before their eyes, as if they were never there.

The Young Princess turns to the Prince. "What kind of love do you want?" she asks. This Princess is wearing a green leather loincloth and not much else.

"I want a Saturday night kind of love," replies the Prince. "And you?"

"I want a Sunday kind of love, the kind that lasts into the next day."

And so they make love for the entire weekend.

And on Monday morning, very early, they walk back to the castle, to civilization, hand in hand, both the wiser for what they have learned.

The Furies

AT fight! That's what the producers of "Donahue" were trying to stage, thought Erica Jong, when they booked her with Andrea Dworkin in the spring of 1987. Both were feminists, both were writers, but the parallels stopped there. Jong, author of the 1973 best-seller *Fear of Flying* and other popular novels featuring frolicsome heroines, was one of the country's more widely recognized voices of sexual liberation. Jong's books spread the idea that women could emancipate themselves by adopting the same jaunty attitude toward sex long held by many men. "The zipless fuck." It was Jong who had coined that memorable phrase.

Andrea Dworkin was a far different creature, a radical lesbian polemicist who viewed sex between men and women as a desecration of the female body. In her latest book, *Intercourse,* she had likened the erect penis to a weapon of war: "The thrusting is persistent invasion. [The woman] is opened up, split down the center. She is occupied—physically, internally in her privacy."

Yes, the fur was sure to fly on this one. Here, on one stage, under the white-hot TV lights, the opposite poles of American feminism were going to thrash away at one another. Phil Donahue, that symbol of male sensitivity and moderation, would have to jump in to restore order. Hose them down with a commercial break. Talk-show melodrama thrived on face-offs like this.

But something unexpected, something full of larger meaning, happened that morning in the NBC studio in Rockefeller Center. Instead of greeting Dworkin's extraordinary sexual opinions with cries of derision and savage barbs, Jong offered her qualified praise. Jong rejected the notion that sexual intercourse was an inherently "invasive and pounding" act; in a "more feminized culture," sex between men and women could be something warm and cuddly. Still, she said, "[Andrea] has asked some very important questions and written a very brave and honest book."

Here was a curious turn of events: the celebrity novelist known for her bawdy heterosexuality paying respects to a feminist intellectual of daunting severity who regarded intercourse as "collaboration" with the enemy. Women who spread their legs for men, Dworkin had written, were in fact "more base in their collaboration than other collaborators have ever been: experiencing pleasure in their own inferiority; calling intercourse freedom."

Donahue seemed unsettled by this unlikely rapprochement. "Do you have any difference at all with Ms. Dworkin?" he pleaded with Jong. But the novelist would not be goaded into attack. His studio audience, however, was less deferential. These were women who already knew what they felt about sexual intercourse. They regarded Dworkin with pity and scorn. "I'm married and I would never give up my sexual intercourse," said one. "What tragic thing happened in your life that made you feel this way?" asked another. A third woman expressed her wonder over Jong's apparent turnabout: "You were the one who coined the term 'zipless'—uh—encounter!" she marveled.

The following year, Erica Jong and Andrea Dworkin renewed their sisterly pact by posing side by side in the pages of *Ms.* magazine. They made an odd couple: Jong, with her soft bouncy mane and her black and sparkling silver designer outfit with matching high heels, flirting with the camera; and Dworkin, fat and impressive as a Samoan queen, looking us dead in the eye, wearing her trademark blue-jean overalls, leather jacket, and running shoes—a costume designed "to keep men and the world at bay," in Jong's words.

In the accompanying article, "Changing My Mind About Andrea Dworkin," Jong explained that she had once been "turned off by [Dworkin's] rhetoric, its 1960s cant, and by what I took then to be its crude overstatement of women's lot. But I was a lot younger and more innocent then, and as

Gloria Steinem says: Women are the sex that grows more radical with age."
Now, wrote Jong, her attitude toward Dworkin was that of a "respectful
dissenter." Jong still had some nagging doubts about "the dimension of paranoia" in Dworkin's work. After all, Jong herself had "enjoyed sex [with]
loving lovers" during her "charmed life." But perhaps Dworkin's brutal portrait of male-female relations was more representative than her own experience, mused Jong. Perhaps Dworkin's lesbianism gave her special insights into
"the hypocrisies of the patriarchal system."

Perhaps men really were, in their dark core, a specter from a Sylvia Plath
poem: "A man in black with a Meinkampf look/And a love of the rack and
the screw."

The press did not take notice of Jong's tribute to Dworkin. But it seemed
to us a cultural marker of sorts, an event that suggested a deepening rancor in
the world of feminism, a growing division between the sexes. We sought out
Jong, finding her in the New York brownstone off Park Avenue where she
lives when not in residence at her Connecticut country home or summering
in Venice. We wanted to know how she had come to sip from the tart and
brackish waters of Andrea Dworkin and call it a fount of wisdom.

Jong was, after all, a writer who had formed a close friendship with Henry
Miller, that old goat of American literature, a man whose work was deeply
reviled by many feminists. She was a woman who had once written a poem
about sucking off her lover just before going on a TV talk show ("My mouth
seeded with your sperm/I talked back to the interviewer"). Here was a
woman who had told *Playboy* magazine, "I can get enormously turned on by
being dominated in bed." Yes, here, it must be said, was a woman who salted
her novels with hot and sweaty acts of "collaboration" and whose fictional
alter ego, Isadora Wing, relished a good "pounding" now and then.

"When Bean entered her," wrote Jong in *Parachutes and Kisses,* her third
Isadora novel, "it was as if she were possessed by a dybbuk. When he rammed
her, she found herself urging him on in a voice that didn't even seem to
belong to her—as if she had truly become a bacchante, as if the boundaries
between pain and pleasure had totally dissolved and he were her master, her
priapic god, pounding her soul as well as her body.

"Ah—she claimed to worship the Great Mother, but she was in thrall to
the penis, cock-bound, cock-mastered . . ."

So much for warm and cuddly sex.

What in the name of the Great Mother, it seems fair to ask, is going on here? Who is the real Erica Jong? Cock-mistress or cock-slayer?

There is, of course, an ungenerous explanation for Erica Jong's changing sexual politics. It could be noted that by the time *Parachutes and Kisses* was published in 1984, bawdiness no longer seemed so fresh or charming. A different mood had settled over the country, and the book was much less successful than *Fear of Flying*. It did not take a writer as finely calibrated to cultural change as Jong to determine that a market repositioning might be in order. One could see her new sympathy for this puritanical strain of feminism as an effort to get back in tune with the country's zeitgeist.

But Jong herself had a different explanation. What she told us was this: She had come to feel soiled by her association with sex, because America has a dirty mind. A mind Andrea Dworkin understands all too well.

"I can't tell you how horrified I am," said Jong, "when I get these letters from men: 'I'm going to be in New York, can I came and fuck you?' Or 'Send me a pair of dirty underwear.' They've taken sex, which should be a feast of life, and put it in their meat grinder. When you get mail like that for fifteen years, you begin to get dismayed.

"We reduce sex to the gutter in this country. It's a vast Forty-second Street of the mind out there. 'The zipless fuck' was just Isadora's fantasy, not something I yearn for. My idea of sex is something sensual, beautiful, poetic, not indiscriminate. It's cuddling in bed, lying in a field of flowers, eating figs. My books are better understood in Europe.

"The sexual revolution was joyless, acquisitive, quantitative. It was an outgrowth of our materialistic, addictive culture. Americans believe that the more they consume, the richer they'll become."

We were feeling an impolite urge to point out that no best-selling author has done more to trivialize sex than she. The men in Jong's novels are seldom more than ducks in a shooting gallery, knocked off in quick succession. But the conversation suddenly turned to erections. "Andrea Dworkin has a profound aversion to the penis," Jong observed. "I don't share that feeling, that fear of penetration. But I honor her as an intellectual."

Dworkin, she continued, was "on to" something deep, something buried in the American unconscious—the boot-in-the-face element of male-female relations. "The extreme reaction to Andrea Dworkin is like shooting the messenger. She says things people are afraid to say. Our society is in deep denial about the violence to women."

The bonds between men and women seem more frayed than ever, Jong went on. "Both sexes are running screaming from one another in panic and dread. Men don't feel they're getting the nurturing they need, and women feel they're getting trashed all the time, getting dumped after falling in love." She herself has crashed and burned more than once in recent years. There was the wrenching divorce from writer Jonathan Fast, father of her daughter, Molly; followed by an outburst of promiscuity ("a grief-and-mourning reaction"); followed by a romance with a much younger man, who left her when he turned thirty "to go out and prove himself"; followed by a year-long engagement to another man; followed by a free-floating period of half commitments that she found melancholy and unsatisfying.

"The culture is not giving us any answers about love or sex or raising babies," Jong concluded, sounding all at sea. "We've torn down the old social structures and haven't replaced them with anything new."

Jong confessed that she was not comfortable with Andrea Dworkin's "confrontational" style. In fact, she objected to the "whole paradigm of the war between the sexes," with its "antagonistic dualism rooted in Western culture." She longed for a harmonic convergence of the sexes: "We have to think holistically or we'll destroy the planet." But in the confusion of the 1980s, with men and women groping for new roles, sexual antagonism had more immediate appeal. It was easier to bash the opposite sex than to set up a new social order.

There was no doubt about it. The war between the sexes was turning as ugly as a Sicilian blood feud.

It had not always been so.

In the beginning, the wolf lay down with the lamb. Sex and feminism were merry cohabitants in the early years of women's liberation, the late 1960s and early 1970s. These were the years when Germaine Greer showed off her backside in the pages of *Suck* magazine (after insisting that the male editors display their hood ornaments for readers' inspection) and sang out, "Lady, love your cunt!" There were feminist masturbation workshops and barebreasted demonstrations. The demand for more sexual pleasure was one of the movement's main rallying cries. Men had their attention directed rather forcefully toward the clitoris and were given new insights into the mysterious splendor of the female anatomy by the wide dissemination of speculums.

Feminists insisted that women's liberation would also free men sexually, by putting fewer demands on their "pork swords," in the words of the ever-colorful Greer, and eroticizing the entire body. Sex would no longer consist solely of piston mechanics but would also involve a mutually glorious exploration of uncharted erotic territory. There was some truth to this grandiose declaration, as many men who came of age in those years can personally attest, including your two authors. One of us still has sweet memories of his college days in a three-story Victorian house in Santa Cruz, California, where a collective of young feminists and lesbians, all radiant and bold with their new understanding of life, taught him the ways of the fingers and tongue. Reeducation can be an agreeable task.

But as the years went by, sexual liberation and feminism grew further apart. The focus of the movement seemed to shift from explaining what gave women pleasure to dictating what should give *men* pleasure. Feminist literature became as prescriptive in its way as those old sex manuals which advised couples that missionary coitus was the only medically sound technique. "The sexual personality is basically antiauthoritarian," Greer had written. But feminism increasingly sought to impose a politically correct design on sex. Any bedroom play that was not gentle or "poetic," in Jong's words, fell under suspicion.

At the same time, men and male sexuality were increasingly demonized in the works of leading feminists. Rape, battering, and child abuse came to be seen as not so much a product of cultural tensions or human imperfection as male instinct. Feminists who once soundly rejected the "biology is destiny" argument began proclaiming the natural moral superiority of women. Man-hating had previously been limited to the more eccentric offerings of the women's movement, such as the infamous SCUM (Society for Cutting Up Men) manifesto by Valerie Solanis, a New York actress who pumped two bullets into Andy Warhol's stomach in 1968. ("The male is an incomplete female, a walking abortion," proclaimed SCUM.) But as the seventies and eighties progressed, a sense of profound revulsion from men could be found in a growing number of women's magazine articles and feminist best-sellers, including Susan Brownmiller's *Against Our Will,* the Hite reports on love and sexuality, Alice Walker's *The Color Purple,* the novels of Marilyn French and Fay Weldon, and the torrent of "men bad/women good" advice books.

Great red-and-gold explosions of fury were lighting up the sky in all directions. In this climate, not surprisingly, consorting with the opposite sex became a strained and perilous operation for many women. If you let men into your home, Marilyn French declared, "In an hour they were in your bed, and after that *whoosh!* they'd taken over your space, your life. Just like that." Sex researcher Shere Hite spoke for many other feminists when she announced that the sexual revolution had been largely invented by "male novelists [and] male-oriented magazines" to win men greater access to women's bodies.

Of course, not everyone in the women's movement regarded sexual liberation as a male conspiracy. A number of New York feminist intellectuals, including Ellen Willis, Carole Vance, Ann Snitow, Lisa Duggan, and Kate Ellis, protested the drift toward prudery in women's culture and the increasingly censorious antipornography movement. These self-styled "bad girls" of feminism organized conferences and published essays that called for a freeing of women's sexual imagination. They charged that by defining male sexuality as brutal and ruttish, and female sexuality as soft and refined, the "good girls" of feminism reinforced traditional sexual ideology, putting women on a pedestal as "the weaker sex." Goody-goody sexuality not only clamped a straitjacket on heterosexual women but also on lesbians, according to the bad-girl feminists, among whom were a number of women who loved women.

The bad-girl intellectuals sought to burst the bonds of shame and taboo. At a controversial conference on sexuality held at Barnard College in the spring of 1982, women at one workshop were asked to write down their deepest, darkest fantasies. "The pieces of paper were thrown in a hat and read out loud," recalls the workshop leader, anthropologist Paula Webster. "One woman wished there were glory holes for women. Another wanted to fuck her brother. After a bunch more of these were read, a woman from Scandinavia stood up and complained, 'I haven't heard the word 'love' mentioned once here today.' I said, 'Well, you're probably not likely to either.'"

Here was a cheeky new attitude on the part of educated middle-class women: Sex was its own reward. Kinky sex too. In 1986, a committee of women that included Rutgers English professor Kate Ellis and ACLU attorney Nan Hunter published a collection of essays on pornography and censorship,

Caught Looking, which was illustrated with the most diverse assortment of obscene photographs and drawings ever gathered in a feminist journal: old French postcards of grinning men in handlebar mustaches sliding between the splayed black stockings of their mistresses; stills from 1950s stag films featuring blondes in bondage and men and women with mouths full of cock; snapshots of performance artist Karen Finley shoving baked yams up the dark side of her moon; orgy scenes of every possible description.

This chaos of raunch was exciting, unhinging. But the bad girls' libertine philosophy failed to light a spark outside a small intellectual circle. Even they themselves confessed to leading lives of quiet domesticity; most were married or coupled off with devoted lovers. Their wild sexual explorations were, for the most part, of a theoretical nature. "We used to joke that the more we talked about sex, the less we got," smiles Paula Webster. "Some of us visited an S&M society once, but mostly to observe. All the real experimenting was probably going on in California. For all our talk, we were pretty repressed."

It was a brazen sensibility borrowed largely from gay male culture—a culture that was itself turning increasingly tame in the shadow of AIDS—and it just did not seem to hang well on most women. Too much in the crotch. Like the Scandinavian woman at the Barnard conference, it seemed, the fairer sex generally wanted to know, Where is the love?

The feminists who struck the deepest chord with women in the 1980s were those who reviled male sexuality, not those who sought to imitate it. These angry women did not find the tag "good girls" amusing; they called themselves radical feminists. And with good reason, for what they were demanding was indeed sweeping in its ambition. They wanted nothing less than a drastic retooling of male sexuality, a feminization of the hairy beast within. Their crusade was "a cultural revolution in progress," declared Shere Hite. And by the beginning of the 1980s, these revolutionaries had established themselves as the dominant force within feminist culture and were extending their influence over mainstream culture as well.

Meanwhile, throughout the grand debates on sex and love that were shaking the Empire of patriarchy, heterosexual American men remained, for the most part, strangely, dumbfoundingly mute. The most intellectually provocative examinations of the realm of the senses were almost exclusively the work of feminists and gay men. Like a husband who sullenly withdraws to his tool shed to escape his wife's temper and misery, American men simply opted out of the cultural dialogue. Occasionally, the old chest-beaters like Norman Mailer or hearth-and-home traditionalists like George Gilder were heard from, but these were the fading roars of the past. Ishmael Reed landed a few blows when he struck out at what he viewed as the growing feminist control of the culture industry and the scapegoating of black men in feminist literature. But he swung so wildly he opened himself up to the KO punch. More interesting was the new masculinism of Robert Bly, but his men's retreats were just that —a flight from the sex wars.

In fact, men were so far removed from the field of battle in the 1980s that the term "sex war" seems a misnomer. The "stronger" sex could only mount an occasional guerrilla raid, leaving women firmly in control of the ideological terrain.

Without a countervailing male voice or a strong expression of feminist moderation, the center could not hold in the 1980s. The ones with the passion, the ones who got the blood going, were the radical feminists. With them in ascendance, the women's movement began to give a different message to American society: sex is dangerous and degrading; desire must be strictly regulated.

As we shall see in the following pages, this was the same odd tune heard on a wide range of feminist channels. It was the song sung by Andrea Dworkin, by Susan Forward, by Shere Hite, and finally, even by that longtime sexual revolutionary Germaine Greer. Such were the times.

Yes, the heavens were filled with strange wonders; planets collided and realigned. Feminists forged alliances with Bible-thumping preachers to enact antipornography ordinances. A woman doused herself with gasoline and set herself on fire in a Minneapolis porn store to protest sexual exploitation—an act of feminist self-mutilation that called to mind the tongueless Ellen Jamesians in *The World According to Garp*. In the spring of 1987, after more than six years of Reaganism, feminists gathered at New York University Law School to attack *liberalism*—in particular the ACLU and the First Amendment—for "fiercely defending the rights of men to control, abuse, and profit from the bodies of women."

Among the more provocative moments of the NYU conference was a declaration by a group calling itself Women Against Sex (WAS). According to the WAS manifesto, not just intercourse, but *all* sex, oppresses women— including lesbianism and masturbation. "All these erotic choices are also a part of sexuality as constructed by male supremacy," stated the WAS position paper, which was accorded serious discussion at the conference. "We have learned that we cannot trust our feelings . . . Genital arousal represents the literal incarnation of women's political subordination. It is politics made flesh." Therefore, stated the women of WAS, until sexuality was "dismantled" and reconstructed according to their own feminist design, the only correct sexual practice was no sex at all, or "radical celibacy." It was all a far cry from "Lady, love your cunt!"

"We have learned that we cannot trust our feelings." It could have been the motto of the decade.

The conference also heard from such feminist celebrities as Gloria Steinem, and Shere Hite. But the true star of the gathering was that orator in overalls, that spellbinder who spoke for the tongueless masses, that bather in the blood of female suffering, Andrea Dworkin. For it was the fiery and ecstatic Dworkin who best captured the Holy Rolling spirit of the days. She did not have the high visibility of the big-name feminists. But the hot breath of her righteous anger was felt throughout the movement. She was, to hear Gloria Steinem tell it, "an Old Testament prophet for feminists." Or, as Dworkin herself put it, "I am a feminist, not the fun kind."

As a teenager, growing up in Camden, New Jersey, Andrea Dworkin enjoyed reading what she called "very high-class intellectual pornography." Books such as the pseudonymous Pauline Réage's *Story of O,* the hallucinatory novel of sexual servitude that created a sensation among the Parisian literati when it was first published in 1954.

> "You are here to serve your masters . . . Your hands are not your own, nor are your breasts, nor, most especially, any of your bodily orifices, which we may explore or penetrate at will."

Dworkin would recall, "I responded to it absolutely."

Later, as a literature major at Bennington College in the mid-1960s, she defended the book in an argument with a young Marxist. He was outraged; he called O's ordeal "the ultimate in alienated labor." "Oh," Dworkin shot back, "but you know nothing about love." She thought *Story of O* "very profound, and very full of ideas about sex, and very full of ideas about what love really was."

> O felt that her mouth was beautiful, since her lover condescended to thrust himself into it, since he deigned publicly to offer caresses to it, since, finally, he deigned to discharge in it. She received it as a god is received.

Of course, Andrea Dworkin would come to have very different ideas about pornography. And about love and sex. But the château at Roissy, the chamber of O's sublime defilement, would continue its hold on her, like a painfully exquisite melody.

Dworkin was propelled toward feminism by two episodes of sexual trauma in her life. The first occurred in 1965, while she was still a freshman at Bennington, when she was arrested during a protest against the Vietnam War and held in the Women's House of Detention in New York City. "I spent four days and four nights in the filth and terror of that jail," she later wrote in *Our Blood,* a collection of her essays. While there, two doctors—she did not say whether they were women or men—"gave me a brutal internal examination. I hemorrhaged for fifteen days after that. The earth moved for me then." "The earth moved for me then." It is a curious way to describe her violation, a metaphor of sexual euphoria. As Dworkin points out earlier in the same essay, it echoes what Maria is asked in *For Whom the Bell Tolls,* after making love with Robert: "Did the earth move?"

The second trauma lasted longer and had an even greater impact on her. In 1969, Dworkin married a young Dutch radical. After taking up residence with him, she discovered he was a violent man, a batterer. She stayed with him for three years. Later, she wrote about the experience in a moving and beautifully crafted article that appeared in *Mother Jones* magazine, "The Bruise That Doesn't Heal": "By the time I was 26 I was still a terrorized woman. The husband I had left would come out of nowhere, beat or hit or kick me, disappear. A ghost with a fist, a lightning flash followed by riveting pain . . . The fear does not let go. The fear is the eternal legacy."

It was a bruise she has kept coming back to again and again in her essays and speeches. By the time the experience made its way into her fiction, she was writing about it with pornographic intensity: "He brought home 4 drunken friends, one of whom kept calling me kike, and they tied me to the bed and fucked me until I passed out and thank god I dont know what happened after that." That's the way she imagined it in her short story "bertha schneiders existential edge."

After leaving her husband and embracing feminism, Andrea Dworkin came to see men and women as two different camps, "one an armed camp and the other a concentration camp." Women in Amerika, as she spelled it for Teutonic emphasis, are viewed as an "inferior gender class," declared Dworkin. Men assert their control over women through a systematic program of sexual violence, which she called "organized gynocide." Rape "remains our primary model for heterosexual relating."

"The penis must embody the violence of the male in order for him to be male," wrote Dworkin, in her incantatory prose. "Violence is male; the male is the penis, violence is the penis or the sperm ejaculated from it." Sex, violence, and death. This is "the male erotic trinity," according to Dworkin.

"Men love death," she announced. "In everything they make, they hollow out a central place for death, let its rancid smell contaminate every dimension of whatever still survives. Men especially love murder."

Men reveal these sinister truths about themselves most nakedly in their pornography, believes Dworkin. "I think that in displaying to us the true opinion that they have of us and the actual content of their sexuality, [men] have made an irreversible error," Dworkin proclaimed. If other women examined these texts with her same analytical devotion, the scales would surely fall from their eyes as well. And they, too, would become free.

So she made pornography her political passion. She denounced it as "Dachau brought into the bedroom and celebrated." She delivered speeches, she led marches, she helped devise a new legal strategy to drive adult bookstores and video stores out of business. She proposed that cities adopt a civil rights ordinance defining pornography as a form of sexual discrimination. The legislation would allow citizens to sue in civil court to ban hard-core materials and to collect damages for the harm done by pornographers. It was a brilliant stroke: instead of relying on the patriarchal state to defend womanhood, the law would deputize women themselves to act as censors. The initiative was passed by the Minneapolis City Council, but vetoed by the mayor. It briefly became law in Indianapolis, before being struck down by the Supreme Court as unconstitutional. But Dworkin vowed to fight on. She compared the antipornography crusade to the long struggle fought by blacks for civil rights protection.

Andrea Dworkin's collaborator in this ceaseless campaign, the coauthor of the model ordinance, her Friedrich Engels, was a feminist law professor named Catharine MacKinnon. The two were as different as the halves of a presidential ticket. Dworkin is the daughter of first-generation Jewish Americans. Her schoolteacher father moonlighted as a postal clerk to cover the medical bills of Andrea's mother, a woman with never-ending heart trouble. MacKinnon, on the other hand, was the offspring of Minnesota's conservative establishment. Her father, George, was a corporate lawyer and politician before being named to the federal bench by President Nixon. According to her father, "Kitty," as Catharine MacKinnon is known to friends, was a chum of Julie Nixon's during their undergraduate years at Smith College. "I wouldn't say that," says MacKinnon herself, who seems discomfited talking about her family background. *How well did she know Julie Nixon?* "I don't see what possible relevance that has," she responds, refusing to comment further on the subject.

In the early 1970s, MacKinnon pursued degrees in political science and law at Yale. It was in New Haven where she began moving toward radicalism and feminism, or as she puts it, "where I became aware of the real political context in which I lived." MacKinnon was particularly enamored of the Black Panthers, an outfit not known for its feminist sensibilities. "I liked their way of confronting racism, their political analysis, the way they used the law in courts," she tells us.

In their war on pornography, Dworkin, as wild-maned and slovenly as a 1960s street fighter, would rally the troops with her "rolling thunder" speeches, as Susan Brownmiller describes them. And the trim, attractive MacKinnon, dangling gold jewelry like a Junior Leaguer and encased in a dignified suit, would gather up her long, gray-streaked brown hair in a bun and do battle in the courts or government chambers.

While their styles and their roles are markedly different, Dworkin and MacKinnon share the same outlook on the world. "There is no separation between us," says MacKinnon. "I count on very little in life, but I count on Andrea. We are in this fight together."

The world in which these two feminist leaders cling so tightly together is a treacherous one indeed. It is a world at war, a world stalked by cruel and brutal men and traders in female flesh. And they, Dworkin and MacKinnon, are underground partisans, living lives filled with terror and bravery. MacKinnon claims she has been threatened by pornographers. "That's why I have lived essentially underground since 1979," MacKinnon tells us in her quiet office at Stanford University one afternoon. "There have been times when I was followed; that is, I believe someone was following me for a period of time. I never verified it. I did what I could do to shake them and was successful. My phone at the same time made a great many strange sounds, and we have also received threats on the phone. And I have received letters about the elaborate sexual things that people want to do to me."

Dworkin, says MacKinnon, draws even more bursts of strange and inexplicable hostility. "It's insane. I mean, people try to run her over with their cars sometimes. It's just because she's not conventional-looking, and she isn't trying to be attractive to men. And I think it's extremely significant that she's a Jew. I do. I mean I just smell anti-Semitism all over the way they treat her. And, of course, simply being female is like being a walking target for males."

"danger. sex . . . I looked for it everywhere," writes Dworkin in her short story "the simple story of a lesbian girlhood."

Bad-girl anthropologist Paula Webster scents a strong sexual aroma in all this female terror. "It's erotic to be enthralled by fear," remarks Webster. "Dworkin and MacKinnon are enthralled by victimization. I understand that attraction, but I feel sorry for them that they live their lives that way."

However, Andrea Dworkin is no shivering maiden. The world she conjures in her writing is one of sadism and submission; yet Dworkin's voice is anything but submissive. Her prose derives power from its jabbing cadence: "Violence is male; the male is the penis; violence is the penis." Here, her speeches make clear, is a woman who likes to give a good tongue-lashing. "She knows how to whip a crowd into a frenzy," observes Susan Brownmiller, a former political ally who grew disaffected from Dworkin because of her "demagogic" style.

But it is in her fiction where Dworkin most shamelessly reveals the dominatrix within. This is fiction with a dark surprise.

Yes, a curious thing happened in the midst of Dworkin's feminist crusade. The scourge of pornography began to write pornography. She denied this is what it was; it was laced with feminist morals and she called it feminist literature. But it was pornography all the same, pornography of a sadistic nature. The sex was violent, degrading; the writing was hypnotic. It owed much to *Story of O.*

Her female characters undergo the worst kinds of sexual humiliation, which Dworkin describes in exquisite detail:

> then one night he had spread her out naked on his bed. he spread her legs as far apart as they could go. he tied her wrists to the bedposts. another man entered and sat on a chair at the foot of the bed. whatever this was had been planned, choreographed, between them. she did not know.
>
> the second man was big, his arms laden with muscles, a square face, athletic, all loincloth and sweat.
>
> her lover fingered her cunt slowly, dispassionately. he was grinning. surprise, Ive taken you by surprise. the second man watched. she was red with shame. they both liked that.
>
> then her lover mounted her and the second man mounted him from behind. then her lover fucked her and the second man fucked him. this double man on top of her, heaving, the weight of that cock inside her driven by this double weight, this two headed, two assed man on top of her, like a mountain, volcanic, erupting, on and on, fucking and fucking, the sweat and the weight, drowning her in lava and ash.

There it was again, the vile château at Roissy. But this time it was in Dworkin's rarely seen short-story collection *The New Womans Broken Heart,* published by a small press in 1980. In her first novel, *Ice and Fire,* which was published six years later, Dworkin's heroine suffers further mortifications of the flesh. A man who chews her clitoris, jailhouse doctors who rape her with speculums (this trauma, once more), a husband who fucks her and beats her until she is "torn and bleeding" (this too). She was a modern-day Justine. And Dworkin was conquering her own very real moments of suffering and shame by inflicting them on her fictional creation.

Andrea Dworkin is a woman who likes to throw her weight around. Here is a woman who grew up with nothing but contempt for her frail and sickly mother; she "experienced her only as an ignorant irritant," Dworkin later wrote. It was Dworkin's father who raised her and encouraged her intellectual development. Yes, here is a woman who once objected so violently to revisions made in her article by former *Viva* magazine editor Patricia Bosworth that she "threw me to the ground and practically pinned me," according to Bosworth.

"She physically held me there and said, 'I won't let this run until the cuts are restored.' If you know how slight I am and how big she is, you can imagine my dilemma. We reached a compromise and the piece, which was about the horrors of Chinese footbinding, ran."

Here is a woman who rejected the limp, temperate philosophy of liberalism —a philosophy that failed to protect women from male savagery. She and other radical feminists preferred a heavier boot. They were drawn to the rawest kinds of power. Ti-Grace Atkinson, an early leader of radical feminism, shocked her sisters in the 1970s by falling in love with Mafia chieftain Joe Colombo and romanticizing his brotherhood of violence. Catharine MacKinnon had her Black Panthers. And Andrea Dworkin turned into a literary terrorizer of women. A master of dark thrills. The bogeyman she had warned her sisters about.

It is one of the more psychologically fascinating developments in American sexual politics, one loaded with Swaggart-like ironies. The dominant figure of radical feminism, the nation's leading intellectual critic of pornography, is moved inexorably to dip her own pen in the inkwell of the Marquis de Sade. More remarkable still, no prominent feminists have been moved to comment on the peculiarity of all this.

Dworkin periodically lashes into the feminist establishment for not fully endorsing her antipornography measures, for being fainthearted, for becoming a "small professional clique" out of touch with the suffering of women. But Dworkin continues to command wide respect within this clique. She is admired for some obvious reasons: for her masterful polemics, for her literary skill, for "being one of the few feminists who keep passionate debate alive" in the doldrums of the 1980s, as *Ms.* magazine editor Letty Cottin Pogrebin told us.

But it goes deeper than this. Dworkin quickens the blood of the feminist intelligentsia the way de Sade and Réage stirred French intellectuals, the way black militants stirred Leonard Bernstein, the way convict-writer Jack Henry Abbott stirred Norman Mailer. They find Dworkin exciting because she is drenched in the violence and viscera of human experience and they call it the Truth.

Germaine Greer, of all people, praised Dworkin's *Intercourse* as "the most shocking book any feminist has yet written: it forces us all to ask ourselves if we have not been deliberately ignoring the obvious." Shere Hite hailed it as "outstanding, original, and an act of forbidden rebellion." Here, in this book, was the logical conclusion of her years of analytical work. It was a wail against the cruelty of human biology. The root of women's misery is not simply male violence, states Dworkin, but the penis itself—and the female body's ports of entry.

"Intercourse," she writes, "remains a means or the means of physiologically making a woman inferior: communicating to her cell by cell her own inferior status, impressing it on her, burning it into her by shoving it into her, over and over, pushing and thrusting until she gives up and gives in—which is called *surrender* in the male lexicon."

Once again, the writing is pornographic. And once again, Dworkin emotionally identifies with both the male tormentor and the female victim. She is the punishing cock, and she is the helpless girl "ripped up the middle of my legs all the way to my throat," in the words of an incest victim quoted by Dworkin. The book, characteristically, is a welter of lust and horror.

"Dworkin touches something deep in a lot of women," feminist writer Charlotte Bunch tells us. "She dredges up the primal childhood fear—*oh no, that thing is too big to go inside there*—the incest fear, the fear of male violence." But she makes her own uses of that fear.

Andrea Dworkin is the voice from deep inside the black forest. *Do not walk alone, little girl, the woods are full of hunters and beasts. Come, I will take care of you.*

Susan Forward, the author (with Joan Torres) of *Men Who Hate Women and the Women Who Love Them,* is showing us around her home, an impressive two-story Los Angeles manor tucked into a canyon near Beverly Glen. The interior has the dark, simple elegance of the lobby in a five-star Tokyo hotel. There is primitive Japanese art on the walls and figurines of Japanese gods on the shelves. A vast, black TV of sleek design sits in the corner of the living room like a modern art piece. The lighting throughout the house is muted. It could be the quarters of a Toyota chief executive (except for the white Jaguar parked outside) or a Honda heiress. Forward bought it with the treasure she made from her number one best-seller.

"I call it the house that misogyny built," she smiles.

Men Who Hate Women and the Women Who Love Them was one of the most commercially successful titles in a tsunami of women's advice books that flooded the stores in the late 1980s. *Women Who Love Too Much; Men Who Can't Love; Men Who Can't Be Faithful; Successful Women, Angry Men; Smart Women, Foolish Choices; Born to Please: Compliant Women, Controlling Men,* and, perhaps the most bluntly worded, *No Good Men.* Like the works of Andrea Dworkin, these books blame women's misery on male cruelty and insensitivity. But unlike Dworkin's grim treatises, they promise relief with a variety of therapeutic remedies and they have sold in staggering numbers. Four hundred thousand hardcover copies of Forward's book were plucked from store shelves, and more than two million copies in paperback were sold. In the 1980s the war between the sexes became big business.

The men who inhabit these advice books are a pathological lot: in love with the bottle, threatened by their wives' success, prone to tyrannical outbursts and violent humors, poisoned with jealousy, a constant drain on their mates' emotional and even material resources. In short, not the sort you would want in your car pool, much less your bed. The women, in contrast, are a long-suffering and generous group, too willing to put these sorry excuses for men before themselves, too ready to be an "ever-flowing breast," in the words of Susan Forward. It's a simple world portrayed in these pages: the men are invariably despots of the heart, and women their pathetic victims.

While Dworkin believes that abusive men such as this are the natural offspring of a patriarchal culture, Forward and the other dispensers of pop feminist psychology contend they are the creations of unhappy homes. "The passive father/smothering mother and the tyrannical father/victim mother are the types of families I have seen most frequently in the backgrounds of misogynists," writes Forward in *Men Who Hate Women.* She and the other best-selling therapists caution their female readers to watch carefully for problem men, providing them with helpful lists of warning signs. Beware of "spellbinding chemistry," advises Forward. Beware of "too quick bonding or fusion." In this world of therapeutic love, passion is a prime suspect.

Women must never relax their guard, according to Forward, because misogynists come out after midnight when the moon is full. These men are creatures of romance one moment and frightening case studies the next. Forward calls this the "Jekyll and Hyde" syndrome. "Between his outbursts, he's liable to be as charming and lovable as he was when you first met."

To help maintain this eternal vigilance, women throughout the country joined the antiaddiction culture and formed clubs to ward off men who were terribly enticing but oh so wrong. They sat in circles and talked of "danger signals" and "obsessive patterns" and tried to convince themselves that tame, sensitive men are better for you. They steeled themselves against romance, which they saw as a neurotic condition, against giving away too much of their hearts to men.

"The other night a woman in our group said, 'I know this man is bad business, but I can taste the desire in my throat,'" recalls a fifty-year-old Cleveland woman who runs a Women Who Love Too Much chapter. "I told her, 'Don't even talk to him. If you do, you're already in the bar.' Of course, I should talk. I'm having an affair with my boss, a married man, and I'm still trying to get out of it. I'm extremely attracted to men who are not appropriate."

In California, as always, the country's psychological frontier, another leader of love-crazed women laid plans to organize a group for "children who love too much." "We want to nip this self-destructive behavior in the bud," she declares.

Like Dworkin and the radical feminists, Susan Forward has a fondness for Third Reich imagery. The men in her book have that *Mein Kampf* look. "I tell women all the time that you can't afford to give Hitler Poland," she writes in her book. It is a metaphor that diminishes the brutality of the Nazi occupation.

And yet, insists Forward, she is no man-basher. "Misogyny is very common, very common, but I'm not saying *all* men behave this way. I *adore* many men," Forward tells us, settling into the lush cushions of her living room couch. She is a short, pretty woman somewhere in her fifties (she will not divulge her age), with lively, girlish eyes and a dimpled smile. She is wearing white slacks and a blouse decorated with the fauna of a tropical rain forest— dazzling, bulging flowers of purple, red, and yellow. Her manner is warm and self-confident; she flirts with the skill of someone who knows her effect on men.

Forward says she is a feminist but would like to believe she is the fun kind. She makes a point of repudiating Andrea Dworkin. "I think she's crazy. I met her on a radio talk show once, and I don't want to be associated with anyone that grotesquely ugly, with that type of repulsive personality," she says unkindly. "I don't believe that all men are these evil, slimy things."

Still, doesn't the very title of her book, with its message that men hate, women love, further polarize the sexes? She does admit to a certain amount of unease about that "red flag" of a title. "My editor and I were fooling around with titles and came up with that one. I said, 'It's too scary, it's too inflammatory.' But she said, 'That's your title.' I guess I may have lost some male readers with it, but I don't know— Men don't usually buy books of this kind anyway and none of this was done for commercial purposes."

Forward was inspired to write *Men Who Hate Women* after the failure of her second marriage, a fifteen-year drama with a handsome and exciting entrepreneur named Walter ("Buzz") Forward. They married after a heart-racing four-month courtship. Here was a man who lived up to his name. "He told me he loved me on our first date," she recalls. "He proposed to me on our second. He was so gorgeous that I was utterly flattered. But it had nothing to do with me. This sort of thing has more to do with a man's idealized fantasy and projecting his needs onto you. That's why getting swept off your feet is dangerous. There hasn't been enough time for you to really get to know each other."

In her book, Forward emphasizes the tawdry side of her marriage. After the honeymoon, she writes, she discovered that Buzz was a man with "a great deal of anger in him" and a penchant for blaming "me for everything from his business problems to the fact that his shoes weren't shined properly." When Forward, a former TV actress, began to prosper in her career as a clinical and radio therapist, her husband's ill temper grew blacker still, according to her.

"Although my work was our major source of income at that time," she writes, "he often ridiculed the psychotherapeutic profession in general and me in particular . . . I had begun my marriage as a cheerful, energetic person; now, fourteen years later, I was anxious and frequently on the verge of tears. I found myself behaving in ways that I couldn't stand, nagging and interrogating him constantly, or retreating into sullen, angry silences instead of dealing directly with my feelings about our relationship."

When *Men Who Hate Women* became a runaway best-seller, *People* magazine tracked down Buzz Forward to solicit his response. But he would not rejoin the battle with her in print. "I have as much interest in what she has to say as I have in whether the sun is going to come up in 2050 when I'm long gone," stated Buzz. "She's a very unhappy lady." In his weary resentment, he sounded precisely like the man she had accused him of being. But the remark also contained a kind of admirable pride. It made you want to hear his side of the story. But Buzz, like most men in the great sex debate, was not talking.

In our interview, Forward is more cognizant of her marriage's agreeable qualities than she was in her book. "This was the great love of my life," she proclaims. "It was a very romantic, very exciting, very sexual relationship." She returns to this theme more than once in the interview. "Oh, he was a fantastic lover; that was one of the big hooks."

Forward says she is still "an incurable romantic," but nowadays, in her new therapeutic mold, she tries to avoid men who make her swoon. "If I'm getting the butterflies in my stomach and a lot of anxiety and that kind of stuff, I know something is dangerous. That's my flashing red light." Her current lover, she says, is the type of man she would never have found interesting in the past. "Because he's not that romantic and he doesn't know the moves or the things to say. And I said, 'Susan, stay open to this, because this is a really nice, smart, adequate, decent guy and he's probably too busy earning a living and becoming successful and taking care of other people to develop those particular skills.' And so I stayed open to it, and I'm not saying this is the love of my life, but it's turned into a . . . really nice relationship."

She does not sound very convincing. Not even, we suspect, to herself.

The huge success of Forward's book and those by the other best-selling feminist psychologists was based on their reputations as practical guides to the lovelorn. While Andrea Dworkin could only promise relief through sexual apartheid, the "men bad/women good" books held out the hope of finding a clinically approved Mr. Right if women followed the correct therapeutic procedures.

But in the end, therapeutic feminism seemed of little use as a guide to finding the deepest love. It preached self-reliance and emotional restraint, but as most of us know in our hearts, these are not the hallmarks of true love. As psychiatrist Ethel Spector Person has written, "It is precisely the lovers' leap out of objectivity and into subjectivity that signals the liberation of love . . . Falling in love confers one of the greatest of freedoms—freedom from the confines of the self. Momentarily one exchanges one's preoccupation with oneself for a consuming interest in the Other."

The best-selling practitioners of feminist therapy seemed utterly mystified in the presence of love, as dumbfounded as Bonaparte's soldiers when they first entered the great tombs at Karnak and Luxor. The spirit and meaning of it all eluded them, the chambers within chambers, the secret scratchings on the wall. They could not fathom the ways of men; they could not even make much sense of their own maddening desires. Why was it that the Buzz Forwards of the world were so captivating? What was this great epic that joined the hearts of men and women and tore them asunder? Yes, "Who wrote the Book of Love—and what the hell were they thinking?" in the puzzled words of cartoonist Lynda Barry. These ageless mysteries were not revealed in Susan Forward's book or in any of its ilk.

The war between the sexes has also been good to Shere Hite, as we discovered the day we dropped by her majestic three-floor New York condominium in a nineteenth-century brownstone off Central Park. Those who have been given the official tour liken the apartment to the Doge's Palace in Venice. Its huge salon features a gilded ceiling adorned with carved cherubs, a black marble fireplace, and red velvet couches. Hite shares these luxurious quarters with her husband, Friedrich Horicke, a West German concert pianist two decades her junior. Horicke has the dramatic good looks of a Romantic composer. Hite too seems like a figure from another era. Her chalklike skin, her wispy curls the color of gold brocade, and her theatrical wardrobe inevitably prompt phrases like "Botticelli angel," "porcelain statue," and "consumptive beauty" from those who meet her.

Hite employed the tools of social science rather than psychoanalysis to try to make sense of modern sexuality. Because her reports on male and female sexuality were based on long surveys collected from thousands of respondents instead of unprofound therapeutic ruminations, Hite's work offered more insights into the hearts of men and women than did the books by Forward and company. Her three reports, published between 1976 and 1987, gave a voice to everyday Americans. These faceless people talked of favorite ways to masturbate, of how intercourse really feels, of fantasies too thrilling and dreadful to say aloud, of how love can turn to hate. It made for juicy—and comforting—reading: "I'm not the only one who likes to come by putting my pussy under a warm gush of water from the bathtub faucet!" And her first two reports sold like condoms on a troop ship. Hite went from being a Columbia graduate school dropout and struggling model, reduced to lounging naked with a Labrador for *Playboy* and posing as a dimwitted secretary for an

Olivetti ad ("The typewriter that's so smart she doesn't have to be"), to being the Fifth Avenue doyenne of feminist sex research.

Scholars marveled at the treasure of intimate material unearthed by Hite. "It's not too strong to say that I find in the Hite reports a massive cry of the human heart," exclaimed Bucknell philosophy professor Joseph P. Fell, "a cry for the open recognition of the [sexual] needs so eloquently revealed." But the extravagant scientific claims made by Hite and her feminist supporters made her a figure of controversy. Her research was superior to that of Kinsey and Masters and Johnson—in Hite's immodest assessment—because "their work continued to view sex through certain cultural blinders which kept them from understanding the whole truth about female sexuality." Hite's critics, however, charged that she replaced this bias with one that was assertively and simplistically feminist.

According to her manifold detractors, Hite's questions were slanted, her samples were self-selected and unrepresentative, and her conclusions were nothing more than rambling, loosely argued feminist sermons. The central theme of Hite's work is that men are sexually and emotionally stunted because of the cultural conditioning they undergo in our patriarchal society and therefore they tend to make unsatisfying lovers. "Would it be too simplistic to blame all our problems on the 'male' ideology with its hierarchical and aggressive motifs," asks Hite rhetorically in her third, and most controversial report, *Women and Love. Yes!* came the booming reply from her clamorous critics, who accused her of doing just that and then dressing her feminist dialectics in the lab coat of science.

Hite "goes in with a prejudice and comes out with a statistic," remarked syndicated columnist Ellen Goodman. "This is not science as Kinsey knew it," commented the eminent sexologist Vern Bullough. "If a male sex researcher wrote *The Hite Report,* his career would be ruined," sniped psychologist C. A. Tripp, a former Kinsey colleague.

Some of the heat that accompanied criticism of Hite was perhaps due to professional jealousy, as Bullough himself acknowledges. "When work that is not very well researched gets so much notoriety and monetary reward, other people in the field, including myself, can get very envious," he tells us. Since the 1950s, when the Rockefeller Foundation withdrew its support of Alfred Kinsey's pioneering studies under conservative pressure, sex research in the United States has been underfunded and academically undistinguished. Shere

Hite came bounding out of the women's movement in the 1970s to fill this scholarly vacuum, going deeply into debt and living in "extreme poverty," in her words, to finance the research on her first book. It was a grass-roots feminist project—her first set of questionnaires was sent out under NOW's letterhead—and the sex research establishment resented the competition from this uncredentialed upstart.

"These university and medical school types who have loads of money sit on their asses and don't do any serious sex research," says Irwin Haeberle of the Institute for the Advanced Study of Human Sexuality in San Francisco. "Then someone like Hite comes along and does something that is not exactly what you would like in a study, but at least contains some interesting nuggets, and she is roundly criticized by these layabouts."

The charges brought against Hite by her sexology colleagues are not always of a profound order. "She's the most inconsiderate human being I've ever met," sniffs one. "She arrives late for lectures; she keeps people waiting. She once invited about a hundred people to her swank place for a cocktail party and there was hardly any food or drink. I think she had *one* little can of dip. People had to run out and buy stuff."

Hite is the type of woman about whom people delight in spreading wicked stories. Tales of her eccentricities abound in feminist circles, among sex researchers, and in the press. It is said that she keeps vampire hours, rising late in the day and working through the night in the Old World splendor of her apartment. It is stated that she arrived for her wedding at St. Vincent's Church on Lexington Avenue in an ornate carriage, smuggling her beloved pet mongrel into the Catholic ceremony with her. It is reported that in the stress of the promotional campaign for *Women and Love,* when her work came under its most severe criticism, Hite exhibited particularly odd behavior, belting a limousine driver for calling her "dear," stalking off talk shows in anger, trying to rouse a critic out of bed at two-thirty in the morning, and creating fictional identities to deal with the press. "She seems to be running at high emotional pitch," tut-tutted *Newsweek* at the time.

But it all struck us as good, loony fun. Just the sort of high jinks the drab publishing industry needed in the 1980s. Hite had some weird fun with us too when we first got in touch with her. "I hate being interviewed," she informed us. "Why don't people just read my books. If I died, they'd have to read my books; they couldn't interview me." That would be a rather extreme solution, we pointed out, but she plunged on in this fashion. "Do you hear that phone ringing? That's another person calling for an interview. *I'm going to kill myself* —then people will read my books.

"I have to go now," she signed off, "my dinner is getting cold. You have no idea how sad it is to have a plate of *cold, limp* zucchini staring at you." This, we decided, was sexology humor of a droll sort. It made us think Hite was the fun kind of feminist after all.

Yes, she has endorsed Andrea Dworkin's strange diatribes against erections and pornography. But she also socializes with *Penthouse* mogul Bob Guccione and his wife, Kathy Keeton. Dworkin's allies mutter darkly about the reasons for this friendship. "As I understand it, Shere made a deal with *Penthouse* that they wouldn't run the [nude] pictures of her," says antipornography crusader Dorchen Leidholt. But Guccione denies this. "That's totally untrue," he tells us. "We certainly have no deal with Shere Hite. She and Kathy are good friends, and I've known her for a number of years. We've had dinner with her loads of times. I have a lot of respect for her as a person, and she has, I assume, equal respect for me." The world of New York feminism in the 1980s was full of amusing alliances.

Less fun, however, was the $15 million lawsuit Hite brought against one of her most vocal critics, writer Philip Nobile, in 1984. Hite retained the law firm of the notorious Roy Cohn, a barrister not known for his enlightened social views, to exact compensation from Nobile for "making false and defamatory statements." Nobile had published an intelligent and damaging critique of Hite's work in *New York* magazine in 1981. Two years later he tried unsuccessfully to engage Hite in public debate at a San Francisco sexology conference; in a subsequent editorial in *Forum* magazine, Nobile suggested that she was one of "the charlatans" who should be driven "out of the erogenous zones." The lawsuit was settled out of court. Nobile issued no public apology or retraction. But he apparently has been silenced as a public critic of Hite.

Over the years, Hite has worked with the diligence of a White House "spin controller" to manage the debate about her work. In 1981, after the publication of her report on men, she was scheduled to speak at a Washington, D.C., sexuality conference. But when she heard that writer Gay Talese was also going to appear, she notified the sponsors that she would not share the same stage with him because "he thinks men are promiscuous by nature and that women are negative because they withhold sex." The sponsors promptly withdrew their invitation to Talese. "She is very antimale and doesn't want to listen to a male point of view," responded the author of *Thy Neighbor's Wife.*

In 1988, following the publication of *Women and Love,* Hite appeared at a colloquium on her work sponsored by the New York Society of Clinical Psychologists. The panel was stacked with female supporters of Hite, a bit of stage-managing that brought forth a protest from a man in the audience. "This fellow got up and said, 'If this were a discussion of white oppression of blacks back in the 1960s, you'd expect there to be some whites on the panel,' " recalls panel member Leonora Teifer. "There was a loud groan from the audience. One woman yelled back, 'If this were a panel on Nazi oppression of Jews, you wouldn't expect Nazis on the panel!' " After this much-employed feminist epithet rang out in the auditorium, "it just became a circus," says Teiffer. "It was pandemonium."

Hite tends to dismiss criticism of her work as the wail of an increasingly beleaguered patriarchal order. "The reaction to *Women and Love* was a collective scream from men," she tells us. " *'Shut up!'* White men are feeling it from all sides. My book came out the day the stock market fell, in October 1987."

"So men felt they needed to get it up again by bashing your book?" we ask.

"Yes, I suppose," she laughs.

But this is a convenient way to tune out opposing voices. It would seem useful for Hite, after years of disparaging men's sexual and emotional competence, to listen to the male response. Her case against the opposite sex was, after all, rather severe. In *The Hite Report on Male Sexuality,* she attacked men for being excessively rational and insufficiently passionate and charged that their approach to lovemaking tends to be mechanical and unimaginative, placing too much emphasis on intercourse. Disregarding the primal force of biology, she went so far as to question whether thrusting is instinctive, asserting that intercourse is "glorified" in our society because it is "a celebration of male patriarchal culture."

In *Women and Love* she broadened her attack, declaring that her latest survey showed "widespread dissatisfaction among women about their love relationships" with men. She accused men of practicing "emotional terrorism" against their lovers, habitually demeaning them, withholding their affection, and lapsing into grunts and silences. "Woman after woman says she is putting enormous amounts of energy into trying to make her relationship work—but that the man doesn't seem to be putting in the same effort," wrote Hite.

This was news to many people who felt that men had grown more sensitive to the female half of the species after two decades of resurgent feminism. But no, stated Hite. She detected just the opposite, a relentless "toughening" of masculinity in the years since World War II.

In protest against their callous bedmates, Hite further claimed, many women—in fact, a staggering 70 percent of all those married more than five years—are having affairs. Many others are looking for their primary emotional sustenance in relationships with female friends or their children.

Our best hope for the future is a "cultural revolution" that will remodel society and sexuality along feminist lines. So Hite concluded in the closing passages of her book, a breathless and chaotic finale that drew unsuccessfully on women's spiritualism, business reform literature, ecological radicalism, Einstein, Heidegger, and animal liberation.

Why can't a man be more like a woman? This is the lament that runs throughout Hite's work. She wants a world where Adam is constructed from Eve's rib, where masculine energy grows soft and gentle curves.

Hite displays an admirable sensitivity to the cries and whispers of her female respondents in her two reports on women. "The statements women sent [to me] were full of beautifully written, moving descriptions of their feelings," she stated after publishing her report on female sexuality in 1976. "Receiving these replies was one of the most emotionally fulfilling experiences of my life." But when it comes to her equally eloquent male respondents, she has limited understanding. The masculine voice does not register clearly with Hite.

This is the problem with Shere Hite, not her eccentricity, not even her loose methodology—which, as Berkeley sociologist Arlie Hochschild observed in the New York *Times Book Review,* may not be scientific but has certainly presented us with "many hypnotizing, sad, sweet, chilling and lurid [life] stories." The personal statements collected in her report on male sexuality are full of touching insights into the hearts of men. There is poetry in this data. But Hite hears only the drumbeat of feminism.

Hite misreads her own research throughout her report on men. Despite her insistence that men worship intercourse above all "as a symbol of male power," most respondents in her survey exhibited a polymorphous sexuality. Most of the men expressed an enthusiastic taste for cunnilingus and other types of "foreplay" and lamented the fact that women did not caress them often enough or skillfully enough. As for intercourse, most men "liked all positions" while "a surprising 35 percent preferred to be on the bottom." And they were more apt to describe penetration in lyrical terms than as an act of domination: "Home." "Like hot velvet; I surrender to it, I'm powerless to resist." "We are one, really one. When I hear her heart beat and her breathing, I don't hear mine, so it's my heart and my breathing."

Hite's data indicates that men are more emotionally refined than her analysis would permit: 55 percent of her male respondents had cried themselves to sleep over problems with a lover, and most spurned sex without love. Her anonymous army of confessors—more than seven thousand strong— filled Hite's pages with desire and torment. They grieved over wives who had closed their hearts like coffins, they fretted about their bedroom performance, they even feigned orgasms to please their lovers. They were not so different, these men, from the women whose dramas had so deeply affected Hite.

But she was fixed on seeing men as "dehumanized" beings, half mortals who disconnected "sex and feelings," "body and spirit."

Of course, there were some differences between men and women demonstrated in the Hite reports. For instance, women put more importance on verbal communication in relationships than men, while men placed greater value on sexual intercourse. But even though men tended to express love differently, they were clearly no less passionate in their feelings. Still, Hite chose to interpret these findings as one more indication of women's emotional superiority. Men rarely look their best in studies with a feminist bias.

"Part of the reason that men seem so much less loving than women is that men's behavior is measured with a feminine ruler," writes sociologist Francesca Cancian of gender studies such as Hite's. "Most research considers only the kinds of loving behavior that are associated with the feminine role, such as talking about personal troubles, and rarely compares women and men on masculine qualities such as giving practical help or being interested in sexual intercourse."

Between the covers of Shere Hite's three massive volumes on men and women was an opera of grand sentiments. But Hite heard only Isolde, not Tristan, only Mimi, not Rodolfo. If she had listened more carefully to both the soprano and tenor voices, she would have found it easier to follow the libretto. Many women were unhappy with modern love; this was certain from reading Hite. But so were many men. Hite takes note of this in her report on male sexuality, but fails to make much sense of it. If she had been less willing to impose a predictably feminist interpretation on her data—if she had resisted the temptation to fault men for all wounds of the heart—Hite might have arrived at more intriguing conclusions.

Perhaps the Darwinian forces that have guided human evolution have instilled very different ideas about love and passion in the sexes, differences that produce inevitable conflicts between men and women. Or perhaps romantic relationships have a natural life cycle, beyond which fatigue and frustration inevitably take command. Or perhaps couples thrive on storm and stress as much as Wagner does. But if life is an opera, then Shere Hite, it must be said, is a half-deaf critic.

Young American men learned there might be something erotic about women's liberation when they saw the May 7, 1971, issue of *Life* magazine. There she was on the cover, reclining on a bench in Central Park, laughing and pointing at something in the distance, too cool to notice the camera. She wore pink lipstick and red clogs and a paisley coat over a blue knit dress that nicely showed off her bosom. Silver jewelry dangled from her like a gypsy and her long chestnut hair was shagged like a British glam rocker. The photograph inside had even more casual sensuality: she sat on the floor of her hotel room with her dress bunched up so high that it revealed the entire white expanse of her calf and thigh. It was a big, impressive leg, as demanding of attention as the robust marble in Rodin's *The Kiss,* and draped across her lap with the sweet familiarity of a happy Labrador was a handsome black-haired man identified in the caption as a "friend."

SAUCY FEMINIST THAT EVEN MEN LIKE—GERMAINE GREER trumpeted *Life.* We were embarrassed to be lumped together like this by the corny Henry Luce prose. She was certainly not the only feminist we liked. But Germaine Greer did seem something special, a 1970s suffragist whose crusade was brightened with wit and flair and sexy Moll Flanders fun.

Other generations of men found the shape of their desire in pinups of Betty Grable's backside and movie stills of Marilyn, blond angel with the floating skirt. But the thinking men of the 1970s immediately recognized the "saucy feminist" in the pages of *Life* as the woman of their dreams. Hers was not a common beauty, with its strong Australian features, prominent nose, big-toothed smile. She stirred something deeper. Her face could be as haughty as a fashion model's or as wry as a music hall comedienne's. One look told you that here was an exceedingly proud, quickly intelligent, yet earthy woman. Here was a woman who could keep you eternally off balance.

Germaine Greer was sharply aware of how men needed to change, but she also had a fine appreciation of men's assets. She knew all the troubles that came when the two sexes rubbed against one another, but she still liked the fit. And she was smart and cocky enough to tell off her sisters when their sexual doctrine grew tyrannically sapphic. "It is nonsense to say that a woman feels nothing when a man is moving his penis in her vagina: the orgasm is qualitatively different when the vagina can undulate around the penis instead of vacancy," she wrote in *The Female Eunuch,* the best-selling book that established her reputation.

Instead of inveighing against the power of the phallus as Dworkin would years later, Greer sang the praises of potent vaginas. "Cunts have extraordinary powers," she wrote in *Suck,* an underground British pornography magazine that Greer attempted, ahead of her time, to feminize. "But the effect of constant indoctrination, Freudian monosex, is to convince women that their cunts are mere holes. Most women would be surprised to learn that the women of Tahiti can draw the penis into them with irresistible force, and keep it there working until it bleeds."

Greer did not reveal whether she herself had ever attempted this South Seas feat, but she had ample opportunity to try it out, for the young Shakespeare scholar who had turned feminist theorist availed herself of the pleasures of many beds in those years. She had an affair with the lead singer of the kick-ass, radical prole Detroit band MC5, though years later she forgot his name. "How awful," she would tell a reporter, "when you can't remember their names!" She married a man whose name she did remember, Paul du Feu, "a very sexy man, in a battered and nuggety sort of way," she would write, a man who posed buck-naked on a freshly waxed floor for the British *Cosmopolitan.* But the marriage lasted only three weeks.

"I have hated coupledom all my life," Greer confides to us. "The moment a dinner or party invitation comes for Germaine and whomever, that man comes within an ace of getting his ass out on the sidewalk. I think, How dare he take me over, how dare he be my official escort."

Greer had a taste for one-night stands "as long as there is no element of fraud or trickery or rip-off." She sampled the fair, firm fruit of many nations and then evaluated their relative sweetness like a shrewd farmer. Italian men made the world's best lovers, she told the press, "because their mothers ate them alive when they were babies and convinced them that they were utterly adorable." She was the original bad girl of feminism. But unlike those feminist intellectuals who followed in her path, her life mirrored the randiness of her prose. "I believed there was no such thing as promiscuity," she tells us in her authoritative way, lying on a hotel bed in midtown Manhattan. "If you have chosen to be with the man you're with—even if he's the fifth man today—if you've chosen him, you are not promiscuous."

But this was the fall of 1987, and by then Germaine Greer was a very different woman.

The change seems to have occurred early in the decade, as the sexual revolutionary entered middle age. Greer had fucked herself out, said some feminists. "I think Germaine, in particular, went further than any other famous feminist in pursuit of Erica Jong's zipless fuck, and I can see where she would be tired," Susan Brownmiller remarked to us. Others said Greer was bitter about not having children; after years of sexual politics and recreation, she was reportedly grieved to discover that it was too late to conceive. But whatever the underlying causes, it was clear with the publication of *Sex and Destiny* in 1984, that Germaine Greer, the women's movement's leading sexual liberationist, no longer held the same views on the mating dance.

Sex and Destiny was a free-swinging attack on Western sexuality, with its emphasis on high-tech contraception, sexual play, and small family units. The "subfertile" societies of the West have grown increasingly masturbatory, Greer charged, making "genital dabbling" a higher pursuit than raising children. She contended that sexual liberation has become a religion in the West, "the new opiate of the people," and orgasm a "sacred duty." So repressive is this new religion, with its clergy of doctors and sex therapists and its nagging insistence on achieving sexual glory, that it makes one look with envy on Islamic societies. Or so Greer wrote: "In some ways modern woman has a harder row to hoe than the woman who knows that her integrity is safeguarded as long as she throws her veil around her whenever she goes out of the house, for the modern woman must be sexually active, must be prepared to take the initiative, and yet is only too open to cold-blooded exploitation and public humiliation, which cannot be righted by her brothers' chastisement of the offender(s)."

Here was another strange twist in contemporary feminism: the indomitable Germaine Greer looking on the bright side of Islamic women's black chadors. The celebrator of cunt power longing for an avenging brother with the wrath of Allah to defend her feminine honor.

Greer took as romantic a view of life in peasant societies as that held by Mao's Red Guards. While the West was narcissistic and sexually decadent, in her analysis, the cultures of the Third World were life-affirming and vigorous, built around reproduction and the raising of children. Greer wrote approvingly of the peasantry's primitive methods of contraception, its custom of making child-rearing the collective responsibility of women, and its complex web of taboos that made sex a dangerous and mysterious enterprise. Sex, she suggested, was "a basically banal experience . . . made more attractive by" repression.

The mother-child bond, with its "whole-body eroticism," is the greatest type of love, declared Greer. Sexual love between adults pales in comparison. This "suspicion was first implanted by the behavior of my female cats," she wrote, "who wept piteously when it was time to undergo the gang rape which is feline intercourse, and purred continuously while in labor, even when the labor was obviously painful, and purred all through their suckling, not stopping till the kittens were weaned. The triumphant tomcat may have enjoyed his brief ejaculation, but the female purred for eight weeks."

Greer's admirers in the women's movement reacted to *Sex and Destiny* as if they had been betrayed. In *The Female Eunuch,* Greer had written, "Sex is not the same as reproduction." But in *Sex and Destiny,* this is just what she seemed to be suggesting—that being fruitful and multiplying was indeed the central point. Barbara Ehrenreich, one of the few leading feminists in the 1980s who still endorsed the sexual revolution, published a particularly stinging review in *The New Republic,* calling the book a "burst of midlife petulance" from a woman who had decided that "apostasy" sells.

We did not want to believe that feminism's most clever and colorful proponent of sexual freedom had turned against her cause. How could Our Paisley Lady of the Park Bench become part of the drab detumescence of the 1980s? Greer still identified herself as "a sexual radical" in *Sex and Destiny,* someone who believed that "human libido is the only force which could renew the world." Perhaps her book had been misinterpreted. We found more to applaud in its pages than its feminist critics. There was no denying Greer's assertion, for instance, that one of the more unfortunate consequences of the sexual revolution was a growing merger between sex and commerce. "Sex," she wrote, has become "the lubricant of the consumer economy." In the process, sex has been "purged" of "passion."

If Greer was trying to restore some of the magic and primitive force that sex had lost, then we were still with her. It seemed important to clarify this. She had been, after all, the woman of our dreams. And so we came to talk with her, that warm September afternoon, in her room at the Orleans Hotel, where she was staying during a visit to New York.

The woman who greets us is not the vibrant lady of *Life*. More than sixteen years have passed since those photos were taken—Greer is now nearing fifty—and time has not tread lightly for her. Ghostly wisps of gray course through her hair. There is no luster to her skin. She seems older, more faded than her years. There is no more polite way to put it.

The year before, Greer had published in *Vogue* an article about aging titled "Letting Go." We liked the earthy, sensible way she wrote about growing older. Why submit yourself to the "tortures" of dieting and cosmetic surgery, declared Greer, when you can give yourself over to the gentle pleasures of decay. "We ought to be turning ourselves loose, freeing ourselves from inauthentic ideas of beauty, from discomfort borne in order to be beautiful . . . I'll keep the hips and heavy bosom." But there seems to be no joy, no sensual release in the way this woman before us has aged.

The spark, we quickly discover, is in Germaine Greer's speech. She is a dazzling conversationalist with a gift for the brassy assertion and cutting remark. As the afternoon progresses, most of her wicked brilliance is directed against the sexual revolution and, more disconcertingly, sex itself.

"I don't think the sexual revolution ever happened," Greer says, settling into a straight-backed chair facing us. She is wearing a sensible blue dress and blue stockings with runs in them. "What revolution? For a sexual revolution to have happened, people would have had to reconquer their innocence. They would have had to make love to each other without knowing what sex they were or what was likely to happen at the end. They would have had to come on to each other out of sheer joy in what they were. We never got there.

"We didn't release the average person on the streets of New York to a full understanding of their own eroticism. What we did do was tie them to a duty of genitality and a duty of sexual response. They weren't allowed even to be bored. Holy shit!

"Look, it seems to me that the basic fact about human sexual conjunction is that it's banal, and the chief problem of the human race has been to render it interesting. In the past, it was made exciting and exotic and faraway, so that when you finally got into the woman's bodice it was like going all the way to Turkey. But nowadays, instead of mystery and excitement, we have a performance ethic about sex. You're supposed to keep your circuits un-jammed, you're supposed to climb on regularly, you're supposed to have good orgasms of the right kind. We've now got a Protestant religion of sex. We have WASP sex. And it is deeply tedious."

Greer's pure, bright anger is invigorating. She sees with a burning clarity how badly sex has been used. But there is a great fatigue in her voice as well. No sexual practice seems to hold interest for her anymore. Masturbation? "Basically dull. I think we can all agree to this. We have all masturbated and we all know that it is deeply dull. Doctors now prescribe it, certain proof that it's deeply dull." Oral sex? "It's like being attacked by a giant snail. I prefer conversation. 'Hey, what's-your-name, what are you doing down there? Do you mind if I smoke while you're eating?' "

By now, Greer is carrying on the conversation from her hotel bed. We have been talking a long time, and she says she is tired. She lies there with her head nestled in the pillows, like a Victorian woman in the fainting room. She does not intend her recumbent position to be seductive, and there is nothing seductive about it. Is Greer really as weary of the dance to Venus as she sounds?

She assures us that she is. "I have found sexual love extremely exhausting, riddled with tensions and hostilities and jealousies and insecurities. I spent most of the best years of my life trying to get it right, and I'm just delighted not to be worried about it anymore. I really couldn't care less. I'm much happier to see that my house [in the British countryside, four miles south of Cambridge] is running well, that friends are well and happy, that we're eating well and the garden is flowering, that the animals are healthy and the trees are growing. I love all that. I can actually wake up in the morning and feel good. And my feeling good does not depend on somebody else's fucking mood.

"My favorite way of living would be with a lot of women and a lot of children and men who are allowed to drop in if they behave, which is the pattern of Islamic society. I think that's a good system because men are not thoroughly domesticated and we don't want them to be entirely tame in terms of genetics or evolution. We need them to be fairly aggressive and fairly competitive for the best reproductive opportunities.

"Believe me," she tells us, propping her head up with one elbow, "I would love to lose interest altogether in the penis. I don't know what's the matter with me that I still think it's so fascinating. It really makes me mad. But at least I prefer boys to men, so I'm not entirely lost."

By this point, the woman's cynicism has begun to enervate us as well. Germaine Greer's premature descent into the realm of the crotchety is profoundly dispiriting. Once upon a time, Greer wrote that "sex must . . . become a form of communication between potent, gentle, tender people, which cannot be accomplished by denial of heterosexual contact." But now she views true communion between the sexes as a hopeless enterprise. Heterosexual desire seems a nuisance.

What has made Germaine Greer feel this way? Her answer is full of weary sarcasm. "Well, you see there are these things called estrogens, my friend. You stop secreting them and everything changes. Mostly for the worse." She makes her voice wind down like an old Victrola.

"Yes, but the world is full of lusty older women," we say, always admirers of the sexy and wrinkled.

"They're all on estrogen replacements, take it from me," she replies flatly.

We have overstayed our welcome. Greer has grown as tired of discussing sex as she is of engaging in it.

"Are there any points we haven't covered?" we ask, preparing to end the interview.

"Oh, lots of things—we haven't covered anything I'm interested in," she sighs, sinking back on the bed and burying her face in the covers.

"Such as?"

"Oh well, never mind about hunger or socialism or the likelihood of war. All this talk of sex is fiddling while Rome burns. But that's what you people from San Francisco are famous for."

"But that's what you're known for as well," we point out. "Books about sexuality and society, not books about war and peace."

She sighs again. "I suppose."

This is the voice of intellectual, not just emotional, fatigue. Germaine Greer has nothing more to say to the world about sex, except for a barbed comment or two. Though we don't all lose our taste for sex in midlife, there's no reason why Greer should not be allowed to. But instead of moving gracefully on to other interests, she seems intent on spoiling the fun for everyone else. Greer's life nowadays may not have no Elvis in it, as they say in Texas, but that's no reason why the rest of us should stop wiggling.

The graying of Germaine Greer was part of the general fade-out of feminism in the 1980s. For over a decade, feminism—along with gay liberation—had provided most of the intellectual energy (and much of the kinetic energy) in the great exploration of the country's erogenous zones. But by the mid-1980s, the boiler had run out of steam. Feminist writings on sex were marked by a dreary cynicism—with occasional exceptions such as *Re-Making Love* by Barbara Ehrenreich, Elizabeth Hess, and Gloria Jacobs, an overlooked 1986 book that made the novel argument that the sexual revolution was actually a feminist project. But for the most part, feminist intellectuals seemed like ragged and lifeless survivors of the sex wars, with no heart left for engaging the enemy and no inspiration for how to reach an armistice.

With feminists of the stature of Germaine Greer renouncing sex and even cheering on crazy-as-birds Andrea Dworkin, women's liberation came to rest on the shore opposite from where it started. The shore opposite desire. The movement was born in the hothouse of love, and its first cry was for more human pleasure. But in the 1980s, feminism took its place alongside Christian fundamentalism, AIDS, and money mania as one of the chief inhibitors of America's sex drive. It was one of the sadder cultural developments of the times.

Fury has a way of immolating itself. And from its bone-white ashes grows human mercy. How long could feminist culture make gargoyles out of men? How long could lust and romance be banished from the feminist cathedral? Toward the end of the decade, a small but growing number of prominent feminists began asking such questions, among them even those who were doctrinally pure. "One wonders when peaceful coexistence between the sexes —a coexistence not predicated on a separatist peace—might become possible," asked the respected feminist literary scholars Sandra M. Gilbert and Susan Gubar in the New York *Times Book Review.* "Surely by now some of the old wounds of the feminist struggle have healed . . . Can the sexes lay down sword and shield sometime soon, or will the year 2001 witness a war of the words between feminists who are 'not the fun kind' and 'wild men' in search of 'the primitive root' of their maleness?"

Gilbert and Gubar were promptly attacked as schismatics by Mary Daly, a former Catholic theologian and a leading figure in feminist spirituality, one of the few dynamic areas of the women's movement in the 1980s. Daly, who has the soul of an inquisitor, accused the two scholars of "linguistic befuddlement" for "reducing [radical feminist thought] to the absurd category of 'sex wars.' " She further suggested that they were guilty of calling for "the defeat of feminism disguised as the healing of 'old wounds.' " Onward, feminist soldiers, cried Daly, who had once called upon her sisters to undergo "misterectomy" and get the men out of their lives.

For some feminist veterans, the thought of de-escalating the war between the sexes was simply unthinkable: the war gave purpose to their lives. It also provided them with healthy incomes. There were hefty academic grants, donations, speaking fees, and book contracts at stake. Feminism may have lost its intellectual momentum in the 1980s, but it was still a boom industry for many women. And they did not look kindly on those peace-loving sisters who were threatening their livelihood.

Still, the new voices of heresy would not be silenced. This budding movement for sexual harmony, for a third path between confrontation and capitulation, found support in a variety of feminist strongholds, from New Age conclaves in California to intellectual circles in New York. One of the more distinctive voices of reconciliation belonged to Starhawk, a thirty-six-year-old priestess (that is, a witch) in the old religion of the Goddess. Her books *Spiral Dance, Dreaming the Dark,* and *Truth or Dare* have brought her an impressively large New Age following. One would expect a feminist witch to take a dim view of the opposite sex, drawing on her dark powers to wither the limbs of men and turn them into newts. But when we dropped by the old, forbidding-looking house in San Francisco that Starhawk shares with the eight other members of the Black Cat Collective, we were relieved to discover that this witch is a great lover of men, as well as of women, and a great sensualist who believes that "sexual pleasure is an avenue to the Goddess."

There are male witches in Starhawk's coven and "every variety of sexual arrangement," she told us. "The Craft is a very earth-based spirituality and our rituals tap deeply into erotic energy. The singing, chanting, and dancing are very sensual ceremonies, often built around increasing someone's fertility.

"You know, in the old Sumerian tradition, the Goddess is a very sexually aggressive being. It's not the same as rape; it's a matter of 'I want you.' We also have a male god in the Craft, and he's a pretty hairy, horned fellow, the god of animal life. It's good for men to reclaim their wild energy; it's good for women too."

Black cat women! Starhawk and her coven seem like perfect matches for Robert Bly's beastly men—if only they would put down their drums and male power objects long enough to take notice.

In New York during the spring of 1988, we put our ears to the ground and heard other sounds of peace. We spoke with feminist intellectuals who were perhaps somewhat less colorful than the California neopagans but no less keen on finding common ground with the opposite sex. "My sense of where we have to go in the nineties," lesbian-feminist theorist Charlotte Bunch remarked, "is to learn how to deal better with diversity, with differences between the sexes, races, and political factions, so we can have vigorous debate without destroying each other.

"The women's movement was a necessary corrective to the sexual revolution. There had been a lot of sexual irresponsibility, a lot of abuse of male power—rape, violence, emotional damage. But it's time now to continue our exploration of sexual pleasure."

Rutgers professor and veteran feminist activist Kate Ellis issued a particularly passionate plea for sexual harmony. "Making enemies can be very gratifying, hating is enjoyable—but feminist politics must change," she said. "Men and women both have reflexive, conditioned attitudes of antagonism toward one another. But should we be committed to antagonism or coexistence? Years ago, the women's movement concluded that relations between the sexes were basically hopeless. Alright, so now what? Do you want to live in Andrea Dworkin's bleak world, that black hole where there is no possibility? I certainly don't. I'd prefer to try to bring forth something new."

There was a good feeling here, and it gave us hope. It was the feeling of reunion, of old lovers falling into one another's arms after years of bitter separation, like Florentino Ariza and Fermina Daza in *Love in the Time of*

Cholera. By now our bias must be plain, but we will make it plainer still: we are for the togetherness of men and women. We are for the rough and tender strife from which life flows. This human pact that drives away death. We like the way poet Sharon Olds played these chords in her 1987 collection *The Gold Cell:*

> The large hard bud of your sex in my mouth,
> the dark petals of my sex in your mouth,
> I could feel death going farther and farther away,
> forgetting me, losing my address, his
> palm forgetting the curve of my cheek in his hand . . .
> I looked at you and I tell you I knew you were God
> and I was God and we lay in our bed
> on the dark cloud, and somewhere down there
> was the earth, and somehow all we did, the
> blood, the pink stippling of the head, the
> pearl fluid out of the slit, the
> goodness of all we did would somehow get
> down there, it would find its flowering in the world.

And where were the men, when women began to write love poems like this? We were still not much for words, at least when it came to sexual debate. Yes, but in our songs and literature thumped a wise and wild new love. Springsteen's *Tunnel of Love,* Prince's *Lovesexy,* García Márquez's *Cholera.* This is how men best communicated their feverish feelings for women in the decade's final years. It was a gush of passion from the tongue-tied sex, and it seemed to us deeper than analysis, truer than cynicism.

The singer and songwriter Leonard Cohen, with his cool and chivalric way of looking at love, summed it all up during his 1988 U.S. concert tour. "For the last two thousand years, men have been asking the question, What do women want?" he told his audiences in his ragged, smoky voice. "And for the last fifteen minutes, women have been asking *themselves* what do women want. And for the last two minutes, men having been asking, What do *men* want? If any of these questions interests you, even for a moment, you are lost . . . I would do anything," he announced, to heated cries of approval, "to be worthy of a woman's caress."

IRTH

Pandora's Mirror:
The Rise of Fem Porn

T

all began, the feminist pornography of the 1980s, at a baby shower for Veronica Hart in the spring of 1983.

Hart was an innocently beautiful woman who sometimes shaved her pubic
hair in the shape of her last name. She had once performed with her hostess,
Annie Sprinkle, in a film called *Pandora's Mirror,* in which the two women
discover a magical antique mirror that allows them to watch again everyone
who has ever made love in front of it.

"While Annie Sprinkle may not be one of the top female erotic performers
of all time," qualifies the *Directory of Adult Film,* perhaps unfairly, "one thing
is true: she is certainly one of the kinkiest."

At the baby shower in Sprinkle's large loft in lower Manhattan, the
women, about thirty of them, soon broke into rival camps, Sharks and Jets.
They sang all the songs from *West Side Story,* especially "I Feel Pretty," which
they sang over and over again. Annie sang a slightly different tune from a
single she once recorded. The record never received a great deal of Top 40
airplay. "I'll Fuck Anything That Moves," it was called. The elegant Candida
Royalle, who had played a "bored, bitchy, and (temporarily) frigid wife" to
Hart's seductive maid in *Delicious,* snapped her fingers and belted out a bebop

version of "The Tomato Song": "I used to be a pear/And people nibbled all around me/Now they sip me through a straw/And call me Bloody Mary." Royalle's father had played drums with Lester Lanin and Louis Prima, and she was very good.

"We'd had sex together, and made movies together," Annie Sprinkle will tell us in her soft, otherworldly voice, "but before Veronica's shower, we never got to know each other in a more intimate way, you know what I mean?"

So the women brought out their baby pictures, and Annie shuffled them. Everybody tried to guess which little cherub of the fifties and sixties had become what porn star of the eighties. Then they played old fashioned baby-shower games like Pin the Tail on the Donkey, only Annie had changed it to Pin the Baby on the Boob. The women blindfolded Candida and spun her round and round, until it was impossible to pin the photo of the suckling baby Annie had given her, to the corkboard with the giant blowup of Mother Veronica's breast.

The women laughed until tears ran down their cheeks. They giggled and screamed like teenagers at a slumber party. This was the first time most of them had been together without cameras or men, and men had been ex-pressly forbidden at the shower in "the Sprinkle Salon," as everybody called Annie's apartment.

Except for Roger T. Dodger, of course. Giant, silent Roger, the gorgeous bodybuilder who was a former Mr. New York, served the hors d'oeuvres. "Annie made sure Roger was wearing a green apron and a black bikini bottom and little else," remembers Veronica Vera, Annie Sprinkle's best friend and the Catholic girl performance artist who wrote that antiseminal essay "Cunt Envy."

"A deep connection came out of that baby shower," says Royalle. "We realized we were kindred souls."

So seven of the women, including Royalle, Sprinkle, Hart, Vera, and Gloria Leonard, the pioneer of phone sex, decided a few months later to form a consciousness-raising group. They called it the Club 90 after the street address of Annie's apartment, and they have met twice a month ever since.

"We earned our living in a very intense way," says Royalle, "making love on camera for money. None of us really fit in anywhere else. The way people who don't understand or approve can treat you, it helps to have women around who love and trust you and who are doing the same crazy thing."

Royalle herself would go on to form Femme Productions, an unforeseen response to the video revolution. Today Femme has become a haven and creative home, a sort of United Artists of what can only be called "fem porn."

What could be more natural—and unexpected—than a group of former porn stars coming together to produce videos for women and what the industry calls couples? It was a commercially compelling concept because a survey of one thousand video stores in 1986 revealed that a majority of X-rated videos were rented by women, or by women and men together. Video pornography is a $600-million-a-year business. The VCR revolution of the eighties put sex tapes in the bedroom, where women and a new generation of young couples felt comfortable watching them. But still—feminist pornography? It was an affront that would catch moralists of all persuasions with their pants down.

Tonight in Femme's soundproof editing room on the West Side of Manhattan, Veronica Vera is sitting before a giant monitor instructing the technician on how big to make the titles. Behind the camera, she looks a little different from the way she does in front of it, more like a children's librarian in her gray flannel skirt and sleeveless sweater. The video segment is called "Shady Madonna," and on it, in freeze-frame, a naked actress is taking a bite out of a red, red apple.

At the other end of the room, squinched into the gray cushions of a new leather couch, is Annie Sprinkle. Annie is rewinding the rough cut of her own new video, "In Search of the Ultimate Sexual Experience," which will be packaged with "Shady Madonna" to form the release *Rites of Passion*. Annie wants to catch the scene with "Starman," who is played by Roger—the bodybuilder, you remember, at the baby shower. Starman is about to teach the "Naked Princess" about tantric love, but first he must explain how she'll never be able to enjoy the ultimate ecstasy until she learns to eat better.

To us, Annie is explaining the difference between the old, male-dominated porn and Femme's new "hard erotica."

"In the old days, the sex was already over before they thought about the woman's orgasm. You'd be lying there on the bed. The guy would be toweling himself off, and the director would shout, 'OK, take a face.' Then the camera would move onto your face for the close-up, and you'd fake the orgasm, like *'Ooh! Ahh! Moan! Groan!'* "

Annie laughs.

Candida Royalle smiles. "At Femme we don't go in for overdubbing moans and groans. We fold the woman's orgasm into the music."

Candida returns to a discussion she's having with a lawyer from MGM-UA. The lawyer wants to cut a distribution deal for Femme in Italy.

Annie turns back to Starman and the Princess. "I think this definitely needs more heavy breathing, don't you?" Starman is starting to put himself into the Princess. You see his back and his legs and face, but the shot of his cock is much quicker than it would be in most porn films.

Candida turns away from the lawyer again. "Very little focus on genitalia in Femme films," she points out.

"Those two are married in real life," smiles Annie as if she were talking of her children. The actors are moving wildly inside each other now.

"I try to get real-life lovers as often as I can," says Royalle. "You get the heat and the love that way. It's wonderful. And if I use real lovers, I don't have to use safe sex."

"Lovers for the dream sequences, condoms otherwise," smiles Annie.

"I think it's important to educate viewers as to how they can eroticize the use of safe sex," adds Candida.

The MGM lawyer is staring at the two women. He is wearing a shiny gray suit and a red power tie perfectly knotted at the center of his white collar. Royalle, thirty-four, is given to open-toed Parisian sandals, magenta capri pants, and little hot-pink plastic Eiffel Towers for earrings. Her hair is a precision cut, too elegant to be called punk. Annie Sprinkle, twenty-eight, is wearing a silk dress, and her neck is wrapped in the same elaborate Egyptian gold jewelry that the Naked Princess is wearing on the monitor. "Don't take this the wrong way," the lawyer has said moments before, "but I come from the days when there were no women in the editing room."

The videos of Femme Productions range from the sensual, like *Christine's Secrets* or *Three Daughters,* to the wacky. Sprinkle's *In Search of the Ultimate Sexual Experience* is definitely the latter.

In this wild river of tape, a jaded but good-hearted city woman who has done everything "from orgies to lesbians to the thing with Japanese guys" ("I guess you could say it's autobiographical," explains Sprinkle with a sweet smile) decides to clean up her sex life by throwing out her wham-bam-thank-you-ma'am lover. Her now-boring nights are suddenly perked up when Starman, a being this New York Princess once saved in another celestial lifetime, drops by Manhattan to repay the debt and shows her the ins and outs of three-day tantric love sessions, not to mention the prerequisites of a healthier diet. (Starman hates Cheez-Its.) Then, in a feminine reversal of an old X-rated story line, Sprinkle's hard-core ingenue teaches old Mr. Wham Bam to take it slow and easy, and for a very, very long time.

At the end of *Three Daughters,* Dad tells Mom, "Your eyes still shine like they always did." Mom, played by Gloria Leonard, lays her head on Dad's freshly pressed chinos. Her hand floats to the zipper. "Oh, I love you," gushes Dad when she wraps her mouth around him. Then, as he begins to have his orgasm, he starts to cry. It's a long, vulnerable jag of sighs and tears, and one imagines that few women have experienced such a sensitive display.

Femme women don't sleep with men until they want to, and if the guys do start things, they usually ask first. And politely. There's lots of kissing and fondling and foreplay. Afterward, the men rock the women in their arms. Royalle likes cuddling.

The men dress like models in Calvin Klein ads. The women are hardly the "Talk dirty to me" fuck-bunnies of older porn but rather normal, if horny, gals with good jobs and "Dynasty" clothes. The sets seem designed by Laura Ashley, all flowered wallpaper, arranged silverware, antique oaken beds, designer sheets, and yards and yards of expensive lingerie. The music is decorous, mostly Wyndam Hill–sounding stuff, and when the soundtrack builds to that called-for crescendo, those crescendos, too, are decorous.

Violence is as forbidden as a male lead with a potbelly. OK, maybe a little giggly bondage with silk scarves looped around the pipes of that Laura Ashley brass bed. But good God, no "golden showers" of love—which is how, if you haven't already guessed, Annie got her name—and definitely no nipple-piercing, a forbidden pleasure Veronica Vera writes about in her short and picante autobiography, *Beyond Kink.* The ladies have gone mainstream!

This seems to bother the old guard. "Sensitivity is wonderful, but it's not grounds for arousal," huffs Jim Holliday, the self-appointed historian of American porn.

"Women want a situation, a tenderness component," counters Royalle. "They want a relationship, more than a body and a sex organ. Of course, I'm filming erotica for men and women together, couples, and that's tricky. I don't want to lose the men to get the women, and they have different fantasies. The big fantasy in many adult movies is to have lots of women throw themselves at a man because that sort of thing almost never happens to men in real life, whereas for women, it's easy to go out and have sex—too easy—so we like buildup and lead-in. But I'm convinced that the new men my age want a lot of the same things women do and that it will be the women who help the men explore.

"Typical porn," she says, "strives to please men who live in a society where hot sex is mostly prohibited. Since your wife is supposed to be that lovely, pure woman who wouldn't dream of giving you a blow job, then the male porn movie provides you with that little girl-woman piece of meat who does offer dirty, nasty sex—on tape, at least. That's why the visible come-shot is so very important in typical porn. It provides these men with visible release. But it's so narcissistic, it gets to the point where the orgasm these guys want to see isn't the woman's. It's their own."

After agreement is reached with the MGM lawyer, most of the people in the editing room leave for dinner. Candida stands in the hall talking about how she got into adult films in the first place.

She yawns at the usual myths of the abused childhood or white slavery, although she admits she's seen some strong things in the porn world. (Royalle "hates" the word "porn." She prefers "adult films.") After quitting the Parsons School of Design in New York, Royalle landed in an office, which she hated. "I was sexually assaulted by bosses, and I had to kiss them good night every night to keep my job." She joined a feminist coalition in the Bronx that ran a free clinic for women. Eventually Royalle burned out on politics and moved to San Francisco to take up drama. Broke, she turned to cheesecake modeling. When a boyfriend acted in a hard-X movie, *Cry for Cindy*, she decided to check out the set.

"The cast and crew were beautiful and healthy. I thought, What the hell, it's good money. This was the early seventies when we were all still in the throes of the sexual revolution. I was twenty-three. Women who didn't jump into bed the first time were either uptight or gay. It was a very different time, a very different time."

In an earlier interview Royalle expanded: "I got into the business because of Catholic guilt over being a very sexually alive young woman. Candida

[Candice is her real name] became a way for me to be that lusty woman without being myself . . . I was being requested and paid . . . yet the pleasure was for men and not for me. I never really got off doing it. It was a way to get male attention. I think that my father left me with a feeling of not really loving and appreciating me . . . I'd lose weight, do the movies, and put on the weight again. I knew I always had mixed feelings about being in the movies, not because I thought they were bad in and of themselves but more because the way they shot them was so embarrassing."

By the late 1970s Royalle was making a name for herself in what were considered in the business to be elegant outings, movies like *October Silk* and *Delicious*, as well as raunch epics that have become fem-porn classics, such as *Hot & Saucy Pizza Girls*. In *Pizza Girls*, the worst fear of a woman in X-rated movies came true: the actor she had contracted to play opposite could not get his erection. "The director was pressed for time. They brought a stand-in whose attractions did not lie above the belt. You feel like a piece of meat then."

In 1979, Royalle decided to quit the business. She had been seeing a therapist who in another life had been a prostitute but now specialized in helping bad girls adjust to strange times without forsaking all desire. And Royalle had fallen in love with Per Sjostedt, a filmmaker from Sweden who supported her acting but refused to watch her make love to others. Royalle found that it became difficult for her to perform with other men "after being so deeply in love with Per."

They decided to create erotica "that came out of our peer mentality rather than the fifties mentality." After Royalle secured a distribution promise from VCA's Walter Dark of the notorious Dark brothers, she was able to borrow start-up money from her father-in-law, who was a major film distributor in Scandinavia.

To save money and capitalize on the VCR revolution, they shot directly onto video, and to escape the robotic look of standard porn, they used a single hand-held camera that "lived" in the bedroom with their screen lovers—and they insisted on authentic moans.

While Candida is chatting in the hallway, an executive from another company has been trying to enter the editing room. He knocks first, slides the door halfway, sticks his head in, then stomps off. Each time he returns, he bangs louder and leaves his head in longer, until Candida stops talking to check out the scene.

Candida opens the door.

"An-nie!"

Annie Sprinkle is still on the new gray leather couch beside the monitor, but now a technician is underneath her. Her silk dress is bunched around her waist. The breasts that shocked the *Directory of Adult Film* swing free. Her hips are nonchalant, but they don't stop rocking.

"Umm, sorry, Candida," whispers Annie as sweetly and tentatively as ever. "Ummm, I guess my video must be OK. At least it turned *me* on."

Annie Sprinkle may be the Mae West of the 1980s. After she rearranges herself, we join her, Candida, and Per, and adjourn to a fashionable bistro called Capito. Above the bar is a bright neoprimitive mural by Richard Toddei. Painted in black chopped letters below the mural is the dictum THE SHORTEST DISTANCE BETWEEN TWO PEOPLE IS RARELY A STRAIGHT LINE.

Annie and Candida begin to sip Capito house cocktails, concoctions called "peaches-at-the-beach." Per is drinking a double vodka.

"Annie, when I came in on you two, I felt as if I'd walked in on my big sister. My face turned all red."

"Did it, Candida, really?"

"Yes."

Last weekend, says Annie, changing subjects, she tossed off a lesbian fuck film. "All these girls were doing it for the money," she explains, her eyes at once as wide as Little Orphan Annie's and as shrewd as Daddy Warbucks's.

"The director ordered everybody as quickly as possible: 'You eat her, OK, you eat her, no, no, open your legs like this . . .' And one girl definitely wanted the shoot to be over. She was eating this other girl out and suddenly she stopped and shouted, 'She's coming! It's over. She came.' But the other girl raised up on her elbows and moaned, 'Wait! Wait! No, I didn't!' "

Everybody laughs.

It is Friday night. The little party moves to Annie's loft. In the taxi on the way over, Per says in his dry Swedish way, "America is so concerned with pornography. Pornography to me is an MX missile."

The Sprinkle Salon is dark, and there is the smell of some esoteric herb being burned or cooked. Annie goes to the kitchen to investigate. It turns out that her houseguest has been in a tantric position with a German model in the back bedroom for several blissful hours and has been unable to turn off the broccoli. Nobody is bothered. The tantric lady, late of Rajneeshpurim, Oregon, slips on a cotton dress in front of us. The German rubs his eyes. They both smile like cats. The tantric lady is staying at the Sprinkle Salon as a sort of script consultant to *Rites of Passion*.

The Sprinkle Salon doubles as Annie's bedroom and a photographic studio. Dressed in leather and lingerie and draped in Nikons, Sprinkle and Veronica Vera shoot dozens of photo layouts for men's magazines and special-edition adult books. FROM THE SCHOOL OF HIGH-HEEL JOURNALISM reads their photo calling card, and it is interesting to note that some of the raunchier male titles frowning out from porn arcades in Midtown, U.S.A., originate with the ladies at the Sprinkle Salon. *Girls Over 40* and *Shaved* were two titles, but the show-stopper has to be Annie Sprinkle's *Bazoombas,* Volume I, Number 1.

Bazoombas could be the *Duck Soup* of goofy erotica: BUY THIS MAGAZINE AND HELP PUT A PORN STAR THROUGH COLLEGE PLUS***SEE ANNIE SPRINKLE'S BREASTS DEFY GRAVITY AND WALK ON FIRE PLUS***PORN'S EIGHT BIGGEST-BUSTED STARS SHOW AND TELL ALL.

This last turns out to be "A Bosom-Buddy Bull Session," with Annie asking her friends how they like their breasts to be treated in a sexual encounter. Mistress Candice replies, "I like my breasts treated very gently unless I'm beating someone in the face with them," and Sue Nero says, "I hate my tits. I would like to have them made smaller, but I don't want to lose the sensitivity in my nipples." Later Annie asks everybody, "If tits could talk, what would your tits say to the world?" Her own answer: "My tits would say, 'Don't just love us, love the woman we live on.' "

This is a long way from the sensual decorum of *Three Daughters*. While Annie sets up *Rites of Passion* on her VCR and plugs in a tape machine to test out soundtrack songs for us, Candida explains how more orthodox feminists have reacted to Femme films.

After *Christine's Secret* and *Three Daughters* came out to good reviews in major newspapers and thousands of women began to rent or buy the videos, Royalle found it odd that feminist organizations seemed reluctant at best to publicize what she felt was a revolutionary development. She believed that women deserved to be able to explore eroticism and felt that if organized women did not support people like her, the project would be much harder.

So she invited half a dozen women from the Media Reform Committee of NOW's New York chapter over to her house in Brooklyn to view *Christine's Secrets*. One was Florence Rush, a founder of Women Against Pornography.

It was both a cordial and a nervous scene. The women were surprised when Per emerged with hors d'oeurves he had prepared himself. Per is the cook of the household. He passed the trays around and discreetly refilled them. The women were impressed, a handsome husband with no ego problem. They had not known what to expect at the home of a former porn star.

Royalle put on some clips from a "real" porn movie just to make sure the women knew what old-style male porn actually looked like. Everybody began to laugh. Royalle told stories, and the women warmed to her. She was more plainly dressed than they had expected, wearing a simple cotton dress. And she was educated. They hadn't expected that either. "I was especially impressed by her garden," Florence Rush would tell us later, "because it was organic and wholesome." Most of all, the visitors did not understand how Royalle could have really been a grass-roots feminist organizer and then made love on camera for money. It was all puzzling. It was not the way things were supposed to be.

Royalle played *Christine's Secret*. The women were even more surprised. All of them seemed to enjoy the movie, and some seemed to like it a great deal. The ones who enjoyed it the most were the most guarded about it.

In the discussion that followed, people told Royalle that her film was indeed more sexually egalitarian. They found her sincere. Florence Rush agreed that *Christine's Secret* was certainly different, much better than the old cock-in-the-face stuff, but she felt that the film showed little concern for the problem of unwanted pregnancies or sexual disease, and she asked, "Can we be exploring women's fantasies now in such dangerous times?"

In a way, thought Royalle, it was as if the National Organization for Women, unlike the women who were buying and renting her videos, actually preferred old garbage porn because the old male-made porn was easy to understand and even easier to hate. It certainly raised no unsettling questions, the most obvious of which was, Weren't a lot of women just as turned on by the sight of men and women making love as men were?

Back at the Sprinkle Salon, Annie is also having doubts, but of a different nature. She decides that Marvin Gaye's "I Heard It Through the Grapevine" will bring the tantra spirituality in *Rites of Passion* down to earth, but shouldn't she make the video more hard-core? There's lots of lovemaking, but the blow job is pretty arty. "I like a good, *long* blow job," says Annie reflectively.

The tantra lady rises off the bed. She is a strong woman with calm black eyes and a raunchy laugh.

"Nah," she says, "don't make it for those guys in the raincoats. They have their videos already. This is the porn of the future."

After most everybody leaves, Annie asks the more Montana of your authors if he would like his feet massaged. A former masseur himself, he accepts. Annie begins to talk about sex and death, the connection the Europeans sometimes make. She shows him a horrible yet exquisite book published in France. On the left-hand pages are pictures of men and women fondling, folding, licking, loving, intertwining; there are dripping pussies and stiff-headed johnsons of every hue and hardness; and the people are real, not models. On the right-hand pages are pictures of war and Holocaust, the Marne, Auschwitz, D day, Nagasaki, Khe Sanh, and here are as many naked bodies in as many contorted positions as on the left-handed pages, but those on the right are hacked, bloodied, burned, and decapitated. No captions anywhere. Porn in Europe, says Annie in the same soft, sweet, knowing voice she has used all evening, is, you know, state-of-the-art. They are an old civilization, says Annie, they know what it is all about, sex and death. Or maybe they don't. She laughs. American porn, like Hollywood movies, is much more fun, and she laughs.

On the same shelf as the Europorn is a folio of piercing pictures, women with golden rings slipped through their labias, and men hanging by thick stainless steel hooks poked through their breasts: *O-Kee-Pa 1964, Sun Dance 1978.* Annie waits for a reaction to these. She slips out of her clothes and pulls on a large white T-shirt. Then she lies back on the bed and talks of AIDS, how she has tested negative twice, findings that certainly confirm her belief, she says, that the virus is difficult to get, really. She does not laugh this time. She raises an eyebrow.

Attracted but shy, shy but attracted, your coauthor thinks and thinks better of it. He leaves to catch a cab. It is very late.

The 1980s saw an explosion in erotic material produced by women. Nancy Friday continued the real-life fantasy that began with *My Secret Garden*. California psychologist Lonnie Barbach published *Shared Intimacies*, and the best-selling *Erotic Interludes*. Anne Rice, creator of sensual vampires, began to write hard-core romantic fantasy under two pseudonyms. Susie Bright, who would become a safe-sex porn star for a day, brought out a line of "fem-top" videos that did not stop at fist-fucking, and started the gloriously eccentric *On Our Backs* ("Entertainment for the Adventurous Lesbian").

A literary bohemian from Ohio named Lilli Pond began *Yellow Silk* ("All Persuasions, No Brutality"), a journal of erotic arts that published what most literary magazines were afraid to. A group of well-to-do suburbanites put together a best-selling book of silken titters titled *Ladies' Home Erotica*.

In the cartoon world, Ailene Kaminsky drew Dirty Laundry Comix, and *Esquire* cartoonist Lynda Barry brought out *NAKED LADIES! NAKED LADIES! NAKED LADIES!* a fauvist coloring book that scandalized Seattle in its art show opening. *NAKED LADIES!* was a captioned tribute to the high school experience in the heartland. A sample: "My girlfriend said she read an article about a lady who had done it with a giant lizard and had a baby with bad skin. Somebody's sister said a mouse filled with the holy spirit had run up the toilet while she was sitting on it and made her pregnant. Someone else said you also get hair on your tits."

These books and magazines could be seen either as explorations of the feminine unconscious or as masturbatory vehicles, or both, and they were met with silent blushes by intellectuals. For once, and quite suddenly, women were doing the fantasizing of naked bodies in unusual positions, aggressive behavior, and games and fun of all sorts.

Women producing pornography broke all the rules. Wasn't porn "a male invention, like rape, designed to dehumanize women, to reduce the female to an object of sexual access," as Susan Brownmiller wrote in *Against Our Will?*

What a dangerous forest to walk through! Some feminists, like Gloria Steinem, have tried to sidestep the problem by distinguishing pornography from erotica. "Pornography is to women of all groups what Nazi literature is to Jews and Ku Klux Klan literature is to Blacks," she wrote in her famous introduction to *Out of Bondage*, the 1986 autobiography of Linda Lovelace, who had been the star of *Deep Throat.* "It is as different from erotica as sex is different from rape."

But other feminists are not so sure. "In practice," wrote Ellen Willis in *The Village Voice,* "attempts to sort out good erotica from bad porn inevitably come down to 'What turns me on is erotic; what turns you on is pornographic.' "

The raucous debate over pornography has divided the women's movement ever since the mid-1970s (see Chapter Six), pitting those who would eradicate pornography as an expression of male aggression against those who want to push the envelope of women's sexuality. It's "good girl" versus "bad girl." And the language has gotten pretty dirty.

During an unsuccessful 1985 campaign to pass an antiporn referendum in Cambridge, Massachusetts, good girl Catharine MacKinnon railed that her bad-girl opponents were "house niggers who sided with the masters," little better than "pimps and pornographers" themselves.

At a Women and the Law conference in 1985, bad girl Paula Webster shot back, "something cold, mean, and unforgiving is being shoved down my throat by steely-eyed women who transmit a feeling of hysteria."

In January of 1986 the good girl–bad girl debate spilled out of the feminist arena when Dorchen Leidholdt, cofounder of Women Against Pornography, seized the microphone at the New York hearings of the U.S. Attorney General's Commission on Pornography [the Meese Commission]. "We demand," she said, "that the Commission acknowledge that the $8 billion a year pornography industry is built on sexual enslavement and exploitation of women. We demand that the commission acknowledge that pornography targets all women for rape, battery, sexual harassment, prostitution, incest, and murder."

First surprised, then elated, the commission's chairman, Henry Hudson, a law-and-order prosecutor from Virginia, kept the mike open. Hudson and a majority of the commission had at last found a welcome audience for their own profamily views. They made strange bedfellows, to be sure, these bluenose conservatives and these feminists who were "not the fun kind." But these were strange times.

Before the joining of the unholy alliance, the Meese Commission had been dunned by liberal media as unscientific, disorganized, ignorant of the First Amendment, and unwilling to hear opposing viewpoints of any kind. Many believed the hearings to be a sop to President Reagan's supporters on the religious Right.

Hudson would not improve his position with the First Amendment crowd when he sent out a letter to the giant Southland Corporation, which owned the 7-Eleven chain of forty-five hundred stores. The commission "has received testimony alleging that your company is involved in the sale or distribution of pornography," the letter read. "The commission has determined that it would be appropriate to allow the company to respond to the allegations prior to drafting its final report section on identified distributors. You will find a copy of the relevant testimony enclosed herewith."

The relevant testimony was by the Reverend Donald Wildmon, director of the National Federation for Decency, headquartered in Tupelo, Mississippi, birthplace of Elvis Presley. A newsletter published by the reverend once castigated NBC's "Golden Girls" as a "geriatric-sex series." Before the Meese Commission, Wildmon had pointed out that 20 percent of the sales of *Playboy* came from 7-Eleven stores. If Southland refused to stock *Playboy* and *Penthouse,* the profits of Hugh Hefner, Bob Guccione, and other smut peddlers would be "seriously crippled."

To the shock of *Playboy* and *Penthouse,* 7-Eleven dropped the magazines before the commission had come to any conclusions or issued its report. In a few months, a federal court forced the commission to retract its letter, and *Playboy,* which had been losing circulation to video onanists, announced a fresh concept in pictorial spreads: "The Girls of 7-Eleven."

After the commission released its report, Dr. Judith Becker and Ellen Levine, two of the four women on the panel, would issue a dissenting opinion that slammed Hudson and the majority. Becker and Levine denied that any credible evidence existed to link pornography to sex crimes, the real nut of the pornography debate.

That the commission was abandoned by half its women members while all the men held fast caused Johns Hopkins University sex researcher John Money to charge that the Meese report was "the most furtively sexist and antifeminist document of our time. It declares that women are so morally delicate that they may not partake with men of the explicit depiction of the frankly erotic."

But the most articulate critics of the antiporn crusaders were feminist pornographers themselves. Women like Missy Manners, the Republican safe-sex porn star and cantankerous significant other to Artie Mitchell of the Mitchell brothers, the producers of *Behind the Green Door* and the tough pixie kings of American pornography. Or like Nina Hartley, a registered nurse who has made more than fifty-five X-rated movies and got her start, she says, when she was only six years old. Her mother told her to get the hell out from under a steel-wool and cotton "orgone blanket" stored in the attic of her parents house. The orgone blanket was left over from her mother's flirtation with Reichian therapy. "I must have had a premonition," Hartley tells us, "or maybe the experience electrified me." And then there is Annette Haven, a rebellious ex-Mormon with alabaster skin and an angry intelligence. Haven fumes over iced Heinekens in a Marin County restaurant, "People are so upset about sex. I don't understand. Those who are guilty of anorexia nervosa or gluttony are not treated as pariahs, are they? You know, sexuality is one of the minor things on the agenda of the universe. There's death, birth, environmental self-extinction, all kinds of hairy and awful and frightening and painful stuff. I can't understand why we can't handle sexuality. How incompetent of a species are we?"

But the most sweetly savage would be novelist Anne Rice, the most famous of them all. "No matter what bad-girl things my heroines do," she smiles, "they never get truly hurt because at heart they are still good girls."

Upstairs in Anne Rice's study on the top floor of her San Francisco Victorian, it's all saints and computers. Somber St. Anthony holding the baby Jesus in his arms; serene St. Gerard clasping a tiny book to his robe; angelic St. Thérèse, "the Little Flower of Jesus," as she was known in the St. Charles district of New Orleans where Anne Rice went every day as a girl in the 1940s; St. Cecilia, headless. Cecilia's head was lopped off in an earthquake two years ago. The heavy wooden bookcase is a Catholic girl's garden of remembered statuary.

"I hope that I may be one of the most famous female pornographers in the United States," smiles Rice, and her smile is as tiny and sweet as one of the antique cloth dolls in her collection downstairs.

Rice is in her late forties and short—five-feet-two-inches tall—although she seems taller. Her bones are small and perfect, her eyes happy and, it would seem, knowing; her hair is long and as black as a moonless night.

Rice touches a red-and-black whip nailed to the wall opposite her Tandy 2000 computer. It is a cat-o'-nine-tails with the softest of leather strands, given to her by a fan who felt Rice's books should contain even more accounts of flagellation.

Has Mrs. Rice ever been whipped herself?

"Let's build up a mystique," she says with another perfect china-doll smile. "Let's not tell everybody how dull I am."

Anne Rice is the author of *The Queen of the Damned, The Vampire Lestat,* and *Interview with the Vampire,* the classic modern horror novel that may be to our sexually ambiguous time what Mary Wollstonecraft Shelley's *Frankenstein* was to the early nineteenth century. Under the mildly lusty pseudonym Ann Rampling, Rice also writes best-selling contemporary novels of exotic sex and romance. And under the French nom-de-plume A. N. Roquelare (Roquelare means cloak), she publishes fairy-tale pornography, hard-core variations on the Sleeping Beauty theme.

"Sexually, the 1980s have become the plague years," smiles Rice. "People are beginning to flee from reality. The vampire novels give me a way to talk about eroticism and sensuality from a context of total fantasy. These creatures are vampires; therefore, they don't exist."

To Rice, a vampire is an elegant, doomed person, beautifully dressed, tragically sensitive, locked into the monstrous nightmare of being a vampire against its will. Rice's vampires are mostly gay, or as homoerotic as supernatural beings can be who must substitute the thrill of the kill and the sublimity of bloodsucking for earthly sex.

In the first few pages of *Interview with the Vampire,* an ancient French vampire named Lestat pulls Louis, a Louisiana plantation owner of the eighteenth century, to his chest "like a lover" and whispers, "Be still. I am going to drain you now to the very threshold of death, and I want you to be quiet, so quiet that you can almost hear the flow of blood through your veins, so quiet that you can hear the flow of that same blood through mine. It is your consciousness, your will which must keep you alive."

"I wanted to struggle," says Louis, "but he pressed so hard with his fingers that he held my entire prone body in check: and as soon as I stopped my abortive attempt at rebellion, he sank his teeth into my neck."

When it is Louis's turn to drink from Lestat's lashed wrist, which is how Rice's vampires are made, Louis says, "I drank, sucking the blood out of the holes, experiencing for the first time since infancy the special pleasure of sucking nourishment, the body focused with the mind."

Rice worked on *Interview* twelve hours a day, or rather night—from five in the afternoon until five the next morning, vampire hours. Her first child had just died of leukemia, a blood disease, and Rice felt she herself "simply had no right to live. Why? Because she was my child and I couldn't save her . . .

"If I have one rule as a writer," says Rice, "it's pursue an obsession, and when I wrote that book, I knew I was obsessed."

As a girl, Anne Rice thrilled to the supernatural tales of Algernon Blackwood and M. R. James, which she read in the New Orleans public library; and from her Irish Catholic mother and father she heard stories of antebellum ghosts and beautiful women who burst into flame while combing their long blond hair. "My mother had a million stories like that."

By the time she was a teenager, Rice felt outside her parents' religion. "I grew up very Catholic, going to mass and communion every day, and I had two aunts who were nuns and a cousin who was a priest. The church in New Orleans was very Latin, very Italian, with candles burning in front of the saints and all the trappings. In college, at Texas Woman's University, I remember speaking to this intelligent priest who told me, 'You are the kind of person who will be Catholic all your life. Any attempt to give it up will just lead to misery.' Kids reared the way I was reared are marked forever. When I left the church, there was a loss of faith I couldn't find anywhere else. Brotherhood is all we have left in the twentieth century."

Rice also felt herself to be an outsider sexually. "The repression was very strict. There was a lot of bitterness. There was no attention to my own desires whatsoever." By her twenties, she even believed she was a man trapped inside a woman's body. "I've never been at home as a woman. It bothered me tremendously. I felt somebody would realize I was an imposter. When you're very young, and people have told you that you're too aggressive and you talk like a man and you don't walk like a girl, and all this southern crap, it can be very upsetting."

For years Rice could not bring herself to believe that men and women could have anything close to an equal relationship. In her imagination, equality existed only among gay men, "dream figures that loved each other like angels." Rice believes that even today, in the face of AIDS, gays are the only

Americans still perpetuating a belief in the wholesomeness and goodness of sex.

The writing in *Interview with the Vampire* is sensual, but the sex is veiled. Not so in the hard-core Roquelaure books, *The Claiming of Sleeping Beauty*, *Beauty's Punishment*, and *Beauty's Release*, all novels of "discipline, love, and surrender."

In a chapter from *Beauty's Punishment* titled "Soldiers' Night at the Inn," Beauty finds herself a captured slave. She is naked as she serves food and ale to the golden-haired Captain and his men.

At once the Captain's strong right hand clamped on her wrists and he rose from the bench lifting her off the floor and up so she dangled above him . . .

"To my good soldiers, who have served the Queen well," the Captain said, and at once there was loud stomping and clapping. "Who will be the first?" the Captain demanded.

Beauty felt her pubic lips growing thickly together, a spurt of moisture squeezing through the seam, but a silent burst of terror in her soul paralyzed her. "What will happen to me?" she thought as the dark bodies closed in around her. The hulking figure of a burly man rose in front of her . . .

The smell of the stables rose from the man, the smell of ale, and the rich, delicious scent of sun-browned skin and rawhide. His black eyes quivered and closed for an instant as his cock plunged into Beauty, widening the distended lips, as Beauty's hips thudded against the wall in a frantic rhythm . . . Yes. Now. Yes. The fear was dissolved in some greater unnameable emotion . . .

The cock discharged its hot, swimming fluid inside her and her orgasm radiated through her, blinding her, her mouth open, the cries jerked out of her. Red-faced and naked, she rode out her pleasure right in the midst of this common tavern.

She was lifted again, emptied . . . As the hungry mouth sucked on her nipple, she lifted her breasts, arching her back, her eyes turned shyly away from those who surrounded her. The greedy mouth fed on her right breast now, drawing hard as the tongue stabbed at the tiny stone of the nipple . . .

Something touched her pulsing clitoris, scraped it through the thick film of wetness. It plunged through her starved pubic lips. It was the rough, jeweled handle of the [Captain's] dagger again . . . surely it was . . . and it impaled her.

She came in a riot of soft muffled cries, pumping her hips up and up, all sight and sound and scent of the Inn dissolved in her frenzy. The dagger handle held her, the hilt pounding her pubis, not letting the orgasm stop, forcing cry after cry out of her . . . All her body had become the orifice, the organ.

Rice touches her wedding band as she talks, seated at the kitchen table. America's most famous female pornographer has been married to her high school sweetheart, poet Stan Rice, for twenty-four years. From time to time, Lucky, her giant bull mastiff, barks deeply from the backyard. A deer's head with comic dentures wedged in its mouth stares down from the kitchen wall.

"When I'm before that computer writing," she says, "I'm fairly sexually aroused. Very frankly, I'm creating a one-handed read. I pace the scenes with my natural feelings. If you don't, then it's only hackwork, which to me is pornography written by people who don't really share the fantasy, to use the cliché, but are only trying to second-guess the market. One of my theories about the rare but violent pornographic film, like *The Tool Box Murders,* in which a man with a nail gun shoots a naked woman—and it's horrible!—is that viewers don't really need the violence to be aroused. The violence is borrowed from television shoot-outs, added by hacks who don't know the market."

But what about the sexual violence of, say, "Soldiers' Night at the Inn?"

To Rice, the wild scene at the inn is not violent at all because it is consensual. "The whole point in my Roquelaure books is that the sexual experimenter doesn't get truly hurt, no matter what bad-girl things she does *because she is a good girl.*"

In fact, one of the things that made Rice begin her pornographic series was her hatred of Pauline Réage's classic *Story of O.* Rice found it "grim, pessimistic, and sinister" because "O" goes mad, is branded, and disintegrates. Rice set out to create a fairy-tale world in which the heroine could enjoy all manner of "fun and games" without being slashed or killed. To Rice, connecting forbidden sex with punishment and death is a form of moral control.

She throws up her delicate hands. "You know the TV version. The cop hero tells the teenybopper prostitute to get the hell off Sunset Boulevard. She refuses, and so by the end of the show, she's about to be killed for a snuff movie when who should burst in but Mr. Cop, who saves her—or almost. She dies lusciously in his arms. If only she hadn't been such a bad girl."

What Anne Rice does is give good girls permission to dream bad girl dreams. "There are thousands upon thousands, if not millions, of women in the United States who would like nothing better than to be dominated in a safe context by some man who they know is not going to kill them," says Rice. "They would love it. They buy tons of romances in which women are dominated by pirates and Yankee soldiers and God knows what."

Why?

"The desire to be dominated in a sexual situation has very deep roots. Maybe these people enjoy it because the responsibility is off their shoulders. They are forced to feel things.

"The heart of the matter," stresses Rice, "is that people want the permission to enjoy. They want to be carried away in the whirlwind and receive all that wonderful attention—and then emerge unharmed. That's the sadomasochistic fantasy, and it appeals," she insists, "to men and women both."

Rice believes that any culture which emphasizes sin and repression will create people who want to be punished before they can enjoy. She believes the pornographic representation of sadomasochism was strongest in Victorian England and that practitioners were typically Church of England gentlemen, straight or gay. She points out that Raymond Chandler and Ian Fleming may be viewed as writers of male S&M, since they subject Philip Marlowe and James Bond to continuous, appalling, excruciating tortures, a good many of them sexual in tone. Rice laughs her fast rich laugh: "And didn't Woody Allen say that he wanted to die smothered in the flesh of Italian actresses?"

But in the end, Rice prefers to beg off. "I'm not a psychiatrist. I'm not a lawyer. I'm not an anthropologist," she says crisply. "I am a writer and I only write what turns me on."

What bothers Rice more than the possibly dark implications of her fantasies is any attempt to rein her in.

"Women as sexual beings haven't been out of the closet for more than about twenty years. What I see now is the closet door being slammed back in our face by an alliance of feminists, Moral Majority conservatives, and old-guard liberals who seek more to protect women as victims of male sexuality than to argue for equal rights or the rights of women to express themselves sexually. To me this is very frightening. I want to know what other women feel. I wish they would write more erotica. It's a big mystery what women want. It's a big mystery what turns them on. We've spent two thousand years telling women what they should and shouldn't feel. It's time now to find out what they really do feel."

Rice is matter-of-fact about this. "I largely see feminists as my enemy. Although I see myself almost as a radical feminist, at this point in history there are many vocal reactionary, repressive feminists who are trying to get pornography banned and trying to interfere with the expression of sexual desire in art.

"The problem for any writer," Rice insists, "is keeping other people's voices out of your head when you're at the computer. You must not be intimidated."

Rice believes that antiporn crusaders such as Andrea Dworkin and Catharine MacKinnon are "idiots" and "fools." She feels that "they have been indulged. If the kind of antipornography legislation which they advocate were pushed by two fundamentalist Baptist ministers from the Bible Belt, it would be laughed out of the public arena overnight. But because Dworkin and MacKinnon are women and are supposed to be feminists, they have confused well-meaning liberals everywhere. People have bent over backward to understand their position when they don't deserve any leeway—because Dworkin and MacKinnon have no respect for free speech, for the Constitution of the United States, or for rights that have mattered to the rest of us for hundreds of years, rights that have evolved out of English common law."

What angers Rice most is her belief that Dworkin and MacKinnon have no regard for legal precedent. "If you link pornography to rape, then, as I understand it, a woman would have the right to sue *Playboy* magazine if she felt *Playboy* incited some man to rape her. But then, logically, the man could turn around and sue *Playboy* for making him rape her. Or he could say, 'The movie made me do it. I was so obsessed after viewing *The Tool Box Murders* that I couldn't stop myself.' Once you place blame outside the man for the rape, it's only one jump to sticking it right back on provocative clothing: 'She made me do it because she wore a red dress and gold bracelets.'

"Dworkin and MacKinnon are really questioning whether people have free will. This is as true for the rapist as for the porn star. But I think people must be held responsible for their actions. When Dworkin and MacKinnon say that a woman who has signed a contract to be in a porn film should not be held to it, what does this mean? That women don't have free will to sign contracts? If it is a question of coercion, fine. Coercion happens. But there are already laws on the books for that.

"Americans don't really want censorship from their government. They don't want Linda Lovelace to be hurt either, but they want to be able to go to that corner video store and rent *Deep Throat* and find out what it's about. Middle-class Americans are renting these tapes by the millions. To me, that shows the sexual revolution is still going on to a large extent, and I think that's healthy and wholesome. The Meese Commission made noise but had little impact."

In San Francisco, the same troubled, debauched city of the 1980s where Anne Rice lives, live also the Mitchell brothers, Artie and Jim. If Rice is the sweet S&M mother of fem porn, the bad-boy Mitchells may be seen as its wise-guy fathers. The Mitchells, whatever else they did, liberated pornography when they made *Behind the Green Door* with Marilyn Chambers in 1972. Before the Mitchells, porn films mostly consisted of grainy loops made in New York by older raincoat producers who felt that sex just wasn't a turn-on unless it was forbidden and dirty. The Mitchells brought a California feel to the business. Jazz scores were mellow. Colors and sets were lush. Lovemaking flashed across the fantasy world of 1970s Northern California: rocky beaches, Victorian mansions, Marin hot tubs, even fishing boats and fields of orange poppies. Blow jobs were fashionably solarized. There was a semblance of plot, sometimes much too much, as in *Autobiography of a Flea* or *Sodom and Gomorrah*. But this was fun, and fun in porn was itself a new concept.

Most strange, the sex was clean, and women appeared to have natural orgasms, even a measure of control. The brothers liked sassy women around them—to a point—and often hired female directors like Sharon McKnight to make their films, as well as employing a raft of independent lesbians in their live sex palace in San Francisco.

Behind the Green Door is still the ultimate "permission" film, a story that gives both women and men the freedom to be swept away, to use Rice's phrase, by the whirlwind. Which is why, perhaps, it is still one of the two most popular erotic films of all time, a movie that cost $60,000 to make, a fortune for a porn movie at the time, but that has grossed perhaps $50–$60 million, including bootleg versions.

Behind the Green Door showcased a nineteen-year-old Marilyn Chambers. Far from seeming to be a coerced prostitute in bondage counting the strokes till her next heroin fix, Chambers was the all-American girl. Her pristine mother's face graced every box of Ivory Snow: "99 & 44/100 percent pure," read the label. Chambers would forevermore be the symbol of California pornography: the good girl gone very, very bad. She did it, and she liked it, and she asked for more. This was something new, something 1970s. For the first time, couples trooped down to the Pussycat Theater in their city and watched, mouths agape, hands in each other's laps. It was the dawn of porno chic.

"The movie was made under conditions so hot," recalls Artie Mitchell, "we just wanted to throw down the cameras at the end of each day of filming and fuck and suck our way to oblivion. Do you understand me?"

Artie Mitchell has a tough little pixie face. Sometimes he is all smiles, cracking up at some insider's joke: *How come it is that the biggest dicks, like the fourteen inches of the late Johnny Holmes, never become truly hard? You understand the connection between the shape of a woman's mouth and the feel of her pussy?* Because Artie Mitchell loves his chosen field of pornography as affectionately as he loves his own mother. At other times, the pixie smile turns as sour as blood in the mouth, and his light blue eyes drill you. This happens so quickly, like a cloud suddenly crossing the moon on a clear night, that those talking to him have been known to feel fright.

Brother Jim Mitchell often frightens people. His face is harder than his brother's; his eyes are black rather than blue, and smaller. Jim Mitchell doesn't drink much these days, and he doesn't make jokes about eating pussy or why big spongy dicks never get hard. Jim Mitchell's the producer, older little brother Artie is the director, and what Jim likes to talk about is money, usually big money or the sorry state of America or both, as in "The Japanese will own most of the country by the end of the nineties, face it." Jim Mitchell says he fucked his way through Tokyo and Osaka and halfway to Hong Kong during his army days.

After the Mitchells made *Green Door,* they retired to their fantasy castle in San Francisco, the O'Farrell Theater, only to return in the late 1980s with *Behind the Green Door: The Sequel,* a full-on rubberized circus that has given our AIDS-terrorized time its first heterosexual safe-sex film—as well as introduced America to its first Republican porn star.

The story of the Mitchell brothers begins at a smoker in the early sixties in Antioch, a dusty California town in the Sacramento River delta, the sort of place where hamburgers are always well-done and most people's dads worked in the nearby steel mill. During the underground film showing, one brother—

nobody remembers which—turned to the other and said, "Hey, bub, an ol' boy could make himself a lot of money with these kind of movies."

Still teenagers, the brothers began to grind out soft-core "beaver shoots" in which one woman on a bed slowly peeled off her dress and then her bra but never bared all, or almost never. "We believed in happy endings," remembers Jim Mitchell.

Their parents were shocked when they heard what the sons were up to. *What did they say?* "They didn't say anything," remembers Artie Mitchell. "They were struck speechless."

Not that Mother and Father Mitchell were babes in the woods. The old man was a professional gambler and con man who often handled security at local card games. When outsiders from Reno or Los Angeles sat in, the stakes could climb surprisingly high. The old man's job was to make sure nobody substituted a "machine deck" for the house cards. A machine deck is one that is secretly sorted before the game so that the con man knows exactly who is getting what. A local player might be dealt the best hand of his life and bet accordingly, only to watch the dealer produce an even more impossible hand. Little dramas like this made items in the back of the Antioch and Vallejo papers: SHOOTING AT LOCAL CARD GAME. So it was worth paying a pro like old man Mitchell to watch out.

"Being an outlaw," explains Artie Mitchell, "it helps to come from an outlaw family. The pressure is less."

The older Mitchell died in the 1970s, but Mother Mitchell is an officer of the brothers' corporation as well as its psychic evaluator. She once told her son after returning from a day at court, "Arthur, we have a problem here. I believe this judge to be a very insecure young man. I believe that he possesses a very small dick, and he will have it in for you and Jim." As inheritors of the old Barbary Coast, the brothers have been targeted by mayors, district attorneys, and the FBI since the huge and messy success of *Green Door*.

In the movie, a woman played by Marilyn Chambers is kidnaped and brought to a kinky sex club where a cult of women prepare her for a night of abandon. The kidnaped woman and the club's audience—in tuxedos and gowns—are told there is nothing they can do to stop the action, even if they recognize the woman. Given permission, the shy but lithe Chambers, much like Beauty at Rice's inn, then makes abandoned love to a Negro god and to many other men on a strange trapeze until the audience slides into a spontaneous orgy of its own.

For the Cannes showing of *Behind the Green Door,* Artie and Jim Mitchell, along with their wives, who were erotic actresses and dancers, and Marilyn Chambers and her boyfriend of the time sat in the balcony of the old art deco French movie house. Artie sported a tuxedo. Jim wore a bowler hat. The brothers thought they were the Coppola and Spielberg of adult films.

At the end of the movie, after the orgy scene with the fat lady and the dwarf, and the football players and the go-go dancers, and the California bohemians and their real-life girlfriends, the lights went on. The packed crowd of twelve hundred people was dead silent. Nobody clapped. Nobody booed.

"They all turned around," says Artie Mitchell, "and just stared at us. A minute went by, two minutes, five minutes—and not one of those frogs said a thing. I thought maybe they were going to tear us apart. I figured Jim and I could take a few of them. I figured Marilyn would get a couple more. Then this Frenchman jumps out of his seat downstairs, and he screams up at us, 'Shit! Shit! Shit! Fuck! Fuck! Fuck!'

"We were in shock now. These were supposed to be sophisticated French people, and except for this one lunatic, they were all numb. I was sure they were going to come for us. Then these four French cops came running down the aisle with their batons, and they just started clubbing people in tuxedos and shoving them and forcing them out of the theater."

Pornography is not what we want to see. It is not what we need to see. But is seems to be what we cannot help watching.

Deep Throat, the sister-film of *Green Door,* would seem to have a different message than permission and bondage. *Deep Throat*'s premise is goofy, harmless, and, one could say, progressive, reflecting the newly radical Masters and Johnson wisdom of the times, which de-emphasized the pure missionary position. A woman, played by Linda Lovelace, has trouble achieving orgasm vaginally. She finally goes to a doctor, Harry Reems, who discovers that her clitoris is lodged in her throat. The only way she can come is . . . Right!

Yet, of course, the joke was no joke. Linda Lovelace Marchiano was by her own account a prisoner behind the green door during the filming of *Deep*

Throat, the bruises inflicted by her husband-manager Chuck Traynor covered up by the makeup crew and her every good-time smile a leer of pain. To read her two autobiographies, *Ordeal* and *Out of Bondage,* is to read the diary of a concentration camp victim. There is gang rape, forced sex with dogs, beatings, whippings, and a reaming by a sadomasochistic lesbian that leaves Lovelace's rectum gushing blood.

Many within the pornography industry will tell us that Linda Lovelace was in reality a voluntary slave in a complicated master-slave relationship. No, says Linda Marchiano when we talk to her, "that's like asking someone if they take pleasure in being raped and beaten." For Marchiano, porn stardom was all coercion, enforced by "a Walther PPK .45 automatic eight-shot pistol, a semi-automatic machine gun, constant threats against my family and friends, daily beatings and isolation. I wasn't the star but the victim." Marchiano has never seen the new fem erotica, and is unsure whether or not actual lovemaking can be depicted without being degrading to the actresses. "I didn't go to college. I'm not a psychologist. All I can do is speak from my experience, and my experience was a lot of people who were cold and callous and treated women as objects. My manager believed that a woman's body was created to be used and abused by men for profit." Marchiano now lives in Long Island and is writing a children's book.

The outer reaches of the American experience are as intense as they are unclear. What is sure, however, is that the experiences of the two women, Chambers and Lovelace, represent the two poles of pornography, unsanctioned ecstasy and unredeemed slavery, and neither, we believe, is entirely exaggerated.

One night as we talk to Artie Mitchell, the older brother, in his office at the O'Farrell Theater in San Francisco, Mitchell sidles around the big pool table and opens the enormous green steel safe that sits in the corner like a Buddha. He sets his vodka and cranberry juice on a shelf next to two pistols and pulls out a shotgun. The shotgun is a fine one, smithed of Spanish steel and engraved CHRISTMAS 1973.

Behind the Green Door made so much money for the Mitchells, so quickly, that it led to problems. The brothers were outlaws operating in an unprotected industry. A wise guy came to them with a contract, remembers Artie

Mitchell, which offered them "the right" to distribute their own film in certain areas of the country. They would be allowed to buy back this cockamamie contract, said the wise guy, for $15,000. The Mitchells, according to Artie, told the man to go to hell, but having developed a sense of caution as well as a sense of humor, they issued Spanish shotguns to the staff for Christmas.

Later, the brothers discovered that the wise guy was not well connected but that other hot shots were pirating *Green Door* all around America, piling up quick fortunes off the porno-chic crowd. They made inquiries, says Artie Mitchell, and somebody introduced them to an older man from New York named Mickey Zaffarano.

"Mickey was funny as hell. Everything was just business to him. He wanted to be involved in porn, sure, but he didn't have a big sex thing. All's he wanted was maybe a girl down on her knees in the back of the limo in Las Vegas blowing him. He was a gentleman."

Zaffarano, one of the top old-style Mafia leaders in the country, was not everybody's idea of a gentleman, of course, and soon, according to Artie Mitchell, the FBI was everywhere. Zaffarano invested $25,000 in a later Marilyn Chambers movie, paying by check, and this did not help either. To the FBI, porn was a priori a Mafia enterprise. The coming concept of the couples film did not intrigue the FBI.

"We finally said, 'Hey, Mickey, we love you, but, you know . . . the heat.' "

When Zaffarano died, long after his relationship with the Mitchells was over, according to Artie Mitchell, the brothers flew east to attend his funeral. They stood out like rabbits at the tortoise's wake. They'd flown in from California, their hair was long, they were young and chipper and blond. The mob bodyguards assumed they were FBI. "No, no, no," joked Artie, "no way! We're the Mitchell brothers, you know." The dead Zaffarano's bodyguards did not know. "Like, *Behind the Green Door,*" prompted Artie. "Oh yeah," said one of the heavies. And the brothers from San Francisco got to pay their respects.

Long after, the Mitchells would be able to affect a wise-guy mien at will, but, thought Artie Mitchell, what was the point? The Mitchells had it all and they represented sweetness and light, as far as porn went. The wise guys and the FBI were pretty much the same thing really: they were both bad for business.

After *Behind the Green Door*, the Mitchells made *Resurrection of Eve* and *Inside Marilyn Chambers*. *Inside* is porn vérité. In one sequence, Chambers refuses to allow semen to be splashed across her face and stalks off the set.

Then the Mitchells got silly. They pumped $350,000 into an apocalyptic fantasy called *Sodom and Gomorrah,* far and away the most expensive erotic movie of all time, the *Gone With the Wind* of American pornography. In the film God is a chimpanzee who lives in a perpetually orbiting space station where the Virgin Mary floats naked in a tank of clear water, while far below on earth the citizens of Sodom worship the backdoor imposter Anu. The Chimpanzee God jumps up and down like Bonzo, President Ronald Reagan's famous film partner, and sends His Archangel Gabriel to set things straight. The whole weird soup was put together on the hills of Livermore, overlooking the nation's Star Wars laboratories.

The problem was not the overreach of the brothers' imaginations but probably the focus on anal sex. For heterosexuals, backdoor romance was largely a specialty taboo and did not sell well in Peoria. *Sodom and Gomorrah* was a bomb.

The Mitchells retired to their "live porn" palace at the corner of O'Farrell and Polk, a building they had painted with fifty-foot murals of undersea life, salmon, dolphins, octopuses, and two humpback whales mating. Inside Japanese tourists sat reverently in the little glass booths that ringed the Ultra Room and watched teams of leathered lesbian strippers mock-maul each other to the crash of "U Got the Look" by Prince or shine long-tipped airport flashlights on the nipples of Caucasian women in the Kopenhagen Room and experience the Western thrill of lap-dancing. The Mitchell boys had built themselves a candy store.

The brothers picked a good time to retire. The times were about to pass them by anyway. Within the world of porn, the Mitchells represented something playful between hard-core men and women. In the 1980s, though, relations between men and women turned tough. Women were more equal, more demanding. Men were more resentful. Porn, always a wild release, suddenly reflected the sex wars. The fun and games of the Mitchells gave way to the bitter, gouging sex of the Dark brothers. Even their name was ominous.

"Hey, I didn't set out to denigrate women," Greg Dark tells us. "I consider men to be morons too. Humans are animals. I do commentaries."

At the time he made his first hard-core film, Greg Dark was a thirty-year-old film school brat from Stanford who was between development deals at Home Box Office. "The adult producers were so stupidly serious. They'd call a scene beautiful when it was only a twenty-year-old girl who couldn't remember her lines for more than thirty seconds, screwing for six minutes. 'It's *sooo* beautiful,' the producer would say. 'Why?' I'd ask, ' 'cause her pussy doesn't have crabs?' "

The Dark brothers represented the resurgence of New York–style porn, down and nasty. But this time the shoots were done in L.A., and it was New Wave: bleach-blond mohawks and scores by the Plugz. They took every sexual stereotype in America and corn-holed it. And they were as manufactured as Madison Avenue. The name was a rip-off of the Mitchells; the logo, two hepcats in porkpie hats and sunglasses, was stolen from the Blues Brothers, although Greg Dark maintains the idea came from the sideshot of Alfred Hitchcock in the TV series. There were no real brothers, only Walter Dark, the thick-bodied eminence of big-time Southern California porn, and hired gun Greg "Not My Real Name."

The Darks made a porn classic, in 1986, and it was a vision of Hell: *The Devil in Miss Jones, Part 3.*

Punk bitch Justine Jones picks up a bozo in a Soho after-hours club. He comes with such vigor that she smacks her head against the bedboard and awakes in Hell. There, she refuses to believe she's really dead. Believe it! barks her black pimp guide. The only way out is to fuck yourself through to the other side! Which she proceeds to do. The only inhibition in the film is the clear plastic raincoat that Justine's Stepin Fetchit Virgil insists she wear so that she will not drown in everlasting come.

In *Devil,* southern belles are damned to take on black shoe shine boys. Black women must fuck Nazis.

"Where are all the black racists?" screams Justine at one point. "There ain't no such thing, bitch!" her jive guide screams back. "What do you call a black man who hates white people then, asshole?"

"I calls him smart."

The Darks were amoral and hot at the same time, the perfect porn combination for the eighties—crossover material, in fact, just like *Green Door* a decade before. Hard-core porno was chic again. The Darks made the annual "What's Hot" list in *Rolling Stone* and were prominently trashed in *Vanity Fair,* which was better than being praised.

What the Darks said about women and men in the 1980s was hardly uplifting. The Darks didn't bother to offer permission, as had Anne Rice or the Mitchells. They just went balls out with borrowed MTV effects: hot backlighting, quick cuts, rock pacing. The emotional logic was urban eighties, a kind of equal opportunity degradation. Women became things, but so did men. Misogyny was only half the picture, since the real message was misanthropy.

The Dark view of life assumes not a retreat from sex but an escape from emotion through sexuality. If an Andrea Dworkin concluded that real love between men and women was impossible, the Darks readily agreed. Dworkin's conclusion led her to a romanticized lesbianism. A prisoner to his glands, Greg Dark would simply call for more and more fucking until hot-hump sex obliterated feeling . . . All is degradation. Let the Bomb drop.

Artie Mitchell once visited the Dark brothers studio, and found it hilarious that on the same production line, the corporation was churning out Bible classics with titles like *Story of Jesus* next to tapes of *Devil in Miss Jones* and *Black Bun Busters.*

But Greg Dark was finally frightened by his own nihilism. As the Meese Commission held hearings in Los Angeles, he jumped out of porn.

"I'm thirty-four now," he tells us. "I feel like an old man. I don't even like to do nudity anymore. No brutality. Heavy feminist parts in all my films. In my last picture this actress was about to take her bra off to make the scene more realistic, and I shouted, 'No! No!' 'cause they'd say, 'There goes that Greg Dark again.' OK, I slid into adult for a few years, but it's the kiss of death. This is not a moral opinion. But the grand scheme of the country is against these sorts of things. Features and TV are safe. You don't hire curious directors. You hire safe people. It's hard to believe, but if they wanted to drive Greg Dark out of the industry, well, they did, 'cause I never made a real wad to retire on like the Mitchells. I don't have the money to defend myself. I'd rather sell shoes than go to jail."

When Greg Dark retreated to hard-R, spouting and whining all the way like one of his never-satisfied characters, the Mitchells saw a chance for a comeback. Perhaps the Darks had gone too far. In their films, sperm sprayed around like water from loose firehoses. Women sucked and licked and swallowed as if there were no tomorrow. Anal sex was regular fare. Like the revelers in Edgar Allan Poe's "Masque of the Red Death," most porn producers and performers persisted with the Darks in thinking that their dream factory was immune to contagion. But by the middle of the 1980s, the AIDS virus had worked its way into the bloodstream—and much more, the consciousness—of the heterosexual community. The Mitchells saw a perfect way to step back into the porn game. Why not remake *Behind the Green Door* as the first safe-sex porn film?

The original brainstorm came from Priscilla Alexander, codirector of COYOTE, a prostitutes union (Cast Out Your Old Tired Ethics). COYOTE realized that prostitutes were at risk from the new disease. A safe-sex porn movie would be the perfect way to educate johns. With women more vulnerable to infection than men, at least straight men, safe sex had become a feminist issue. COYOTE founder Margo St. James took the idea to the brothers.

"I first approached them when the Meese porn commission hearings were being held in L.A. I said, 'You guys should take the offensive here before they shut you down. Show that you're responsible citizens—help men get over their prejudices against rubbers. Make it smart and sexy to wear them.' "

The Mitchells liked the idea of staving off the porn hunters by wrapping themselves in the hygienic flag. They also realized that a few bisexual men acted in X-rated films. Some of these men moved from gay movies to straight. There was the possibility, too, that an actor could catch AIDS through needle use off the set and then pass the virus to a partner before the cameras. In 1986, even the king of porn, Johnny ("Wad") Holmes, had tested positive for the virus. Since the Mitchells had been in and out of court since they had entered the business, they were always looking for ways to protect themselves legally. It would be harder to sue the new paragons of promiscuous virtue. Besides, to the brothers the project looked to be big fun, and the Mitchells liked fun.

Not that they didn't think it was a bit of a gamble. "A lot of men believe wearing a rubber is like wearing a raincoat in the shower," said Artie Mitchell just before the movie was released. "There was resistance to the first *Green Door* also," added Jim Mitchell in his soft growl. "The New York distributors said there were too many blacks, that they couldn't sell *schwartzes* to their audience. But we've never been dictated to by the market. If we were, we'd be like all the other scumbags in the industry."

The set of the film was both a tight ship and a typically eccentric Mitchell production. We would like to introduce Susie Bright to tell the story. Bright is a character for the eighties. Tall and strongly built, twenty-nine years old, she is the editor of *On Our Backs*. Her mien often switches from reference librarian to charming firebrand, from shy and polite to sexy and animated. Her glasses are thick and old-fashioned. Her hair hangs to her softly rounded shoulders or is tucked away in a bun. Her father is linguist John Bright, who for many years was an editor of *Language,* and her mother is a woman who, believes Susie, never made love after her daughter and only child was conceived.

Bright, who was intrigued by the fact that nearly all of the actors in the safe-sex movie would be amateurs, decided to try out. Later she would write an article on the experience for *Forum* magazine. "I always wanted to be a film star," she tells us. "I admit I'm just a little bit of a ham."

When Artie Mitchell asked what her "sexual expectations" were for the movie, she quickly replied, "Girl-girl, and no sex."

However, the ham in Susie Bright did her in.

The plot of *Behind the Green Door: The Sequel,* is very close to the plot of the original except that any allusions to a kidnaping are cut and almost all the action is now fantasized by a perky airline stewardess played by Missy Manners, Senator Orrin Hatch's former aide and a budding Republican porn star, soon to be a true-life character in our story, as well.

Bright came with two friends, Fanny Fatale, who was a dancer at the O'Farrell, and Vanessa. Once they were seated at their table and the other orgy extras were seated at theirs, director Sharon McKnight shouted out, "Raise your hand if at any time you believe you are not having safe sex. The staff will now be handing out a bag of condoms, surgical rubber gloves, dental dams, and nonoxynol-9 lubricant. No penis will be touched without a rubber on. No fingers will get stinky without a rubber glove. All pussies must be covered with a dental dam before they are licked. I want to be able to smell your lubricant a yard away. Is that clear?"

It was five hours before the cameraman reached Bright's table. Her friend Fatale worked on her tax forms while others in the room orgied on cue. Finally, the overhead videocam zoomed their section.

Bright describes the scene: " 'Alright, cast, loosen up,' " Jim Mitchell said. " 'We're coming over to your tables, one by one for close-ups. Start your action.'

"Close-ups and action? We grabbed our tabletop. Panic was setting in, and I must admit, vanity as well. Could we afford to sit there with empty smiles on our faces just stretching our condoms?

"Fanny cocked her head at Vanessa. 'I think you have the nicest breasts, Vanessa . . .' She looked at me apologetically.

" 'Perhaps,' I said like a kitten, 'we could pour the champagne on them?'

" 'No,' said Vanessa, 'we're supposed to use the latex, aren't we?'

" 'OK. Well, I could kiss your rubber fingers after you put them in the champagne. Then you nip my neck. We'll both cup your breasts.' "

Susie giggles as she remembers the scene.

"We rehearsed like a last-minute audition [for] 'The Gong Show.' When the floor camera rolled into our view and Fanny hiked her hips above the table, I realized that I was probably the only woman in the room who had not properly clipped and pruned her pubes. There was no time to regret that now, however.

"So I fished around in what the Mitchells called our safe-sex kit and pulled out a dental dam. This sucker was like a file card and thick as glass! It was suppose to be the equivalent of a guy's condom. I thought, Isn't that just like an all-male group of safe-sex experts! They had chosen the ultimate barrier to cunnilingus. You well could have blindfolded someone with this wad of rubber. But Fanny was getting into it, serving up some impressive Method moans, arching her back like a fish. I laid the dam over her pussy and took a tentative plastic lick. When Vanessa rolled her eyes, I became extremely annoyed. You could say my Amazon imagination went into overdrive. No-body was about to destroy my moment of glory with a strip of wallpaper. I don't know what I thought, but I knew I had to do something raunchy and safe at the same time, and very quickly. So I rolled the dental dam into a nice little rubber cone and started flossing Fanny's inside lips. I may have been dreaming, but I think she raised her hips toward me. So I began to play her like a cello. The latex bow hummed to and fro between her little pink clit and her labia. Real safe sex and hot too. I was ready to latex every pussy in the room.

"When we were done, Fanny slid down on her seat, but now the big camera was focused on another table.

" 'Well, so much for girl-girl, no sex,' I said.

" 'Let's admit it, Susie, we're a couple of vain suckers,' said Fanny.

"But I say, big deal if we were prima donnas for a day. We did a credible job putting safe sex on the X-rated map, and I was probably the first porn starlet in history to keep her glasses on for a sex scene. I cradled my head in my arms. It was long past my bedtime."

The porn of the 1980s was becoming a very strange slice of ginger indeed.

After the sequel was released, Jim Mitchell bragged that it would make other porn films "obsolete." And if those other porn producers didn't like that, "tough shit." "It's a whole new sexual world out there, and they're going to have to change with the times."

We talked to one well-known producer who was not convinced. "The only people who worry about AIDS in the straight end of the business are hypochondriacs," he said rather optimistically. "This is a gay problem. Girls don't get the disease, period."

This man takes great pains to screen out unhealthy ingenues during the casting process. "I'm a regular gynecologist after the hundreds of films I've made. I can tell by taking one peek if she's healthy." Of course, now and then a bad apple slips through his rigorous examination. "Occasionally, when we go in for a close-up during filming, I'll notice some venereal warts or something on a girl." But that's show business.

The Mitchells' film and the growing reality of AIDS had a great influence on others in the adult industry, however. Candida Royalle began to show women putting condoms on their men or using real-life lovers in sex scenes. Marilyn Chambers began to require all performers in her new movies to undergo the AIDS antibody test before shooting. "Then we plan to keep them under our control while we're filming so they can't run around and get exposed to something," added her manager, Chuck Traynor, the man Linda Lovelace had accused of being her slavemaster. "We'll pay them a little extra to stay in isolation with us." And platinum-blond porn queen Seka told us, "The AIDS test will become standard practice in this business."

A star like Seka or Traci Lords "can pretty much dictate whatever she wants," said Dave Friedman, chairman of the Adult Film Association of America. "Female stars are coming to the forefront of this business, in some cases financing and producing their own films." But very few porn performers have the clout to protest and walk off a movie set until safe-sex working conditions prevail.

And, yes, condoms can lead to performance anxiety in male porn stars just as easily as in anyone else.

"Performing under those bright lights has never been my forte," said performer Richard Pacheco. Pacheco is a short man of boyish energy. His wisecracking manner undoes the image of porn star as simpleminded stud. In fact, Pacheco, whose real name is Howie Gordon, decided to become a porn actor the same week that he turned down a fellowship to the Hebrew Theological Seminary. "I have to be surrounded by safety in order to perform nowadays," he laughs. "I've got three small kids, and I want to stick around."

After the Mitchells made *Green Door: The Sequel,* Pacheco agreed to do a scene with siren Hyapatia Lee only after he was assured he could wear a condom and no bodily fluids would be exchanged.

"Hyapatia and I get into foreplay. I'm up. I'm down. She's about to slip the rubber on me and suddenly my penis is in Bermuda. I mean, she was gorgeous and I hadn't had sex with anybody but my wife in a year and a half—but I was really having trouble. The cameras were rolling, panic was setting in. Suddenly, against our rules, she took me in her mouth. By that point, I was so concerned about my professional image that I let her do it. But it was dumb —immediately afterward I regretted it. And my wife was definitely not happy about it when I told her later. I mean, her health is at stake here too."

In our files is a picture of Missy Manners, the star of *Behind the Green Door: The Sequel,* with Senator Orrin Hatch, the conservative and powerful Reagan stalwart from Utah. The date is 1981. Senator Hatch looks like a sincere game-show host. Missy, nineteen years old and Hatch's Senate intern, looks to be an ungainly goof-bug in an oversized sport coat and sweater, high collar, and bow tie. Her frowsy hair is clipped behind her ears. Her grin says, *Aw-shucks.*

Four years before she made the *Green Door* sequel, Missy became a model and a dancer at the O'Farrell Theater in San Francisco, as well as girlfriend to the boss, Artie Mitchell. Hers is one of the stranger political transformations of the times, at least at first glance.

"I remember very clearly walking out of the O'Farrell Theater after the filming was over and feeling, Did that really happen to me? Because I had sex with ten people that day. I thought, What's my sex life going to be after this? How jaded am I going to get? Oh God, am I going to have to do little dogs or goats or girls?"

Missy's real name is Elisa ("Missy") Florez. Her father is John Florez who is the former chief of staff of the Senate Labor and Human Resources Committee and has served as a White House consultant and Reagan appointee to the U.S. Civil Rights Commission. Missy herself worked as a staff aide for the Republican National Committee.

"I'm not sure my dad and Senator Hatch saw the movie," she tells us. "I know they had a discussion with a reporter to find out what happened. They wanted to know, 'Did she take off her clothes?' The reporter said, 'Oh yeah, she took off her clothes!' Then there was this pause. What do you say—'Uh, yeah, your daughter just made a porno movie. I saw her fuck six guys wearing goat costumes, and she was really great'?"

Once on the Rona Barrett show in Los Angeles, Barrett asked Missy how a nice girl like her had ended up in "trash" like *Behind the Green Door*. Again and again, Barrett asked what the reaction of Missy's powerful family had been. "Leave my family out of this, Rona," Missy shot back. "I love them and they love me."

After the show Missy went to a bar and downed two shots of tequila. Then she called up her younger sister, "my cute little sister," and told her, "Look, I'm sorry about what's happened. I love you all very much." But her sister replied, "Why can't you just keep down in the gutter where you belong, Missy and shut up, because we all hate you very much."

On the plane, Missy cried all the way back to San Francisco. "I mean, I just couldn't believe, like, Oh God, what have I gotten myself into here." When she got home, Senator Hatch's press secretary was on the line. "Missy," he said, "we stayed up late to watch your interview on TV and we just want you to know: we love you."

"That meant a lot to me," Missy says today. "I'm still a Republican inherently."

Still, although some Republicans have attained high political office after careers in acting, none has taken off quite so many clothes as Missy. Like Candida Royalle, Richard Pacheco, Annette Haven, and Marilyn Chambers, Missy Florez is not what most people imagine a porn star to be.

Missy grew up in Salt Lake City, a bookish but enthusiastic little girl. Her father chose her over her brother to follow in his footsteps as a political wheeler-dealer, first in Utah, then in Washington, D.C. She idolized him to the point of always buying the same expensive power briefcases he affected. But with her baggy pantsuits and goofy grin, Missy saw herself as the ugly duckling. Her mother told her again and again that her breasts were too big, that she would never be beautiful like her sisters. Missy wanted desperately to be seen as a sexual person as well as a bright young girl. She was very aware that politicians flirted with her at the parties the Republican National Committee threw, but she was still convinced of her homeliness.

"I had to get away from my beautiful sisters. I moved to California, and I would go to aerobics every single day, and there would be these pretty blondes again, so skinny, great suntans, perfect teeth. After a while I looked down at myself and realized I had better tits and ass than these women. I wasn't so bad. In California I realized I was no longer the ugly duckling."

So Missy, not unlike a few porn actresses, saw adult films as ego-enhancement. Not that lust, a contradictory feminist lust hardly imaginable since the time of Mae West, did not play a considerable part.

"I knew I wanted to do *Green Door*. If you really want to know, I get off ten times more than most women do. I'm not one of these people into orgasm retention, like one a year. I could have ten great ones in a day and not feel guilty.

"The way I look at it," explains Missy in her firm high voice, "I'm still a good Republican. I worked hard to get Reagan elected, twice. I consider myself the Pat Robertson of porn. This is my fight for individual rights." She throws back her head and laughs. "Once I was a freedom fighter. Now I'm a freedom fucker."

This morning the freedom fucker is behind the wheel of Artie Mitchell's long white Mercedes 500 SEL. Mitchell points out that with a flick of a switch he can "toast our buns" with the special heaters inserted under the seats. "You know the difference between a Mercedes and a Rolls-Royce?" he asks from the passenger seat. "In a Mercedes you have to take off the girl's panties. In a Rolls-Royce she takes off her own."

"Oh, Artie!" protests Missy Manners.

It is 9 A.M. in Berkeley, California, and the fog is still on the ground. We are on our way to Sacramento. The California state legislature wants to tighten significantly the state's operating definition of obscenity. In the year since the *Green Door* sequel has appeared, Missy Manners has become America's unofficial spokesperson for safe sex (and lots of it), and she wants to testify against the bill.

Manners is wearing little black slippers with the face of a cat outlined on them in rhinestones, and an electric-blue silk dress that fits her like a sheath, except around her breasts, where it is open like a robe.

Artie Mitchell is dressed down for the occasion, as he is for most occasions: old blue jeans, lace-up lumberjack boots, gray-and-red wool socks, and a T-shirt from the skateboard magazine *Thrasher* that shows a human skull with a snake wrapped around it. On Mitchell's tight bald head is a Rommel desert hat that he had ordered through *Soldier of Fortune* magazine, and at the crown of the hat is a little brass pin in the shape of an old-fashioned movie camera.

Between the leather seats, front and back, always moving, is Mr. T. Mr. T is a dog, a tiny teacup poodle the size of two fists. "T," as everybody calls him, is as white as the color of the car's carpeting.

Mitchell swigs a couple of morning Heinekens and puffs the butt of a joint. Pretty soon he is dancing away in his seat to the oldies blasting from the marvelous speakers—"Ain't That a Shame" by Fats Domino and "You've Got a Friend in Jesus" by Norman Greenbaum. Accidentally, his foot taps down on Mr. T, and Mr. T lets out an incredibly loud scream for a cup of fur.

"Artie!"

Artie Mitchell puts down the joint and lights up a cigarette.

"You can fuck up your own lungs, Artie, but don't fuck up Mr. T's."

"Life is hard," replies Artie Mitchell, and more than once today he will expand upon this theme: "Life is hard for a couple of old pornographers like Jim and me. We're burned out old men. Our time in porn is done. I wish I knew where all the money went. Just two old pornographers . . . living alone—with nine children . . . and a Brazilian maid."

Sometimes it seems the Mitchell brothers have gotten where they are as much for their developed sense of humor as for their sense of depravity. The part about the money has been debated by the IRS and most others, but it is true that the brothers live together in a large house in a wealthy suburb across the bay from San Francisco, with the nine children of their four previous marriages, and some order is kept by a South American maid.

We arrive in Sacramento before noon. Mitchell saunters forth from the Mercedes. His needs are primitive. He looks up at the capitol dome only a few yards away. Beside the building is a block of lilac bushes. Artie Mitchell decides to mosey through the lilacs and relieve himself of most of the Heinekens. When he parts the flowers again, his hand is still on his zipper but his mind has turned to Missy's upcoming testimony.

"Tell 'em lies, Missy, but only to save lives."

"Freedom fuckers!" laughs Missy.

Mitchell likes to paraphrase Lieutenant Colonel Ollie North, who is also testifying this week, in Washington. In the 1960s, Mitchell was in army intelligence, attached to NATO in Germany. For sport, some of Mitchell's cohorts used to inflate the estimates, "like '15' Soviet tank divisions in Czechoslovakia instead of '1–5,' " he claims. "The army loved to hear that stuff," he says. "In my life I've just gone from soft estimates to hard fantasies."

On the way to the Senate offices we walk up a long sidewalk between two cement-pillared buildings. Mitchell waves his hands like Lincoln and shouts out the inscriptions on the cornices. INTO THE HIGHLANDS OF THE MIND is writ across one cornice. "Yes!" says Artie. BRING ME MEN TO MATCH MY MOUNTAINS is chiseled across the other. "That's it!" shouts Mitchell once more. "Men to match your mountains, Missy! That's your slogan!"

Clearly, the pornographers are ready to meet the assemblymen. But first they want to strategize with Jack Davis, chief of staff for San Francisco's state senator, Quentin Kopp.

Davis is a thick, muscular man in a suit. He is a techno-pol and very careful about what he says. But he is young, forty-one, and he's San Francisco. The Mitchells threw a party for Davis's fortieth birthday at the O'Farrell Theater. The bash was also a benefit for Bread and Roses and a hospice organization. Two large naked candy buttocks were iced across the top of Davis's birthday cake. Still, Davis has noticed the pop-eyed stares of the young aides in his office as Missy shakes hands and holds Mr. T at the end of his pink leash. Davis is not happy to see us.

Missy Manners is oblivious. She chirps away, rapping of *Green Door: The*

Sequel as if it were some sweet safe-sex educational film sent out by the Centers for Disease Control. She makes no mention of the fat lady and the dwarf or of Susie Bright's latex orgy or of Missy's own trapeze scene with three men dressed as satyrs.

Davis stares at his hands, which are folded in his lap.

"Yes, Missy," interrupts Artie Mitchell, "tell the assemblymen *Green Door* is not your usual wad-in-the-face porn movie. Tell 'em it's safe."

Davis is even more quiet. He refuses to go to lunch with us. He refuses to let Manners use the Xerox machine. Each side has run out of things to say.

"Could it be possible that your office has already sold its vote, Jack?" asks Mitchell.

"We voted."

"Oh, Jack," says Missy.

The cramped office grows quiet for a second. Artie Mitchell is smirking. Without knowing why, everybody turns their eyes to little Mr. T, who has stopped scampering across Davis's desk. Mr. T is lifting his leg. Mr. T stares at us blankly. Mr. T covers Jack Davis's desk in a rich pool of doggie urine.

The laughter is hysterical. Even Davis laughs. He finally understands that he must offer some bit of advice to the porno invaders or they may never leave.

"Missy, I beg you. Do not show the assemblymen your video. Tell them that twenty thousand San Franciscans are dying of AIDS. Tell them that every district in the state will soon have many, many cases. Tell them that censoring a safe-sex video is contradictory when the legislature is spending $40 million this year to control the disease."

"That's right, Missy, get heavy," suggests Artie Mitchell. "Tell the assemblymen those twenty thousand AIDS deaths will rest on their collective legislative souls!"

The large chamber where the Assembly Committee on Public Safety is meeting is packed with reporters, profamily lobbyists, and state bureaucrats, all bored and hoping for a circus. The room has high ceilings. Green brocade curtains cover one wall. Several dozen people are standing, and they press forward as the committee chairman, Larry Stirling, bangs down the gavel to end debate on the previous bill, which would have made pit bull fighting a felony rather than a misdemeanor. This is a bill of interest only to Mr. T.

Senator Wadie Deddeh then brings forth his antiobscenity motion. Deddeh is a Persian-born Christian who now represents an important part of the Central Valley. For the hearing the senator is wearing a white-and-black pin-striped sport coat that almost perfectly matches his salt-and-pepper hair.

Essentially, Deddeh wants to change the definition of obscenity so that an "average person applying contemporary community, rather than statewide, standards" will find material such as *Green Door: The Sequel,* or, for that matter, the Jack Nicholson–Ann-Margret film *Carnal Knowledge* to be "prurient."

A representative of the American Civil Liberties Union speaks of a possible chill factor if the old law is changed. He reminds the assemblymen that *Carnal Knowledge* had once been banned in Georgia as obscene and that, as a result, college film festivals throughout the South had been censored for a decade.

A woman from a library association lectures the legislators that certain books by classic authors (Twain, Faulkner, Hemingway, Salinger) may have to be removed from the shelves if the bill is passed. A spokesman for California's sheriffs testifies that busy sheriffs do not have time to enforce obscenity laws.

Senator Deddeh seems peeved at such mainstream opposition when supporters of the bill include the Archdiocese of Los Angeles, San Francisco's Mayor Diane Feinstein, California Lieutenant Governor Leo McCarthy, Concerned Women for America, the California District Attorneys Association, and Black Americans for Family Values.

"I am disturbed," he says, "that witnesses with law degrees have the gall and audacity to claim that my legislation will have a chilling effect on the arts, as if this law were born in Russia or Nazi Germany. When are we going to grow up and realize that these people who invoke the First Amendment are in fact preying on the minds of the young? I pray to God that history will record our votes."

And then it is Missy Manners's turn.

Manners is nervous at first, and she stumbles. "I am here to speak for the bill—I mean, against it," she begins. "That's a Freudian slip."

A young lobbyist for "family protection" named Karen Grimm loudly whispers, "What an airhead!" and somebody sitting behind us asks, "Was she really Hatch's personal secretary?" But the gallery loves the spectacle of the big-bosomed porn star in the blue silk dress confronting the legislators. It sure beats pit bulls.

"My name is Missy Florez, although I believe that many of you legislators may know me as Missy Manners," she pauses and looks each of the men in the eye. "Missy Manners, the star of *Behind the Green Door: The Sequel,* which is a safe-sex video. You live in a world where political survival is paramount, but I live in a world of life and death where survival itself is at stake. I think you could say," and here Manners treads water for her big line, "that I have a hands-on perspective about safe sex."

The room is silent, and then, of course, the audience breaks into laughter. The legislators stare down at their yellow legal pads and do not laugh. Against Jack Davis's advice, Missy Manners immediately begins to pass out copies of *Behind the Green Door: The Sequel.*

"I would like to put this safe-sex video on the record," she says.

"No way!" answers a young blond assemblyman from San Diego.

Manners waves the video above the heads of the committee like a hussy goddess. The assemblymen do not appreciate this.

"Obscene videocassettes such as this woman's are worse than pornographic cinemas because these cassettes can be taken home and shown to minors," says an assemblyman who has been a prosecutor.

"You don't *want* my video?" asks Missy Manners, pretending to be hurt. Missy is taking control, beginning to enjoy the spectacle.

"No, ma'am," says the careful Deddeh. Deddeh stares at the shrink-wrapped box as if it is slathered with AIDS virus. THE REALITY—THE FANTASY— THE SENSUALITY promises the cover. In the photo, Missy Manners is without bra under a white T-shirt. Her brown nipples stand at attention, and she is smiling like a rebellious Republican.

And then it is over. Manners drops the videos into her Halliburton aluminum power briefcase and shrugs. Her large breasts shake. Stirling bangs down the gavel as he did for the pit bulls.

Ever cynical, Artie Mitchell has skipped the hearing in favor of more Heinekens at a nearby bar. But afterward, on the lawn outside, he is sweetly encouraging: "Gotta rat-fuck those guys, Missy! It's the only way."

Missy is on a roll. She wonders if we should stay another hour or two in order to crash a Pat Robertson reception. The two debate whether Rev.

Robertson wears nylon panties. "Let's go home," says Mitchell, "I'm already a member of the LORD Club: Let Oral Roberts Die."

Manners drives. Mitchell fires up another joint. At a red light on the way to the freeway, a thin little woman with straw-red hair gawks at us from the sidewalk. A black Harley-Davidson T-shirt is stretched across her bony ribs.

"Hey, Mama!" shouts Mitchell. He whistles.

"Women do not like to be whistled at, Arthur," says Manners.

"Hey, Missy," says Artie Mitchell, "I'll suck little titties if I have to."

The woman with the green-apple breasts leers at Mitchell, and Artie Mitchell returns the leer.

Missy Manners floors the Mercedes. On the drive back to San Francisco, she grows more jealous. Mitchell begins to talk of the time he served as fluff-boy to Ginger Lynn and, almost, for Traci Lords. It is a story he will tell in more detail later—without Missy.

Artie and Jim Mitchell were filming *The Graffenberg Spot* around a swimming pool. It was seven in the morning, the beginning of the shoot, and Artie Mitchell was meeting star Ginger Lynn for the first time. Over coffee and donuts Lynn told Mitchell that she might require a fluff-boy. Now, thought Artie Mitchell, porn producers often employ fluff-girls to keep the men hard between takes, but this was the first request he'd ever heard of for a fluff-*boy*. Porn had indeed changed in the 1980s. And Ginger Lynn was then the queen of adult films, a tongue-between-the-lips blonde. So Artie Mitchell answered, all gallant, "I'll be your fluff-boy, Ginger."

As Artie Mitchell recalls what happened, Lynn and costar Harry Reems, who had been the male star of *Deep Throat,* were inside on a large bed, waiting for the crew to set up. A fluff-girl who had a yen for Reems began to service him. Ginger Lynn motioned to Artie, "I think, Mr. Mitchell, I could use that fluff-boy now."

Artie Mitchell was on the spot, prince of his own jaded world. Photographers from Larry Flynt's *Hustler* magazine were there, and his own crew was staring.

"It was a profile in courage. Had to rise to the occasion. Got down on my little bony knees, licked my lips, and just turned into the Human Vibrator. *Vrroomm! Vrroomm! Vrroomm! Vrroomm!* Sweet Jesus, but Ginger had a nice little clitoris!" Mitchell shakes his head. "Life is hard."

Next day, Mitchell drove to Half Moon Bay to film a scene with Traci

Lords, the notorious underage porn star of the Dark brothers' video *New Wave Hookers*. Lords was sixteen at the time. ("She claimed to be eighteen," insists Mitchell.) Artie Mitchell had never met Lords, who was in her dressing room when he arrived. She was putting on her lipstick.

"I hear you really know how to eat out, Artie."

"Traci Lords's first words to me!" laughs Mitchell, his mouth goofy, his eyes hard.

Missy Manners hates these stories.

Although she tells one about a wild night at the O'Farrell when, after a few drinks, she felt like jumping up onstage with the dancers. Somebody handed her a whip and everybody scattered, afraid, but laughing, and then Artie Mitchell, the padrone, jumped onto the stage with her. Mitchell dropped his trousers and bared his buttocks, and Orrin Hatch's former aide flailed away.

Or the time when Mitchell, Manners, and three women were dining at the back booth of an elegant San Francisco restaurant, and Missy Manners crawled under the table and started giving oral sex to everybody during dessert, and then the women sent a note to the head waiter requesting that a particularly young and handsome busboy be turned over to them so that they could strip off his clothes and truss him up like a turkey and ream his ass.

"I didn't really tell the headwaiter that, did I?" asks Missy Manners.

"Yeah, you did," says Artie Mitchell.

"Ah, the good times," says Manners.

But a few months later, the times turn bad for the first couple of American porn. As usual, jealousy is the trip wire. We are at Harry's Bar and American Grill on Van Ness Street in San Francisco. Harry's is the old-line bistro with mahogany-paneled walls and oriental carpets that sponsors the annual Hemingway writing contest. Invent a good page of ersatz Papa, and win a trip to the Harry's outlet in Florence, Italy.

At Harry's, Artie Mitchell orders quail in ragout sauce, pretending to mispronounce the French. Missy Manners has a fancy meat pie, and little Mr. T is allowed to chew butter patties off the china dishes.

Mitchell makes a joke about a scene in a porn movie where two guys "hard-pack" the star.

"That's so gross, Artie! Two dicks hitting each other in there."

"Oh, I don't know," smiles Mitchell with his usual tough pixie smile. "Such things help a man get over his homophobia."

This is advanced humor, but Missy is having none of it. "Oh, let's listen to Artie talk about old girlfriends." Here she means Marilyn Chambers.

So Mitchell does. "I am not in love with these people," he says, "but I'll tell you, everyone I've ever fucked, I've gotten hard for." Manners rolls her eyes. "I have a nice little dick," says Mitchell. Manners laughs at that but soon enough she says, "A book should be written about what gets women off, because most guys can't bring a woman off." "Well," says Artie Mitchell, not missing a beat, "that's been your experience in life. You take such a long time."

After this the discussion quickly slides downhill. Artie begins to explain why, sociologically, the first *Behind the Green Door* with Marilyn Chambers was so hot, and Missy counters with something like, "Well, maybe I don't make a porn film every week, Arthur, the way some of these actresses do, like the immortal Marilyn Chambers, Artie." Mitchell points out that Chambers only made five films in her entire career, and then he confides that he and his brother may make *Green Door III,* this time with Nina Hartley, so that *Green Door* would become the James Bond and Superman of porn films—a never-ending series of juice wrapped around the timeless fem-porn theme, women given permission. Manners says, "That's really original, Arthur, that's creative, another *Green Door,*" and then, backtracking swiftly and considerably, Manners calls one of Mitchell's old girlfriends, "a monkey-faced Australian."

Artie Mitchell stands up. He has a flash temper. "I think I want to go home," he says. He says it quietly, but the wise-guy mien washes across his face and instantly turns the pixie smile into something very dark.

Harry's is the perfect place to have a loud argument because the mahogany walls and the oriental carpets absorb everything. Outside, the valet carefully draws the long white Mercedes to the curb. Mr. T is placed in the backseat inside his curved little leather cage. Artie Mitchell revs the smooth engine, once, twice, until it screams, and then, like a teenager back in the Sacramento Delta, he burns rubber for a hundred yards, but now, twenty-five years later, he roars up the widest street in San Francisco. Smoke from all four tires covers the enormous car like a cloud of delta dust.

But Artie Mitchell and Missy Manners could not not keep their hands off each other for long. In the coming months there would be more scenes like the one at Harry's—and rumors of much worse—and then the inevitable rapprochement. Then the two would separate again.

The safe-sex Republican porn star and the co-king of American pornography were birds of a feather in a unique American forest. Both were serious fuckaholics, yet each was intelligent and ferociously independent as well as politically shrewd. And they were outlaws. Missy Manners had exploded her bridges. Artie Mitchell was born with fewer limits than the rest of us. They were a match.

But Mitchell and Manners were also a volatile mix. She craved respectability, not the respectability of the chaste and churchgoing, obviously, but rather the respectability of being somebody. She wanted to influence events. She was still her father's daughter. To Manners, safe sex was just as much a way to make the talk shows and sell videos as it was a crusade to save lives. She even toyed with the idea of running for public office, the way the Italian porn star Ciccioline had stood for Parliament and won. This would have pulled the conflicting parts of her life together. But if her young ambition made her more interesting to Artie Mitchell than many of the other women he had known, it could also be a pain. She was always trying to change him, and this he could not abide.

Artie Mitchell was old and unchangeable, an outlaw of excess with a mercurial temper, saved perhaps by his sense of humor. "Artie is the funniest man I've ever known," Missy Manners would say from time to time, and Missy Florez needed humor. On the other hand, *everything* could be a joke to him, with the exception of his children, his mother, and sometimes his brother. This lack of values would anger Manners, who, as she reminded herself from time to time, really was a Republican at heart.

Then there was the little matter of jealousy. The green-eyed monster followed different rules in a world of safe-sex orgies and live sex shows. Playing around was assumed by both parties. But each got very angry if they thought the other might be growing serious about someone else.

It was all crazy, a wild true love affair. Yet it made perfect sense. Artie Mitchell and Missy Manners were at once very different from you and me, and not so different at all.

"Hold on, kids!" Susie Bright is shouting to a roomful of a hundred goggle-eyed Stanford freshpersons, "I think you're all old enough to handle this." Then Bright, editor of *On Our Backs,* amateur porn starlet for a day, and critic of X-rated films, rolls the montage. First, it's *Body Heat* to warm up the students with Hollywood atmospherics. Then, a loving clip from *Three Daughters* to beguile them. And then, suddenly, there's sloe-eyed, beach-blond Jesie St. James attacking Richard Pacheco's curvaceous ass with her shiksa lizard tongue.

"The kids have a conniption!" laughs Susie. "Macho football players are gagging 'cause Jesie's the aggressor, running the fuck. Sorority gals can't believe where Jesie's going to put her mouth. Half the room is wheezing and shouting and the other half is yelling 'Shut up, will you!' After the show, these kids can't stop talking. They're not hung up on the old criticisms. Is this degrading to women? is a cliché by now. The debatable question these days is, Was it sexy or was it stupid? Women and men both."

At twenty-nine, Bright believes that the future of fem porn is in the next generation. This evening she is sitting on the bed in her apartment. In front of the bed, the VCR is stacked with titles like *Smoker* and *Legends of Porn.* Susie pushes those thick glasses up onto her brown bun of a hairdo, and rubs her eyes with her palms. She can't stop laughing.

Perhaps the only time the public Susie, who also runs a road show workshop called Safe Sex for Sex Maniacs, has ever been embarrassed was when the Dark brothers' atrocity *Black Bun Busters* somehow got jammed in her VCR. "How was I ever going to face the repairman?"

The staid world of radical lesbianism was shocked when Susie Bright and Debi Sundahl, who is a stripper, published the first issue of *On Our Backs,* especially when the magazine quickly became the best-selling lesbian journal in the country. "Most other lesbian publications are written by thought police," Bright maintains. "There's such an awful whining aesthetic to them. When it comes to pictures and love, they all go for that soft, defensive, seashell sort of eroticism. We were fed up with gossamer-winged romance when we started *On Our Backs.* We like lusty, fierce, horny women! Hard feminine sensations! Unquenchable romance!"

Bright feels that "fundamentalist feminists" such as Andrea Dworkin are only "flimflamming heterosexuals." Young lesbians such as herself, says Bright, have left the Dworkins behind.

Susie Bright's criticism is slyly earnest. "Andrea is a pornographer—and a great one. She just doesn't know it. I can't tell you how many women I know who masturbate to the dirty parts of her novel. Andrea Dworkin is the de Sade of our times, although she reaches different conclusions and has no sense of satire. I'm afraid it's the old cliché: the more repressed a woman is, the more you know she wants to do the spanking."

"Feminists understand sexism," she adds. "But they don't know shit about sex."

The younger generation will be different, she believes. At Yale there is an erotic magazine with the delightful title *Stench*. At Brown, two undergraduate women have published the one-shot magazine *Positions*, which is thoughtful and ardent and contains pictures of both men and women.

"Some people think this is a joke," one of the young publishers tells us, "feminists printing pornography. It's not. It's feminists proving that pornography does not have to be the product of a moneymaking corporation dominated by men." This student is a shy, curly-haired woman who seems to be as bothered by older porn-hunting feminists as she is by traditional moralists and skin-mag dinosaurs.

"It's so funny when you think about it," laughs Susie Bright in that high thoughtful laugh that she has. "Porn was definitely the last old-boys club in America, an all-male business if ever there was one. Then a bunch of dykes and sweet, horny feminist porn stars cracked it. Affirmative action had nothing to do with it, honey."

Dancing in the Dark

VEN

by San Francisco standards, it's a strange and wondrous party. Men and women are lining up outside a cozy, refurbished warehouse in the South of Market district, a neighborhood where machine shops, artists' studios, and leather bars are giving way to radicchio salad restaurants. Once inside the door, the party guests undergo an immediate transformation: capes, jackets, skirts, pants—even some panties and Jockey shorts—are shed and whisked away by a young black clothes-check man in circus-red bikini briefs who obviously relishes his job. "You should leave your shoes on," he says with a knowing wink, and so the guests cluster around one another in the softly lit room in high heels and Reeboks and make awkwardly polite conversation.

It's hard not to stare. There is something about the curve of a thigh or the slope of a breast or the funny, impudent droop of a cock that demands attention. But, of course, feasting one's eyes is the whole point of this exotic evening. There are undraped bodies to satisfy everyone's curiosity; it's a democracy of flesh. Many eyes are fixed on the young, lean blond with the bottle-brush haircut and the perfectly shaped salami dick, and he obviously knows it as he walks around the room casually working on himself to maintain a state of semiarousal. Then there's the handsome, middle-aged redhead encased in a black leather bodice, with portholes for her jutting breasts, and black leather crotchless panties. She can't seem to take *her* eyes off a stunning man-woman, a transsexual-in-progress with jet-black Cleopatra hair who glides gracefully across the floor, proudly showing off her new jouncy, little milk-white tits. Meanwhile a group of men is gathering around an elegant one-legged woman with a shimmering, diaphanous blouse and a beatific expression, while a band of gay pranksters known as the Cathar-sissies flits among the tropical plants and fluffy old sofas that adorn the room, sprinkling "fairy dust" on the partygoers and "dusting their auras" with rainbow-colored feathers to help break the ice.

The merry Cathar-sissies, in their cock rings and glitter, add a festive touch, but the evening is picking up speed on its own. People are drifting upstairs in twos and threes to the loft, unlikely attractions are forming, the music on the tape shifts gears from Phil Collins to the eerie desert wail of Middle Eastern disco star Ofra Haza. Over in the corner, Buzz Bense, the tall, handsome party host with the red-gold locks and the revealing leather chaps, is grinning as he surveys the growing throng, because he can feel it: it's *working,* the evening's peculiar chemistry is working. The event that has been billed as "the World's First Jack-and-Jill-Off Party" is clearly headed toward success. Buzz is about to witness a safe-sex orgy that will stir together men and women, gays and straights, young and middle-aged—but not commingle dread bodily fluids. "No intercourse and no oral sex and no rude behavior," the invitation had read. "Other than that, we're limited only by our imaginations."

The historic event had been fantasized about and privately discussed by some of San Francisco's more sexually adventurous souls for some time. A couple of women finally broached the subject with Buzz, who as founder of J/O Buddies, a gay masturbation circle, had become the "Pearl Mesta of the jack-off scene," as he liked to put it. The women found the idea of being in a roomful of naked men, greased and hard and straining toward some collective ecstasy, enticing. "Let us watch sometime," they half-joked with Buzz. "We won't touch them: you can put us in a cage." Buzz thought a cage full of lustful women might be too odd an addition to one of the regular J/O Buddies events. But he was intrigued by the idea of sexually integrating the jack-off scene.

So, indeed, were your authors, who—while exploring the frontiers of American sexuality—had come across the early tremors of this event.

Thus, we found ourselves, one brisk fall afternoon, in Buzz's warehouse, taking part in the planning meeting for the ground-breaking party. All was not harmonious during the hour-long discussion, and at one point it seemed as if the long-awaited event might not come off. The meeting had brought together a disparate collection of sexual renegades, including Buzz; Missy Manners and her beau, Artie Mitchell, accompanied as always by the hyperactive ball of fur, Mr. T; a phone-sex performer named Janet Taylor (who shall cross our paths later); a balding erotic poet; a middle-aged female swinger eager to find more hygienic ways of multiplying her pleasure; and a beautiful young German émigré with the face of Mariel Hemingway and an abiding fascination with *Cabaret*-style decadence.

Some matters were easily disposed of by the group. Should bowls of snack food be provided, along with the beer, wine, and mineral water? No, it was quickly decided, because hands slick with baby oil and other slime dipped into the potato chips was simply not an appetizing notion. But other questions proved to be more sticky.

A few of the party planners were extremely concerned about semen splatter. "Look, this thing is being billed as a safe-sex event," observed Missy Manners, "so guys should be told to wear rubbers. I mean, who wants to be squirted in the face by some stranger?" Buzz, however, strongly objected. Gay men had seen so much of their pleasure circumscribed by medical guidelines during these plague years. Now they were being ordered to strap themselves into latex even when they masturbated! "Forget it," snapped Buzz, "I'm pulling out of the party if that's the rule."

The fragile coalition of underground sex cultures behind the World's First Jack-and-Jill-Off Party suddenly seemed in danger of coming unstrung. The women had, of course, raised a legitimate health issue. But buried within this safe-sex debate was a schism about jism. It came down to the way you felt about men's sexual fluid itself. Gay men tend to exalt their "cum," as it is styled in gay and porn literature. Big splotches of sticky sperm smack against a car windshield in one of the erotic prints prominently displayed on the walls of Buzz's warehouse. It's a sign of sexual power, of virility. Men in gay and straight pornography shoot copious amounts of fluid and they often drench their partners with it. Women and straight men, on the other hand, tend to feel a stranger's sperm is, well, icky. Even if it's not tainted with virus.

Disaster was finally averted when the female swinger proposed a compromise: male revelers would be required to ask someone first before they anointed him or her with their virile essence. This was not enough to put Artie Mitchell's mind at rest. "I ain't going," muttered San Francisco's leading commercial-sex outlaw. "I've got six kids to worry about." But the rest of the party committee found this an agreeable solution. And so it was on with the show!

Buzz was still apprehensive as the big night drew near. Had he done the right thing by opening up his jack-off space to heterosexuals? Would the two cultures clash? He knew that some gay men who frequented his Saturday-night affairs were put off by the prospect of having their sexual salon invaded by horny heterosexuals. One man had even ripped up a stack of Jack-and-Jill-Off flyers in a rage.

Buzz believed in periodically recharging the J/O Buddies. That's why his group and the San Francisco Jacks, the city's other main J/O club, staged theme nights from time to time in the Folsom Street warehouse: Military Uniform Night, Primitive Night (war paint and leopard skin), and Bondage Night ("You're tied down. Can't move . . . but others are all over you, stroking you, pumping you"). But this time, he might have gone too far. The Jack-and-Jill-Off Night was sure to be a strange brew, a riot of polymorphous perversity. There was no telling what might happen once this assortment of male and female desires started to collide.

Buzz felt protective of his little demimonde. Joining the cult of Onan had changed his life. He would always remember his first jack-off party, back in October 1984. Years later, he still talked of it with the same passion with which people describe spiritual conversions. Buzz had been plodding through his days in despair. He had broken up with his lover the year before and was finding no pleasure in the gay singles life. San Francisco, in the gathering darkness of the AIDS epidemic, was no longer the carnival it had been when he arrived from St. Paul, Minnesota, in 1979, at the age of twenty-nine. "I was feeling extremely lost," he recalls. "I felt victimized and angry. I felt like screaming. 'Those doctors out there have taken my sex life away and I'm pissed!' "

Then, as usually occurs in these tales of conversion, a friend suggested that Buzz attend a small gathering of the devoted. But nothing in his Lutheran upbringing had prepared him for this meeting. For this was a coming to-gether, as it were, of the San Francisco Jacks, the city's divine order of Priapus.

"I was overwhelmed as I walked in that door. I felt like I had been catapulted to another planet. In those days, the meetings were held in an experimental theater space. Under soft stage lights were fifty or sixty naked men in various states of excitement. I was immediately struck by how different it was from the old bathhouse scene. Because of the brighter lighting, everything was out in the open."

The sexual charge in gay bathhouses had come from the shadowy anonymity. Each dim cubicle held a different mystery man. It was desire at its most elemental, freed of conscience, of concern for the other. But at J/O parties, the thrill derived from the public and comradely display of naked flesh. "The openness is J/O's single greatest invention," says Buzz. "For gay men, taking off your clothes in a well-lit room in front of other men often produces great panic. People say, 'I'm too fat or bald or ugly—no one would like me.' They're afraid of being the one left in the corner. But no one is left out at J/O parties, at least the ones I've been to. There is more a sense of fraternity. People tend to treat each other with more affection and respect."

The exposed nature of J/O parties also made it virtually impossible for overheated celebrants to break the rules and conjoin their bodies in unwise ways. "Gay men often complain that they have a hard time getting passionate nowadays, because they're afraid if they get too hot, they'll lose control and do something dangerous. It's like driving with the parking brake pulled halfway up. But at J/O parties, you know that you can pull out the stops, because if you start to go too far, the group will hold you in check. Every jack-off group has its set of basic rules that the group will enforce. But you can still go wild, grab every man you can, pour body oil all over them, come six or seven times a night, have someone fondle your balls while you get off. The possibilities are endless."

Though many gay men perceive it to be a safe-sex invention, the J/O phenomenon actually precedes the AIDS era. In the 1970s, private masturbation parties were held in the homes of jack-off enthusiasts in San Francisco and New York, men who remained tantalized by the circle jerks of adolescence. A retired gay businessman in San Francisco maintained a bulging Rolodex of group masturbators, along with their phone numbers and proclivities (this one favored uncircumcised men, that one was into hairy chests). But as the disease swept through the gay community in the 1980s, the J/O ranks were swelled by a new wave of men seeking an alternative to the dangerous bathhouses.

The membership of New York Jacks, which was founded on the eve of the epidemic, quickly doubled. New J/O clubs sprang up in Washington, D.C., Kansas City, Cincinnati, Chicago, Los Angeles, Atlanta, Houston, and other cities. The idea soon spread to Europe, where clubs were organized in Paris and Amsterdam. San Francisco Jacks, established in March 1983, began publishing a quirky journal of masturbatory erotica, *The Penis Mightier,* which contained J/O news from around the world. By 1986, San Francisco would boast no fewer than four jack-off clubs, including Buzz Bense's J/O Buddies and a special club for "uncut" men (those with intact foreskins).

Although these far-flung masturbation circles maintain fraternal relations with one another, each has its own identity, often reflecting the cities where they are located. The J/O club in Amsterdam receives government funding. The clubs in New York and Los Angeles are more exclusive than the others, allowing only a carefully screened list of members and their guests into their parties. "We want to avoid a certain type of person," said one of the leaders of New York Jacks, a forty-three-year-old junior high school teacher named Paul. "We don't want those who will 'perv' on the scene, just stand there staring, or those who are very unattractive and overly aggressive."

In 1984, New York Jacks, which has met in a succession of Greenwich Village bars during its history, made headlines in the gay press when it ousted a member suspected of being sick with AIDS. "The issue was not whether or not he was sick," said Paul, "but the person's behavior. He was licking others and allowing himself to be licked. We tried to talk with him, but he became very defensive, threatening to sue us and so forth, so we had to deny him membership. He was lashing out because of his illness." As a result of this incident, New York Jacks now prohibits licking and kissing, a more stringent interpretation of safe-sex guidelines than those of other clubs.

Our first descent into the J/O underground took place in Washington, D.C., after the Third International AIDS Conference in June 1987. The gathering had brought together thousands of scientists, doctors, public health officials, and journalists from around the world, many of whom—particularly those from Europe and Africa—were a sexy and stylish lot. They would stay up until the wee hours, smoking Gitanes and sipping Courvoisier in the bar at the Washington Hilton, where the conference was held. But after last call, they would retire to their separate rooms, for this was not the type of conference that inspired torrid little affairs. Sitting through days of lectures on blood tests, diarrhea, and lesions tends to take the edge off one's sex drive.

"The joke going around is that our wives were perfectly content to let us go to this conference," remarked a bearded epidemiologist from the Centers for Disease Control with a silver stud in one ear and wire-rim glasses. "None of my colleagues is having sex anymore," sighed a sultry young Italian scientist with big brown eyes as she leaned against her research display on the ravages of Kaposi's sarcoma. "Or they're requiring AIDS tests of their lovers."

So in this global forum, from which sex had been regretfully banished, it came as something of a shock to spot one day in the hotel lobby, amid the clutter of leaflets announcing roundtable discussions on AZT treatment and the ethics of mandatory testing, a crude poster with a shot of a hunky bare torso inviting convention delegates to a special meeting of Washington's Jerk-Off Enthusiasts (JO/E) club. It was like being flashed at a funeral, a raunchy reminder that even in the shadow of death, the party went on. Interested delegates were advised to meet on a street corner near the Hilton at 6 P.M. on the closing day of the conference. Wrapping up the Third International AIDS Conference in a roomful of greased dicks? It was a wild notion. We knew we had to be there . . . Journalism can be a strange and demanding mistress.

Thus, it came to pass that your man from Hollywood was standing on a residential street corner in the nation's capital, the din of the mate-and-die cicadas in my ears, waiting with a half dozen equally nervous men from Amsterdam, London, and other far-off places to be escorted to my first jack-off party. Soon we were being led down an alley, through a rear gate, and into a compact two-story town house, where another cluster of men awaited us. The security precautions and the foreign accents in the air gave the proceedings a dash of intrigue. But glamour fled the premises as soon as the party began.

A grizzled, ashen-skinned J/OE functionary in a sweat-stained jockstrap and tank top kicked things off by running down the list of club rules in a brisk, no-nonsense manner. We were then crowded into the "action room," a cramped chamber whose windows had been masked for privacy and whose floor was covered with a splotched old tarpaulin that obviously had seen *loads* of action. An industrial-size can of Albolene lubricant and rolls of double-strength paper towels were the room's sole amenities, save for a VCR on which a porn film appropriately titled *Men in Action* was silently playing.

As our host continued to inform us of the house rules (there would be absolutely no chitchat in the action room), the increasingly despondent group of revelers studiously avoided one another's eyes, staring forlornly instead at the video screen, where a handsome blond army recruit was following his black sergeant's orders by kneeling before him and taking a long drag on his impressive cock. "Oh, for the good old days!" whispered the man to my left, a paunchy, thirtyish scientist.

By the time our host had concluded his welcoming remarks and the assembled guests had begun to strip down halfheartedly, folding their pants neatly and placing them in plastic bags, the stuffy room had begun to stink like a gym. Your coauthor was not alone in taking an early leave from the party; apparently others felt that if this was sex in the plague years, it was preferable to snuggle up with a good book.

The Washington party left us with a sour feeling about the jack-off underground. But our attitude was to change a few months later, after that San Francisco satyricon, that three-ring circus of carnal showmanship that would go down in history as the World's First Jack-and-Jill-Off celebration. Images from the weird, lewd night would stick with its celebrants for days, for weeks afterward, like flashes from a disturbingly erotic dream.

We are back in the Folsom Street warehouse. Upstairs, in the softly lit loft, the party guests are getting to know each other better. The angelic one-legged woman has been tumbled backward onto a sofa that is draped with a clean white sheet, and she is being kissed and caressed by her retinue of male admirers. Lips find her nipples, fingers tease her clitoris. Her head is thrown back, her eyes are closed, her graceful hands play idly with the back of two men's necks as they work away at her. Her crutch is cast aside, she is floating to heaven. Never, she would later tell Buzz, had she felt so adored.

Cleopatra, too, has found her suitors, a man and a woman, who have bookended her on another sheet-covered sofa and are sucking hungrily on her creamy, little breasts. Do they know what's tucked delicately away in her pretty, turquoise panties? Do they care?

Meanwhile, at the other end of the loft, another intense sexual vignette is under way. A tough-looking woman with hair like a mowed lawn and pendulous breasts is putting her young Chinese boyfriend on display. She has slid his Jockey shorts down to his ankles and is slathering his long, thin cock with baby oil. As his shiny, purple-knobbed affair jolts upward, he looks shyly away. But she boldly meets the stares of those who have gathered around them, as if to say, *Go ahead, take a good, hard look. See how excited I make him, see the power I have over him?* Directly across from the couple, perched on another couch a few feet away, two naked young men are stroking each other in rhythm with the woman's hand, each slick slide down their shafts a musical rejoinder to her movements. Now her Chinese consort's sinewy thighs lock tight. He feels on the edge. A look of panic and exquisite pleasure contorts his face: *Oh God, not here, not in front of all these people!* But she pumps mercilessly on, eager to explode whatever is left of his modesty.

Some of us have to look away. It would happen more than once during the evening. You would suddenly catch yourself staring at some of the most primal moments you had ever witnessed, and you would be struck by the impropriety of it all: I shouldn't be watching this; it's very wrong. And superego and id would crash crazily against one another. But at other times, it all seems perfectly natural, like watching the dancers on a nightclub floor.

Over there, a woman is slipping into a pair of custom-made safe-sex panties with a latex crotch so her girlfriend can lick her pussy without violating club rules. And in a far corner of the loft, a buck-naked man has been handcuffed to the heating pipes and is being spanked until his cheeks are hot-pink. "For being bad?" we ask Buzz, as our host drifts by with a can of Budweiser. "For not being bad enough, my dears," he replies, with an eyebrow raised in our direction. For your authors, working hard to maintain professional dignity in the midst of sweaty chaos, are still dressed in swimming-pool-blue Calvin Klein briefs, in the case of Mr. Hollywood, and a three-quarter-length terry-cloth bathrobe, in the case of Mr. Montana. There had been a parting of the ways concerning how best to dress for the world's first safe-sex orgy. Mr. Hollywood, the more romantic of your authors, felt that the experience could only be great fun. You may be dreaming, replied the cautious Mr. Montana, who spent the rest of the evening with his arm around a sweet Brazilian *gostosa* with a bad Italian temper who had bought a red teddy and black heels for the event.

As he wades among his party guests, Buzz has a triumphant look. Everyone is behaving themselves and everyone is pleasuring themselves. Nobody has complained of being bedewed with unwanted juices. Spunk is not spurting through the air or splooshing into people's wineglasses. In fact, the male guests seem rather meticulous in their orgasms, carefully shooting their seed onto their own bellies, for the most part, and then carefully cleaning up after themselves.

It's true that a few straight men fled the premises soon after walking through the door, repelled by the sight of so much oiled maleness. But the greatest marvel of the evening, Buzz feels, is how smoothly the different sexual categories are rubbing elbows and other body parts. Here we are in this era of sexual fear and loathing, Buzz is thinking, with straight people avoiding restaurants that employ gay waiters, steering clear of clothes stores where gay men might have tried on the merchandise, even fumigating airplanes that gay passengers have flown in. And yet here, in his twilit sex salon, close to a hundred nude and seminude men and women—running the full range of sexual expression—are engaged in a bold experiment in collective intimacy.

Over there he spies a straight man nursing on a woman's breast when suddenly a gay man starts fondling his cock. Startled at first, the straight man quickly returns to his work and allows himself to grow hard under the other man's caresses. Later Buzz sees a gay man exploring a woman's body for the first time with his hands. "You know what we did?" Buzz will later exclaim. "We created a safe environment for people to cross boundaries for a night, to try something entirely new." It seemed, in the climate of the eighties, like a radical act of cultural defiance.

As the World's First Jack-and-Jill-Off Party blows into its final hours, however, we are not dwelling on the cultural significance of the event. The wine and the barrage of sensual stimuli are beginning to cast a spell. The members of the party planning committee are no longer graciously greeting guests at the door but, with bared fangs, have joined the rest of the beasts in this erotic menagerie. From upstairs comes the giddy wail of Missy Manners: "Oh God! But I'm into penetration!" The safe-sex porn star has apparently overcome her preparty jitters. She has been encircled by a pack of male and female fans and they have popped her plump, tanned breasts from her low-cut gown and begun to feed on them. In the amber party light, her breasts glow like tropical gourds. Our sense of journalistic detachment is starting to crumble.

Then it is party host Janet Taylor's turn, she of the phone-sex fantasy trade. Janet is hoisted onto a table with a black leather top, a hand-me-down from an old S&M club. A dozen pairs of hands roam all over her supine body, caressing her cheeks and massaging her feet and making forays into her black lace bustier. It looks as if she's the subject of a fiendish lab experiment. By now, one of your authors has succumbed and is running his hands along the pleasure victim's legs.

But Missy, who has proclaimed so loudly that she is "into penetration," wants to take this operation a notch higher. After lubricating a gloved hand with nonoxynol-9 gel, she proceeds to slip her fingers under Janet's black silk panties like a spider. With a queer little smile, she plunges them into her pussy. Poor Janet is pushed beyond her tolerance. She squirms, she wriggles, she finally sits bolt upright like the Bride of Frankenstein come to life, her eyes wide, her hair an electric frazzle, and breaks free of her tormentors. It was all too much, she will say later, even for her. As she leaps from the table, her place is immediately taken by a man as boyishly handsome as Harry Hamlin.

We, too, have been pushed beyond our limits; we too must find release. As the clock strikes midnight, we make our exit. On the streets outside, San Francisco's dandies are lining up to get inside the Paradise Lounge, Club DV8, and ten other dance palaces of the moment. But it all seems strangely pale after our trip through Buzz Bense's looking glass.

There were those who attended the party on Folsom Street that night who felt they had glimpsed the future of the sexual revolution. The party had somehow combined, they said, the wildness of the 1960s and 1970s with the prudence of the 1980s. There were no drugs or hard liquor to be had; it was strictly a mineral water and nonoxynol-9 affair.

The future of the sexual revolution? This, like much about that night, was a bit overheated. Jack-and-Jill-Off-Parties were not destined to become a national craze. Still, as the AIDS mortality figures mounted throughout the decade, more and more people searched for healthy new ways to enjoy themselves. Phone sex, computer sex, latex sex, "noninsertive" sex. The country's more pioneering spirits were busily redesigning Eros. The point was to free the imagination. Your Brain Is Your Biggest Sex Organ became a popular slogan among this sexual vanguard.

No one knew all the right steps. No one was sure where it was all leading. It was dancing in the dark.

Most safe-sex inventions originated out of the desperation of the gay community, which has borne the brunt of the AIDS epidemic. The dramatic transformation of homosexual America in the 1980s was an extraordinary event. Not all gays found it possible to adapt to the new times. In summer 1987, a hospice for dying AIDS patients in San Francisco was forced to launch a "Shhhhhh!" campaign because gay cruisers in a nearby park were making too much noise—a particularly vivid example of the conflicting impulses at work within the gay world. But studies conducted in Chicago, Pittsburgh, San Antonio, and other cities that year indicated that the vast majority of homosexuals were responding to the epidemic by reinventing their sex lives.

Gay health organizations maintained this mood of vigilance by flooding homosexual neighborhoods with advertisements and brochures that exhorted men to practice safe sex and discussed in frank terms how to protect oneself. As a result, the AIDS infection rate among gay men dropped sharply; in San Francisco, new exposures were cut from 20 percent in 1984 to less than 1 percent in 1987. That same year saw the city's last gay bathhouse close its doors.

Heterosexual America, on the other hand, faced with less alarming statistics and buffeted by contradictory messages, was slow to change its way. A 1987 Gallup poll found that only 13 percent of those surveyed were choosing their sexual partners more carefully and using condoms as a result of AIDS. (Younger adults, according to the poll, were more likely to behave cautiously.) The 1988 Women's View Survey, published shortly afterward by *Glamour* magazine, indicated that women were beginning to exercise more sexual discretion. But only one in five of those surveyed said they made sure their partners wore condoms.

The general public's perception of the threat posed by AIDS swerved between extremes throughout the 1980s, in response to changing bulletins from the media. While some reports summoned up a horrifying picture of a world laid to waste by the plague, others brushed off the disease as a threat only to limited segments of the population. These widely divergent assessments sometimes appeared within weeks of one another. In January 1988, *Cosmopolitan* magazine blithely assured its female readers that the AIDS virus could not be spread through "ordinary sexual intercourse." Shortly afterward, famed sex researchers Masters and Johnson stunned the country with a report claiming the exact opposite; according to them, the AIDS virus was "running rampant" among unsuspecting heterosexuals.

While leading AIDS authorities immediately dismissed the Masters and Johnson claim as alarmist, it was well documented by the mid-1980s that the virus was indeed being transmitted through "ordinary sexual intercourse." Like a jackal lurking on the edge of a herd of gazelle, the infection was carrying off a few here, a few there, at a rate that made heterosexuals the fastest-growing group of AIDS victims. And the herd was still not taking serious protective measures.

The times were crying out for strong public health leadership, for a prominent official to cut through both the hysteria and the complacency and warn the citizenry exactly how to avoid infection. This message particularly needed to be delivered to those inner cities where needle use was widespread, such as the South Bronx; public health officials estimated that, by 1987, as many as one in five sexually active men in the South Bronx carried the virus.

But long into the AIDS crisis, public discourse about the disease continued to be dominated by moralists inside and outside of the Reagan administration, who rejected explicit safe-sex education in favor of sermons against homosexuality and sexual license. "In the future, everyone will know someone who is sick or dead from AIDS," we were told by an aide to Senator Orrin Hatch, who played a key legislative role on AIDS throughout the Reagan reign. "One of the ways that people with overactive hormones will have to deal with that is by finding religion, because religious values provide people's lives with structure and discipline. Those who don't embrace religion are going to die. It's that simple." It was a vision of the future with biblical gravity: on the dark side of the chasm wailed the infected and dying, on the radiant side stood the saved.

There is nothing new about this moral approach to venereal disease, as Harvard historian Allan M. Brandt documented in *No Magic Bullet*, a disturbing account of the ways medical, military, and federal authorities in the United States have handled the clap problem for the past hundred years. "Venereal disease came to be seen as an affliction of those who willfully violated the moral code, a punishment for sexual irresponsibility," Brandt wrote. "These infections were employed to argue for a more restricted sexuality."

As Brandt noted, the discovery of penicillin in the 1940s did not elicit euphoria throughout the medical community. Some prominent doctors feared that society would descend into debauchery once freed of the terror of syphilis. "If [a physician] debases the spirit of man by the methods he employs to save his body, he is indeed the Devil's servant," declared Dr. John Stokes, one of the country's leading venereal disease experts.

Stokes need not have worried. America's leaders have only tried to stamp out sexually transmitted diseases on rare occasions during this century, most notably in wartime, when it was feared that the country's military effort would be crippled unless heroic measures were undertaken. But as soon as peace broke out, federal VD-control programs were slashed and VD rates soared again. From syphilis to herpes to AIDS, the nation's public campaigns against sexually transmitted diseases have repeatedly been hamstrung by prudish concerns. Morality has continually vied with medicine, and the former has generally prevailed.

It was therefore a historic occasion when, several years into the AIDS epidemic, the Surgeon General of the United States—a man known for his deeply conservative moral convictions—released a report on the disease that was devoid of pious rhetoric and full of straightforward language about the mechanics of human sexuality and prophylaxis. The report made Dr. C. Everett Koop a national celebrity, jolted the forces of Republican moralism, and changed the way America talked about sex.

"I think that people will look back and say, 'He was a lone voice crying in the wilderness. He rose to a position of notoriety because in an era when there weren't many heroes around, he appeared to be one.' " There is absolutely nothing modest about the U.S. Surgeon General. His office at the Department of Health and Human Services is a shrine. Gold plaques, framed awards, and flattering photos cover the walls. Though his term as the nation's top physician is not yet finished, Dr. C. Everett Koop has already located his proper place in history. "I'm the only sane voice on AIDS that is nationally heard," he tells us.

Over six feet tall and barrel-chested, with a chin beard like his Dutch ancestors and a "Rock of Ages" voice that sounds as though it should be delivering sermons in the desert, Koop certainly fits the part of someone chosen to make history. It is the look of an Old Testament prophet, of Abraham Lincoln, of someone touched with glory. "I think he feels that all his efforts now are God-directed," says one of Koop's best friends, pediatric surgeon John W. Duckett.

Five years after being appointed, at the age of sixty-four, to the Surgeon General's post by President Reagan, following a distinguished surgical career at Philadelphia's Children Hospital, "Chick" Koop found his final calling. He was to fight the plague that was desolating parts of the country, by shedding light where there was darkness, saying forbidden words like "condom" and "penis" and "anus," and by preaching good will toward those rendered "untouchable" by the disease.

It was hard to imagine a less likely savior of gays, drug addicts, and the "sexually active." Here was an evangelical Christian who had crusaded throughout his life against legalized abortion and other manifestations of the new sexual morality. He had made scornful speeches about homosexuality and feminism, which he accused of undermining the family. He had loosed his fearsome anger against the disciples of hedonism, those who pursued lives "of convenience, of pleasure, of permissiveness, of undisciplined morality."

Senator Jesse Helms enthusiastically endorsed President Reagan's choice for Surgeon General. But congressional liberals like Edward Kennedy held up Koop's nomination for nearly a year. They were unnerved by his moral fervor; he even *looked* like the wrath of God. His opponents labeled him "Dr. Kook." "He frightens me," said Henry Waxman, the Democratic congressman from West Hollywood who turned his House subcommittee on health into a gauntlet for Koop.

There were times during the long confirmation battle when Koop would return dispiritedly to the little Georgetown apartment he and his wife had rented on the assumption that they would soon be moving to the more comfortable quarters reserved for the Surgeon General and would suggest that they give up and go home to Philadelphia. It was a galling experience, "the most difficult period of my life," he would later recall. He was one of the founding fathers of pediatric surgery, a man who had separated three sets of Siamese twins, a miracle worker who had performed heroic operations on horribly deformed infants no other surgeons would go near. And yet the New York *Times* was calling him "Dr. Unqualified."

Weathering all this abuse to win a job that had become in recent years nothing more than a figurehead position . . . well, it hardly seemed worth it. Washington mudwrestling just seemed too demeaning to the proud Dr. Koop, a man long used to a respect that bordered on adoration. But Betty Koop, the woman he had married when he was still a Dartmouth undergraduate, who had raised their four children almost single-handedly while he maintained his frenetic schedule at the hospital, who knew him better than anybody, refused to let him give in. She thought he would always regret it.

Even after he was finally confirmed, it was not apparent he had done the right thing. By 1983, the Reagan administration had declared AIDS to be the nation's "number one health priority." But Dr. Edward Brandt, the Assistant Secretary for Health, the man to whom Koop reported in the federal bureaucracy, was making sure that the Surgeon General got nowhere near the AIDS issue. Brandt, a conscientious but politically careful administrator, was working in his low-key manner to turn down the panic and moral uproar around the disease. The soft-spoken, jug-eared physician from Texas faced the daunting task of keeping White House ideologues and fire-breathing conservative activists at bay, while maintaining lines of communication with suspicious gay groups and carefully building pressure for bigger AIDS budgets. At one point, Brandt was forced to jump in and derail an alarming plan for a quarantine and mass firing of homosexuals that was being cooked up within administration councils. The last thing he needed under these circumstances was a Bible-quoting Surgeon General getting in his way.

The rational types at the upper levels of the federal health bureaucracy strongly distrusted Dr. C. Everett Koop. It wasn't just the reputation he brought with him. Maybe it was the way he strutted around the halls at the Humphrey Building in his starched white uniform with the gold epaulets—a getup abandoned long before by his predecessors in the Surgeon General's office. He seemed like a pompous martinet; his Washington critics prayed he would stick to smoking, about which, unsurprisingly for a Surgeon General, he had nothing but bad things to say.

Though Koop was largely corralled during his early years in office, he did bolt briefly into the headlines in 1983 when he intervened in what became known as the Baby Jane Doe case, fighting to keep alive a severely impaired infant against the wishes of her parents. Koop had operated on thousands of Baby Does back at Children's Hospital in Philadelphia. Many of those who had grown up and become success stories still stayed in touch with the surgeon. The idea of abandoning infants who were helpless, but not entirely hopeless, filled him with righteous anger. That way lay Mengele, Koop sincerely believed, the medical ethics of the Third Reich.

"We're not fighting for this baby," he thundered at the time. "We're fighting for the principle of this country that every life is individual and uniquely sacred." Baby Jane Doe's doctors did finally take measures to keep her alive. But the Baby Doe regulations that Koop helped write, which would have forced hospitals to treat severely handicapped infants over the objections of their parents, were later declared unconstitutional by the Supreme Court.

With the exception of the Baby Doe controversy and a flare-up over cigarette advertising, the lofty voice of the Surgeon General was unheard during Reagan's first term, to the immense relief of liberals on Capital Hill. In the meantime, AIDS cast a longer and longer shadow across the land, and Ed Brandt struggled, with little success, to mobilize the government against the epidemic. The administration's tightfisted attitude toward domestic spending and its moral rigidity were proving to be insurmountable obstacles. Each year, the White House asked for less money to fight AIDS than was recommended by its own Public Health Service, and each year Congress was forced to tack on a higher figure to the budget. The nation's leading AIDS laboratories were financially strapped and important research went unfunded.

It was a recipe for disaster, as Daniel Greenberg would note in *The Nation:* "The simultaneous arrival in the United States in 1981 of an uncompassionate, overtly homophobic presidency and a mysterious, fatal affliction transmitted mainly through the sex practices of male homosexuals" was a truly "horrific coincidence."

As it became clear that a vaccine or effective antiviral drug were years away, safe-sex research and public education aimed at preventing wider transmission of the virus became of paramount importance. Was deep kissing safe? Cunnilingus? Fellatio? What were the safest condoms? Did spermicidal gel provide another line of protection? These were the kind of life and death questions that the public needed answers to. But the Reagan administration, wedded to the notion that abstinence before marriage and absolute faithfulness in marriage was the only proper design for living, resisted disseminating this information in the belief that it would encourage promiscuity.

In 1984, the Mariposa Education and Research Foundation, a Southern California institute run by gay health expert Bruce Voeller, began exploring the possibility that nonoxynol-9, a common ingredient of spermicide gels, could kill the AIDS virus in sufficiently high concentrations. After a long delay, the federal Centers for Disease Control in Atlanta conducted tests in conjunction with Mariposa that confirmed this hypothesis. Here was an important breakthrough in AIDS prevention. The research suggested that spermicide gel, in conjunction with rubbers, could block transmission of the virus and save lives. Dr. Donald Francis, the lead scientist on the project, wanted to rush the findings into print, but CDC officials stalled publication for more than a year, claiming they were unsure of the research methodology. Francis had another explanation: the federal government did not want to publicize the value of nonoxynol-9 because it might be interpreted as condoning morally unsanctioned sex.

For the same reason, it was not until mid-1987, over six years into the epidemic, that the Food and Drug Administration began to step up its inspection of condoms, in an effort to improve their reliability. Similarly, not one of the hundreds of federally funded scientific papers presented at the Third International AIDS Conference in Washington, D.C., that year dealt with safe-sex techniques. Throughout the Reagan years, practical AIDS prevention research was left almost entirely to folk practitioners—sexologists, prostitutes, porn stars, amateur scientists—many of whom used their own bodies as laboratories. Safe-sex education, too, would fall to the private sector, with gay organizations and civic-minded celebrities showing citizens how to roll on rubbers. The federal government steadfastly refused to teach the public how to shield itself from the virus. Until, that is, the U.S. Surgeon General saw the light.

Near the end of 1984, Ed Brandt, reportedly frustrated with the administration's politicized response to AIDS, announced he was stepping down as Assistant Secretary of Health. For over a year, his post would go unfilled; no reputable physician or public health official wanted to step into the same slippery ditch. The administration's war on AIDS, never a marvel of coordination and dedication, seemed more rudderless than ever. One day the President was buttonholed by a reporter: What exactly was he doing about AIDS? The question stumped Reagan. He mulled it over a long time. Finally, the President declared that he would tell his Surgeon General to prepare a report.

White House conservatives were pleased with the idea. The report would help forestall criticism that the administration was asleep at the wheel on

AIDS, and anything written by Koop would certainly follow conservative doctrine. But gay groups and the career civil servants who worked on AIDS at Health and Human Services were deeply alarmed. "Dr. Kook," whom sensible Ed Brandt had kept on a short chain for so long, was finally unleashed. They knew what he felt about homosexuality, about modern morality. They dreaded the outcome.

In our interviews with Koop, he would insist that while he was critical of the homosexual lifestyle, he had always been comfortable with gays as individuals: "Some of my closest medical colleagues have been gay. I have always been, I think, a broad-minded person." But HHS staff members who worked with him had seen a less tolerant side of Koop. "He would make remarks about gays, ugly stuff—'homo this' and 'homo that,'" recalled a longtime HHS employee who worked on AIDS-information projects and often conferred with gay groups. "He and his wife would give a Christmas party each year at their house out at the National Institutes for Health. I went with my husband in 1982 or 1983, and as we went down the receiving line, Koop—who was kind of in his cups by then—introduced me to his wife by saying, 'Here's the woman who helps the homos.' My husband and I were offended."

But as he labored over his AIDS report during the first nine months of 1986, meeting with more than two dozen organizations and steeping himself in information about the disease, the Surgeon General seemed to undergo a transformation. "That terrible plague had begun to consume me," he would later say. "It changed my life." The wrathful moralist in Koop was giving way to the compassionate physician. The gay leaders with whom he met were impressed with his concern and attentiveness. "He didn't cut [the meeting] short with some excuse like he had to meet with the President or have tea with Nancy," said Richard Dunne of New York's Gay Men's Health Crisis. As for Koop, he "was very pleased to see the problem through homosexual eyes."

HHS staff members who read early versions of the AIDS report, which went through a total of twenty-seven drafts, found a number of judgmental "them versus us" statements on high-risk groups. "He had one line, for instance, like 'Everybody finds homosexuality offensive . . . ,'" recalled a former Koop aide. "I told him, 'You can't say that.' He was very gracious in accepting my suggested changes." What began to emerge, as Koop carefully wrote and rewrote the report, spending nights and weekends at the stand-up desk in his basement at home, was a document that was remarkably free of conservative dogma and startlingly blunt in its medical advice.

"As soon as I read the final draft, I knew it was going to be important," remembered the Koop aide, who had long been pushing for a more aggressive educational program on AIDS. Koop, too, realized the report's significance, and he was not about to let it be tampered with before it could be released to the public. "I mean, we had people high up in this department who thought you could get AIDS from shaking hands!" exclaimed Koop's aide. The Surgeon General wisely decided to circumvent bureaucratic channels at HHS, brashly telling the new Secretary of Health and Human Services Otis Bowen, "I don't want one word changed." Koop was also shrewd enough to print five thousand copies of his report before taking it to the White House domestic policy council, realizing, in the words of his former assistant, that "a published document looks inviolable; a draft just invites revisions."

Koop's timing was fortuitous. His report was presented to the domestic policy council at a moment when there was no conservative hardliner taking a leadership role on AIDS within the administration. After giving it a quick once-over, the White House council quickly approved the report. The council's haste was due in part to the fact that "there was a little bit of discomfort in talking about [the report] because it mentioned condoms, and Elizabeth Dole [then Secretary of Transportation and the only female Cabinet member] was there," a council member would tell the Washington *Post*.

The thirty-six-page *Surgeon General's Report on AIDS*, released at a packed Washington press conference on October 22, 1986, was an immediate bombshell. It used explicit language to describe how the AIDS virus was sexually transmitted ("Small tears in the surface lining of the vagina or rectum may occur during insertion of the penis, fingers, or other objects . . ."). While advocating monogamy as the safest practice, it acknowledged the realities of human behavior by counseling those who did not know the antibody status of their partners to wear condoms. It called for AIDS education "at the lowest grade possible," including "information about heterosexual and homosexual relationships." It rejected panicky proposals from the Right, such as compulsory blood testing and quarantine, as medically unwise. And it urged public compassion for those stricken with the disease.

"I was stunned," said Gary MacDonald of the AIDS Action Council. So were Koop's conservative supporters. What in the world had happened to their pillar of righteousness at Health and Human Services? How could the White House let him stray so far from the reservation?

There was nothing in Koop's report that AIDS scientists and doctors had not been saying for a long time. But Koop was a high federal official and his words carried more impact. Up until his report, the government and the media had preferred vague and prissy language when discussing AIDS transmission. (President Reagan could not even bring himself to mention AIDS in public at all.) So America heard only about "the exchange of body fluids," rather than about semen and rips in the sensitive lining of the rectum. For a country whose culture is drenched with sex, the United States remains remarkably prudish. Even in the face of a dread epidemic that demanded straightforward discussion, the country opted for the sanitized version. But Surgeon General Koop was refusing to play this game.

In the months following publication of the report, Koop's former comrades on the Moral Right denounced him in the bitter words reserved for those who have betrayed a cause. While liberals once called him "Dr. Kook," conservative leaders now called him "Dr. Condom." They accused him of corrupting the nation's youth by promoting "safe sodomy" in the schools. They charged that he had turned himself into "the instrument of the homosexual lobby." Under pressure from Phyllis Schlafly, three 1988 Republican presidential hopefuls—Senator Robert Dole, Representative Jack Kemp, and Pete du Pont—withdrew their support from a testimonial dinner on behalf of Koop.

Meanwhile, the administration moved to muzzle him. In the wake of the report, Koop was besieged with interview requests from the media. But his two press aides were ordered not to schedule any more interviews after the initial flurry of press attention, and a speech Koop was to deliver before the National Press Club was suddenly canceled. Soon afterward, his press aides, who had been criticized for the effective way they had launched the AIDS report, were both transferred to dead-end bureaucratic posts. And congressional committees that wanted Koop to testify were told he was unavailable. "The administration has the Surgeon General under wraps," complained Tim Westmoreland, an aide to Representative Henry Waxman, in June 1987. "It practically takes a subpoena to get him up to the Hill nowadays."

Koop's enemies were not above the pettiest types of harassment. While Koop was recovering from neck surgery in fall 1986, Dr. Robert Windom, the undistinguished physician who had finally replaced Ed Brandt as Assistant

Secretary of Health, had Koop's office moved from an adjoining suite to a more remote corner of the building. "It was just playpen stuff," said one HHS staffer, shaking her head.

Windom, a big, red-faced geriatric doctor from southern Florida who had raised money for the Reagan-Bush campaigns, resented all the publicity Koop was getting as a result of the AIDS report. Eager to eclipse the increasingly well known Surgeon General, Windom began taking diction lessons so he would fare better in radio and TV interviews. But those who worked with him were unimpressed with his grasp of the health crisis confronting the nation. "If his IQ were any lower, you'd have to water him," remarked one congressional aide. Windom was destined to remain in Koop's shadow throughout his Washington stint.

Despite the flak bursting around his head, Surgeon General Koop refused to lapse into a discreet silence. As the attacks from the Right grew more withering, Koop became ever bolder in his public remarks. In February 1987, he slipped his chains and appeared before a House subcommittee chaired by his old nemesis, Henry Waxman, to advocate condom advertising on television. "Well, I'm glad your mother's dead," Betty Koop told her husband that morning before he went off to testify. At a Philadelphia press conference two months later, he declared that sex education should begin in kindergarten. "You have to tell [children] about AIDS and that requires sex education," he said. "If parents don't do it, they've abrogated their responsibility and somebody else has to do it." He also stated that some high schools should begin handing out condoms to students—an even more stunning piece of advice from a Reagan administration official.

But his biggest philosophical shift occurred when Koop announced that a pregnant woman diagnosed with AIDS had the right to be counseled about abortion. He reiterates this position during our interview with him: "I'm not going to judge her on that; a woman with AIDS is a person in crisis. That's not like the woman who says, 'Hey, Harry, we're going to spoil our vacation to Europe this summer if I'm pregnant.'" This shift was too much for his former comrades in the right-to-life camp. March for Life promptly rescinded the annual award it had bestowed upon the Surgeon General.

Stung by the criticism from old allies, Koop lashed back at them with equal venom. He, too, preferred a family-oriented society founded on the monogamous bond between man and woman, he said. But conservatives were living in a dream world if they thought that was the dominant American landscape in the 1980s. Unlike Phyllis Schlafly and the rest, Koop roared, he was not prepared to "sacrifice that half of the adolescent population that was sexually active just to keep the other half from knowing there are condoms!" Nor would he join conservatives in flaying the homosexual population. "Some of these people seem more concerned with homosexual genocide, and with things like William Buckley's suggesting that AIDS victims be tattooed, than with the human tragedy," Koop told the New York *Times* in a remarkable display of passion.

He was utterly exasperated with conservatives' sexual squeamishness. There was no more time for priggish posturing. Didn't they realize the AIDS crisis had changed everything? Why, under the circumstances, he had no problem sitting down with his own nine-year-old grandson and discussing sodomy and vaginal intercourse, Koop informed *The Village Voice* in another provocative interview. "None of it is frightening to him . . . and when you say some things to him, he says, 'Oh, gross!' and just walks away."

Through his frequent speeches and interviews, the Surgeon General was turning himself into the nation's wise, bearded grandfather, giving us practical advice about sex and health—even if some of us thought it all too gross. To Koop, there was nothing immoral about medical wisdom.

Koop was still the evangelical Christian who believed that science could not fully explain the wonders of life, the devout man who took the word of the Bible literally, starting with God's six-day creation of the universe. But he also understood that faith alone would not rid the land of the plague which had befallen it. Turning his office into a pulpit would only alienate those he most needed to reach, Koop decided. "I'm not the nation's chaplain general," he liked to say. "I'm the Surgeon General."

His conservative critics said Koop was a victim of his overweening ego. Traumatized by liberals and the media during his long confirmation ordeal, they charged, he was now basking in the warm glow of Teddy Kennedy, Hollywood and New York gays, and the TV lights. Even his friends would admit there was some truth to this. "He's in hog heaven in the Washington spotlight," said former colleague Dr. Duckett. "He absolutely thrives on it."

But there was more to the Surgeon General's dramatic metamorphosis than this. Chick Koop had become imbued with the importance of his office, the importance of his medical mission. History, he told Secretary of Health

Bowen one day, would judge them for what they had done to stem the AIDS epidemic.

Koop came to see himself as the heir to Dr. Thomas Parran, President Franklin Roosevelt's great Surgeon General, the man who shattered American taboos in the 1930s by openly discussing the country's syphilis problem in nonmoralistic terms and organizing a public health campaign to stamp out the disease. "We both used words we weren't supposed to use in public: 'syphilis' and 'condom,' " Koop told us. "We both decided you couldn't play that game. We saw a health issue and treated it as a health issue."

Parran's pathbreaking work helped convince FDR to become the first President to directly address the problem of venereal disease. Similarly, in the months after his report was released, Surgeon General Koop angled to get President Reagan to break his increasingly bizarre silence and make a public statement about the AIDS crisis. More than 20,000 Americans had died from AIDS, including the President's old Hollywood friend Rock Hudson, and 1.5 million were thought to be infected. But Reagan had yet to publicly acknowledge he was even aware of the scourge. "You know, it's not the most pleasant subject in the world, and the President is an optimistic kind of guy; he likes upbeat things," a White House aide told us at the time. "So who wants to be the one telling him negative stuff?"

When Koop's attempt to brief the President on AIDS failed, he tried unsuccessfully to arrange a meeting with Nancy Reagan, according to one report (later denied by Koop). The Surgeon General felt a deep sense of urgency because he knew he was not the only one in administration circles pushing an AIDS battle plan. He worried about the "loose cannons" in the conservative movement who had the ear of White House officials—"the type who push the idea that AIDS can be spread through casual transmission or who are so homophobic that it blinds them to the fact the disease is no longer limited to an exclusive club."

By early 1987, the Surgeon General found himself in a critical battle with two other administration officials, Education Secretary William Bennett and White House adviser Gary Bauer, over the future of the government's AIDS policy. After the release of Koop's AIDS report, Bennett and Bauer became his counterpoint within the administration, presenting their ideas as the moral alternative to the Surgeon General's nonjudgmental, medical approach. It was Bennett who got the headlines, calling for "value-based education" to teach teenagers sexual restraint and questioning the reliability of condoms. Like Koop, Bennett was an effective manipulator of the media.

But while Bennett was Koop's main public adversary, it was the little-known Bauer who functioned as the Surgeon General's most effective opponent within the administration, working quietly at the White House to undermine his AIDS strategy. Bauer was a latecomer to the AIDS debate, brought over from the Department of Education in January 1987 by White House Chief of Staff Donald Regan to shore up his credibility with the far Right. Bauer was known primarily for chairing an administration task force on the American family which concluded that "two liberal decades" had resulted in more crime, illegitimate birth, drug use, teenage pregnancy, divorce, and venereal disease.

Once in place as the President's chief domestic policy adviser, Bauer, whom Senator Lowell Weicker referred to as the administration's "philosophical enforcer," lost no time in bending Reagan's ear about AIDS and other issues high on the Right's social agenda. Not long after joining the White House staff, Bauer succeeded in arranging for the President to finally speak out about AIDS—something Koop had been unable to do.

In his April 1, 1987, speech before the College of Physicians of Philadelphia —Koop's home turf—Reagan said AIDS education in the schools should stress sexual abstinence rather than a "value-neutral" prophylactic approach. Just Say No, his wife's antidrug slogan, was also "a pretty good answer" when it came to premarital sex, he later told reporters. The President's comments marked a defeat for the Surgeon General. He had been bested by Bauer, the shrewd political operative who had worked himself up from a dollar-a-week gofer job in the 1980 Reagan-Bush campaign to a top White House position. "I've always been pretty good at infighting," Bauer would later tell us with an impish grin in his unadorned office in the west wing of the White House.

Bauer, who joined the White House staff at the age of forty, was utterly lacking in the Surgeon General's commanding physical presence. Short, doughy, with tiny hands, pop eyes, and a pug nose, he looked like he had stepped from a Saturday-morning TV cartoon. Where Koop was boastful and fond of the limelight, Bauer was soft-spoken and shy, and preferred to work behind the scenes. But the presidential aide was fired with conservative idealism and was as determined in his mission as Koop was in his. "The Mouse That Roars," was the title pinned on him by *The New Republic*.

Bauer and Koop came from similar philosophical backgrounds. Like the Surgeon General, Bauer was an evangelical Protestant, raised in the bosom of the Southern Baptist Church in Newport, Kentucky. And like Koop, he was sorely troubled by the moral state of the nation. In his youth, Newport was known as "sin city," a honky-tonk town where painted ladies paraded up and down the main street and men of weak flesh spent their last dollar in strip shows and gambling joints. Bauer's entry into politics came in 1961, when, at the age of fifteen, he volunteered in a campaign to clean up the town by electing a reform sheriff.

Later, he would come to see America as a larger version of Newport, a Sodom wallowing in sensuality and desperately in need of moral purging. What clearer indication of the country's degraded condition was there than the AIDS epidemic, he thought. Gays and other sexual revolutionaries had been defying the natural order for years, and now nature was exacting a terrible revenge. "We went through a period where people threw out all the rules and now nature, in the sort of difficult way that only nature does, is telling us how unwise this was," Bauer tells us. "What I think is incredible is that we didn't have some sort of terrible disease come down the pike sooner than this one."

Medicine could not fully explain this viral blight, says Bauer, who is unable to conceal his contempt for "experts" and scientific rationalism during our interview. There is a moral genesis to this epidemic, argues the White House adviser, and there are moral lessons to be learned from it. Bauer even talks of a "silver lining in this tragic situation." AIDS, he says, "may get people, young people in particular, to behave in a way that it has been hard for the commu- nity of adults to get them to do until now. There is nothing like the threat of death," adds the diminutive aide with a chilling little smile, "to get the glands under control."

Bauer himself, married at the age of twenty-seven and the father of three children, is a happy family man. But, he confesses, Washington does have its temptations. He has never been the type who turned women's heads. But, as Henry Kissinger had discovered during his years at the political summit, power is an aphrodisiac. "I think it's clearly true that in Washington, there's a certain type of woman who is attracted to individuals they perceive to have power," says Bauer, eager to discuss the subject. "And there have certainly been times when, if I had sent out the right signals, I'm sure I could have worked something out."

How does he manage to ignore the flattery and flirtatiousness, to keep his own "glands under control"? It comes down to his faith and his love for his family. That may not have been enough to protect people like Jim Bakker and Jimmy Swaggart. But Bauer feels his bulwark is made of stronger stuff. "When I think of the worst possible things that could ever happen to me, right at the top of the list would be the breakup of my family."

The battle between Bauer and Koop came to a head in the spring of 1987 over the issue of mandatory AIDS testing. Administration hardliners, led by Bauer and Bennett, were pushing for widespread, compulsory testing of immigrants, prisoners, hospital patients, those applying for marriage licenses, and other groups. Koop and other public health officials vehemently objected, charging that nationwide testing would produce many false results among low-risk groups and drive high-risk groups underground. Gays and others on the AIDS front lines were already fearful, for valid reason, of breaches in medical confidentiality and discrimination. These fears were fanned when right-wing leaders like Senator Jesse Helms periodically raised the specter of quarantine, with some gay activists charging that compulsory testing was the first step to detention.

Koop, by now deeply sensitized to the human component of the epidemic, realized that if the White House handed down a mandatory-testing order, those in greatest need of help would be even less likely to cooperate with the public health system. Education and gentle persuasion were the best weapons in fighting a disease with such a noxious social stigma, stated Koop.

The confrontation over testing brought Koop's and Bauer's philosophical differences into stark relief. Bauer was determined to take tougher measures to protect God-fearing America—the upright citizens like himself who had resisted the siren calls of the sexual revolution and dutifully raised families— from the legions of sexually (and morally) diseased. The goal of the White House hardliners, as one told the press, was "to make ourselves the champion of all the people who don't have the disease yet."

But Koop would not put his faith in this Maginot Line between the infected and uninfected. Like Bauer, he was a strong family man, but he had developed a wider conception of the American family. He might still think of gays and other sexual minorities as black sheep, but he refused to abandon them. "When I was a young surgeon in the emergency room and they brought in a wounded policeman and bank robber," he would tell us, "I didn't go over and say, 'I'll take care of the cop first because he's a cop.' I took care of the one that was in worse shape." Koop had come to see infected and uninfected, gay and straight, needle users and drug-free as all part of the same community when it came to critical matters of public health. It was a philosophy that was summed up by Albert Camus when he wrote, "The only means of fighting a plague is common decency."

Reagan was to finally announce the administration's policy on AIDS testing in a May 31 speech before the American Foundation for AIDS Research, a group chaired by his wife's old friend Elizabeth Taylor. Again, both sides fought to put their own words in the President's mouth. Again, it looked like Reagan was about to side with Bauer and the hardliners and call for mandatory testing. In the days leading up to the foundation dinner, there was intense negotiating over the precise wording of the President's speech. Koop would later call it "the most important week in the history of AIDS as far as government action is concerned."

On Wednesday, May 27, the Surgeon General was abruptly called back from Salt Lake City for a White House domestic policy council meeting where the final recommendation to the President was to be decided upon. "I came racing in from the airport, arriving at the southwest gate of the White House on two wheels at exactly 2 P.M., when the meeting was to begin," recalled Koop. Reagan was not present, but Bauer was, and so was his forceful ally, Education Secretary Bennett, who proceeded to argue strongly for the mandatory-testing approach, hammering away at his points like the big collegiate football tackle he once was. "When Bill Bennett talks, he's on the table, chest, shoulders, both elbows, and he's like the turkey in the middle," said Koop.

Otis Bowen, the aging, white-haired Secretary of Health and Human Services, was no match for Bennett, realized Koop, so it fell to the big-chested Surgeon General in the gleaming white-and-gold uniform to argue for restraint. Koop conceded the necessity of testing certain groups, like inmates of federal prisons, where the disease could be spread through forcible sodomy. But he continued to hang tough against nationwide testing. By the end of the meeting, it was still a stalemate, and the White House staff was ordered to review the opposing arguments and come up with a compromise position.

The wording was to be presented to Reagan at a Cabinet meeting the next day. Koop showed up, prepared to continue battle. "But when I picked up the agenda and looked immediately at item four," he said, "I couldn't believe my eyes. It said, 'The President urges the states to offer routine testing.' Well I know what 'routine' means and I know what 'offer' means and they don't mean mandatory. It was a great victory, not just for me but for the world."

Bauer, too, would claim victory. "I'm glad that Dr. Koop feels good about it," he tells us, "but the bottom line is that we're going to have more testing than we had before—federal prisoners, immigrants, and so on."

But Koop was convinced that he had stifled the administration's worst instincts. Three days later, under a steamy tent filled with Washington socialites, gay activists, and medical celebrities, President Reagan would call for "understanding, not ignorance . . . This is a battle against disease, not against our fellow Americans." It was a rare display of compassion, but for many of those in attendance, who had suffered much loss and anguish during the epidemic, it was too little, too late. As Reagan read that part of his speech calling for limited AIDS testing, he was met with a growing chorus of boos.

Dr. C. Everett Koop, on the other hand, was greeted with a standing ovation when Elizabeth Taylor presented him with a special award from the AIDS foundation. By then, Koop's former liberal adversaries on Capitol Hill were also hailing him as a hero. Henry Waxman, once "frightened" by Koop, now called him "a man of tremendous integrity. He's done everything a Surgeon General should do, and more, to protect the health of the public." Liberals marveled at Koop's transformation. He exemplified, in the judgment of Wahington *Post* columnist Colman McCarthy, "the growth-in-office theory of political appointments. The seemingly worst can turn out to be among the certifiably best."

But Chick Koop insisted he was the same man. Just as his deep religious belief in the sacredness of human life had impelled him to become one of the more zealous leaders of the antiabortion movement and had driven him to champion Baby Doe, so it now directed him to stand up for those whose lives were menaced by AIDS. Every life deserved protection, believed Koop, even those he felt had been badly led. No one was to be left behind. He would never give in to the forces of social triage.

In November 1987, Koop, long mute about his religious convictions out of fear of liberal criticism, felt bold enough to reveal the biblical foundations to his AIDS philosophy in a speech before the Union of American Hebrew Congregations in Chicago. Ironically, the physician had found inspiration in the same story from the Book of Genesis that made his fundamentalist critics burn with righteous conviction. "The Lord wants to destroy Sodom," Koop told the gathering of Jewish leaders in his rich Old Testament voice. "But Abraham argues that the Lord might have to save the lives of thousands of not very nice people in order to also save the lives of as few as ten righteous people . . . [In this] dialogue over the fate of Sodom, I think the Lord was hearing more than just bravado and 'chutzpah' from the newly named Abraham. I think he was hearing a new voice of awareness, of compassion, of human dignity. Call it what you will, but it was clearly a new voice of faith."

The AIDS crisis compelled America to "quickly act upon that powerful Abrahamic tradition of reverence in action." The tendency to blame, to scorn those who "either recklessly engaged in sodomy or swapped dirty needles while shooting dangerous drugs" had to be morally resisted, Koop continued. There were physicians and nurses who violated medical ethics by shunning AIDS patients, he said, and neighbors who had turned against neighbors. But this was unacceptable, he declared. "In this terrible and fearsome period, I maintain—as a physician, as a scientist, but also as a human being—that man *cannot be denied*. AIDS itself would have us do that. People who live in total fear of AIDS would have us do that. And people weakened by the despair of AIDS would have us do that. But we cannot."

Medicine was still no match for the death force of AIDS, Koop told the gathering. "We have no drugs, no vaccines, no magic bullets, nothing that can accomplish that lifesaving job." All we have, he stated, is a commitment to life, a reverence for our fellow human beings. "If mankind is now the victim of a hideous mystery, we cannot give up on him . . . we cannot abandon him for that reason. Rather, as Martin Buber [has] argued, we must affirm his life and his condition. We must 'liberate him from the dread of abandonment' —the *dread* of abandonment—'which is the foretaste of death.' "

Laced with his fundamentalist values, Koop's speech was nonetheless a moving rejoinder to the forces of conservative moralism. "Yes, I thought it was remarkable too," he would tell us with characteristic modesty.

During the final months of the Reagan presidency, it was the judgmental view of the AIDS tragedy advanced by Bauer's hardline faction that would continue to dominate administration policy. Bauer succeeded in stacking Reagan's national AIDS commission with like-minded conservatives, including a San Diego sex therapist who said AIDS could be caught from a toilet seat and an Illinois state legislator who accused gays of engaging in "blood terrorism" by deliberately donating infected blood. But the commission, under the leadership of retired admiral James Watkins, stunned the White House with its final report, which called among other things for new federal initiatives to prevent discrimination against AIDS patients and coordination of the government's disparate anti-AIDS efforts under the command of the Surgeon General. Administration officials decided to accept the report "without fanfare," ignoring its bold recommendations and continuing the policy of benign neglect to the end.

In contrast, Surgeon General Koop continued to use his bully pulpit to promote compassion and condoms, offsetting the doctrinaire tendencies of the administration and fighting against "the dread of abandonment." He spoke out against panicky state initiatives that mandated AIDS testing and that required infected persons to be reported to health authorities. He pushed for more AIDS education aimed at teenagers and drug users. He demanded a halt to the practice of barring students and teachers with AIDS from classrooms.

Koop knew Bauer could not shut him up; his success with the media protected him from White House retribution. The hardliners continued to win the political battles. But, in a sense, Koop had won the larger war. Through his forthright AIDS report and candid public statements, he had changed the national dialogue on sex. The country's top physician had repeatedly used the taboo word "condom"—a word with disturbingly graphic associations for many Americans—and thereby legitimated its entry into the public arena.

It was an American tale that could only have taken place in these strange days of death and desire. The square-jawed Surgeon General with the old-fashioned chin beard and Old Testament zeal had pushed the country one step further along its rocky path toward sexual enlightenment.

She stared directly into our eyes, this young blond woman with the delicate cheekbones, and we knew what she was about to say was serious. Her gaze was unblinking, her lips were unsmiling. "I enjoy sex," she confided, "but I'm not ready to die for it." Just like that.

She went on to say that the Surgeon General recommended condoms as the best protection against AIDS for those who were sexually active. That's why she insisted that her partners wear LifeStyles condoms.

With these words, Kirsten Frantzich Allen, a twenty-five-year-old actress-model from Wayzata, Minnesota, broke the American media barrier against condom advertising. During the early months of 1987, Kirsten's pretty face, a face that projected innocence but not naivete, suddenly seemed everywhere—in magazines, on local TV, on drugstore posters. Only the television networks resisted airing her earnest message, still fearful of offending religious groups and other moral watchdogs. Kirsten was to become the nation's safe-sex pinup girl. She spoke for all those emancipated young women who had come of age as the plague came creeping into nightclub conversation. They had reveled in their sexual freedom, in their ability to date and drop men as they pleased, but now they were getting scared to death of bringing home the wrong man.

American culture had long resisted the public display of prophylactics. As Leslie Savan observed in The Village Voice, "It's not just the inevitable endorsement of nonprocreative sex that makes TV execs reluctant to run condom ads. It's the actual object: More than anything else on the tube, condoms evoke the image of a penis." Even after the three major TV networks finally lifted their ban on condom advertising in the late 1980s, many TV stations remained reluctant to use the C-word. Federal officials went to absurd lengths in their 1988 condom ad campaign to avoid upsetting the more prissy TV viewers, with one spot featuring a young man slipping a sock on his foot and telling the audience, "That wouldn't really save my life, but there's something as simple that could." Get it?

Still, under the impact of mounting AIDS casualties and the Surgeon General's propaganda campaign, this excessive public modesty began to break down. Hotels started placing complimentary condoms in their rooms, along with Gideon Bibles. Colleges installed condom machines in campus dormitories and sponsored condom-awareness weeks. (Harvard public health students took this vigilance too far for many parents' and alumni's taste when they air-dropped packets of rubbers onto the university's 1987 commencement ceremonies.) A Seattle confectionery began marketing chocolate condom mints. A Unitarian minister in Amherst, New York, distributed three-packs of Trojans to his congregation. Perhaps most astonishing, Catholic bishops decided that while it was still impermissible for Catholics to use condoms, it was appropriate to teach—even in Catholic schools—that condoms help prevent the spread of AIDS.

Inevitably, this condom mania produced a backlash. Conservative students and professors at Dartmouth and Stanford issued loud protests when their university health departments launched safe-sex campaigns. So did the International Banana Association when its favorite fruit was used to demonstrate how to put on condoms in a PBS special hosted by Ron Reagan, Jr. ("The banana is an important product and deserves to be treated with respect and consideration," complained the bruised president of the association.) And the tranquil resort town of Traverse City, Michigan, turned into a battleground, with citizens squaring off angrily against one another, when the city commission granted a local businessman the right to stock his vending machines with rubbers.

But America's public morality was changing. Men and women, often mere acquaintances, were having the kinds of explicit conversations that were once heard only in sex parlors and on the juicier segments of "Donahue." In the shadow of death, it was now possible to talk freely about life's most compelling force. It had the smell of the morgue, this new sex talk. But there was still something exhilarating about the candor.

The story of Kirsten Frantzich Allen, America's first condom pinup girl, is in some ways the story of the country's changing sexual consciousness. How did a fresh-faced young woman from a devout Christian family in Minnesota become the first person to hawk rubbers in the national media? It's one more revealing tale from the plague years.

She was hard to locate. We left messages with Ansell, Inc., the maker of LifeStyles condoms; we left word with her New York agency. Weeks went by without a response. Ansell officials told us it had been very difficult to find an actress for their ad campaign. Half of the young women they had considered for the role had turned them down; the campaign was just too graphic, too embarrassing. They worried about the potential impact on their career. Maybe Kirsten was beginning to feel the same way; maybe she wanted to forget the whole thing.

But when she finally returned our call, apologizing that she had been traveling, Kirsten told her story without any hesitation. The young woman who had sold her image to the latex trade turned out to be someone who had thought it seriously through, someone who had pondered sex and death in America and decided she would be providing a public service. Before the ads appeared, she did feel a moment of panic. "You suddenly realize, 'Hey, this is not like doing a candy bar ad.'" Yet these doubts disappeared when four people she knew in the New York entertainment world died of AIDS within days of one another.

It was the man who worked as the dresser for her husband, a featured performer in the Broadway musical *Big River,* who made the biggest impact on Kirsten. "We went to see him in the hospital. My husband was very close to him. He looked up at me and said, 'Kirsten, I know that commercial must have been very hard for you to make, but I want you to know that you have my thanks, you have all of our thanks.' And he grabbed my arms and started sobbing. That was the turning point. After that, I just felt, 'Forget all the moral baloney. You have to do something.'"

Kirsten had met her husband, Clint, in acting class at the Juilliard School. Like her, he hailed from the heartland, a small town in Indiana, and he had her same wholesome good looks. He played Tom Sawyer in *Big River,* and the part fit him like an old fishing cap. Their courtship, according to Clint, was a "cat-and-mouse affair: we batted each other around for a while. Kirsten was doing her Laura Ashley good-girl act." That was her image at Juilliard. When she played a hooker in acting class one day, the other students couldn't stop laughing. It was just too out of character. "But once I opened the door to her heart," recalls Clint, *"wham!"* He smacks the flat of his hand against his thigh like a crashing cymbal.

Kirsten is slighter, even more delicate-boned in person. She has pale blue eyes as clear as a Minnesota lake and a boyish, Peter Pan haircut. Minnesotans tend to have placid exteriors, she tells us, "but once you get them behind closed doors, watch out." *Wham!* "Technically speaking," Clint interjects, "Kirsten was a virgin when we got married, unlike me, but she was a lot more experienced."

But it was not the "experienced" woman in Kirsten that drew the attention of Ansell. The condom manufacturer was looking for "the girl next door" for its LifeStyles campaign, says Kirsten. "They wanted to convey the message that AIDS could strike anybody." Condom advertising in the United States strains to be unsexy. It's fear these commercials sell, not fun. In other countries, condom makers are not afraid to be a little naughty. The Australian ad for Lifestyles showed a woman getting ready for a date as a cheerful voiceover said, "If you want peace of mind as well as pleasure, choose LifeStyles condoms." But when Kirsten pitched Lifestyles to the American public, the message had to be all gloom and doom: "With everything I hear about AIDS these days, I'm more than uncomfortable. I'm afraid."

When preparing its commercial for the American market, Ansell, the biggest manufacturer of condoms in the United States, was too timid to even use the word "sex." The original script given to Kirsten read, "I'll do a lot for love, but I'm not ready to die for it." Kirsten objected. There were many people she respected who had died for love. "I mean, look at Martin Luther King or anybody who has died for a cause." She told the director, "Look, we've misused this word 'love' enough. What you're really talking about here is, 'I want to get laid, but I don't want to end up in a grave'—so why not say that." To Kirsten's delight, the wording was changed to "I enjoy sex . . ." But when the ad later appeared in *Time* and *Newsweek,* it was back to "love." Some magazines felt their readers could just not tolerate an earnest young woman telling them in bold type that she relished sex.

Indeed, there were readers who were jolted when they first saw the ad. Saundra Frantzich, Kirsten's mother, was one of them. She shuddered when she opened her Minneapolis *Star* one morning and saw her daughter's sweet face reproduced in a news article about the controversy that had been ignited by the condom ad. "I didn't give a rip about what the neighbors thought or anything like that," says Mrs. Frantzich. "I was concerned about her integrity and credibility. A lot of younger girls in our community look up to Kirsten because of the field she's in."

Saundra Frantzich is a sturdy, handsome forty-nine-year-old woman of Norwegian stock. She wears her blond hair pulled straight back in a no-nonsense bun. Her eyes are wise. She and her husband, Bill, an oral surgeon, tried to instill a strong moral compass in Kirsten and their three younger children. Each Sunday the Frantzichs worshiped at the nearby Evangelical Covenant Church, a religious sect with Swedish roots. "My kids know that I'm not some uninformed conservative Christian. I'm not a stuffy and rigid person." But she believes that people should try to lead their lives according to the Scriptures. And she had serious misgivings about the LifeStyles ad.

"I thought the line 'I enjoy sex' and so on was sort of stupid. It was not an admirable quote. It indicates the promiscuity of the society we live in. Twenty-five years ago you would never have seen something like that. I preferred the ad with 'love' in it, because at least it indicated a strong relationship."

Mrs. Frantzich thinks American society does not practice enough "self-control. Without that, people are just led around by their gonads." The sex drive is a howling force, she says. "Why we've had neutered dogs who've gone charging out of the house looking for it in thirty-below snowstorms."

This evening, however, it is sticky and hot outside. Kirsten has invited us to her family's home, forty-five minutes outside of Minneapolis on Lake Minnetonka, which she and her husband are visiting for the summer. Through the living room window of the two-story white clapboard house, you can see powerboats skimming across the lake. On a nearby pier, golden Nordic boys and girls dangle their legs in the water. Prince, the decadent musical monarch, resides in purple splendor not far away on the lake. Minnesota blizzards probably do not stop him either when he gets the urge.

Later, we drift next door to the Reeds' house, where friends and family are gathering to see Kirsten and talk about her controversial ad. The coffee table in the living room is spread with plates of smoked cheese, ham, grapes, and crunchy Norwegian crackers. Propped up on the piano is a hymnal and the sheet music for *Godspell*. The Frantzichs live in a tightly knit cul-de-sac, a neighborhood bound together by a shared commitment to family and religion. If her neighbors harbor Mrs. Frantzich's concerns about the ad, they are keeping it to themselves. The Reeds have even stuck a copy of the LifeStyles pitch on their refrigerator door. "We were a little surprised at first," Stephan Roufs, an old high school friend of Kirsten's, tells her. "But we're proud of you. It's an important message, and we know you didn't do it for the money."

The conversation is now all AIDS. There are words of praise for the Surgeon General's compassion and condoms campaign. There is sympathy for victims of the disease. Bill Frantzich has operated on two people with AIDS. AIDS talk is now spoken even in idyllic villages like Wayzata. But this gathering of hospitable Minnesotans still thinks of those infected or most threatened by the virus as the *other*.

David Reed, a forty-six-year-old research scientist, says he stopped going to the haircutting salon on the corner run by a gay couple "when AIDS came along. Not because I was afraid of casual contact—I know better. But because this lifestyle is . . . disreputable." He adds a little sheepishly, "Scientists aren't any more rational when it comes to this stuff." And Mrs. Frantzich, who works part-time as a school nurse, confides that while she can imagine taking care of AIDS patients, she cannot help but think "homosexuality is a serious threat to our society. I wonder if the reason this disease is so lethal and mysterious is because God is unhappy with homosexuals."

There is an underlying feeling here that New York and San Francisco are moral cesspools that are threatening to contaminate the rest of the nation. Kirsten won't go entirely along with this New York–bashing. Manhattan, with its license, its raucous diversity, has been too liberating for her. "You're not judged there; I can be myself. There's not enough passion here. I feel a little stagnant." But she does concede that sex has been stripped of its "sacredness" in the frenetic New York nightlife. "People have slowed down there, but they're still promiscuous. I know people in the acting world who still sleep with dozens and dozens of people a year. That's a problem of the soul."

The gathering bursts into laughter when we tell of the coastal expeditions into the uncharted territory of safe sex: the latex devices, the J/O parties, the experiments in voyeurism. They're embarrassed, they're titillated, they're amazed. They listen as if hearing exotic tales of bare-breasted jungle savages. No, that's not for them, they quickly agree. The consensus here is that the only truly safe sexual union is a faithful marriage.

Mrs. Frantzich sets the moral tone. "Condoms are not the answer to this disease," she says emphatically. She has joined the gathering late because she knows that with her strong convictions and her voice of maternal authority she can dominate conversations like this. But now she has heard enough of sexual confusion and kinkiness. She speaks as if hers is the final word.

"Sex has a soul, and when two souls come together, that's when you have the ultimate experience. As a woman, you have to be stupid to jump into bed time and time again with men. Like Elvis Presley said when I was growing up, 'Why buy the cow when you can have all the milk you can drink for free?' My husband and I waited until our wedding night. That was the icing on the cake."

There are murmurs of approval around the living room. But not everyone is comfortable with the way the conversation is going. "I can't relate to this," pipes up Stephanie, a lean thirty-four-year-old woman with a head of tight blond curls. She is a friend of the Frantzich family; Mrs. Frantzich thinks of her as a daughter. "It just isn't feasible for a single person in her thirties never to have sex." Stephanie, who works for a Minneapolis insurance company, says she is very alert to the threat of AIDS. She has no qualms about bringing up the subject of condoms when a relationship becomes serious. Stephanie is the woman at whom Ansell was aiming its pitch when it hired her friend Kirsten.

The dozen or so men and women assembled here, who vary in age from their late teens to their late forties, are remarkably confessional. Tim Frantzich, Kirsten's twenty-four-year-old brother, is suddenly struck by the revelatory nature of the evening. "Sex seems more public now: it's in everyone's living room." But *he* is not telling all, at least not in front of the group.

Later, as the gathering breaks up, Tim's twenty-three-year-old girlfriend, Carrie, plops herself down next to us on the couch. She's a little nervous; there's something else she wants to confide. "Tim and I have been going out for almost nine months," begins Carrie. A pretty, olive-skinned woman with brown eyes and hair as black and silky as an Indian's, she makes a particularly striking impression in this Scandinavian sea of blondness. "But we still have not, uh, slept together. Tim feels strongly about not having intercourse before marriage. It was hard for me to shift gears. It can be kind of frustrating: I'd been sexually active before with other boyfriends. My friends can't believe it when I tell them."

Moments later, Tim joins us. It's easy to understand Carrie's frustration. Her boyfriend is heart-wrenchingly handsome. He's tall and has long, wavy brown hair and a swimmer's chest and arms, which are now encased in a tight, navy-blue Nike T-shirt. His shy and thoughtful manner makes him all the more engaging. "We kiss and do everything but . . ." Tim's voice trails off. He's embarrassed talking about this, but it's something he believes in deeply. His decision has nothing to do with AIDS, insists Tim. It was prompted not by a fear of sex but a reverence for it. "I've always felt that if you waited until your wedding night, there would be nothing like it. It would be something spiritual."

It's a different type of safe sex Tim is practicing. What he's trying to protect himself from is cultural contamination, the belief that sex is primarily recreational. "I've been raised a certain way. And it would be very hard to detach myself from that without feeling guilty. If Carrie and I were to sleep together, the sex would not be completely free."

The following night, the Frantzich clan and their friends all troop off to hear Tim and his younger brother, Paul, play with their rock band at the Uptown Bar and Grill in Minneapolis. Proud Mr. Frantzich brings along a video camera to record the event. Over the last couple of years, A Few, as the band is called, has penned some punchy original tunes and has built a local following. They have opened for the Replacements, the city's fabled rockers whose raunchy, hard-drinking ways gave Mrs. Frantzich pause. Prince has dropped by to catch their act.

While waiting for the band, we fall into conversation with Carrie. "I respect Tim's decision, I really do," she says over drinks at a table near the back of the club. "This is the most serious, meaningful relationship of my life. But, yeah, it can get really hard . . ." She pushes around the ice in her drink with a finger. Sex without intercourse can be the safest and most tantalizing kind of erotic play. As Tim noted, there is something ecstatic about the excruciating wait. But to what extent can lovers merge without sinking deeply and exquisitely into one another's flesh?

Suddenly Carrie looks up: the band has taken the stage. The spotlight hits Tim as the lean young man rips into a power chord. "I want to get *closer!*" shouts Carrie above the crashing music and she dashes toward the stage.

It's another quiet evening at home for your coauthor, the man from Hollywood. I'm watching Janet Taylor make love with a twenty-five-year-old stranger named "Randy"* on my living room couch. Randy, who says he lives in Dallas, is nervous and inexperienced, but Janet is rolling her hips and moaning like she's never had it so good.

"Why don't you put your hand under my butt," she coaxes.

"It's so nice and hard," says Randy sweetly.

"Yeah, I work out a lot. Now why don't you start rubbing my thighs and licking me."

"It smells good," sighs Randy, his senses fully alive to the moment.

---

* Certain names in this section have been changed.

"Oh, yeah, keep licking me, Randy, oh yeah, oh yeah, awwwww. I don't know what you're doing, but don't stop."

"You're going to make me come big tonight." Randy's excitement is palpable. He has not had sex with anyone for over three months, the young man confessed earlier to Janet.

"You better believe it, I'm going to make you come *real* good," she says in a voice thick with lust.

This is Janet Taylor's fifth man tonight, and she's still going strong. It seems that I'm constantly spying this woman in compromising positions. When last spotted, Janet was spread-eagled on the leather-topped torture table at the Jack-and-Jill-Off party, being groped by a circle of admirers. Now she is sprawling on my couch, her long dark hair strewn over the cushions and her pink velour dress wiggled way up her thighs. As she breathes huskily into Randy's ear, she shoots me a fetching smile.

"Do you really like this too?" asks Randy touchingly. He may not be a sophisticated lover, but he is a considerate one.

"Of course, I do. OK, now I'm going to sit on you, Randy. I'm going to ease my cunt down real slow on your dick, and then I'm going to pull up again. Because I don't want you to come just yet, I'm going to put you through the fucking ropes." Janet is the salacious tutor, teaching her young pupil the ways of Eros.

"OK, I'm going to sit on you good now, oh yeah, I'm going to tighten my cunt right around you. You feel that? I got my cunt clamping down tight."

"Ohhh," moans Randy. His breathing grows louder and louder.

"You're real close, aren't you?"

"I'm real close," sighs Randy.

"Well, now I've got my hand on your balls, honey. And when you start to come, I'm going to squeeze them real gently. Do you feel that, Randy? I'm squeezing your balls. I'm not hurting you, am I? Now I'm digging in my high heels and I'm just eating up that fucking hard dick of yours . . . yeah . . . yeah . . ."

"Ohhhhhhhhhh!" Randy explodes with months of bottled-up longing. His breath is wrenched from him like sobs.

"That's it, baby, shoot it inside me, shoot it all the way inside me . . ."

"Oh, oh . . ." It takes a minute for Randy to come back. When he does, he's even sweeter than before. "That was good . . ."

"Thank you, Randy."

"I need it in real life now . . ."

Janet's eyes fill suddenly with motherly sadness. She often must make this emotional transition from cock-mistress to comforter.

"Well, OK, how do you find it in real life?"

"I don't know."

"Well, goddamn, if you can call me up and ask for it, you can figure out how to get it. There are lots of women just as horny as me. You just go up and start talking to them real nice and slow. Look it, honey, when you're hungry and needing it, any woman can tell. Now, look, you have a wonderful evening."

"Alright, well, thank you for talking with me. I appreciate it. Goodbye." And Randy hangs up.

Phone sex is the safest sex of all. Partners exchange nothing but sighs and whispers, and even those are relayed by satellite. In today's forbidding viral and social climate, it is perhaps the only realm of complete sexual freedom. Men and women engage in flights of sexual fantasy that, if acted out in "real life," in Randy's words, could ravage their bodies with disease or subject them to hard stretches of prison time.

The women who work the nation's phone-sex lines have heard it all: men who want to be spanked by sadistic schoolteachers until their bottoms are raw (and then want to have cold cream rubbed on their burning fannies by kindhearted school nurses), men who want dirty underwear stuffed in their mouths, men who want rolls of adhesive tape wrapped around their hairy balls and then ripped viciously off, men who want to be pissed on, men who want to lick little girls, men who want to fuck heifers after snorting bulls have been into them, men who want to pierce women's nipples, men who just want a good, old-fashioned blow job. Then there are the occasional women customers (who, goes the joke in the trade, you pray have good vibrators or else you're in for a long call), and couples on extension lines seeking to liven up their sex lives.

"You learn a lot about America's fantasy life on this job," says Janet, who works for two national phone-sex services. She's reclining on my couch, her bare legs gathered underneath her, waiting for the next call. She is an attractive forty-year-old woman with the high cheekbones of a former model. "It seems that the number-one fantasy of the American male is to be sexually dominated. Guys are brought up to always be in charge, but what they really want is a strong woman. 'Goddamn it, get your fly down and give it to me!' " She laughs at the leather-strap sound of her voice.

"Some callers, particularly the ones experienced at S&M, can say exactly what they want," continues Janet. "They have a precise list of ten things they want you to incorporate in their fantasy—and you sure as hell better do them or they get very upset. But others are more shy, and you have to feel out what they want, what their triggers are.

"We're half-baked actors: you have to use your voice in just the right ways. You try to create a hypnotic trance. You get them on the edge, keep them on the edge, building, building, then push them at just the right moment."

When she's not performing, Janet tends to have a timid disposition. She swallows her words and covers her mouth when she laughs, like a teenage girl embarrassed by her braces. "If a guy approached me on the street, I wouldn't know what to do. But on the phone, I'm a different person. It's great to hear these men hanging on your words, treasuring the experience. I can be anyone I want to. The guys don't know how old I am or what I look like. I'll probably still be doing this when I'm sixty. I love all the different roles I play. I can really *feel* being on that ranch in Wyoming, getting thrown in the hay by a sweaty, muscular cowboy. I can *feel* that hay. I lose myself, my self-consciousness on the phone."

As phone sex grew during the 1980s into what telephone consultants estimated to be a $300 million industry (excluding services that bill through credit cards), with everyone from pornography tycoons to enterprising house-wives crowding the field, it drew increasing fire. The Reagan administration's efforts to disconnect the phone-sex business proved unsuccessful. But as a result of the growing controversy, Mountain Bell banned "aural sex" services from its 976 dial-a-message network. Other phone companies were sued by angry parents who charged that the sex lines were corrupting their children. Critics pointed out that the 976 lines featuring recorded messages instead of live performers had no way of screening impressionable young callers. Some state utility commissions tried to remedy this problem by passing rules that enabled telephone customers to block 976 calls from their homes. But the legal pressure on phone-sex merchants continued to mount.

Janet Taylor acknowledges that children can abuse tape-recorded sex messages. But she believes the live calls she engages in can have therapeutic value.

"Phone sex gives you access to guys in pain and trouble you would normally never reach," says Janet, who also works as a sex therapist. It's a hotline, she believes, to the dark soul of American men. Some aural sex performers will suffer through the most sadistic and scatological fantasies imaginable without complaint. "If the guy is mad at his wife and wants to beat some woman to a pulp, better he do it to me over the phone than to a woman on the street," says Janet's friend Jackie. But Janet says, "I can't let something like that go on. I'll say, 'Hey, man, you're hurting. What's going on?' "

Janet is always primed to switch to a therapeutic role, trying to guide those fantasies she regards as too twisted in more wholesome directions. "If men are into fucking little girls, I have to be careful not to promote that kind of thinking. I talk to them and tell them I can't play along with that. I'll say, 'How else can we work this for you? What if I'm really eighteen, but I look fourteen?' "

Janet's entire adult life has been devoted to the arts of sexual healing and pleasure. She has starred in explicit sex education videotapes. She has run workshops on safe-sex techniques. She has counseled groups of transvestites and transsexuuals. And she has worked with a wide range of sexually disabled men, taking cases others have refused, including a Chicago man with forty personalities. "That was the roughest one. There were times during a session when he would suddenly turn into a scared ten-year-old boy, locking himself in the bathroom and whimpering."

She is a Florence Nightingale in black lace. As a girl, growing up near Windsor, Canada, Janet took care of her mentally retarded sister and worked in a nursing home run by her grandmother. As a woman, she has found a way to wed her caretaking instincts with her equally strong sexual drive.

Janet's line of sex work is not terribly lucrative. She lives in a low-rent apartment building in San Francisco's hard-luck Tenderloin district. She dresses in clothes that were stylish in the swinging sixties and seventies. Some phone-sex entrepreneurs, such as Gloria Leonard, publisher of *High Society* magazine, have reportedly made fortunes off the 976 lines. But not the women who work the phones. Janet's employers pocket $20 of the $25 they charge for a fifteen-minute phone call.

Aural sex is in some ways a labor of love for Janet. Sometimes she will draw her lovers—a varied lot, in recent years, including men, women, and trans-sexuals—into her performances. "My lover may start licking me in the middle of a call, and I'll tell the guy what she's doing. Or a couple of male friends of mine will be over at my place and we all play roles. Those callers get more than their money's worth," she says with a mischievous smile.

We have turned the lights down low in my living room to create a more intimate mood for Janet's phone performances. A certain tension has crept into the room. I'm sitting cross-legged on the floor, studiously taking notes. We're both avoiding looking too long into each other's eyes as we talk. The jarring ring of the phone comes as a relief. The customer's name, ironically, is David. This time, Janet is completely transformed. She's on her knees on the couch, rocking back and forth, her skirt working itself higher up her thighs, her mouth screwed to the phone receiver. She speaks as if entranced, her voice is that of another woman. "Ooooh, David, that's it, I can tell you're ready . . . give it to me now, and make some noise." Our eyes meet.

It happens during the next call. This one's name is "Fred" and he wants Janet to play "kinky nurse" with him. He also wants to know if she's "got a doctor friend there too?" Janet has a glint in her eye. "Why, yes, Fred, I do happen to have a doctor friend here tonight, and I bet he wouldn't mind getting on the phone too. He's my . . . uh . . . lover." We both blush.

Fred, who says he's calling from Colorado, has a take-charge kind of voice. He sounds like the kind of man who is used to giving orders. But in no time flat, Janet has him on all fours in his hospital bed, propped up on both elbows, his gown shoved high up his back to reveal his hard melon of a butt. "Ooh, I just love to feel a firm ass," says Nurse Taylor lustily, as she proceeds to subject Fred to a rectal examination. "OK, I'm just going to slip on a latex glove and grease my fingers with a nonoxynol-9 lubricant," she continues, ever the safe-sex educator. "You're gorgeous. I'm getting pretty hot doing this, even though it's not very professional. I'm just sliding my fingers in real slow, back and forth. Does that feel good now? Just easing it back and forth, while you're stroking your cock. How does your cock feel?"

"Oooh, real hard." Fred is a model patient.

"OK, now keep stroking it, but if Dr. Talbot walks in, whatever you do, don't scream out, baby, because I could get in a lot of trouble for this. He's making his rounds now, and he could come in any second . . . Oh God, Fred, I hate to tell you this, but he's at the goddamn door right now!"

It's my cue. With practically no warning, I'm about to make my debut as a phone-sex performer. As I crawl quickly toward the couch, I suffer a spasm of stage fright. Just what am I supposed to say to keep Fred's fantasy going? But there's no time to worry. The show must go on.

"Nurse Taylor! What kind of medical procedure is this?" I boom out theatrically. "Are you sure that you're qualified to carry it out?" Show business is in my blood. Janet is straining not to burst out laughing.

"Well, what about it, Fred. Do you think I'm qualified? I think you better consult with the doctor."

Janet thrusts the phone at me, and suddenly I'm in dialogue with a man thousands of miles away, caught in the throes of a feverish fantasy. "Hi, Fred, this is Dr. Talbot. I'm just double-checking to make sure you're not in too much pain. At this hospital, we want all our patients to feel very good."

"What are you, uh, going to do with me?" I've never heard a man's voice this yielding, this expectant. It's slightly unnerving. What *am* I going to do with him?

"Well, I'm going to be watching to make sure the procedure goes correctly."

"Aren't you going to be checking me out?"

"Well, I think you're in very experienced hands with Nurse Taylor. So I'm just going to be supervising." The voice of medical propriety, of professional detachment. Wise not to go any deeper into Fred's fantasy, I'm thinking.

Janet can't contain herself any longer. "It sounds like the nurse is giggling," says Fred. "What is she doing?" I quickly relinquish the phone.

"Hi, Fred," she says, right back in character. "As you can see, I'm doing pretty good right now. I have my little white nurse's uniform up around my waist. And I have a black garter belt and stockings underneath. And, in fact, the doctor is spreading the cheeks of my ass as I bend over to suck your cock. Oh God, Dr. Talbot is keeping me awfully busy here, goddamn . . ."

Our faces are bent together over the phone, like Jimmy Stewart and Donna Reed in *It's a Wonderful Life*. I can feel each breathy whisper on my cheek. "I think you better work on yourself for a while, Fred. This is just too hot for me to give up right now. Uhhh, yeah, ummmm, yeah." Only our knees are touching as Janet and I huddle over the receiver. We are still maintaining a certain decorum. But as Dr. Talbot, I have abandoned all protocol and have slipped deeply and satisfyingly into Nurse Taylor from behind.

Fred suddenly shakes us from our dreamy union. "Would you let him fuck me?" he says in a clotted voice.

Gulp. I look to Janet for help, but she just shrugs. There's no backing out now. Fred is directing this fantasy and he knows exactly what he wants. Like most heterosexual men I know, I have been carried off from time to time by homosexual reveries. But I have never acted on these fleeting desires. The dawning of the AIDS era made it even less likely that I would do so. But now a horny stranger is demanding that I plunge inside him. We are only disembodied voices to one another, but it still gets under my skin. His desire is disturbing, it's stimulating. I'm about to cross into foreign sexual territory.

"What are you doing now?" Fred asks, urging me along. I can practically *feel* how hard he is.

"Well, uh, I'm going to take your temperature, Fred, and, uh, you know how we do that," I say, struggling to keep it in the medical realm. "I have a very sensitive thermometer here." Janet's eyes are dancing with delight. She is charged by watching me get further entangled in this fantasy. We smile weirdly at one another as I slide my instrument between Fred's greased cheeks.

"How does that feel, Fred? I'm sliding it in all the way now, just the way you like it. I'm going to see how high your temperature can go."

I'm beginning to get into this. It's just the way Janet has described it, a heady sense of power. Finding a man's sensory buttons and pushing and pushing until . . . I want to hear Fred groan as I pump his ear full of burning words, I want to make him burst. But, suddenly, as his breath comes quicker and quicker, he blurts, "Why don't you put the nurse back on?" I feel an odd stab of rejection. I've marched him to the pinnacle. But he wants her voice to make him leap.

Janet swiftly finishes it all off. "That's it, Fred, now give it to me. You've got that thermometer up your ass, oh yeah, and I'm rubbing your balls. You're both going to shoot all over my tits. Oh goddamn, Fred, yeah, I can't hold on, I'm going to come. Oh, ohh, ohhhh, Fredddddd." And we all collapse like winded runners across the finish line.

Afterward, Fred acts a bit ashamed. "Well, that was a little kinky," he tells Janet. His take-charge voice has returned. "I may change it next time."

"Maybe you want two nurses next time," she laughs.

"Maybe . . . I think so."

Dr. Talbot has been used and discarded.

But that's the way it is in this world of make-believe sex, once the shameful scenario has been played out. Phone sex *is* the safest sex, emotionally as well as medically. There's something sterile in the utter anonymity of it all, in the quick, efficient disposal of these dreams.

Safe sex was invented out of medical necessity. But it took on a larger symbolism. It is the perfect form of intercourse for an era of sexual estrangement, when men and women often regard each other with the mutual suspicion of superpower arms negotiators. Safe sex leaves no lingering marks, no sticky thighs, no musty scent. And, too often, no feeling.

But if safe sex conjures up the antiseptic image of a laboratory, it can also evoke the spirit of free inquiry and experimentation. The search for alternatives to piston sex can be a liberating experience, as Julia Kristeva observed in the Paris newspaper *Liberation:* "There is the possibility of discovering new erogenous zones, the arousal of tenderness, and (at last!) the erotic use of speech. Could the threat of AIDS be the harbinger of a new libertine practice, one less performative but more diverting, more narcissistically perverse?"

Public figures like C. Everett Koop and Kirsten Frantzich Allen, the condom pinup girl, helped free the nation's tongue. Sexual pioneers like Buzz Bense and Janet Taylor helped free its imagination. In doing this, they sparked a new wave of sexual innovation. It was not as carefree as the sexual revolution of the 1960s and 1970s, and it was not as widespread. But in private chambers across the land, adventurous Americans were demonstrating just how creative they could be under duress.

Home Fires Burning

HE
twenty couples scattered around the lecture room at the Virginia Mason
Medical Center cannot take their eyes off Penny Simkin, Seattle's legendary
birth coach and the coauthor of the classic *Pregnancy, Childbirth, and the
Newborn*. At the front of the class, Simkin, a pleasant brown-haired grandmother with four children ages twenty-two, twenty-three, twenty-five, and
twenty-seven, is down on her hands and knees. A plastic doll is wedged
between her thighs. She moans low and in pain like a woman about to give
birth. Then, running a hand along her belly, she assumes a deeper voice:
"Come on, baby, come on!" This is the voice of the prospective birth partner
—in this room, all men, except for one lesbian who is half of the only couple
expecting twins. "OK, OK," Simkin returns to the voice of the mother,
sucking deep belabored breaths, "thank you, partner."

In a few weeks the moans and encouragements will be live and unsimu-
lated. The mommies will scream with real pain and the nervous, proud,
loving, and very serious daddies will be standing scrubbed and scared beside
the obstetrician in a hospital room upstairs, something that would have been
unthinkable to all but a handful of their own fathers.

At an earlier class, recalls Simkin, a prospective father stood up and said that giving birth was a new and creative way to make love, that the birth process had elements of a sexual experience. Simkin thought about this and decided the young man was right. After all, birth begins with conception, a sexual moment, and a woman in labor loses touch with her surroundings much like a woman in intercourse. Ideally, a loving partner is present both times. "For many women," says Simkin, "birth is like orgasm. Pain and pleasure are almost indistinguishable." So she began to show the class a series of slides called "Joyous Beginnings." In one, the woman is straining, the man cradling her in his arms, kissing her moist face. "This generation, with its freer and more experienced past, is better equipped to handle the sexual challenge of pregnancy," states Simkin.

It is now the couples' turn to simulate contractions like Coach Penny. The women in their maternity silks and pastel sweats hunker down on hands and knees on the carpeted floor. Their partners in black jeans and aerobics shoes, and a few in sport coats, kneel beside them.

"Pelvises out," instructs Simkin, standing. *"Whooh! Whooh! Whooh!* Breathe. Blow it away. The contraction is gone now. Blow it away."

A beautiful young doctor rests her head on a chair while her husband, a software executive, begins to massage her back. All around them, pregnant— very pregnant—women are being caressed and massaged by their husbands or partners. The room looks like a beach full of sea turtles straining to give birth.

Later, Simkin demonstrates how fathers can insert a thumb inside their pregnant partners to massage the perineum, which lies between the vagina and the anus. Massaging the perineum makes it more elastic and should lessen birth pain and tearing, lowering the need for an episiotomy. "Of course," explains the down-to-earth Simkin, a tulip fancier on weekends, "your hands must be clean. Trim those nails and no hangnails. That would scratch and be uncomfortable."

"Last week it was like a live sex show," the pregnant doctor tells us after class, as the expectant mothers waddle slowly toward the door, arms tight around husbands and lovers. "Penny got down on the floor with an artificial vagina." She laughs. "It was wonderful."

For the new young families of America's baby-boom generation, sexuality is changing in many ways.

Most couples no longer shut off intimacy in the months and weeks before birth. In the 1970s, nearly all medical authorities concurred that intercourse would not harm the fetus in most cases, and this was happy news to women who had grown much more accustomed to initiating than their mothers had, as well as to men used to the greater frequency of their bachelor days.

But this generation, "while freer in emotion," as University of Washington sociologist Pepper Schwartz will tell us, "is more sparse in time." The shrinking ability of the modern economy to support a family with one paycheck and the simultaneous entry of women into the workplace has made the home a harried place and coordinating parallel lives a new American obsession.

Then there is the age-old problem of how to keep the home fires burning under the constant threat of kiddie interruption. But the new generation seems to be facing this conundrum with gusto. Sex with baby around is becoming less a Freudian taboo and more a Polynesian reality. This has led to extreme controversy in an era of forming and reforming families, of live-in stepfathers and stepmothers, and simultaneously a time of white-hot concern about child abuse. No wonder that Sue Miller's best-selling novel *The Good Mother* and its film adaptation stirred boomer passions the way *Fatal Attraction* did, as we shall see.

The baby-boom generation is also the first generation to postpone reproduction, and this is perhaps the biggest change of all, one that has led to an irony inconceivable in the past. For many thirty-something couples there is now great pressure to have children. But many anxious men and women are finding that they are no longer so physically capable as they were in their twenties. "This is the first generation to have control of conception," explains Seattle clinical psychologist and sex therapist Dr. Julia Heiman, the coauthor of *Becoming Orgasmic*. "Since they were teenagers, the concern of baby boomers has been how *not* to get pregnant, and they were successful. It never occurred to many of them that after a certain age getting pregnant might not be so easy. It can be terribly upsetting to them when they find out." Science has entered the bedroom, and what was once the most spontaneous of acts has become for some a high-tech chore. Yet even this "technologizing of sexuality," as Dr. Heiman phrases it, has given new hope to infertile heterosexuals and created new options for groups such as lesbians, who in past decades might have remained childless.

Seattle is the perfect place to chronicle the changing ways of a new generation of parents because it is a city where children matter and parenthood is taken seriously but the prudery of other family-oriented cities, Salt Lake, for instance, is mostly absent. This is part of Seattle's can-do heritage: safe, efficient, and sexy in a wholesome Liv Ullmann sort of way. The greater Seattle area, a muscled metropolis of over two million people, has become a boomtown for baby boomers. Giant Boeing, in decline a decade ago, is now swamped with new plane orders. High-tech corporations like Microsoft employ thousands. The port has become a major Asian gateway to America. The few freeways are gridlocked from six in the morning to eight at night with spanking new pickups and imports, and every Volvo station wagon or Nissan King Cab seems to sport a proud BABY ON BOARD sign or carry a toddler safety seat or contain a real, live infant or two or three. Maternity leave is widespread. Paternity leave is catching on. There has long been an unusual marriage between the downtown hospitals and the natural-childbirth and feminist health movements. Young couples looking for big-city culture and a small-town feel are flocking to Seattle from all over the West.

"It's such a sweet town, the best place to raise kids in America—it's enough to make you scream," laughs cartoonist Lynda Barry, a Seattle native.

Seattle's shift to home and hearth was hardly unique, however. By the mid-1980s, with the simultaneous aging of the baby-boom generation and the unsettling fear of sexual disease, the culture was calling for commitment. All America seemed to be with child. In Hollywood, family and sobriety were increasingly in. Playtime for adults was often out. Home fires epics like *Three Men and a Baby* and *Baby Boom* became big box office.

As a generation of young couples settled down, many of Hollywood's more dissolute stars struggled to change their image, making every effort to come across like members of TV's Cosby family.

"Miami Vice" playboy Don Johnson uttered envious remarks about those couples who "struggle through seemingly impossible odds to stay together . . . those people have a richness and a depth of value and meaning in their lives that other people just don't have." Johnson wound up the decade by returning to the arms of his ex-wife, actress Melanie Griffith.

Johnson also played up his close relationship with his young son, Jesse, just as David Bowie, another symbol of decadence from an earlier period, did with his own son. In the seventies, Bowie had teased fans with his sexual ambiguity. By the eighties, the trendy pop star had put his finger up and felt a new wind blowing. He began to present himself as a responsible father.

Some stars were too set in their ways to change. Lady killer Warren Beatty was rumored to be settling down, finally, but he turned fifty without walking down the aisle. In the sixties and seventies, he might have been envied. In the eighties he appeared to be a man out of his time. Hollywood columnists and film biographers ridiculed his endless sexual prowling. His own sister, Shirley MacLaine, poked fun at him onstage at the Oscar ceremonies.

First, the public demanded to see marriage licenses. Then, it wanted its favorite celebrities in a family way. Baby-boom rock star Sting recorded the birth of his child in the documentary *Bring On the Night,* modestly making sure that the camera closed in on his expression of parental concern and adoration. The pregnant actress Debra Winger showed off her wonderful full-moon belly to her fans. As more and more of us became mothers and fathers, we wanted our favorite stars to glamorize the role.

And they were not allowed to fake it either. Even in death, John Lennon was put under surveillance by that master of tacky investigations Albert Goldman, who claimed the musician's widely-publicized final days as a doting father and a househusband were a fraud.

Yes, we expected our stars to take their vows seriously in the eighties. Bruce Springsteen might extol home and sexy commitment in his songs, but that still did not spare him from the wrath of the *People* when he dumped his young and innocent wife Julianne for his Jersey girl backup singer Patti Scialfa. "He talks about scruples and commitment, but the sad thing is, he's having an affair," said one friend.

Commitment was not a problem for the settled young couples we talked with in Seattle: it was a given. Their problems were not those of image.

A few days after the birth class we eat dinner with "Karen," the pregnant doctor of Penny Simkin's birth class, and her husband "Nelson," at Burk's, an upscale Cajun joint in Seattle's waterfront Ballard district.* Karen felt her first labor contraction earlier in the day. Although she is over eight months pregnant and the baby is officially due in only three weeks, her arms and face do not look heavy. The weight is concentrated at her stomach, and the baby bulges straight out like a bowling ball concealed under her black silk pantsuit. Circling her neck is a string of charms, tiny watermelons and jeweled oranges on a gold chain. It is a schoolgirl touch for a medical doctor. Nelson wears a

---

* Certain names and identifying details in this chapter have been changed.

western shirt, white cotton and expensive, fashionably buttoned at the collar, like a Ralph Lauren model.

Karen is a woman who postponed pregnancy until it was almost too late. During medical school she had an abortion. Although she felt psychologically ready for motherhood, she believed she did not have the energy to raise a child and complete her residency at the same time. The day she finally finished her training, she had only one goal: to become pregnant. She was very excited. But for twelve months, nature would not cooperate. It was as if, she thought guiltily, she had been given her chance and not taken it. Now every menstrual period was a loss. "I used to say I got postmenstrual depression rather than premenstrual syndrome."

Karen, who is thirty-five and Nelson, who is forty, did not know what was wrong. They subjected themselves to four months of tests at the Special Infertility Program at the University of Washington Hospital. Nelson's sperm was checked for shape and motility and then counted and "washed" of white blood cells. Karen's fallopian tubes were plumbed for obstructions. A probe was threaded into her uterus, and a tiny piece of the lining was sucked out for analysis. Perhaps the fertilized egg could not adhere properly. Except for the fact that Nelson had a low-grade prostate infection, all tests proved negative. They still did not know what was wrong. The clinic staff proposed a high-tech solution. Several of Karen's eggs would be removed from her ovaries and fertilized outside the womb with Nelson's washed sperm. In a process known as *in vitro* fertilization, the eggs would then be surgically implanted inside her uterus. The procedure cost $5,000 for each try, and it was necessary to alter Karen's hormones with daily injections administered by Nelson at home. "The needles were two inches long. Karen's hips were covered with bruises. This wasn't procreation," says Nelson, "it was surgery."

Nelson would be led into a clinic room and told to masturbate into a sterile plastic cup. Then the sperm would be applied to Karen's isolated eggs. "It was embarrassing, degrading, a bit funny, and very humbling," he remembers. "There was this old *Penthouse* I was supposed to look at. The cover was torn off, and it was stamped PROPERTY OF THE UNIVERSITY OF WASHINGTON. I had been faithful to my wife for thirteen years. This was not my idea of love."

Karen looks at Nelson with sympathy. But she laughs bravely at her own memory. "The first time they put the turkey baster inside me, I wanted to ask the young doctor—he was younger than me—'Doctor, was it good for you too?' "

Karen and Nelson are a love story. They met very young. She was eleven. He was sixteen and her older brother's best friend. She had two sisters too, both redheads like her. The family lived far out on Long Island at the beach, and there were always lots of young men around, visiting her brother, stealing a weekend away from their own parents in Manhattan, and of course, sneaking hot looks at the three growing girls. Either her mother approved of Nelson or she saw the writing on the wall. She would trot out young Karen for Nelson's inspection, "dressed in the most shocking miniskirt, frosted lips, and braces," she remembers. They both laugh. In college they dated, but mostly each other. Afterward, they moved in together and, five years after that, decided to get married. They wrote their own vows. Nelson, he remembers, cried at the wedding.

"There's a sensuality as well as a sexiness to pregnancy," the father-to-be says at one point, stroking three fingers across his wife's enormous stomach.

"When our bellies were touching," adds Karen, "he could feel the baby kicking, just as I could."

Karen and Nelson were euphoric once they discovered she was pregnant. "Every second of every day for months we had thought about what was wrong," says Karen, especially during the clinic program, and then their luck, or whatever it was, changed. Ironically, success did not necessarily come from the high-tech methods at the university lab. After four months, Karen and Nelson rebelled against the alienating environment and the pain. They thought the scientists had taken advantage of their anxiety and their desire to become pregnant quickly. They considered the low-tech option of monitoring Karen's menstrual cycle. But, within a month of doing nothing, Karen found herself pregnant. Karen still does not know what went right. "Friends and relatives had been saying, 'Just relax, enjoy it. That's your real problem.' The message there was that we had been making ourselves infertile. It was like blaming the victim. And even if I was furious at these people, I still had to consider the possibility. It added to all our other guilt feelings. You feel that at bottom your body has turned against you. We'll never know if the clinic treatment helped or what."

Nelson recognized the change first. "She smelled differently, her sweat—"
"And down below," finishes his wife, laughing. Nausea and exhaustion

gripped the doctor for the first trimester, but after a brief vacation on Maui at the beginning of the fourth month, sex became "terrific," climaxes growing in intensity.

As we talk of love, orgasm, two-inch needles, and the washing of sperm, Burk, the proprietor, wanders over. He inspects the barbecued prawns that Mother and Father are chewing on, pleased that only the tails are left. Then he begins to stare at Karen's bowling-ball middle. "Didn't want to say anything the last time you were in," he drawls, "but I thought it was more than my cooking. You've put on some weight."

"Might happen tonight," says a guest, "here."

Burk doesn't miss a beat. "They say spicy foods bring on labor," he offers, and he tells the Seattle baby-boom story of last week when an overdue woman decided to induce birth with gumbo. At one point, she attained a flush, says Burk, and her two friends began to walk her around between the big tables under the sculptures of life-size alligators and bayou bullfrogs. It proved to be a false alarm. The baby wasn't born for two more days but, he smiles as graciously as the attorney for Dennis Quaid in *The Big Easy,* "We are always ready to lay down a fresh tablecloth."

Seattle is a very accommodating town.

There is even a billboard on the way in from the airport that proclaims the city to be a good place to raise kids. Certainly, the message has caught on in Seattle's growing lesbian community, where women are now making babies with the same high-tech procedures and low-tech desires of heterosexual couples like Karen and Nelson. We talked with "Lonni," who at thirty-seven is two years older than Karen. Lonni is the director of a large church day-care center located not so far from Burk's restaurant.

"Lesbians used to be able to have only dick babies," smiles Lonni in her office below the playroom.

Dick babies? we ask.

"Sorry," she says cheerfully, "but that's the term. Some lesbian moms had children when they were married, before they came out. The others are through artificial insemination."

Lonni is wearing white Reeboks, blue jeans, and a red sweater-vest over a white shirt. She herself has two children conceived very differently. The first, a boy, was created by traditional means, and she lost him to his father in conservative Utah after a bitter and messy custody battle. Now she has a two-year-old girl as well. Her female lover inseminated her. "You find a man who's willing to ejaculate into a clean jar, and you get the sample to the woman reasonably warm within half an hour." Lonni's partner inserted the sperm into her using a needleless syringe, what Karen called her "turkey baster." Many women make a loving ritual of the process, lighting candles, talking to each other about the baby to come, kissing and caressing, while the mother-to-be lies quietly with her hips and legs raised.

"Sometimes it can be intimate, sometimes not," says Lonni, depending on how many times it takes. Her partner became pregnant on her first try, "which I found really amazing." But it took Lonni over two years and twenty tries. "Every menstrual cycle you wait and see. Then you get your period and you're disappointed. Then you have to kind of get excited and try it again. It can be frustrating. You're kind of on a roller coaster."

In the past, many lesbians preferred to make babies with gay men, but now they are afraid of receiving AIDS-infected semen, even if the man tests negative for the virus. This is about the only limitation to the process, explains Lonni. She talks of a woman who used sperm from her partner's brother. The partner and her brother were Hispanic and the lovers wanted to keep "the cultural background." Ironically, the majority of children born to lesbians through artificial insemination seem to be boys, since women naturally choose the optimal point in their cycle to try to conceive, and this happens to be a better moment for male sperm.

"That used to be kind of an issue," says Lonni. In the era of dick babies, Seattle lesbians tried to preserve all-women spaces in which men and boys were not allowed. With the increase in boy children, the lesbian community, believes Lonni, has become more accepting.

Lonni believes that lesbians and straight couples handle the whole process of pregnancy and child-rearing differently. She feels lesbians demonstrate more commitment to their children. Lesbian mothers more easily accept part-time work so they may spend more time with their kids, for instance, and they spank them less. But unlike Karen and Nelson, and most other heterosexual couples we talked with in Seattle, Lonni believes that sexual desire falls off during pregnancy, and certainly when children are around the house. This is a bit of a sore point.

She remembers once reading a report by Pepper Schwartz, the Seattle sociologist who coauthored *American Couples,* that concluded sexuality tends to decrease vastly more for long-term lesbian partners than it does for married straights. (Forty-seven percent of lesbian partners together for ten or more years have sex only once a month or less, compared to only 15 percent of married heterosexual couples, the majority of whom are still pumping away one to three times a week or more.) "I became so angry, I threw the book down and made love to my partner immediately!"

Nevertheless, all of her friends "validate the study," she says. "It's depressing." This phenomenon is called "lesbian bed death" (a reworking of "crib death") by Susie Bright and her raucous sisters in San Francisco, but for Lonni's lesbian-mother support group here in Seattle, it is "a real big issue," and Lonni and her partner are in therapy "to see if we can figure it out." Lonni lists a number of reasons why lesbian desire seems to fade more quickly. "As women, we have not been socialized to be initiators in the sexual act. Another factor is that we don't have to make excuses if we don't want to do it. We don't say we have a headache. We just say no. We also do a lot more cuddling and touching than heterosexuals, and we get fulfilled by that rather than just the act of intercourse . . . Another thing is that such a sisterly bond develops that the relationship almost seems incestuous after a while. The intimacy is so great. We know each other so well." When Lonni first came out of the closet, nonmonogamy was considered to be a heterosexual sin, politically incorrect. But these days, "all my friends are nonmonogamous, especially those with kids. There's been a big change in the community over the years."

Little "Drake," the child of "James and Sara Jamison," is what might be called a "trouser snake" baby, conceived the old-fashioned way, although his entrance into the world was precipitate.

"We went to bed at eleven-thirty that evening and made love," explains Sara, who is an attorney for the state of Washington at the appellate court level. "My water broke at three-thirty that morning."

"During pregnancy," adds her husband, a forty-two-year-old TV news producer as well as a dealer in primitive art, "that child was *bombarded* with hormones," referring to the prostaglandins in sperm that can cause the uterus to contract.

"I felt like I was sixteen again or something," laughs Sara Jamison, who is thirty-five. "I was constantly chasing James around. During my whole pregnancy I was a lot more, shall we say, horny."

Sara and James steal glances at each other as we talk. There is a lot going on here. The mood is alternately giddy and tense.

She has beautiful peach-colored skin. She wears large, clear-framed glasses, a black sweater, blue-striped cotton pants, aerobics shoes. He has on hand-made open-toed leather slippers. His jeans are well worn. His button-down blue oxford shirt is untucked. They are both strikingly good-looking people. He speaks formally, with well-chosen words, measured and calm, or at least calm-sounding. She smiles more and tosses in the jokes. ("That first day, I didn't know whether I was pregnant or whether I was just desperately ill.") She plays with him verbally, which he seems to enjoy immensely.

The living room is small but tasteful, original art on the wall, baby gear arranged everywhere. The Jamisons are selling their house in the Bryant district and deciding where to move, either the Virgin Islands or Friday Harbor in the San Juans. Both are a little bored with television and with the law. ("I guess we all have high hopes in television journalism that we are going to change the way people feel about their world. Then you end up year after year cranking out the same story about the weather or whatever.") The Jamisons want to devote more time to art and the children.

They met a decade ago in Arkansas, where she was just finishing college and he was a reporter for the local NBC affiliate. He was having trouble setting up an outdoor shoot for a story about college loans. She was eating her lunch beside the campus fountain and laughing at him. He retaliated by asking her to dinner. The only problem was that they were both already married to other people and in the process of trying to secure divorces.

"My attorney had advised me," explains Sara in her soft accent, "not to be seeing men in public because in Arkansas you have to have grounds, and there are only a few: insanity—"

"Not owning a handgun," James interrupts.

"Well, adultery is one," she continues. "My attorney thought my ex might be having me followed. James wanted to take me to a restaurant. I kept changing the subject. Then I told him why I didn't want to go out. He said, 'Well, I'm a great cook. Why don't I cook, and you come over to my apartment?' Out of the frying pan and into the fire! Oh my God! He made *boef bourguignonne*. I ended up staying until five-thirty in the morning. Talking. Making love."

James and Sara laugh. This was ten years ago.

The only "down" part of the pregnancy came when Sara found out what sex the baby was. Waiting until birth to hear the doctor say, "It's a girl!" like some actor in a forties movie is an anxious pleasure relegated to past generations, like waiting until Christmas morning to open presents. Baby boomers, at least those thirty-five and over, can find out the sex of the baby with the results of the amniocentesis test, should they choose to have one, and most do. "The clinic called with the results," remembers Sara. " 'It's healthy,' the nurse said. 'Do you want to know the sex?' 'Yes,' I said. 'It's a boy,' she said. 'Oh.' Tears formed in my eyes and everything. I cry fairly easily anyway, but tears were running down my face, and I felt guilty for feeling that way, like I should just be glad it's healthy, but I had sort of wanted a girl. I really couldn't see myself as the mother of a boy. I thought of little boys as having frogs in their pockets."

Except for that moment, Sara was elated during her pregnancy, and her sexual drive continued to heighten until the last few weeks, when she had trouble maneuvering. "Those ladies who blossom sexually during pregnancy," says Penny Simkin, "are the ones who feel ripe and gorgeous. They keep their confidence, and they enjoy the experience."

Sara would examine herself in the mirror "and go, Oh my God, I look like one of those laughing Buddha statues with the big tummy and the belly button in the middle. I thought this little alien being was coming in and taking over." But she wore sexy nightgowns, partly for reassurance, partly for the fun of it, and she never stopped importuning James, day and night.

James did not feel he had to reassure his wife verbally that he still found her attractive. "Actions speak louder than words," he says, and Sara laughs at that.

"One cannot generalize," says Simkin, laughing as well, when we talk to her in her office. "I only guarantee that your sexuality will change."

Those who do tend to generalize about pregnancy and sexuality, such as Libby Colman and Elisabeth Bing, authors of *Making Love During Pregnancy*, mention a common euphoria in the first trimester caused by the relief at no longer having to use contraception. This relaxation ("no interruptions," one woman tells us) can be countered by a fear of miscarriage and by morning sickness, both of which often go away around the fourth month when genital engorgement and confidence take over, especially among "those ladies who blossom." In the last month or two, many women are slowed down by size.

This is a time to switch positions since ladies-on-top, Donkeys in the Third Moon of Spring, the Tiger's Tread, and other exotic positions probably not entertained by one's mother become more comfortable than the missionary posture.

We found that many men of the new generation greatly enjoy sex with their pregnant wives. "Sharing this effort to bring a child into the world added a dimension to our lovemaking," says James Jamison. "It enhanced the bonding and it helped sexually." "It was like making love to a new woman each month," another father tells us. "Sex has become the best we've ever had," says an expectant man. "I've really grown in my respect for what women go through. I was there for the amnio. They put this enormous needle right into her belly with no anesthetic. The way she took it, my heart went out to her. Plus I like big tits, I really do. I go for that rounded Aztec look."

Not all men are so accepting. One Seattle man, a shipping company comptroller, told his pregnant wife that he was turned off to her big belly and increased vaginal discharge. "You can either buy a vibrator or have an affair, but I just can't get it up," he said in a calm and clinical tone that bothered her. "Just make it safe." Husband and wife loved each other and wanted the baby, but the wife's libido was strong. She decided to take her husband at his word.

She recalled that another man, a friend of her husband's, had told her that for his part he found pregnant women incredibly sexy. The wife and the friend bumped into each other at a party when the husband was working.

"She came on to me," says the friend, a handsome, athletic man who, like James Jamison, displays a formal manner that masks strong desires. "She was very flirtatious, but she established that I was not to construe what we were about to do as a long-term affair. So we went into a bedroom at the party and fucked. Every couple of weeks, we would meet until she got too uncomfortable, physically. The first time was fun, but after that, it got a bit arranged, a little clinical. And after the baby was born, that was it. And the husband, my friend, became completely cool to me. He'd sanctioned the thing, but he meant for her to go after somebody farther afield. Actually, to this day I'm not positive he sanctioned it. She may have just told me that."

This lover of pregnant women tells us he has had three similar affairs since the first. "I meet these women, and I say, 'God, I think pregnant women are sexy!' And a few of them answer, 'You do? My husband sure doesn't!' And we go from there.

"I can't exactly explain my motivation. For me it was more tenderness and spirituality than pure lust. It was like being closer to the life process somehow. To me, sex is part of life and babymaking—and, I just love that big, hard belly and those expanded nipples. And their faces get so radiant. The color of the skin gets good. Even the eyes shine."

"I want a C-section! I want a suicide pill!" Sara Jamison shouted in the middle of labor, but she thought better of both and recovered, and Drake was born naturally enough. Birth was an experience that strengthened her love for James and his for her. "We all felt so close," she says, "so tight together. It's much more intense than when you first fall in love. It's not like the initial infatuation, when you can't get enough of the other person. You feel you have accomplished the most wonderful thing that could possibly be, the making of a new life. I didn't move around much for the first few days because of the swelling and the stitches and all that kind of stuff. James waited on me, and there was this incredible coziness and loyalty. We were a unity that could not be disturbed."

"We were in our little cocoon," remembers another Seattle woman, also a lawyer. "There's a glass roof above where we sleep, and I don't think we got out of bed for two days. People brought us food, and the pediatrician came to our home."

"If the father is separate from the experience," says Nelson, Karen's husband, "he might resent things because that intense physical feeling will be directed elsewhere, to the new being, and the man is naturally displaced, but if he takes part in the exercises and classes and he's present for birth, the love is deepened. What could possibly connect you more?"

A father's participation in birth was not always taken for granted. Everyone remembers the days when anxious dads chattered and chain-smoked waiting for a nurse to hold up a swaddled baby behind a glass wall. "Is it a boy? Is it a girl?" The dad knocks on the glass. The other dads in the waiting room laugh. Their turn will come.

In a way, America's new fatherhood could be said to have begun in a Seattle hospital in the mid-1950s when a father and mother decided to experience the birth of their child as a couple. It was a revolutionary demand at a time when birth was considered a wholly medical procedure, something like removing a diseased kidney, and mothers were as shot full of drugs as a Frank Purdue chicken.

When the young couple arrived at the hospital with the wife in the advanced stages of labor, the husband asked to be present at the birth. The doctors refused. The husband insisted. Security was called, but the father-to-be had already handcuffed himself to his wife. Now the doctors were outraged. But it was too late. The baby was born with father present. "Incredible, don't you think?" Penny Simkin asks us.

Yes, we agree. The new fatherhood is one of those developments that is rarely talked about which, nevertheless, augurs serious societal change. As some mothers become more like fathers—by bringing home the bacon, sharing in workplace stress and achievement—some fathers become more like mothers by bonding with their newborns, sympathizing with the pain and magic of birth, realizing what life is all about. In this shakedown period between the sexes that is our time, it would seem baby-boom couples have found a romantic key to togetherness.

So for these randy and caring new parents who have made love throughout pregnancy, testing new smells and laughing at mom's svelte dolphin shape, then bonding in a sublime threesome at birth, the postpartum period can come as a shock, sexually. Biology has a way of whacking us over the head.

"After Drake was born," says Sara Jamison, "my sexuality went down like a 747. There was some vaginal tearing at birth," she explains. "We repaired that and started trying to have intercourse about three weeks later. But there were some stitches that were still catching, and they were extremely painful. I finally went back to the midwife and said, 'Gee, this is hurting like crazy! Something must be wrong.' The problem was that the end of a little stitch hadn't dissolved, but we had gotten off to a bad start. I also felt extremely ugly after birth because of the big wrinkles and the flabby stomach and the stretch marks. To be able to give freely to someone, you have to accept your own body, and for several months I couldn't bear to look at myself after I stepped out of the shower."

Sara shoots a glance at James as she finishes. James is calmly staring at her from the couch.

How did you feel about that, James? we ask.

"How did I feel?" he answers. "Deprived."

"Once we started trying it, and it was painful for me, that acted to divide us," says Sara. "He was afraid to approach me, and I would avoid him. I was afraid I would either have to grin and bear it, or turn him down. It was this vicious circle. It started building a wall."

So this was the source of the tension in the well-appointed living room, the flip side to the giddy discussion of filmy nightgowns and chases to the bedroom during pregnancy.

How did it work itself back?

"It hasn't," says James.

"For one thing," say Sara, "breast-feeding Drake is so close and intimate; it's so wonderful to have this child totally dependent on you that I really don't want James to touch my breasts because—they're Drake's. They're sacred. They have another purpose now. They are no longer sexual.

"In the past we would hug a lot. Before I left for work in the morning, I would tell him I needed a nice hug . . . Now it's like I'm getting all my touching and stuff from Drake. It's sad and it's weird."

"I've become philosophical and have found consolation in other men who are going through the same thing," says James, and here he sounds like his father might have—but, he stresses, his own father would never have talked about such things. This is another difference between the generations, but it doesn't solve the problem. Only time will.

"I'm *tired*. I'm nursing," a thirty-seven-year-old Seattle mother of a toddler says to us, a woman who in another life is a geophysicist. "This is something the Leche League doesn't tell you. It's population control. You stop ovulating, or at least I did. Desire is lessened. I led a wild youth in a scientific sort of way," says this intense mother, who looks a little like Genevieve Bujold with short red hair. "I had a lot of lovers, some married, some not. I didn't care. People said I was like a man. Then my father got ill. I decided family was high-priority. It was time to settle down. I wouldn't go back, except in a wistful way."

"Babies are sucking those breasts ten times a day," Professor Gayle Kimball, author of *50–50 Parenting*, tells us. "You don't have that need for cuddling. Some women also have the postpartum blues. But the main thing is the fatigue. Sex is connected to feeling good about yourself and being full of energy, at least for most women. If you're awakened every two hours around the clock, it's like being tortured. Pregnancy is a sexually enhancing time for women. Nursing is not."

And yet we talked with a mother of two girls who says, "I loved breast-feeding. It was a very sensual experience. I never had an orgasm during feeding myself, but I came close, and I know people who have."

This woman "Betsy Gilbert" is forty years old and the Seattle coordinator of a television series for the Public Broadcasting System. She is full of sparkle, like a favorite high school teacher, with thick glasses, light gray eyes, and full breasts that haven't nursed in some time. To us, Gilbert represents a mother who has managed to keep the home fires burning with children present and pestering.

Her first marriage broke up in Los Angeles when her older daughter, "Angie," was only a year old. Scriptwriter for the TV series "Eight is Enough" and the TV film *Having Babies,* Gilbert was the story consultant on the movie *Heartland.* During filming she met "Jake," the cameraman. "We had what they call in show business 'the location romance.' But this one grew. I decided to move to Montana to be with him. Before that for several years, Angie had me all to herself. She would always slide into bed with me, and at dawn neither of us could remember how she got there. Now here was this guy in bed with her mother. She'd cry, 'Mommie doesn't love me anymore.' And Jake had to adjust because suddenly here's this little kid.

"Finally, we went to see a therapist, this hard-bitten Montana gal, who looked me in the eye. 'If you want this relationship to work, you and Jake have got to stick together because Angie's going to wedge right between you and break you up. You gotta be tough.' So we tried some behavior modification techniques. When Angie started having her tempers, we would ignore her rather than paying more attention and rewarding her bad behavior. Jake spent time alone with her, and he built her a tire swing in the backyard and took her fishing. Under it all, she had been dying for a father. They got to be buddies, and in a few weeks it all worked out beautifully."

Two years later, Betsy and Jake had a child of their own. Once the couple had built their family unit, cementing together as best they could the cracks between stepparent and first child, first child and second, the stumbling block to sexual intimacy became *time.* "There has never been a period when Jake and I were together without children," Betsy Gilbert laughs. Now it is the younger child, age six, who wants to sleep with them. She's still afraid of the dark. Recently, when the couple wanted to watch a porn movie without being disturbed, they wedged a cedar chest against their bedroom door.

"Having a baby hits you like a truck . . . You view your single or childless friends as adolescents," she shrugs. "There is no such thing as the extended family anymore. Everybody is so damn mobile." There are no willing grandparents to take the kids for the weekend. "Who lives in the same town as their parents anymore?" she asks. "You make your own network. We rely much more on friends in the same situation than our parents did."

Betsy and Jake are problem-solvers. Some of their solutions are simple. "One of the things you learn early on when you have children and you don't have time for a whole long buildup into good old penetration-type sex, is short hand-servicing. You masturbate each other. You have oral sex more. We feel real comfortable doing this. There's a lot of affection involved. It's no big deal. We just know that's all we have time for sometimes." Once a month or so, the two try for "the Wild Weekend." They park the kids with friends and retreat to a hot springs in the San Juan Islands. And, resolutely, they take off one night a week to orgy out at the local multiplex cinema, sneaking into the different shows one after the other and gorging on junk food. Another approach is more complex. They attempt explicitly to increase the intimacy of their family. "We try to spend time together talking. With all the pressures and tensions of what two workaholics go through day after day, we make sharing and intimacy a conscious priority."

In the end, Betsy Gilbert's goal is nothing short of making America a more child-oriented society. She believes that "the evolution of feminism took the dignity away from being a mother." Baby boomers are returning this esteem, "and the next step is to endow the father as well, to make him a conurturer, which means acknowledging that your value as a parent is greater than your ability to make a lot of money. That's a stiff order in America, but you can be successful and still have a family. Both parents need to work to afford a minimally decent home in a minimally decent neighborhood, and if I didn't work, I and the kids would both go crazy anyway. But a balance must be struck. Attitudes need to change. That's the battle for the nineties. We are all so addicted to pleasing ourselves. We need to realize we can't give birth to children and then expect them to raise themselves."

But these are long-range goals. Just maintaining intimacy in the home remains for Betsy's family a practical but tricky matter.

"All four of us crawl into bed and hug each other in the morning because we've always been expressive about that. When the kids were a lot younger, we'd all take showers together. We stopped at a certain point. It's not that we made an issue out of it. It's just that the younger girl was getting older and more modest. It is," she laughs, "certainly harder for Jake and me to do it in the shower now because the kids inevitably barge in."

Sex between the parents is not something Betsy Gilbert believes children have to be shielded from. They should not be "introduced precociously" either. "You never want to create an embarrassing situation for yourself or the child. Jake, particularly, is real modest about that kind of thing, and I think that's good." The point, she says, "is affection and context."

As psychologist Dr. Julia Heiman explains, "It can be just as difficult on a child never to see her parents acting physically affectionate as it is to see them once having sex together. I have a lot more clients seeking sexual therapy who were raised in families where nobody ever touched. It's unusual for anyone to suffer irreparable damage from accidentally seeing or hearing their parents have sex."

Real-life mothers like Betsy Gilbert are learning to balance romance and maternity. The characters of the powerful *Good Mother* are not so lucky. In the novel, a young divorced mother has sex with her new boyfriend in the presence of her young daughter, who barges in after a nightmare. Later, the daughter touches the man's penis and innocently tells her father about it. The father, who is a lawyer, takes his ex-wife to court and gains custody of the child. The forlorn mother winds up losing everything—her daughter, her relationship with the new man, and her interest in sex.

This is a single mother's worst nightmare, the culture trying to warn once again that something evil lurks. Although the novel is clearly on the side of the loving yet sexy mother, the book must be taken on two levels. Its bottom line, a very old one, is that erotic motherhood is a risky venture.

Yet we randy baby boomers push on.

We talk to a very different sort of woman, a tall, dark-haired environmentalist from Brazil, who says at one point, "I want my baby on one breast and my husband at the other. What's wrong with that?"

Which brings us swiftly to your authors, since we know this woman well. The man from Hollywood, no longer so confused in his heart, now lives at the top of a hill with a cat-eyed Sicilian, their sex wars over, and Mr. Montana has actually married the above-mentioned environmentalist of the two nursing breasts. She was the belingeried Brazilian of Buzz Bense's safe-sex orgy. Now Mr. M. is doing personal research when he attends birth classes, mixing business and immortality, since the blessed event is due very soon. He lies awake with his hand on his new wife's wondrous beach ball of a stomach feeling the future Mr./Ms. Baby kick like a soccer player in the dark, and sometimes the mother-to-be slides on top of him then, smooth as a seal in the night, and then he feels the baby's kicks between their rocking bellies like drumbeats. From "Obsession" to "Home Fires": the harder they come, the harder they fall. One of your sex-tour guides will soon be changing Pampers.

It is only too easy to imagine: It's 2 A.M. The computer's down. Little Cody's finally asleep. Your coauthor has finished feeding and burping him. Now he's rinsing and drying the trusty Evenflo portable breast pump, about to throw the baby clothes in the washer, mix up some tasty soy formula in the fridge, the usual, when— What's that noise? The sound of falling water. It's only Mom in the shower. Ummh, the sound of falling water . . . Brazil, Salvador da Bahia, the Hotel Pelhourinho, Carnivale, hot sweat in February, those grandfather drums wailing in the street below--naked samba! Remember? Yes, the soap, that nice, hard bar of Ivory, where is it? Bathtime for Papa.

Burning desires.

A week after we ate shrimp and gumbo at Burk's in Seattle the news came that Karen, the doctor at Penny Simkin's class, had given birth. Nelson, Karen's husband, was there. Early in the morning the day of the birth, Karen experienced a bit of bloody show. She was gripped with a horrible thought: she was getting her period. It was the same disappointment she had felt each month for the twelve months before she had been able to get pregnant. But this, she almost started to laugh out loud in the toilet, was a flashback. No period was possible now. Labor was beginning. She called up her doctor, but the doctor said, "No, it's just part of the mucus plug. You could have another week." Even so, Karen decided to stay home from work that day, and so did Nelson. It was the first time they had both been home together in five months. They went out for provisions, and they took a long walk in the woods, and when they got home, they ended up making slow love in bed. Strong contractions soon began. They entered the hospital's home birthing room at exactly midnight, and she noticed two things right away. The moon was full and it was shining onto the bed. The midwives kept the lights low. And the second thing was, she realized she had lost control of her body. Something had taken her over. She held on to Nelson, her arms around his neck, grabbing on to his hair, trying to focus, but she could focus only on his face. She could not take in all of his body at once, and she had lost track of everybody else. The pain was greater and it came faster than she had imagined and she herself as a doctor had seen many women give birth in this same room, in this same bed. But her own contractions came faster, two or three every couple of minutes. She couldn't catch her breath. She couldn't do the breathing she had practiced for. She was off on the roller coaster. It took her only four hours to dilate, and then came the visceral feeling to push. This was good though, she thought. For the first time, she was aware of what was going on in the room. Her doctor was there. The midwives stood beside her. Nelson held her legs while she pushed. She tried not to scream. She wanted desperately not to lose purpose, rhythm, control. Nelson's clothes were wet from holding her in the hospital shower earlier when she still had thoughts of holding back the contractions. There was no holding back now, and this was good. She was glad, hysterically glad suddenly, because she understood she could harness this feeling to enable her to bear the baby. And then came intense searing pain. The sensations had been anal. It had felt, she said, like a watermelon exploding inside her. Good in a way, she said. Now they burned. But it was quick, and there he was. There was the baby. The relief was instant. She saw his head. She lost count of the next seconds. The doctor was laying the baby on her stomach. She started to talk to the baby: "Oh, baby! Oh, baby!" She told the baby how glad they were to see him. She told the baby how much she loved him. She told the baby how very long they had waited. By now Karen was sobbing, and so was Nelson. But Jack, the baby, just looked at them with his serious baby face, half covered in vernix, and he blinked and watched them cry, or appeared to.

Nelson thought suddenly of all the months when it could not happen and about sticking the two-inch needles into Karen's hips to change her hormones, and he saw the bruises, and he could not stop thinking, and he remembered the nausea, Karen's swollen feet, his own not daring to hope that there was nothing really wrong and that they would get pregnant, and he thought of making love in Maui too, Karen's belly beginning to rise between the strips of her bikini, and then the doctor plopped his son on his wife's chest. The doctor offered to let him cut the umbilical cord but he could not because his feet, he felt, were not on the ground. He felt as if he were actually floating.

It was then that Karen noticed that the moon was gone. It was almost exactly six hours since she had been helped into the room and now the clear, white dawn of a dry August morning in Seattle streamed through the window. She could see the entire city spread out below, the Space Needle, the skyscrapers, Puget Sound black-green, the Olympic Mountains to the west, the shadows coming alive with the light. She thought, We started at midnight and we worked all night, and then with this dawn came the baby. She thought next, Anything and everything is possible for this child. And she thought immediately after that, Every parent thinks exactly the same thing. But Karen believed it with her heart open in the dawn, and then she looked at Nelson, who was still crying, softly now, and she thought, This is the start of the next phase of our lives.

About the Authors

Born at the foot of the Beartooth Mountains in Montana, **Steve Chapple** now lives in San Francisco's North Beach with Brazilian environmentalist Maria Ines de Pentagna Salgado and their first child, Cody. He is the author of *Don't Mind Dying* and *Outlaws in Babylon*.

David Talbot was born in the wilds of Hollywood and now lives with writer Camille Peri on San Francisco's Telegraph Hill. He is the coauthor of *Creative Differences*, a study of Hollywood's political rebels, and is a former editor of the San Francisco *Examiner* and *Mother Jones* magazines. Chapple and Talbot have written for *Rolling Stone,* the New York *Times, The Christian Science Monitor, Playboy,* the Los Angeles *Times,* and other publications.

Index